BASCOM AVR Programming with practical projects

Authors: Jurij Mikeln, Vladimir Mitrović

Editor: Jurij Mikeln

Technical Editor: Samo Gregorčič

Proof reading: Brian Millier

Publisher: AX elektronika d.o.o., Ljubljana, Slovenia

Design & DTP by: AX elektronika d.o.o., Ljubljana, Slovenia

CIP - Kataložni zapis o publikaciji
Narodna in univerzitetna knjižnica, Ljubljana

004.43(035)
681.5(035)

MIKELN, Jurij
BASCOM AVR programming with practical projects / [author] Jurij Mikeln. - Ljubljana : AX elektronika, 2012

Translation and adaptation of the book:
Programirajmo z BASCOM AVR

ISBN 978-961-6680-04-2
1. Jurij Mikeln

262361600

Introduction

Dear reader!

In front of you is a book – well not just a book, but more than that. This book will not only show you how to program AVR microcontrollers with Bascom-AVR software, but it will also show you microcontroller hardware which, with the help of your program, will breathe new life into your projects.

When I talk to people involved into programming microcontrollers, I often hear that the only way to enter this world, is to use either C or assembly language, because these two languages offer the best possible results. I partially agree with that statement. It's true that an engineer, who is fully-occupied with microcontroller designs, should use C and assembly language. One reason is that they have to switch from one microcontroller family to another very quickly – due to project targets, of course.

But for newbies to microcontroller programming, it's different – much different! Give them a C compiler, a development board and a goal to display some data on an LCD, and it is not a piece of cake. Often a newbie will even have problems with that simple a task.

It is a much different story with Bascom-AVR: ask the same newbie to perform the same task and it will be done in no time. People, who have attended Bascom seminars that I have presented, are impressed with Bascom's ease of programming, in fact, many say that they love to use Bascom. Once attracted to world of microcontrollers, there is no way back – he or she will probably program microcontrollers as either a hobby or professionally. I have, as a test, given our development boards along with a few minutes of lectures, to my son and his friend, when they were 10 years old. In no time at all, LEDs were blinking in various ways. Later, my son built himself an LCD scheduler for his school classes, as well as other projects.

In this book you will find the basics needed to start programming AVR microcontrollers. From the basics you will advance to the programming and use of some modern electronic devices, such as a graphical LCD with a touch-screen, GPS, various sensors and many other interesting devices which interface to microcontrollers.

I have known Mr. Vladimir Mitrović for more than 15 years, and I still remember the day when I showed him how to program with Bascom. He has truly embraced it and upgraded many Bascom programs with very clever assembly language programming - a winning combination. The ease of programming that is offered by Bascom combined with full access to the microcontroller, using assembly language, can beat any C compiler that we know of, when time-efficient programming is concerned.

I am very pleased that Mr. Vladimir Mitrović has decided to contribute some of his fine articles to this book. Without them, this book would not be the same. In the book, articles by other authors can also be found. The reason is simple: we found them to be very interesting and they fit the concept of the book. Thanks to Mr. Vladimir Mitrović and all of the contributing authors for their articles and programs. I also acknowledge the lecturers and the proof-reader, Mr. Brian Millier, well known Circuit Cellar writer and regular Bascom-AVR programmer, who adapted this book for English speaking readers.

I dedicate this book to my late son Miha who was a real inventor who loved designing- including microcontroller design.

Jure Mikeln

Table of Contents

9 INPUTS & OUTPUTS

In microcontroller applications push buttons are used in most cases. How to use them without unwanted contact «bounce« (what is debouncing anyway?), how we can intelligently increase the number of I/O pins of a microcontroller, driving DC motors and becoming familiar with PWM, are topics of this chapter.

Get your hands on an AVR microcontroller with help from Bascom-AVR and start controlling the world around you!

57 DATA DISPLAYS

Data displays are very important in the world of microcontrollers. With modern graphic LCD displays, one can design smart-looking products. But in some cases the »classic« 2x16 alphanumeric LCD or even 7 segment LED display is better-suited. If you have a limited number of I/O pins on your microcontroller, you might even want to connect your LCD via an SPI interface. All this is covered in this chapter.

Pick the right display and make sure that your product will stand out!

77 DATA MEASUREMENT

Human beings live in an analogue world and feel comfortable there. But this is not so for microcontrollers, which live in a digital world. After successfully measuring data, we have to transform it into digital values. We can do this in many ways, by using smart sensors (and smart programming) to get temperature, air pressure or even a GPS location – all with AVRs.

Get familiar with data measurement using Bascom-AVR!

105 DEVELOPMENT TOOLS

Having programmed microcontrollers for many years, we have become regular users of development boards. There are many available on the market. Some expensive ones attempt to achieve universality by handling many different MCU models and including many different peripherals onboard. Others are nothing more than a »break-out« board for a specific MCU device.

In contrast, we have designed optimal development boards, that will meet most of your requirements while writing/testing your AVR programs. These boards emerged from extensive usage in our daily work, so there are very good reasons why our tools are designed as illustrated in this chapter.

Use smart tools when writing your Bascom-AVR programs!

161 PRACTICAL PROJECTS

There should be many practical projects in every book for programmers and this book is no exception. Bascom-AVR, in conjunction with AVR microcontrollers, is a winning combination when designing a simple (but very powerful) I2C analyzer. Other projects, like a Frequency generator, Frequency counter, a simple but accurate clock and a Metal detector are just a few of the projects that can be found in this chapter.

AVR microcontrollers are user-friendly, so get to know them better!

211 PINOUT FOR THE AVR MICROCONTROLLERS

Inputs & Outputs

9

In microcontroller applications push buttons are used in most cases. How to use them without unwanted contact «bounce« (what is debouncing anyway?), how we can intelligently increase the number of I/O pins of a microcontroller, driving DC motors and becoming familiar with PWM, are topics of this chapter.

Get your hands on an AVR microcontroller with help from Bascom-AVR and start controlling the world around you!

Short introduction to programming microcontrollers with Bascom-AVR

By Jurij Mikeln

We are witnessing great progress in all areas of technical science. Much of that progress we can attribute to the development of processing power in our PCs, which have enabled development of new powerful programming tools running on our PCs. In the field of electronics there are many tools that we use daily and which are indispensable to our work. The same goes for electronics components, especially microcontrollers, which have progressed tremendously in the last 15 years.

This progress can be seen in both lower component prices and better technical specifications. Today, a 32-bit ARM microcontroller, with extensive peripherals like A/D (analogue to digital) and D/A (digital to analogue) converters, Ethernet, CAN and USB interfaces built in, can be bought for few Euros. However, we should clarify a few terms: in a PC there is no microcontroller, but a powerful 64-bit (possibly multi core) processor which sends and receives signals to various peripheral units such as video, memory, hard disk drive etc. The difference between a microcontroller and a processor is basically in the peripheral units: a processor does not have embedded peripheral units.

This book will not deal with ARM microcontrollers, nor with processors but will outline the basic information which will be a foundation for your AVR microcontroller programming. Typical AVR microcontrollers will drive motors, relays, receive signals from sensors and display data on LCD display, for example. Further on in this chapter we will show the basics of how to program microcontrollers. Upon completing the last chapter, you will know how to write a microcontroller program on your own. We hope that this knowledge will encourage you to develop an understanding of microcontroller programming.

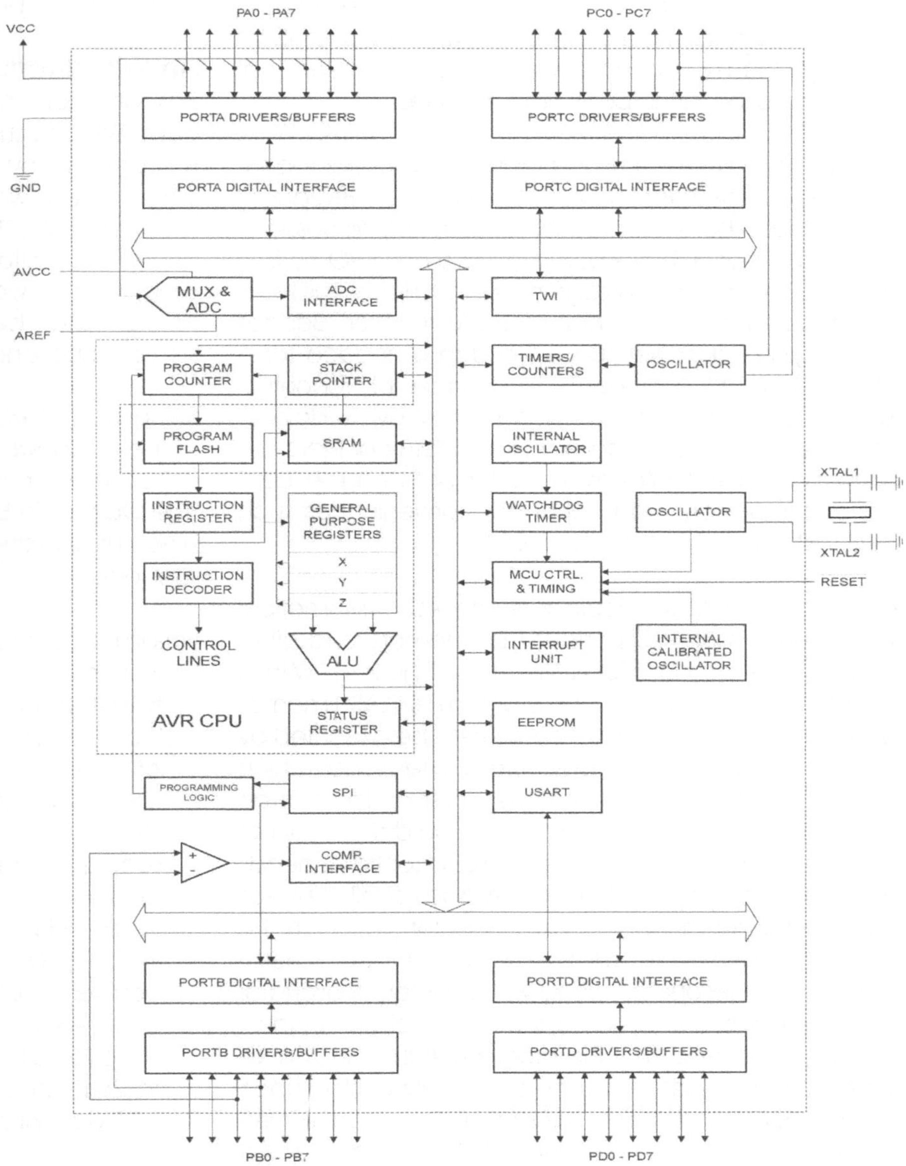

Figure 1: Block diagram of ATmega 16

Microcontrollers, processors, controllers

Let's try to define the differences between the terms microcontroller, processor and controllers. The term controller is normally used when referring to a PLC controller, i.e. a controller like Simatic etc. used for industrial automation. A PLC controller is therefore a device enclosed in a box equipped with I/O (input/output) connectors, and sometimes also containing buttons, LED or LCD displays etc.

The term processor has already been described as a chip having no built-in peripheral units such as A/D or D/A converters. A processor receives data, and performs computations on them within a powerful arithmetic logic unit (ALU) core (or cores) and then sends them back to the bus.

The term microcontroller refers to a chip which includes a modest processor (compared to a PC processor) and a rich set of built-in peripherals.

Microcontrollers can be characterized by the number of bits in the microcontroller's core: 4, 8, 16 and 32 bit ones are the most common. The microcontrollers that we will describe in this book are 8-bit ones.

AVR microcontrollers are one of the popular microcontrollers available over the last 10 years or so. Because I want to describe a microcontroller as simply as possible, I will refer to it as a "black box", having several I/O ports. A microcontroller with no program yet installed in it is like a "dead bug" i.e. it will perform no useful function. Besides this program, a power supply voltage is needed for a microcontroller to start performing its task. Microcontrollers are currently being used in virtually every device: be it a toy or a PLC controller. In a modern car there are numerous microcontrollers used for both engine control, safety devices and occupant conveniences such as entertainment systems and GPS.

AVR microcontrollers incorporate an ALU (arithmetical logical unit), more I/O ports, FLASH memory and other units that will be described later (see Figure 1). With a suitable programmer, we can program its FLASH memory with our own program, which will then be executed by the ALU step-by-step. I/O ports are bi-directional, which means that they can function as either an input or an output. The port's data direction must be defined by our program. As mentioned earlier, a microcontroller needs a power supply voltage to operate. Additionally it needs an external crystal or ceramic resonator (although this function is commonly built-in to newer microcontrollers). The crystal or resonator, along with an internal oscillator circuit generates a clock for the ALU. Lacking a clock, the ALU stops executing the program. If the clock is restored, the ALU starts executing again. Depending upon the microcontroller, it may not start back up where it left off. Most AVRs contain an internal RC oscillator which generates the clock needed by the ALU, meaning that no external crystal or ceramic resonator is needed. Selection between the internal RC oscillator and external crystal/resonator is done during programming, and will be described later in this book.

The AVR program being executed is actually machine code instructions, which "tell" to ALU what to do. Since the ALU operates on binary numbers, coded with zeroes and ones, each instruction is made up of zeros and ones. When microcontrollers were first introduced, this machine code language was the only way that programmers could write their program code. Because this was very inconvenient, programmers soon switched to assembly language (using an Assember program). Even this was cumbersome, so today high-level compilers such as C, Pascal and Basic are more commonly used. Such high-level compilers translate your program into machine code. Among Basic compilers, a notable one is Bascom-AVR, which has both good and bad points. However, I believe that Bascom is an ideal compiler for both beginner and professional programmers, as it combines the advantages of the high-level Basic language along with the ability to embed assembly language in your program

An introduction to Bascom-AVR

Bascom exists in two versions: Bascom-8051 and Bascom-AVR. The suffix tells us which microcontroller family is supported by the compiler. In this book we will use Bascom-AVR, which can be downloaded from: www.mcselec.com. The free DEMO version is fully functional but with a limitation on program length. As beginner programmers we should find that the DEMO version fulfils our needs, because our programs will be short, but still fully functional.

Being a Windows program, Bascom is similar to many of the Windows program that most of us already know hence we will not waste much time describing icons like "File Open, File Edit" etc. We will however, spend some time outlining the various variable types which BASCOM supports.

Variables that we can use in Bascom compiler are:

» Bit (1 bit),
» Byte (8 bits = 1 byte),
» Word (2 bytes, variable can have a value from 0 to 65,535),
» Integer (2 bytes, variable can have a value from -32,768 to + 32,767),
» Long (4 bytes, variable can have a value from -2,147,483,648 to + 2,147,483,647),
» Single (32 bits, variable can have a value from 1.5 x 10^-45 to 3.4 x 10^38,
» Double (64 bits, variable can have a value from 5.0 x 10^-324 to 1.7 x 10^308,
» String (a collection of text characters with a length up to 254 bytes, A string dimensioned with a length of 10 bytes will occupy 11 bytes in memory).

We can assign variables any »name«. I suggest that we use names that will describe the function of variable: i.e. a variable with name *B_left* can be used for *button_left*, while *B_right* can be used for *button_right*. There are however, many so-called reserved words which cannot be used for variable names. Here are a few of them: OFF, ON, OUT, OUTPUT, LCD, LEFT, RIGHT, LINE, TIMER etc. Reserved words show up in a different colour within the Bascom Editor, making it easier to avoid using these names for your own variables. When I program I try to use as normal a name as possible for variables, like Button, Sensor, Temperature etc. I avoid using names like *A1, A2, A3*, because, as your program grows, you will have difficulty distinguishing the meanings of A1, A2, A3 later on in the program.

Before we start to program, let's start off by getting familiar with Bit and Byte variables. Both terms have been seen in elementary school math. The Binary number system contains of only 2 digits: 0 and 1. The smallest variable size is Bit, which can hold 2 values: 0 and 1, while Byte can hold 256 values, from value 0000,0000 to value 1111,1111, which in the decimal number system corresponds to 0 and 255 respectively.

Our First program

Our first program will be simple and will use the most commonly used command:

```
Do - Loop
```

This is a so-called never ending loop, in which the program loops from the Do statement, where it starts executing the program, to the Loop statement, where it loops back to the Do statement. Most of our programs will contain the *Do – Loop* statement: few programs exist without it.

With our first program, we will turn one LED, connected to the microcontroller, on and off. LEDs (light emitting diodes) are ideal for use with microcontrollers since LEDs require only few milliamps to glow. All AVR devices can easily deliver those few milliamps to one or more LEDs. The circuit diagram is shown in Figure 2.

Note that each LED has a resistor connected in series. This resistor limits the current through the microcontroller output port and LED to a safe value. The formula to calculate the resistor value is:

$$R_{LED} = (U_{VCC} - U_{LED})/I_{LED}$$

U_{VCC} in most instances (at least in this book) is 5.0 Volts, while U_{LED} is from 1.5 Volts (for red or yellow LED) and up to 3.2 Volts for white LED, while I_{LED} is in a range from 1 to 10 mA for small signal LEDs.

We also see in Figure 2, resistor R1, which is connected to the Reset pin, which ensures the correct start of the microcontroller when the power supply is connected to our circuit. We also see a ceramic resonator (RES1), CON2 which serves as programming connector and of course our microcontroller IC1. Good electronics practice dictates that we use capacitor C1 in our circuit: it blocks interference that may be caused by our microcontroller.

Our first program will be like this:

```
$regfile = "m16.def"
$crystal =8000000
Dim Led as Bit

Do
    Config PortD = Output
    PortD.0 = Led
    Led = Not Led
    Wait 1
Loop
```

The first statement tells the BASCOM-AVR compiler that we will use the ATmega16 micro controller. The second statement defines the frequency at which the microcontroller runs. This frequency (8.0 MHz) is generated within the microcontroller itself using either an internal RC oscillator (8.0 MHz) or the external 12.0 MHz resonator that we may have chosen to use in our circuit. Next is the so-called *Dimension* statement, where we <u>define the name</u> of the variable and <u>its type</u>. In our example we have defined a variable with name *Led* which is of the Bit type.

You will recognize the *Do – Loop* structure that has been mentioned earlier. Within *Do*

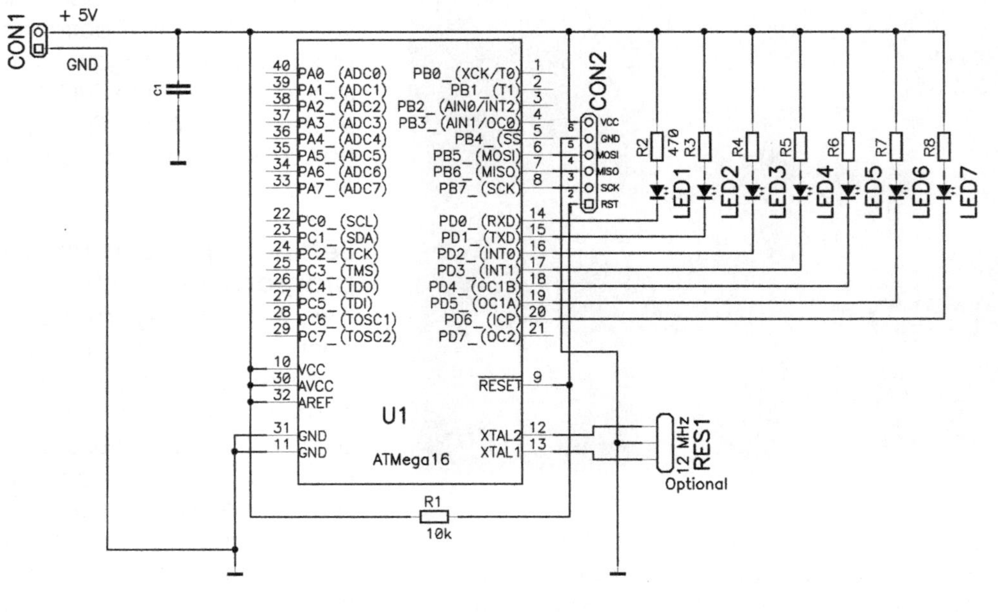

Figure 2: Simple use of microcontroller with LEDs

– *Loop* you will see a statement that configures I/O port D as output. With the statement *PortD.0 = Led* we assign the variable *Led* to a certain pin of the microcontroller, which in our case is PortD.0. We could have assigned variable *Led* to any pin from PortD.0 to PortD.7, which is very handy from a hardware point of view. In other words, it's easier to assign a different pin name in your program than changing the PCB (printed circuit board) layout in your device if so required.

The next statements are:

```
Led = Not Led
Wait 1
```

The first statement inverts the value of the *Led* variable. If its value was 0 then it will become 1 or vice versa. The *Wait 1* statement means that the program will wait for 1 second before proceeding. This simple program will cause the LED to blink with a frequency of 1/2 Hz on PortD.0. (1 second on, one second off, for a total period of 2 seconds or ½ Hz).

OK, you have written your first program, which works as expected, but now we have to realize this in a real life circuit. We can use a soldering iron and solder it or use a

NOTE

"Note: when using Sample Electronics programmer with MiniPin II make sure that you connect 5V power supply to J16!"

development board along with suitable programmer. If you join the microcontroller world, I would certainly recommend using one of the AVR development boards. Such development boards contain all that is needed to develop programs on the microcontroller. Some such boards require an external programmer to program the microcontroller, while others include a programmer. An example of the latter is the MegaPin development board, described later in the book.

MiniPin II development board

At this point we will briefly describe the MiniPin II development board, which is a PCB with all the necessary parts needed to program microcontrollers and to test their behaviour in real life.

You can see in Figure 3 a photo of MiniPin II with its description.

Figure 3: MiniPin II board features: keypad, I/O connectors, 2x 8 LEDs, Reset Button, USB connector, sockets for microcontrollers, crystal/resonator socket, I/O connectors; 2x 8 LEDs, 1Wire sockets and its connectors, socket for external crystal oscillator; programming socket; trimmer for external V_{REF}

MiniPin II is basically the same as the device seen in Figure 2 with some extensions which are not used in our example. What is common to Figure 2 and Figure 3 that both devices need a programmer to program our microcontroller. A simple, easily-built programmer that can be connected to an LPT port is shown in Figure 4.

Whichever programmer that you use, Sample Electronics programmer or Proggy II, you should connect it to PROGGY socket on MiniPin II. Proggy II has a built-in connection for 5V power supply.

Setting up Bascom to program MiniPin II

If we want to program microcontrollers with a program that we have written in Bascom, then we have to make a few settings within Bascom. In Figure 5 you will see setting for the Sample Electronics programmer, like the LPT address, that you can find by looking at the BIOS set-up screen of your PC. If you use

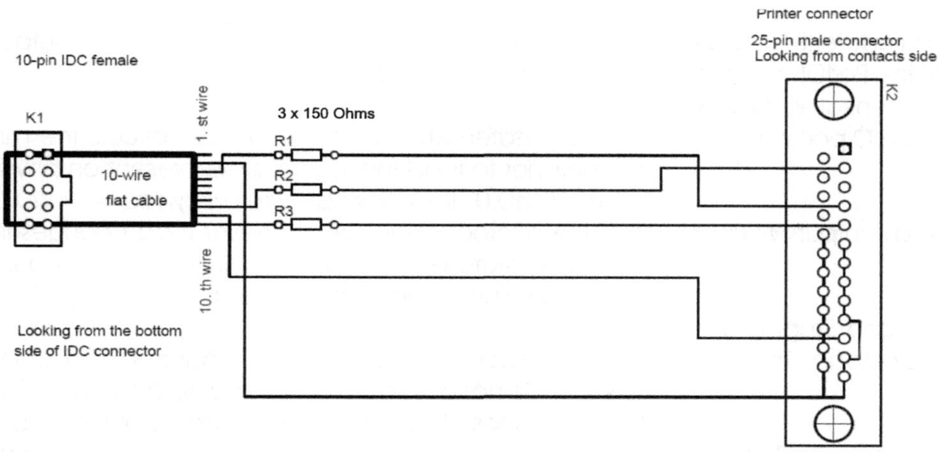

Figure 4: Simple LPT programmer – Sample Electronics programmer

Proggy II however, set Bascom as seen in Figure 6. In settings (System / Device manager / COM-LPT ports) find the No. of the COM port, which is labelled "USB Serial COM port". Below the COM port section, set the path for STK500.exe file. This file is part of Atmel's AVR Studio Ver.4 program which can be downloaded for free from www.atmel.com. STK500.exe is normally at "C:\Program Files\Atmel\AVR Tools\STK500". These are all the SW settings needed within Bascom-AVR for the programmer.

The first program that we wrote can now be saved and compiled (press F7, or click the icon Compile, or click right mouse button and select Compile). Then the microcontroller can be programmed (press F4, or click the icon Program, or click right mouse button and select Program) into our microcontroller. If all went OK then our LED should blink nicely.

Keypads & transistors

Microcontrollers need to be able to receive data to their input pins and perform specific tasks as defined within their program. Those input signals can come from various sensors, keypads or other electronic elements. For the next example we will show how to use a simple keypad. The schematic diagram can be seen in Figure 7. You will notice that this schematic diagram is the same as the schematic of MiniPin II, where we also see LEDs and resistors. Keypads are connected between the microcontroller and GND. Note that this is the generally used convention when wiring keypads in microcontroller applications. In this schematic a logical state will change from 1 to 0 if a keypad will be pressed. Check out the program Program1.bas, written in Bascom-AVR, which detects pressed keypads.

```
Config Portb = Output
Config Pind.0 = Input
PortB = 255

Dim Led As Bit
Dim Keypad As Bit

$regfile = "m16def.dat"
$crystal =8000000
Do
Set PortD.0
Keypad = PinD.0
PortB = 255
If Keypad = 0 Then
   PortB.2 = Led
   Led = Not Led
   Wait 1
Else
   PortB.1 = Led
   Led = Not Led
   Wait 1
End If
Loop
```

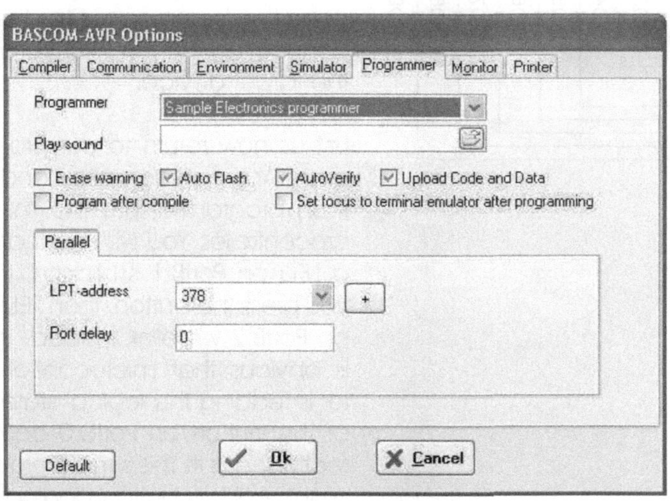

Figure 5: Set Sample programmer within Bascom-AVR

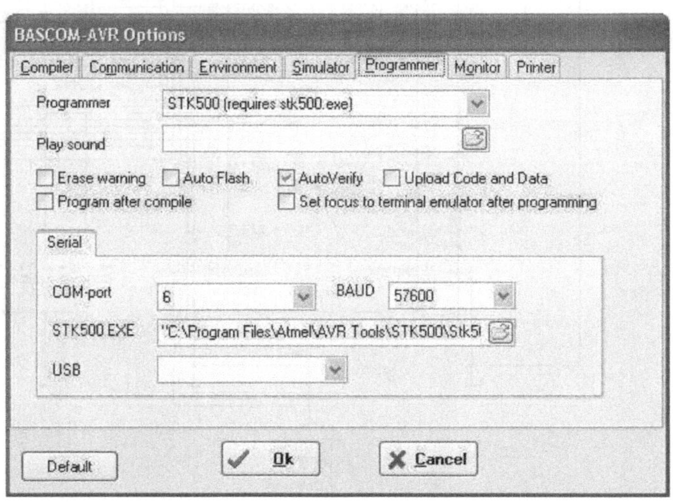

Figure 6: Set STK500 programmer within Bascom-AVR

You will notice that we have configured PortB as Output and PortD.0 (that is the first bit of the PortD) as Input. The rule with AVRs (and all other microcontrollers except 8051 family) is: before manipulating an I/O port we have to define whether it's Input or Output!

The next statement *PortB = 255* sets all outputs of PortB to logical 1, which turns all LEDs off.

We already know the *Dim* statements and *$regfile* and *$crystal* statements, as well as the *Do-Loop*. The next statement is new: *Keypad = PinD.0.*

The careful reader will notice that we wrote ***PinD.0*** and not ***PortD.0*** – why is that? Well, let me briefly say that the AVR has 2 registers associated with each physical I/O pin: the PIN and PORT registers. The PIN register is intended for reading the logical state of the I/O pin, while PORT register acts as an output: driving the physical pin with a logical 0 or 1 (and providing a suitable output current, either sink or source).

DDRn	PORTn	I/O	Pull up	Comment
0	0	Input	No	3-state (Hi - Z)
0	1	Input	Yes	PORT n will source current if ext. pulled low.
1	0	Output	No	Push - Pull Zero Output
1	1	Output	No	Push - Pull One Output

Table 1: Explanation of DDRn registers, where n stands for Port name, i.e. A, B, C, D, etc.

Therefore statement *Keypad = PinD.0* instructs the microcontroller to read the logical state present on physical pin PortD.0. If we instead wrote *Keypad = PortD.0* then the microcontroller would never read changes in the logical state of the physical pin, but instead would return the value of the output register.

This fact often causes problems to programming beginners, but do not despair - you will get used to those Pins & Ports. For those that wish to know more about this topic let me say that AVRs contain a DDRn register, for each I/O Port "n". The DDR register defines whether an I/O pin is input/output or 3-state. See Table 1 for explanations of DDRn registers.

Next, let's set-up PortB with some physical pins set as output, some as input and some as high impedance:

```
DDRB  = &B11110000
PortB = &B11000011
```

What does that mean? PortB.7 and PortB.6 are configured as Push-Pull Outputs with an output value of "1" or high. PortB.5 and PortB.4 are configured as Push-Pull Output with an output value of "0" or low, PortB.3 and PortB.2 are configured as Inputs without Pull-up resistors and hence they act as high impedance input. PortB.1 and PortB.0 are configured as Input but with Pull-up resistors activated. As a beginner one would ask himself: why do I need high impedance inputs? Well, there are electronic circuits – like VHF receivers that are intended for remote control or toys etc. Some of those receivers have a high impedance output which means that on the microcontroller side you must also have a high impedance input. Another application of the Hi-Z input is if we want to "disconnect" a microcontroller's pin from the target device. In this case putting a microcontroller's I/O pin in a high impedance condition is analogous to disconnecting the pin itself from the target device.

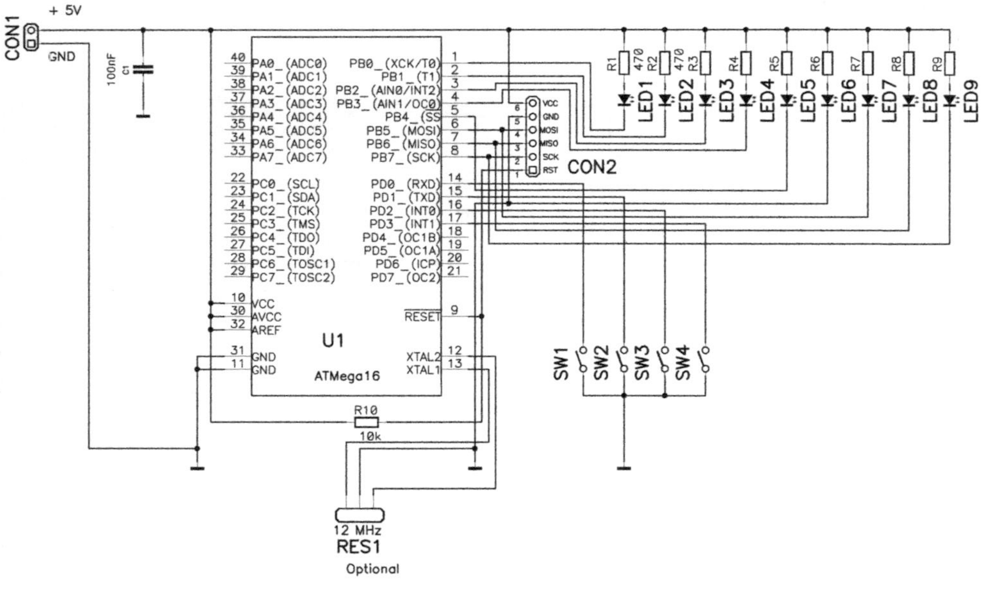

Figure 7: Schematic diagram of keypads connected to a microcontroller

Let us now return to our program. You can compile it and then program it into the microcontroller. You will see that a LED on PortB.1 s blinking. If you press the button, then LED on PortB.2 will blink instead. It is obvious that microcontroller is reading the logical state of the button on PortD.0 correctly. That's it! This simple program reads a button's logical state on one of the microcontroller's pins. No big deal, it's that simple. You can now use as many buttons as you like in your microcontroller devices providing that reading is done from the PIN register as shown above.

Debounce

Well, life is never as simple as it looks at first a glance. The above program(ming) sample of reading a keypad's logical state works OK in an electronically "calm" environment without interference. Even if we had an ideal, electronically calm environment, you should be aware that all electrical switches "bounce". When we press the button and see how the LED state changes, our eyes react much too slowly to see all the quick changes of signal (the "bounces") that have occurred when the button changes state from on-off and vice- versa.

In Figure 8 you can see that there are many bounces when a button is pressed and rest assured that a microcontroller can easily detect all of those bouncing signals. This can result in disaster if we don't take suitable precautionary measures to prevent that. Imagine a worker who is loading metal parts below a 10 Tons press while holding his hands under the press. Sudden interference could activate the press, resulting in all that force being applied to the worker's hands... We have to prevent that and similar situations! One way to prevent this is to use the Debounce statement. Its usage is simple:

```
Debounce Pinx.y , state , label [ , SUB]
```

You will note that the *Debounce* statement is also reading a button's logical state from the PIN register. *Debounce* can be performed at either the logical state 0 or 1. When the condition is met, it will jump to a label or subroutine.

Debounce works briefly as follows: when a button is pressed, the microcontroller detects this and waits for 25 milliseconds (the default setting of debounce time) and then re-checks for that logical state again. If the logical state is not the same as it was previously, then this means that the microcontroller has sensed interference and no further action should be taken. If the logical state is the same as it was previously, then program jumps to the indicated label or subroutine.

Let's look at an example of debouncing in program Debounce.bas:

```
Config PortB = Output
Config PinD.1 = Input
Config PinD.2 = Input

Dim Led As Bit, Led1 as Bit
Keypad Alias Pind.2
$regfile = "m16def.dat"
$crystal =8000000

Do
PortB = 255
Debounce  Keypad, 0, Turn_LED1, sub
Debounce  PinD.1, 0, Turn_LED2, sub
Loop
End

'subroutines
Turn_LED1:
While Keypad=0
   PortB.1 = Led
   Led = Not Led
   Wait 1
Wend
Return

Turn_LED2:
While Pind.1=0
   PortB.2 = Led1
   Led1 = Not Led1
   Wait 1
Wend
Return
```

I trust that most of the program is clear, however, there is a new structure called *WHILE-WEND* used in this sample. The *While-WEND* structure (or loop) uses the following syntax:

```
WHILE condition
  statements
WEND
```

If we now look at the whole program it is clear: if no button is pressed, then nothing is happening and no LED is blinking. When we press any of the buttons then the *Debounce* statement executes a suitable subroutine. In this subroutine we check within the While loop to see how long the applicable button remains pressed. As long as it is pressed, the subroutine will continue to execute in a loop, blinking the corresponding LED. When the button is released, the program returns to the main *Do-Loop*.

Let me add that the *Debounce* time can be set with:

```
Config Debounce   = xx
    'where xx = time in milliseconds
```

As mentioned earlier, the default setting is 25 milliseconds.

Driving a transistor

Microcontroller can drive various electronic components as long as these components don't draw too much current (i.e < 20 mA). That is a price that we must pay for the miniaturisation of microcontrollers. But that does not matter much, since we can drive powerful relays and other electronic devices with the help of transistors which are connected between the microcontroller and the powerful device. In electronics there are many types of transistors, but in this book, we will focus on bipolar and FET transistors. With both types of transistors, there are P and N types. P types are driven with a logical 0 while N types are driven with a logical 1. Figure 9 shows a basic circuit

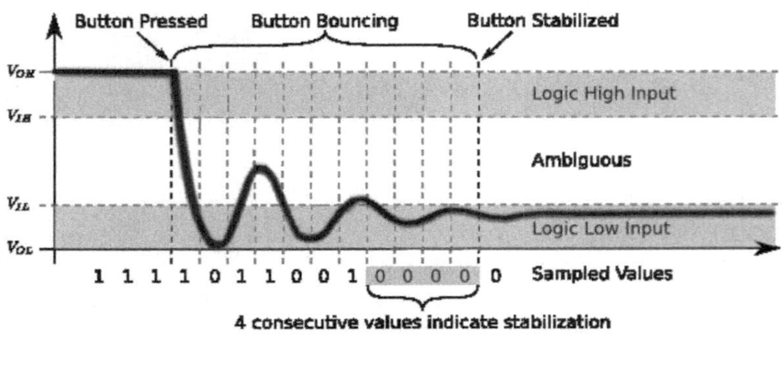

Figure 8: Typical bouncing signal when button was pressed

where P and N type bipolar transistors were used, while in Figure 10 you can see the use of FET transistors instead.

In Figure 9 you will notice that both transistors have a resistor connected to their Base pin. These resistors are there to protect the transistor's base from too high input current. The value of that resistor can be in the range from 1k Ohm to 10k Ohm. In this circuit, the relay functions as a load. With the NPN transistor, the relay is connected to + 12V, while with the PNP transistor, it is connected to +5V, so one has to choose a relay with a suitable coil voltage rating. You will also notice in this circuit a diode is connected in parallel with the relay's coil. This diode serves as a protection for the transistor when the relay is turned off. With the NPN transistor, we turn the relay on with a logical 1 and with the PNP transistor a logical 0 is output to the microcontroller's port instead.

Figure 10 is similar to Figure 9 with a note that FET transistors do not need a protection resistor in series with the Gate pin because no current flows to the FET's gate, but we need one connected to GND.

The Bascom program for turning the relay on and off is identical to the program for turning On/Off LEDs.

Driving a small DC motor

A DC motor can be connected to our microcontroller in a few ways. The first circuit can be seen in Figure 9 or Figure 10 where we could connect a motor instead of a relay.

Doing it this way has a disadvantage: we can turn a DC motor On/Off, however, we cannot change its rotation from clockwise to counter clockwise, nor can we change the speed of rotation. To do that we need 4 transistors connected in a "bridge" configuration. Using modern IC technology, we can instead use an integrated circuit (IC). For our purposes, we can use the L272M chip, which includes 2 powerful operational amplifiers, that can drive up to 1.0A current to a load - more than enough to drive small DC motors.

The schematic diagram seen in Figure 11 is simple - not much different from those already discussed. The only thing new is the L272M chip. Its connection enables you

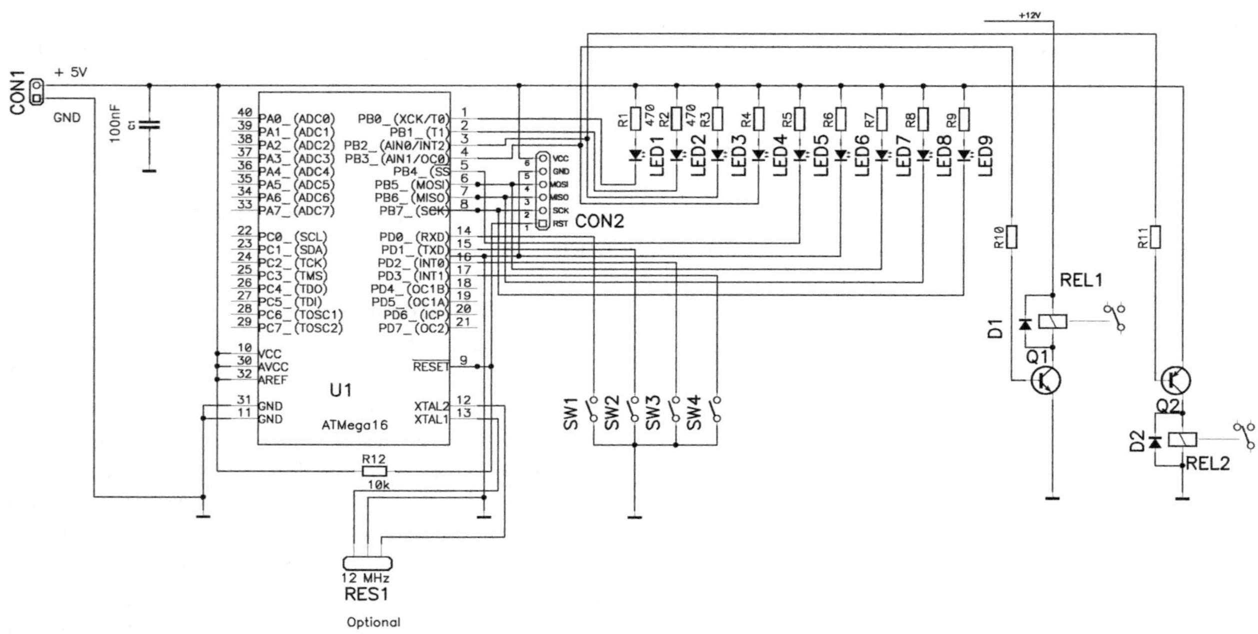

Figure 9: Basic circuit for driving bipolar transistor P & N types

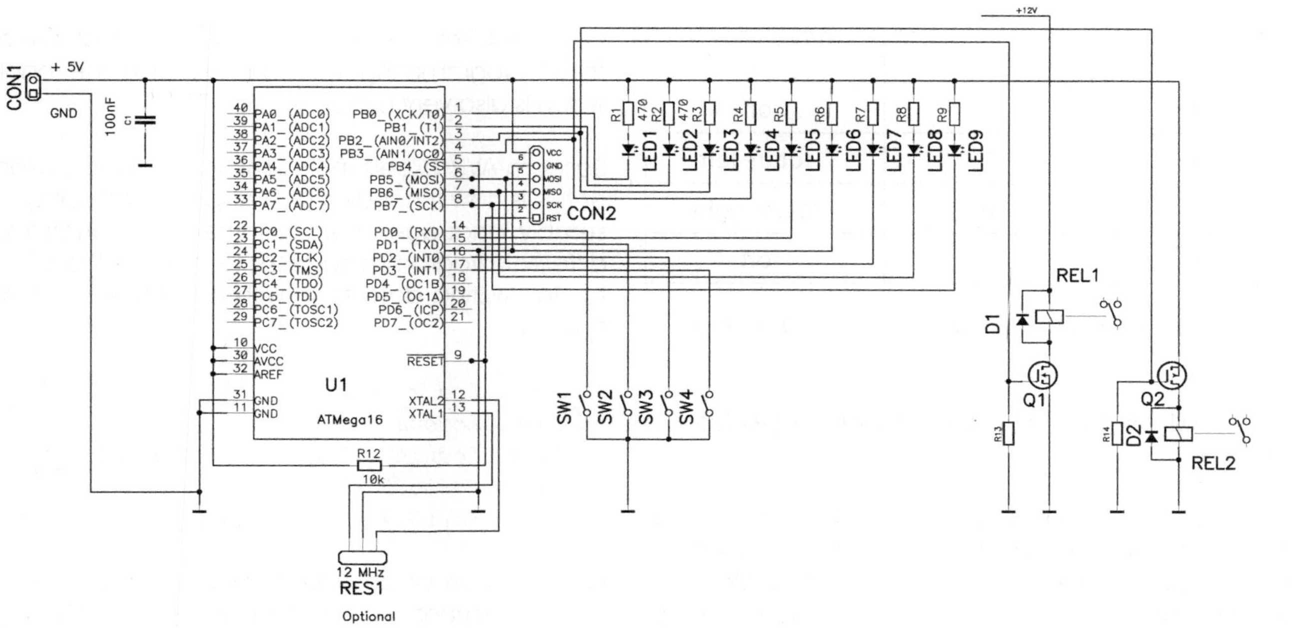

Figure 10: Basic circuit for driving FET transistor P & N types

to turn a motor in either direction with only 2 logical signals. The motor can also be quickly stopped. See Table 2 for an explanation of the logical states.

Please note that the expressions clockwise or counter clockwise depend on how you connect up the motor's wires to your circuit. If you notice that the motor turns opposite to Table 2 then just reverse the wiring to the motor's terminals – or be wise and change the logical states in your program instead.

If you want to drive larger motors, with currents up to 3A, then use an L298 chip. The schematic is similar to Figure 11, for the pin-out of the L298 please refer to its datasheet.

Displaying data on LCD

Displaying data on an LCD display has been the wish of all those involved in electronics ever since LCDs were mass-produced. Most devices that we use today use LCD displays. In this chapter we will use an alphanumeric 2x16 LCD module that is widely available.

Let's first say a few words about the LCD module. The description 2x16 means that this LCD has 2 lines, each of which contains 16 places to show an ASCII character. There are many LCD modules available on the market and one can buy LCD displays with different character sets. Most LCD displays have the capability to also display up to 8 custom-designed characters which a skilful programmer can program into the dis-

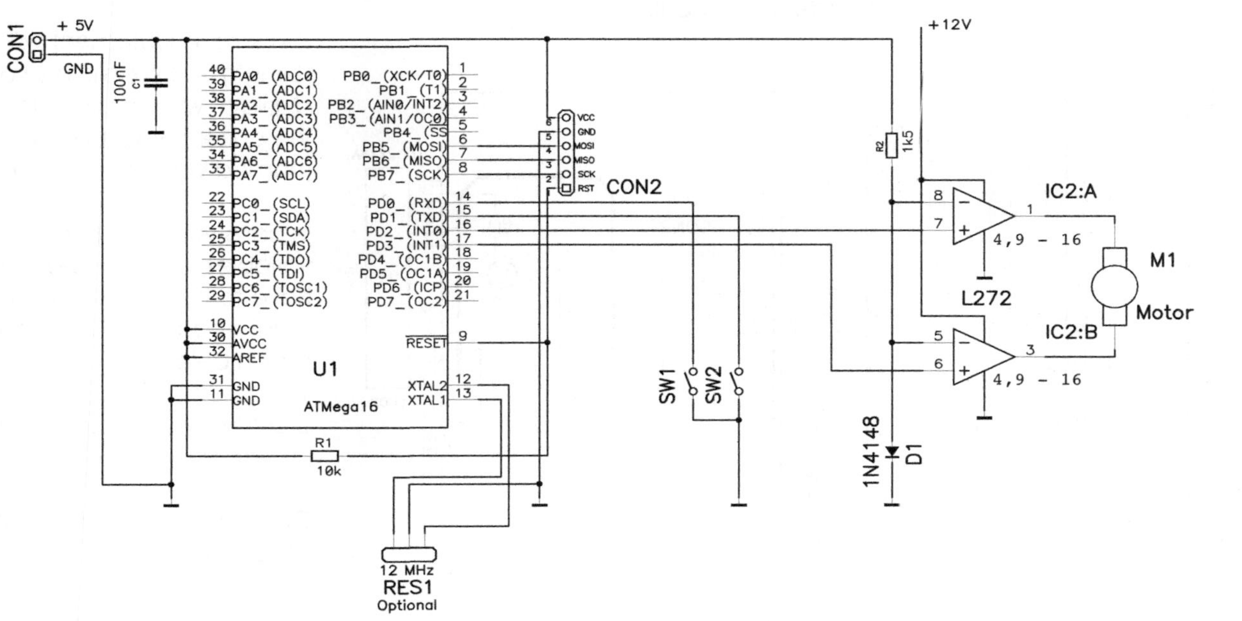

Figure 11: Schematic diagram where an L272M drives a small DC motor

PD2	PD3	
0	0	off
0	1	rotate left
1	0	rotate right
1	1	off

Table 2: Logical states for driving a motor with L272M

play's RAM memory which will be discussed later in the book.

LCD displays need a power supply and some logic signals which determine which characters will appear at the different positions available on the display. Most LCD displays have 8-bit or 4-bit addressing, while the power supply voltage is generally 5V. Additionally there is a pin for setting the contrast, Enable and Register Select pins. Most frequently, 4-bit addressing is used, as it minimizes the number of microcontroller pins that are needed for the interface. 8-bit addressing is faster than 4-bit, however I have seen no application so far that would require the faster 8-bit LCD addressing.

A schematic showing an LCD connected to a microcontroller can be seen in Figure 12.

Note in Figure 12 that a trim pot is used to set the contrast on the LCD screen.

The value of this trim pot is not critical, and it can range from 5 kOhm to 50 kOhm. Most LCDs also contain a built in backlight for easier reading in a low-light environment. To use this backlight, connect its pins in series with a 10 Ohm resistor (some LCDs will require a larger resistance) to + 5V and GND. In schematic Figure 12 we have used a FET to turn the backlight On/Off under microcontroller control. You will see later in the book that with some smart programming we can also dim the backlight which is also very useful.

Bascom-AVR excels in its simplicity. A good example of this is how it handles LCD display interfacing. In assembly language, one would need to perform seven different programming tasks to initialize the LCD and to start writing data to it. With Bascom-AVR it's much simpler:

```
Config Lcd = 16 * 2
Config Lcdbus = 4
Config Lcdpin = Pin, Db4 = Portd.4, _
Db5 = Portd.5, Db6 = Portd.6, _
Db7 = Portd.7, E = Portd.2, Rs = Portd.1
```

Configuration of an LCD display is that simple. Within three statements we define the type of LCD (*Config Lcd = 16*2*), the way that we have chosen to drive it (*Lcdbus = 4*) and have configured the I/O ports for all the necessary pins on the LCD display (*Config Lcdpin*).

So, you have now configured your LCD display. At the start of your program you could use the *CLS* statement (Clear screen). Also, you must define where the LCD should display your specific messages with the statements *Upperline* or *Lowerline*, which define the upper or lower line of the LCD. The statement used to display text on the LCD is very simple:

```
LCD "text"
```

This simple statement will display the word "text" on your LCD. Could it be any simpler? Generally you will be displaying text and variables from your program. You can do that as follows:

```
LCD "Length = "; variable; " m"
```

This simple statement will display "Length = xxxx m" on your LCD display where xxxx represents the current value of the variable (named variable, above).

In case you want to display more variables on one line, then you have to be careful to add some blank spaces between them, as shown below:

```
LCD "Txt1 = "; variable1; " ";
    "Txt2 = "; variable2; " "
```

One can also use the statement Locate as follows:

```
Locate 1, 1
LCD "Txt1 = "; variable1" ";
```

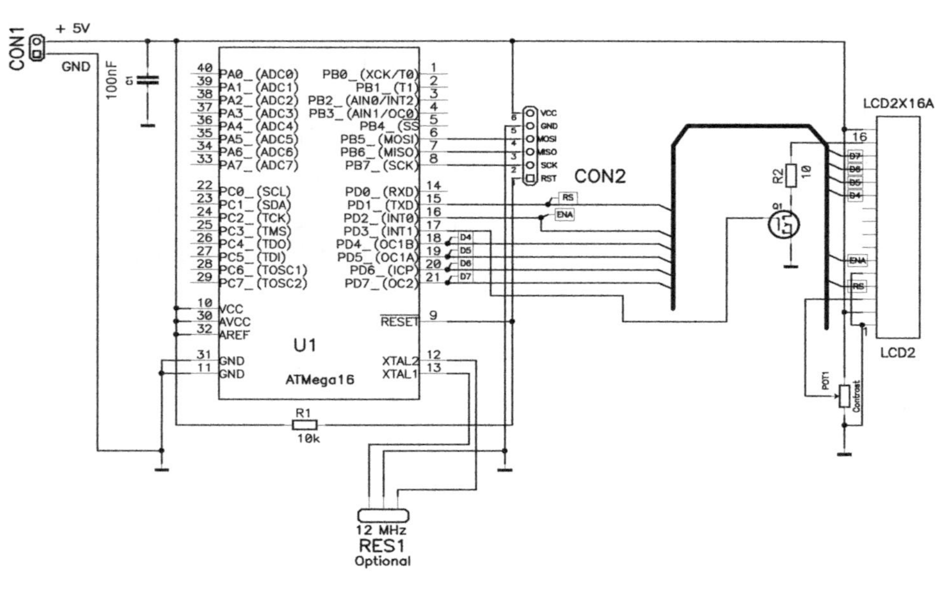

Figure 12: Connection of LCD to a microcontroller

```
Locate 1,6
Txt2 = "; variable2; "  ";
```

It is good practice to add a few blank spaces after each variable. These blanks will over-write digits previously displayed for that variable, when the value of that variable decreases by a factor of 10. For example, if we display variable = 1234 and next moment we display variable = 56, then LCD will display 5634. You may ask yourself why that is so. Well, to begin with, we did not use the *CLS* statement in-between the two LCD commands. That however is not the problem. The problem is that digits on the LCD display remain on until we power the display off. That means that those digits "34" remained on LCD because we displayed them previously and had not replaced them with blanks. With a few blanks we would have removed the unwanted digits from being displayed.

This technique only works if you have plenty of free space on your display., For advanced programmers I recommend using the format and fusing statements, in most cases.

Sample program LCD 2x16.bas also includes use of Timer0 at generating 1 second pulse. It's usage is simple. We have to configure Timer0, enable interrupts and Timer0:

```
On Ovf0 Tim0_isr
     'define interrupt subroutine
     'interrupt subroutine
Config Timer0 = Timer, Prescale = 1
     'configure timer
Enable Timer0
     'enable timer
Enable Interrupts
     'enable interrupts
```

The statement *On Ovf0* defines name of interrupt subroutine, *Config Timer0* defines mode that Timer0 works in (in our case it's a timer, but could be also counter) and defines Prescale factor. Prescaler within AVR divides system clock (8.0 MHz). While, in this case it's not needed, on other occasions it's handy to be able to divide the clock frequency by a certain value.

Conclusion

The simplicity of Bascom-AVR is very attractive. I have seen many people from different occupations, i.e. biologist, chemist, mechanical engineers and also retired people who all recognised Bascom-AVR as a wonderful tool which has widened their knowledge in the field of microcontroller programming. Everyone who came to Bascom courses that I hold at my company have told me that they understood that programming microcontrollers is something that is meant for professional engineers who program microcontrollers nearly 24/7. They were also under the impression that the only way to program microcontrollers is with C or assembly language. Well, I know many professionals use C or assembly at work but for personal projects (where they do not work in a group) they use Bascom. Since many companies use Bascom-AVR in their products, there is absolutely no reason why you would not consider it. Besides, Google the word "Bascom"; you will receive more than 6 million results! If you narrow search to Bascom-AVR then we receive 770.000 results. That says something doesn't it!

Example program ID	
Name:	Program1.bas
Microcontroller:	Any AVR microcontroller
Testing circuit:	Figure 2
MiniPin compatibility:	yes
MegaPin compatibility:	yes
Program turns On and Off LED	

Example program ID	
Name:	Program2.bas
Microcontroller:	Any AVR microcontroller
Testing circuit:	Figure 7
MiniPin compatibility:	yes
MegaPin compatibility:	yes
Program generates a blinking LED if a keypad is pressed	

Example program ID	
Name:	Debounce.bas
Microcontroller:	Any AVR microcontroller
Testing circuit:	Figure 7
MiniPin compatibility:	yes
MegaPin compatibility:	yes
Program generates a blinking LED if a keypad is pressed (using Debounce command)	

Example program ID	
Name:	LCD 2x16.bas
Microcontroller:	Any AVR microcontroller
Testing circuit:	Figure 12
MiniPin compatibility:	yes
MegaPin compatibility:	yes
Program displays data on 2x16 LCD using Timer	

Example program ID	
Name:	LCD 2x16_1.bas
Microcontroller:	Any AVR microcontroller
Testing circuit:	Figure 12
MiniPin compatibility:	yes
MegaPin compatibility:	yes
Program displays custom characters on 2x16 LCD	

Programming AVR microcontrollers without a programmer

By Jurij Mikeln

Our task here is to program our target microcontroller with a Bootloader program. What is a Bootloader? It's a short program that is placed at the upper end of a microcontroller's Flash memory which is normally inactive. We can activate it by pulling the Reset line low or pressing the Reset button.

Setting Up

The Bootloader program can be downloaded from our web page for free. When you open the file with Bascom-AVR, you will see some configurations pre-written for most common AVR MCU's, as follows:

```
$regfile = "m16def.dat"
Const Loaderchip = 16

'$regfile = "m32def.dat"
'Const Loaderchip = 32

'$regfile = "m88def.dat"
'Const Loaderchip = 88

'$regfile = "m162def.dat"
'Const Loaderchip = 162
```

From amongst these configurations, choose the pair of statements that correspond to your target microcontroller, and un-comment them. In our case it's the ATmega16, and you can see that these statements have no leading comment symbols. The program should be compiled with Bascom-AVR and programmed using any suitable programmer that can set the Fuse bits. Next, the Fuse bits should be set to the Bootloader memory

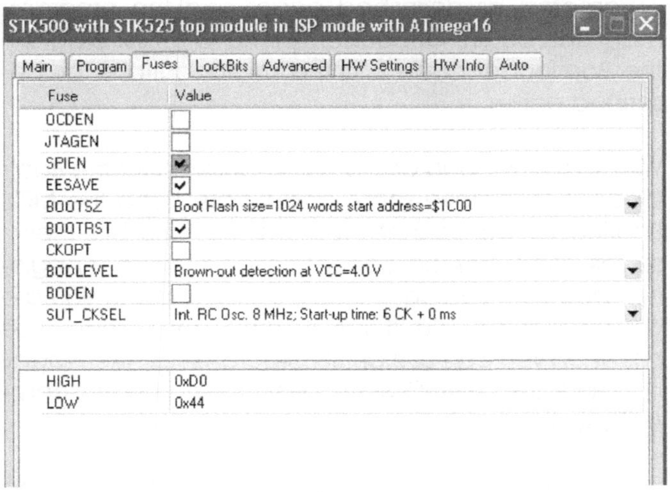

Figure 1: Fuse bits settings

space as shown in the Bootloader program. For example, in the case of the ATmega16:

```
#if Loaderchip = 16          ' Mega16
    $loader = $1c00          ' 1024 words
    Const Maxwordbit = 6     'Z6 is
                             'maximum bit
    Config Com1 = Dummy , Synchrone = 0 , _
    Parity = None , Stopbits = 1 , _
    Databits = 8 , Clockpol = 0
#endif
```

You can see from the statement *$loader = $1c00 ' 1024 words* that the loader size is 1024 words, and its starting memory address is $1C00: that is the value that we have choosen within AVR Studio's ***Bootsz window***, as shown in Figure 1.

Within the Fuses menu, also tick the BOOTRST box and then click the ***Program*** button. That's all there is to do for the Fuse bits settings. You have successfully programed Bootloader program to AT Mega16

Now, let's continue with other settings within Bascom-AVR. Using ***Options/Programmer*** you must set the Programmer listbox to MCS Bootloader, as shown in Figure 2.

Make sure you set the Baud rate to value shown in the

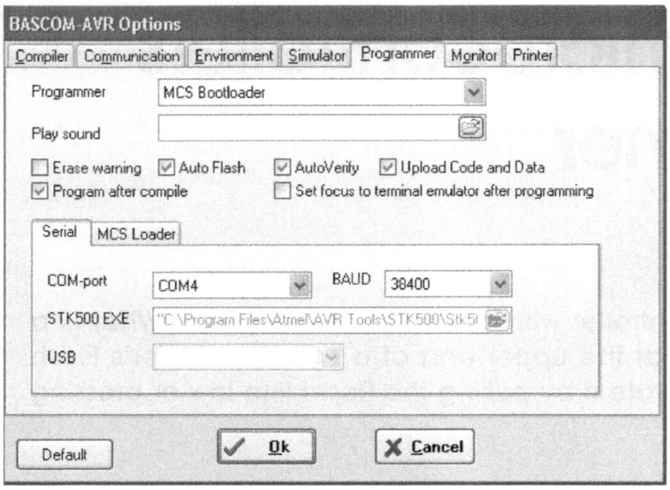

Figure 2: Programmer setting within Bascom-AVR

Bootloader program itself. Also set the COM port to the correct number. How do we know the correct COM port number? Well, connect MiniPin II to your PC via a USB cable and examine the COM/LPT Ports within the ***Device Manager*** on your PC (Control panel/ System/Hardware/ Device Manager). There is one last setting that we must set within the ***MCS Loader*** tab, as shown in Figure 3.

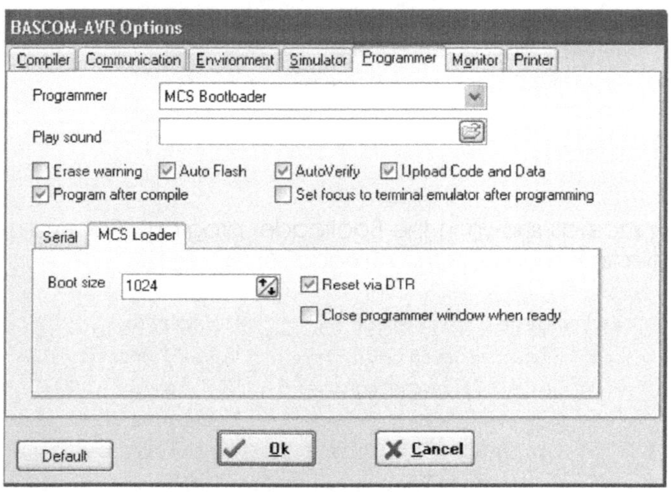

Figure 3: Additional setting within Bascom-AVR

Here we must set ***Boot size*** equal to the same value that we used when setting the AVR Fuse bits (from within AVR Studio as shown in Figure 1). Also we must check off the ***Reset via DTR*** box. Now, all the settings are done and programming via the USB cable can begin!

Programming

Mount a microcontroller (containing the Bootloader program) in the appropriate socket on the MiniPin II board, or on your target circuit board. Connect the MiniPin II board to the PC with a USB cable. Load your desired program into Bascom, compile it and then click ***Program***. A new window will open, as shown in Figure 4.

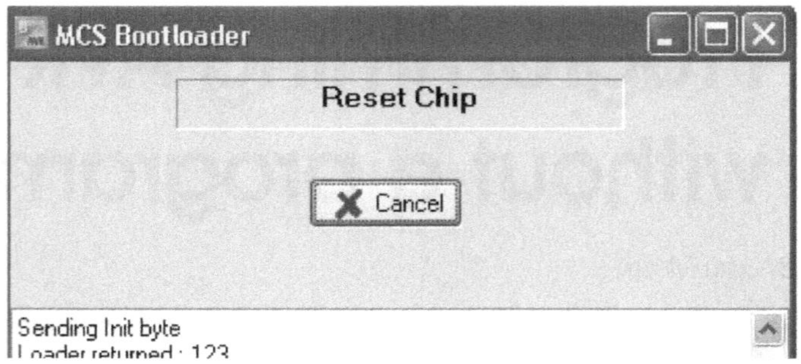

Figure 4: Window showing the start of programming using the MCS Bootloader programmer

Within a couple of moments you will see a window showing that the program is being uploaded and then you will see a message that the program was successfully programmed, as shown in Figure 5. If, by any chance you did not check off ***Reset via DTR***, as shown in Figure 3 (maybe you do not have the DTR signal available on your COM port), then you will have to press the Reset button when you see the message shown in Figure 4.

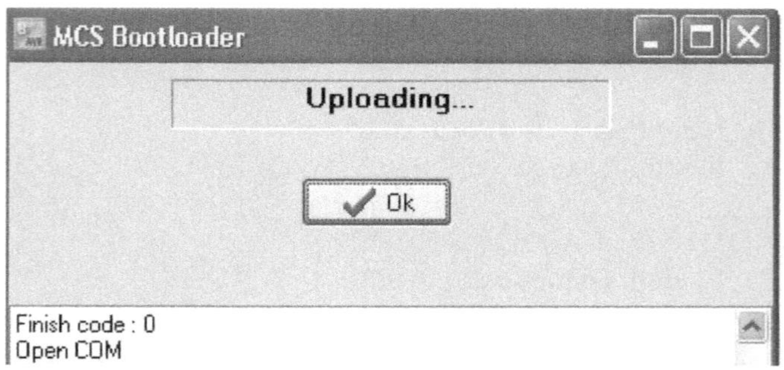

Figure 5: Successful programming

What if we do not have a MiniPin II board and/or USB? For these situations, there is also a solution. Say that you have any board containing an AVR microcontroller with the Rx/Tx and GND pins available. To program via the Bootloader, use one of the RS232 to TTL (or USB to TTL) adapters and connect it to your board using the Rx/TX pins on the AVR (and GND). Then set all the parameters as described earlier and the programming can begin. Of course, you have to first program the Bootloader code into the microcontroller as described earlier.

With so many good points, it is impossible for the Bootloader not to have some bad points. Using the MCS Bootloader we cannot program the Fuse bits themselves. That's not too bad restriction if you're a beginner, because you can't "mess up" things that you are not familiar with. But if you do have to change Fuse bits, then you can use an SPI programmer (like Proggy II) or use the $PROG statement within your Bascom-AVR program.

There is only one more thing to mention: When using an AVR MCU with the Bootloader code installed, the normal I/O functions of PortD.0 and PortD.1 are disa-

NOTE

$PROG statement may however lock your microcontroller (sometimes called "bricking it") if you do not know what you are doing, so be careful.

Example program ID	
Name:	BootLoader.zip
Microcontroller:	Any AVRs with bootloader
Testing circuit:	/
MiniPin compatibility:	yes
MegaPin compatibility:	yes
Bootloader program for many AVRs	

bled, because they serve as the UART's Rx and Tx pins during the bootloading process. We can, however, disable UART transmit and receive functions using these statements:

```
Ucsrb.3 = 0
Ucsrb.4 = 0
```

If we include these statements in our Bascom program, we regain the normal I/O functions of PortD.0 and PortD.1, but of course we cannot use the UART for serial communications unless we re-enable the UART, using the normal Bascom serial configuration statements.

Improved Debounce Routines

By Vladimir Mitrović

Anyone who has ever tried using a microcontroller to count how many times a switch or any other mechanical contact has changed state, will certainly agree that this is not a simple task. The problem is that mechanical contacts "bounce" when changing state. The microcontroller is fast enough to register not only the "real" change of state, but also those unwanted changes caused by contact "bounce". Therefore, it's common that a single push of a switch can register as multiple switch closures.

Bascom's *Debounce* statement solves this problem, by checking the switch's state over again a bit later, when a level change is detected at an input pin. For example, if *Debounce* is configured to recognise a falling edge at an input pin (a logical level change from *High* to *Low*), it will delay the program execution for 25 ms and then check the input pin again to see if it is still at a logic "0" or not. If it is, an associated subroutine will be executed. If not, the level change will be considered as just a "bounce", and will be ignored. This reduces the probability of false readings significantly. Also, the *Debounce* statement reacts to any change of input state only once, and does not block program execution while waiting for the desired state change to happen.

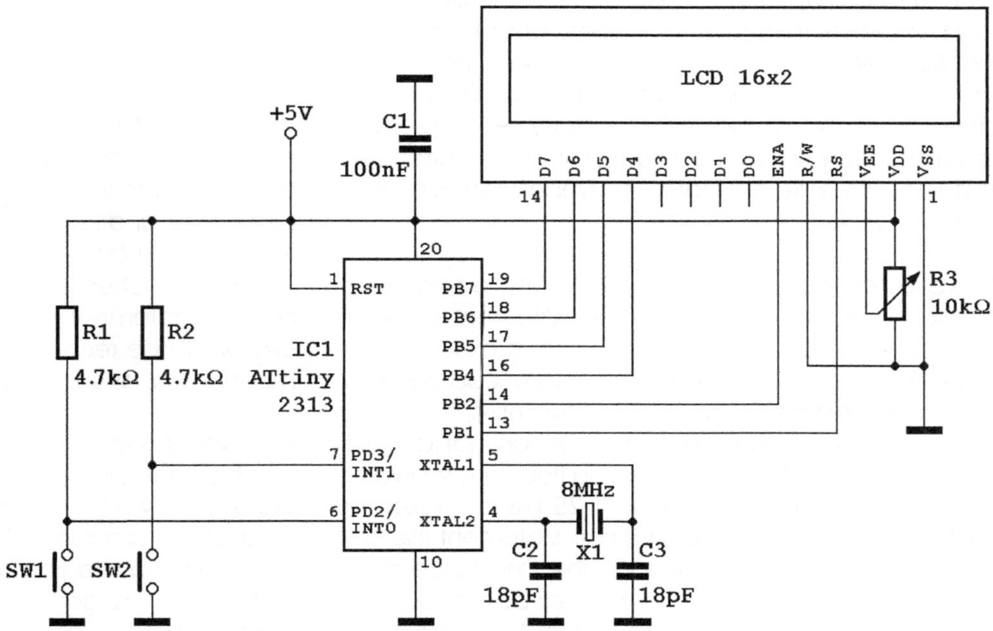

Figure 1: Test circuit for an improved Debounce

From my early days with Bascom, I realised the value of the *Debounce* statement and have even succeeded in expanding its capabilities. Let's see how!

Debouncing using external interrupts

The test circuit shown in Figure 1 is designed for testing the behaviour of the *Debounce* statement. An example of a suitable test program follows:

```
'Program *** Debounce1 ***

Dim Up_dn_counter As Byte

Sw1_pin Alias Pind.2
Config Sw1_pin = Input
Sw2_pin Alias Pind.3
Config Sw2_pin = Input
```

```
Up_dn_counter = 100

Do
   Debounce Sw1_pin , 0 , Sw1_sub , Sub
   Debounce Sw2_pin , 0 , Sw2_sub , Sub
   Home L
   Lcd "Counter = " ; Up_dn_counter ; " "
'do whatever
Loop

Sw1_sub:
   If Up_dn_counter > 0 Then
      Decr Up_dn_counter
   End If
Return

Sw2_sub:
   If Up_dn_counter < 255 Then
      Incr Up_dn_counter
   End If
Return
```

It is assumed that an LCD display is configured to match the wiring shown in Fig 1, but those statements are not shown, for simplicity. Pressing push-buttons SW1 or SW2 briefly will decrement or increment the value of the *Up_down_counter* variable, which will be immediately displayed on the LCD. Normally, each press on a push-button will be counted only once - erroneous readings are extremely rare. The *Debounce* statement works very well!

However, there is one detail that must be emphasized. To work properly, the *Debounce* statement must be located inside an endless loop, which is executed frequently. The time between consecutive loop iterations should be as short as possible. For example, if we want to reliably detect a push-button activation that lasts only 150 ms, the time between two loop iterations should be less than 125 ms (the remaining 25 ms are taken up by the execution of the *Debounce* statement itself). In other words, the loop containing the *Debounce* statement should execute at least 8 times per second. We can illustrate this problem if we insert a *Wait 2* statement at the end of the loop structure, in the previous example. Most short switch activations are now missed, and sometimes it's necessary to press the button for a pretty long time before the counter changes its value.

If we have a complex program in which the main program loop takes more than 100 ms to execute, and yet we need to effectively read the state of one or more push-buttons, we are forced to use external interrupts. The structure of such a program might be:

```
'Program *** Debounce2 (initial) ***

Dim Up_dn_counter As Byte

Sw1_pin Alias Pind.2
Config Sw1_pin = Input
Sw2_pin Alias Pind.3
Config Sw2_pin = Input

Config Int0 = Falling
On Int0 Int0_sub
Config Int1 = Falling
On Int1 Int1_sub

Up_dn_counter = 100
Do
'do whatever
   Home L
   Lcd "Counter = " ; Up_dn_counter ; " "
Loop

Int0_sub:
   If Up_dn_counter > 0 Then
      Decr Up_dn_counter
   End If
Return

Int1_sub:
   If Up_dn_counter < 255 Then
      Incr Up_dn_counter
   End If
Return
```

Again, the LCD display configuration statements are omitted for simplicity. External interrupts INT0 and INT1 are configured to detect a high-to-low transition on input pins PIND.2 and PIND.3. The associated interrupt service routine *Int0_sub* or *Int1_sub* will be executed when either of these switches is pressed. There is no need for *Debounce* statements anymore, since a push-button activation will be recognised via the appropriate interrupt mechanism, as soon as it occurs.

However, if you try out this program, you will be disappointed: one push-button activation will often be recognised as two or more presses. The reason is that there is no longer a double-check of the input pin's state, as was previously integrated into the *Debounce* statement. It seems like a good idea to include the *Debounce* statement within the interrupt service routine, as in this example:

```
'Program *** Debounce2 (correction 1) ***

Int0_sub:
   Debounce Sw1_pin , 0 , Sw1_sub , Sub
   Set Eifr.intf0
Return

Sw1_sub:
   If Up_dn_counter > 0 Then
      Decr Up_dn_counter
   End If
Return
```

A high-to-low transition on the PIND.2 will trigger execution of the *Int0_sub* routine, and the *Debounce* statement within that routine will check whether this transition was caused by a "real" press of the push-button, or if it was caused by switch "bounce"... However, this does not work properly! The *Debounce* statement has internal flags and will not execute the associated subroutine again until it detects that the push-button has been released and pressed once again. This occurs naturally if the *Debounce* statement is within the main loop and executes frequently. However, if it is written within an interrupt service routine, we have to allow the *Debounce* routine to sense input pin level changes in both directions. To do this, we must change the *Config Int0* statement as follows:

```
Config Int0 = Change    'correction 2
```

Note that the INTF0 bit within the EIFR register must be cleared (by writing "1" to it!) before the interrupt service routine returns control to the main program. By clearing this bit, we ignore any SW1 "bounces" that might occur during the execution of *Int0_sub*. Although the *Debounce* statement will prevent switch "bounce" being misinterpreted, each "bounce" will set the INTF0 bit and the interrupt service routine will needlessly execute again (because a pending interrupt exists!), as soon as control is returned to the main program.

A second possibility is shown in the *Int1_sub* interrupt service routine example, which looks like the following:

```
'Program *** Debounce2 (correction 3) ***

Int1_sub:
   Waitms 25
   If Sw2 = 1 Then
   Elseif Up_dn_counter < 255 Then
      Incr Up_dn_counter
   End If
   Set Eifr.intf1
Return
```

Now, the *Debounce* statement is simulated by inserting a 25 ms delay, followed by the *If Sw2 = 1* statement. If this condition is true, it means that input pin PIND.3 is no longer at a logic "0", and the interrupt service routine was triggered by a "bounce". Since there is no executable code in this case, program control returns to the main program. However, if the *If Sw2 = 1* condition is false, then SW2 is still pressed and the program executes the statements associated with this condition. Don't forget to clear the INTF1 bit in the EIFR register (by writing "1" into it!) to clear any pending interrupts, before returning to the main program.

Checking to see how long a button has been pressed

Sometimes it's useful to know not only if the button has been pressed, but for how long it has been pressed. A simple test circuit is shown in Figure 1. The program loops until the SW1 push-button is pressed. This is detected by the *Debounce* statement, which calls the *SW1_sub* subroutine:

```
'Program *** Debounce3 (part 1/3) ***

Sw1_pin Alias Pind.2
Config Sw1_pin = Input

Do
   Debounce Sw1_pin , 0 , Sw1_sub , Sub
'do whatever
Loop

Sw1_sub:
   Sw1_counter = 2
   While Sw1_pin = 0
      Waitms 10
      Incr Sw1_counter
      If Sw1_counter > 250 Then
         Exit While
      End If
   Wend
```

The *SW1_sub* subroutine executes a *While-Wend* loop until the button is released or 2.5 seconds has elapsed - whichever happens first. The program counts how many times the loop has been executed. As each loop takes (approximately) 10 ms, the value in the *SW1_counter* variable will be:

- 2-250 if SW1 was closed for 25 to 2500 ms or
- 251 if SW1 was closed for more than 2500 ms.

As the *Debounce* statement tests the condition of the specified pin two times within 25 ms (unless configured differently), intervals less than 25 ms will not be recognised. Therefore, the *SW1_counter* variable cannot hold values of 0 or 1. The value of the *SW1_counter* variable can be examined within the *Sw1_sub* subroutine itself, or within the main program loop. In the following example, it is done within the *SW1_sub* subroutine, immediately after the *While-Wend* loop:

```
'Program *** Debounce3 (part 2/3) ***

   Home L
   If Sw1_counter > 250 Then
      Lcd "pressed > 2.5s"
   Elseif Sw1_counter > 200 Then
      Lcd "pressed 2-2.5s"
   Elseif Sw1_counter > 100 Then
      Lcd "pressed 1-2 s "
   Else
      Lcd "pressed 0-1 s "
   End If
   Disp_counter = 200
Return
```

Here we display only an appropriate message. Before returning to the main program loop, the *Disp_counter* value is set to 200. This will ensure that the message is automatically erased from display after approximately 2 seconds:

```
'Prcgram *** Debounce3 (part 3/3) ***

Do
   Debounce Sw1 , 0 , Sw1_sub , Sub
'do whatever
   If Disp_counter > 0 Then
      Decr Disp_counter
      Waitms 10
```

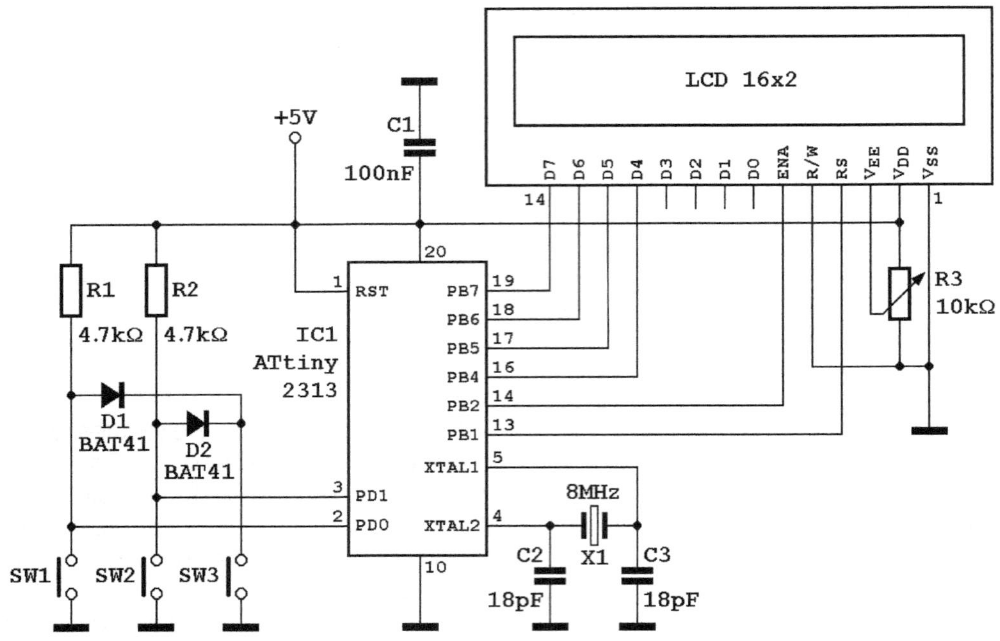

Figure 2: Two I/O pins are sufficient to read the state of three push-buttons

```
    Else
       Home L
       Lcd "Press SW1!"
    End If
 Loop
```

In programs containing no messages related to the *Debounce* statement or if messages are treated differently, omit the *Disp_counter* variable and any related statements in the main loop.

I usually use this time-measuring extension to *Debounce* when I want to associate more than one function to a single push-button. If you want to use it in your own program, keep in mind that, as opposed to the standard *Debounce* statement, this extension blocks program execution until the button is released or a time-out occurs (2.5 s in this example).

Using Debounce to read the state of more than one push-button

Often you will run into a situation in which you need one or two more pins than you have available, to monitor switches. If you don't want to invest in a more sophisticated microcontroller, you can try a circuit that reads the states of three push-buttons with only two input pins, as shown in Figure 2. Two of the push-buttons, SW1 and SW2, are connected to their own input pins PD0 and PD1, while the third push-button will activate both input pins simultaneously via Schottky diodes D1 and D2. Similarly, you can read six push-buttons with three input pins, ten push-buttons with four input pins, etc. The principle is always the same:

» if there are n inputs, connect n push-buttons directly to these inputs;
» the remaining push-buttons connect via two Schottky diodes to any distinct pair of inputs.

If we want to use the *Debounce* statement to monitor a push-button that is connected to two input pins, and keep the full functionality of the statement, we have to modify the way that it is usually used. Let's investigate this in the following program example, which repeatedly displays the value of the counter on the lower line of an LCD display. Pressing SW1 will decrement the counter, while pressing SW2 will increment its value. Pressing SW3 will reset the counter to its initial value of 100.

NOTE

With three or more inputs, we could connect one push-button to more than two input pins (using more diodes) and, this way, connect even more push-buttons than described above. However, we won't explore this option here.

The program uses byte variable *SW_flags* to store the state of the push-buttons, where bits 0 and 1 correspond to the input pins labelled *SW1_pin* and *SW2_pin* respectively:

```
'Program *** Debounce4 (part 1/2) ***

Sw1_pin Alias Pind.0
Config Sw1_pin = Input
Sw2_pin Alias Pind.1
```

```
Config Sw2_pin = Input
Sw_flags = 0

Do
   Debounce Sw1_pin , 0 , Sw1_deb , Sub
   Debounce Sw2_pin , 0 , Sw2_deb , Sub
   ...
Loop

Sw1_deb:
   Set Sw_flags.0
Return

Sw2_deb:
   Set Sw_flags.1
   Debounce Sw1_pin , 0 , Sw1_deb , Sub
Return
```

If *SW1_pin = 0*, indicating that the SW1 or the SW3 push-button is pressed, the first *Debounce* will execute the *SW1_deb* subroutine, which will set the *SW_flags.0* bit.

If *SW2_pin = 0*, indicating that the SW2 or the SW3 push-button is pressed, the second *Debounce* will execute the *SW2_deb* subroutine, which will set the *SW_flags.1* bit.

As a result, the value in the *SW_flags* will be:

» 0, if no push-button is pressed,
» 1, if only SW1 is pressed,
» 2, if only SW2 is pressed and
» 3, if SW3 is pressed.

Here we do not analyze the situation where two or more push-buttons are activated simultaneously.

Notice the third *Debounce* statement, within the *SW2_deb* subroutine. This is necessary to properly interpret the case in which SW3 is pressed at exactly the same time as the first *Debounce* has finished but before the second *Debounce* executes. In this (extremely rare) case, SW3 would be detected as SW2, which we want to avoid; that is why we need the third *Debounce*.

Normally, the *Debounce* statement is used to execute an associated subroutine when the input state changes as expected. In this example, we have done nothing except setting appropriate bits within the *SW_flags* variable. The execution of associated subroutines is delayed, until all *Debounce* subroutines have finished. At this point in time, the value of the *SW_flags* variable is valid, and we can use its value to conditionally branch the program, or to execute subroutines related to the pressed push-button. This can be done using either the *If-Elseif-Endif* or the *Select Case* structure, or we can use the *On value* statement, as shown in the following example:

```
'Program *** Debounce3 (part 2/2) ***

Do
   Debounce Sw1_pin , 0 , Sw1_deb , Sub
   Debounce Sw2_pin , 0 , Sw2_deb , Sub
   On Sw_flags Gosub Dummy_sub ,"_"
      Sw1_sub , Sw2_sub , Sw3_sub
   'do whatever
   Home L
   Lcd "Counter = " ; Up_dn_counter ; "  "
Loop
End

Dummy_sub:
Return
Sw1_sub:
   If Up_dn_counter > 0 Then
      Decr Up_dn_counter
   End If
   Sw_flags = 0
Return

Sw2_sub:
   If Up_dn_counter < 255 Then
      Incr Up_dn_counter
   End If
   Sw_flags = 0
Return

Sw3_sub:
```

```
    Up_dn_counter = 100
    Home L
    Lcd "Counter reset"
    Wait 1
    Sw_flags = 0
Return
```

SW1_sub, *SW2_sub* or *SW3_ sub* will execute only if the *Debounce* routines detect that a push-button of the same name has been pressed. These subroutines execute code appropriate to the switch that was pressed. Notice that, prior to returning to the main program, the value of the *SW_flags* variable is cleared, in order to ensure that one push-button activation causes just one execution of the subroutine. Alternately, a single *SW_flags = 0* statement can be added following the *On Sw_flags Gosub* statement. The *Dummy_sub* executes if no push-button is pressed; this can be an empty subroutine, or it can contain some code, but its presence is necessary to ensure that the conditional branching works properly.

Example program ID	
Name:	Debounce1.bas
Microcontroller:	ATtiny2313 and most AVRs
Testing circuit:	Figure 1
MiniPin compatibility:	yes (with appropriate μC)
MegaPin compatibility:	yes
The program illustrates the use of the Debounce statement.	

Example program ID	
Name:	Debounce2.bas
Microcontroller:	ATtiny2313 and most AVRs
Testing circuit:	Figure 1
MiniPin compatibility:	yes (with appropriate μC)
MegaPin compatibility:	yes
The program illustrates the use of the Debounce statement within an interrupt subroutine.	

Example program ID	
Name:	Debounce3.bas
Microcontroller:	ATtiny2313 and most AVRs
Testing circuit:	Figure 1
MiniPin compatibility:	yes (with appropriate μC)
MegaPin compatibility:	yes
The program illustrates the use of the extended Debounce statement which measures for how long the Debounce condition lasts.	

Example program ID	
Name:	Debounce4.bas
Microcontroller:	ATtiny2313 and most AVRs
Testing circuit:	Figure 2
MiniPin compatibility:	yes (with appropriate μC)
MegaPin compatibility:	yes
The program extends the use of the Debounce statement to multiple conditions.	

Wait a minute!

By Vladimir Mitrović

It is pretty difficult to find a program without a single time-delay statement. In Bascom-AVR, we can explicitly wait in seconds, milliseconds and microseconds, but delays are embedded in other statements, too. For example, the *Debounce* **statement will wait a bit and then re-check an input pin state, communication routines often wait while data is transmitted or received, etc.**

All of Bascom's wait statements and the delays embedded in other statements are essentially loops that execute the required number of times to achieve a desired time-delay. There is an internal Bascom-AVR routine that lasts 1 ms, *_WAITMS*. During program compilation, the Bascom-AVR compiler checks the *$crystal* directive and uses a specified parameter to calculate the values needed for the counting registers in order to achieve a 1 ms execution time of the *_WAITMS* routine (or as close as possible to 1 ms). The *_WAITMS* routine is used in a loop for larger delays. For example, *Waitms 100* executes the *_WAITMS* routine 100 times. Furthermore, the *_WAITMS* routine is a building block for another time-reference within Bascom-AVR, namely the 1-s-routine *_WAIT*. Once again, larger delays are achieved by executing the *_WAIT* routine an appropriate number of times within a loop.

It is obvious that no accurate timing is possible with such statements for several reasons:

- It's impossible to calculate values for counting registers to achieve a precise 1-ms or 1-s reference, for every possible crystal frequency;
- when the basic delay routines (_WAITMS, etc.) are executed in a loop for larger delays, the execution time of the assembly language commands which make up the loop structure, get added to the basic time reference;
- when interrupts occur, their execution will extend the total duration of wait statements, if both occur simultaneously.

The Bascom-AVR compiler is written cleverly and you can rely on the wait statements as long as you don't expect very high accuracy. The main factor affecting reasonably precise timing is to correctly specify the *$crystal* directive: if you use a 10 MHz crystal with *$crystal = 8000000*, you can expect a significant deviation from the specified time delays.

Wait and the clock division factor

There is another factor worthy of consideration, and that is the clock division factor. The option to set the clock divisor is available in most new AVR microcontrollers. For example, the ATtiny2313 microcontroller offers division factors of 1, 2, 4, 8, 16, 32, 64, 128 and 256. The ATtiny2313 is shipped with the CKDIV8 Fuse programmed, which results in a division factor of 8 at start-up. In other words, if you use an 8 MHz crystal to run the ATtiny2313, the internal clock will be only 1 MHz and you should either change the division factor at the beginning of the program or specify the *$crystal* to match the 1 MHz frequency.

What will happen if the clock division factor is changed dynamically during the program execution? You can specify only one parameter in the *$crystal* directive and the counters for the *_WAITMS* routine are defined during program compilation. They cannot be altered during execution. This means that all wait statements within a program will be accurate for only one clock frequency;

current consumption [mA]		supply voltage			
		3 V	3,5 V	4 V	5 V
internal CPU frequency	20MHz/1	5.72	6.94	8.50	14.6
	20MHz/4	2.21	2.74	3.64	8.40
	20MHz/16	0.85	1.11	1.75	6.12
	20MHz/64	0.45	0.62	1.18	5.40
	20MHz/256	0.35	0.50	1.05	5.20
	idle	0.33	0.47	1.02	5.20

Table 1: The ATtiny2313 current consumption with a 20 MHz crystal as a function of the clock division factor and the supply voltage

if we change the clock frequency during program execution, wait statements will execute at an inappropriate speed and will not last the expected time.

Why would we want to change the program execution speed? In battery-powered circuits, where the current consumption is an important issue, it's good practice to slow down the CPU during idle periods and run it at full speed when there is something to do. The current consumption of an ATtiny2313, measured with a 20 MHz crystal oscillator at various clock division factors and various supply voltages, is shown in Table 1.

The current consumption is notably lower at lower clock frequencies, especially at lower supply voltages, and similar results can be expected for other microcontrollers. So there is a good reason to optimize the program execution speed!

If there are parts of the program that always run at full speed, while others execute at a slower rate, say with clock division factor 8, there is a simple method of adjusting wait statements to the actual clock frequency used in the slower part of the program: just use *Waitms 125* instead of *Wait 1* to obtain a 1 s delay. The program becomes "less readable" but everything works OK.

It is a bigger problem if the clock division factor changes unexpectedly, for example as a result of an interrupt or if some kind of delay is programmed within an interrupt service routine. In such cases, it is necessary to find out the actual clock division factor, and we can read it from the lower nibble of the CLKPR register. The relationship between the CLKPR register contents and the clock division factor for the ATtiny2313 is shown in Table 2.

Let's explain how this works using the example of a "handwritten" 25-ms delay, which can be used in the *Debounce* statement simulation (see page 27, Improved Debounce Routines). Unlike a Bascom-AVR *Waitms 25* statement, this one will generate a 25 ms delay regardless of the current clock division factor.

```
'Program *** Wait1 (part 1/3) ***

Waitms_25:
Dim Wait_counter As Byte
   Wait_counter = Clkpr And &H0F
   Wait_counter = Lookup_
     (wait_counter , Wait_table)
   Do
      Waitus 96
      Decr Wait_counter
   Loop Until Wait_counter = 0
Return

Wait_table:
Data 0
Data 128
Data 64
Data 32
Data 16
Data 8
Data 4
Data 2
Data 1
```

CLKPR	clock division
xxxx0000	1
xxxx0001	2
xxxx0010	4
xxxx0011	8
xxxx0100	16
xxxx0101	32
xxxx0110	64
xxxx0111	128
xxxx1000	256

Table 2: The relationship between the CLKPR register and the clock division factor for the ATtiny2313

At the beginning of the *Waitms_25* routine we fetch the lower 4 bits from the CLKPR register and use them as an index into the *Wait_table*. This table contains coefficients that are used later on as a clock division correction factor. The first coefficient, 0, is interpreted as 256. Therefore, a product of the current clock division factor and the correction factor is always 256 and the following *Do-Loop* structure lasts (approximately) 25 ms regardless of the clock division. The factor 96 in the *Waitus 96* statement was chosen experimentally, with a little help from the Bascom-AVR simulator. Accuracy varies from -0.3% to +1.3% for clock division factors from 1 to 64. Slightly worse accuracy is measured at clock division factors 128 (+2.9%) and 256 (+6.1%).

A similar routine can also be written for a 1 s delay:

```
'Program *** Wait1 (part 2/3) ***

Wait_1:
   Wait_counter = Clkpr And &H0F
   Wait_counter = Lookup(Wait_counter ,_
     Wait_table)
   Do
      Waitus 3904
      Decr Wait_counter
   Loop Until Wait_counter = 0
Return
```

The two routines, *Waitms_25* and *Wait_1*, share the same *Wait_counter* variable and the *Wait_table* table, and differ only in the *Waitus* coefficient. The value "3904" is chosen as was previously explained and we can choose appropriate coefficients for other delays in the same way. Accuracy is better for larger delays: for the *Wait_1* routine, the deviation from the ideal 1 second is 0.14% at clock division factor 256 and totally negligible for all other factors.

NOTE

With the introduced procedures, we can achieve any fixed time-interval longer than several milliseconds and make it almost independent of a change in the clock division factor. The same does not apply to other statements that use the *$crystal* parameter to adjust their internal delays - a change in the clock division factor will still have a strong influence on their timing.

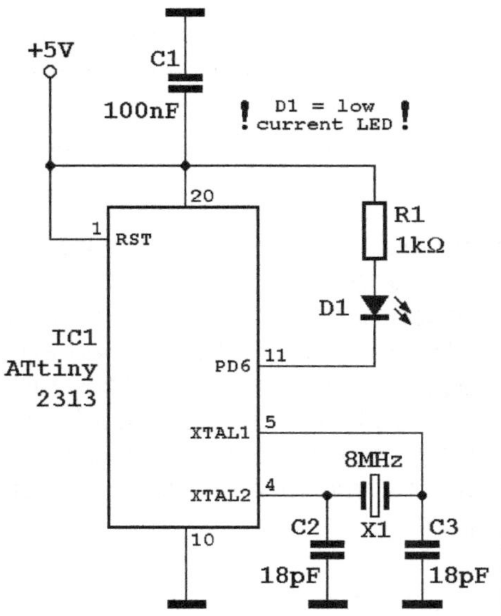

Figure 1: Test circuit for a Wait_1 routine which is independent of clock division factor

The demo program Wait1.bas was written to illustrate the use of the *Wait_1* routine. The program constantly changes the clock division factor from 1 to 256 and yet the LED D1 (see Figure 1) toggles ON and OFF once per second:

```
'Program *** Wait1 (part 3/3) ***

Config Pind.6 = Output
Portd.6 = 1

Do
   Config Clockdiv = 1
   Gosub Led_on_off
   Config Clockdiv = 2
   Gosub Led_on_off
   ...
   ...
   Config Clockdiv = 256
   Gosub Led_on_off
Loop

Led_on_off:
   Portd.6 = 0
   Gosub Wait_1
   Portd.6 = 1
   Gosub Wait_1
Return
```

Power-saving Wait

Earlier in this chapter we have analyzed how the clock frequency affects a microcontroller's current consumption. From this you would conclude that if you want to minimize power consumption, you should run microcontrollers at the lowest possible clock frequency. This is the opposite of what we usually want: to finish a task as quickly as possible. A good compromise is to run important parts of a program at full speed and wait with the lowest possible current consumption. This is especially effective with programs that:

» wait most of the time for some event to happen or
» poll some devices regularly but infrequently, to check their state, but do nothing in the meantime.

The first example in the list is handled by putting a microcontroller in idle or power-down mode. In idle mode the CPU sleeps and power consumption is consequently reduced. Any interrupt, either internal or external, can wake up the microcontroller to handle the request. In power-down mode the external oscillator is stopped; power consumption is reduced even more, but the choice of interrupts that can wake the microcontroller up is limited.

Let's investigate how we can exploit this technique to minimise power consumption in programs which extensively use wait statements. The idea is to replace wait statements with intervals in which the CPU sleeps, and allow a timer to wake it up when the wait interval has finished. Since timers have to be active, we are forced to use idle mode, but the current consumption can be reduced even further if we reduce the clock frequency just before putting the CPU to sleep. Here is how it works.

Subroutine *Wait_and_sleep_1* replaces the ordinary *Waitms* command. It puts the CPU in idle mode and uses a properly configured 16-bit Timer1 to wake it up as soon as the given wait time elapses. At the very beginning of the subroutine, the actual clock division factor is fetched from the CLKPR register and stored in the *Wait_clkpr* variable:

```
Dim Wait_clkpr As Byte

Wait_and_sleep_1:
   Wait_clkpr = Clkpr And &H0F
```

Now we can reset the prescaler and configure Timer1 to count system clock pulses divided by 64.

```
   Set Gtccr.psr10
   Config Timer1 = Timer , Prescale = 64
```

The configuration simultaneously starts Timer1. At this point we can slow down the clock and enter the idle mode:

```
    Config Clockdiv = 128
    Idle
```

Let's assume that the microcontroller runs on an 8 MHz clock. After division by factors 64 and 128, Timer1 will count milliseconds (actually, it will advance every 1.024 ms). When Timer1 overflows, the CPU will wake up and start to execute the following instructions. First, we have to restore the original value in the CLKPR register and thus restore the original clock division factor. The wait interval is over; it's time to stop Timer1 and return to the main program:

```
    Clkpr = &H80
    Clkpr = Wait_clkpr
    Stop Timer1
Return
```

The *Wait_and_sleep_1* subroutine will only work, as explained, if the Timer1 interrupt is enabled. Consequently, it's necessary to enable this interrupt at the beginning of the main program, although there is no interrupt service subroutine provided (as it is not needed):

```
    Enable Timer1
    Enable Interrupts
```

If we want to delay the program execution for a while, we write the desired time interval in milliseconds to the Counter1 register as a negative number and then call the *Wait_and_sleep_1* subroutine:

```
    Counter1 = -1000      '1000 ms
    Gosub Wait_and_sleep_1
```

If the frequency of the main oscillator differs from 8 MHz, we will adjust the *Clockdiv* parameter in the *Wait_and_sleep_1* subroutine:

```
    Config Clockdiv = 64  'for 4MHz
    Config Clockdiv = 256 'for 16MHz
```

The value in the Counter1 register will be in milliseconds in both cases. For other frequencies we can calculate the value in Counter1 in the following way:

$$\text{Counter1} = -\frac{\text{time-delay [ms]}}{\text{Clockdiv-factor}} \cdot f_{quartz}[\text{kHz}]$$

Here the "Clockdiv-factor" is the product of the factors specified in *Config Clockdiv* and *Config Timer1 Prescale* statements. The same formula allows for an accurate calculation of the value in the Counter1 register for an 8 MHz clock frequency, too. For example, we have assumed that *Counter1 = -1000* results in 1 second delay, but the real time delay will be 1024 ms. The formula gives a more precise value, *Counter1 = -977*, which results in almost perfect accuracy (deviation is less than 0.05%).

It is possible to write a value between -1 to -65535 into Counter1 and thus achieve time delays from approximately 1 ms to 67 s. For longer time-intervals, put the call within the *For-Next* loop and execute it several times. For example,

```
For I = 1 To 60
    Counter1 = -58594    '1 min
    Gosub Wait_and_sleep_1
Next
```

will produce a delay of 1 hour with very good precision. Note that in this case the *For-Next* loop executes at full speed, but most of the time the microcontroller is in idle mode.

Of course, it is possible to use Timer0 in the same way. If we use the *Wait_and_sleep_1* as a template and change all references from Timer1 to Timer0 we arrive at this wait routine:

```
Wait_and_sleep_0:        'version 1
    Wait_clkpr = Clkpr And &H0F
    Set Gtccr.psr10
    Config Timer0 = Timer , Prescale = 64
    Config Clockdiv = 128
    Idle
    Clkpr = &H80
    Clkpr = Wait_clkpr
    Stop Timer0
Return
```

This routine works well and all previous remarks can be applied here, too. Don't forget to enable Timer0 instead of Timer1! However, as Timer0 is an 8-bit timer, it is possible to achieve delays of up to 262 ms (approximately) with a 1.024 ms resolution. This can be extended to more than 8 seconds if we increase the prescalers to their maximum values, but the resolution will then be a bit less than 33 ms:

```
Wait_and_sleep_0:        'version 2
    Wait_clkpr = Clkpr And &H0F
    Set Gtccr.psr10
    Config Timer0 = Timer , Prescale = 1024
    Config Clockdiv = 256
    Idle
    Clkpr = &H80
    Clkpr = Wait_clkpr
    Stop Timer0
Return
```

For both versions of the *Wait_and_sleep_0* routine, and for others that may be written with various prescale factors combinations, the following formula is valid:

$$\text{Counter0} = 256 - \frac{\text{time-delay [ms]}}{\text{Clockdiv-factor}} \cdot f_{quartz}[\text{kHz}]$$

Note here that the Bascom-AVR compiler does not allow for the direct transfer of a negative value to the Counter0 register and the formula has to be modified appropriately. If we use the first version of the subroutine and need a 100-ms delay, the formula gives 158 as a result. The subroutine call is as follows:

```
Counter0 = 158          '100 ms
Gosub Wait_and_sleep_0
```

The value of 158 is difficult to associate with a 100-ms delay. If we are satisfied with time intervals that deviate somewhat from a given value, there is a simpler way to call the subroutine:

```
Counter0 = 256 - 100    '100 ms
Gosub Wait_and_sleep_0
```

There is no need to calculate anything and with the expression *256 - 100* we have tricked the compiler into accepting a negative value. However, the resulting time delay will be about 2.4% longer than expected. This simpler version is applicable only to version 1 of the *Wait_and_sleep_0* subroutine.

Demo program Wait2.bas has been written to illustrate the use of the *Wait_and_sleep_0* (version 1) and *Wait_and_sleep_1* subroutines. The program causes the LED (shown as D1 in Figure 1) to flash briefly every 2 seconds. The microcontroller is active only during short intervals when the LED state changes. Most of the time, it just waits in the idle mode, consuming minimal power.

```
'Program *** Wait2 ***

Config Pind.6 = Output
Portd.6 = 1

Enable Timer0
Enable Timer1
Enable Interrupts
Do
   Portd.6 = 0
   Counter0 = 158          '100 ms
   Gosub Wait_and_sleep_0
   Portd.6 = 1
   Counter1 = -1855        '1900 ms
   Gosub Wait_and_sleep_1
Loop
```

Both *Wait_and_sleep* subroutines are identical to those explained before and are therefore not shown here. Of course, the 100- and 1900-ms delays could be achieved using only one timer, Timer1. This example wastes resources, but the intention was to illustrate the use of both subroutines. An average current consumption has been measured and the results are shown in Table 3. The same table contains measurements on the same circuit programmed with an equivalent program that uses ordinary *Waits*. Note that the program that uses *Wait_and_sleep* routines consumes significantly less power than the program with ordinary *Waits*, especially at lower supply voltages.

supply voltage	Wait_and_sleep	Wait
5 V	4.70 mA	8.90 mA
4 V	0.75 mA	4.15 mA
3.5 V	0.27 mA	3.23 mA
3 V	0.15 mA	2.66 mA

Table 3: Average power consumption with Wait_and_sleep and with an ordinary Wait (using an 8 MHz crystal)

CAUTION

Program Wait2.bas slows down the system clock a few statements after it starts. It is recommended that you insert an appropriate wait statement (for example, Waitms 500) at the very beginning of such a program - otherwise you might experience problems when you try to reprogram the microcontroller.

Example program ID	
Name:	Wait1.bas
Microcontroller:	ATtiny2313 and similar AVRs (with CLKPR register!)
Testing circuit:	Figure 1
MiniPin compatibility:	yes (with appropriate μC)
MegaPin compatibility:	yes
The program illustrates the use of the Wait_1 subroutine, which is used as a substitute for Bascom-AVR Wait 1	

Example program ID	
Name:	Wait2.bas
Microcontroller:	ATtiny2313 and similar AVRs (with CLKPR register!)
Testing circuit:	Figure 1
MiniPin compatibility:	yes (with appropriate μC)
MegaPin compatibility:	yes
The program illustrates the use of Wait_and_sleep subroutines	

I/O Expansion

By Vlado Berend

Bascom users probably know the PCF8574A(P) chip, which is an I²C 8-bit I/O expander that expands the number of available I/O ports via I²C. If we just need a larger number of output pins on a microcontroller, we can also use a cheaper device- the CD4094, which is a serial shift register.

I had a requirement where a 20-pin microcontroller had to drive one LED display plus other peripherals. To drive the LED display, required 8 pins that were not available, because they were already used by other peripherals. After a literature search, I found a cheap shift register which performs like the PCF8574 (which is not cheap at all!). Using shift registers has been mentioned in various places including the Svet elektronike magazine, but none contained a practical example. In this chapter I will show you a practical way to implement this. For this purpose, PCBs were designed to drive four 7-segment LED displays as well as a 32 LED circular bar-graph display.

The basic circuit is shown in Figure 1. The shift register is driven using the pins Strobe (ST), clock (CLK) and data (DATA).

Before we write the data (which will be shifted into the shift register), we must first set the strobe pin to logical 1 (note that the pin on the microcontroller is also labelled STR). Then on the data pin we set a data value (0 or 1) followed by setting the clock pin to logical 1. By setting the clock pin to a logical 1, the shift register shifts that data by one bit, into its 8-bit register. After that, we reset the clock pin to a logical 0, set a new data value, for the second bit, and raise the clock pin to a logical 1 again. This sequence is repeated until all 8 bits are shifted in. At the end of this sequence, we must reset the strobe pin to a logical 0, which transfers the register data to the output pins (Q1 – Q8). Let's look at a Bascom program (Out_port.bas) which does this.

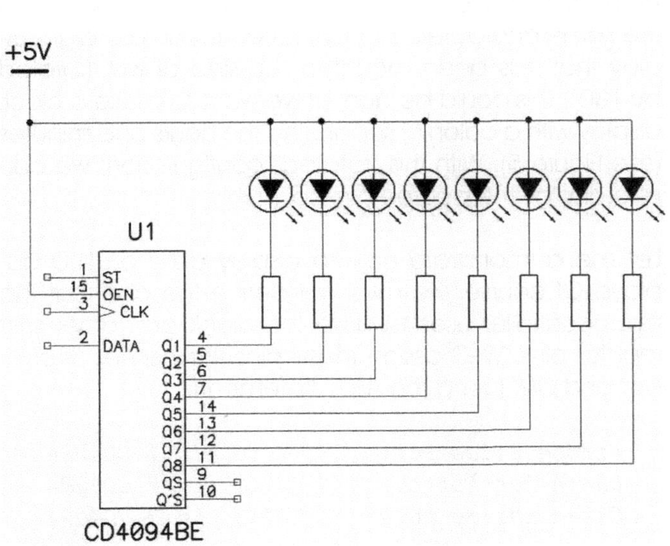

Figure 1: The schematic diagram of a shift register driving LEDs

```
Dim I As Word , N As Byte , V As Byte ,
C As Byte , Z As Byte
Config Portd = Output
Portd = 0
Strobe Alias Portd.2          'to pin 1 CD4094
Dat Alias Portd.3             'to pin 2 CD4094
Clk Alias Portd.4             'to pin 3 CD4094

N = 255                       'all outputs are
                              'set to high
Gosub 4094

Do
 Input I
 N.i = Not N.i
 Gosub 4094
Loop
End

4094:
   Set Strobe                 'enable writing
   For C=7 To 0 Step-1        'each bit of
                              'variable
      Dat = N.c
      Set Clk
      Reset Clk
   Next
   Reset Strobe               'shift register
                              'changes do not
                              'affect output
                              'until strobe
                              'goes low
Return
```

By setting *N = 255* (binary = 11111111), we set all bits to a logical 1 and therefore no LED is lit. If we want to turn on one LED we have to pull down that particular bit. Many newbies don't know that one can change a bit within a variable very easily. For example: if a variable (N) has a value 255 (binary 11111111) and you want to change only the least-significant bit to 0, (binary 11111110) you can do that very easily using the statement *N.0 = 0*. With this simple statement you can change single bits in your byte variable.

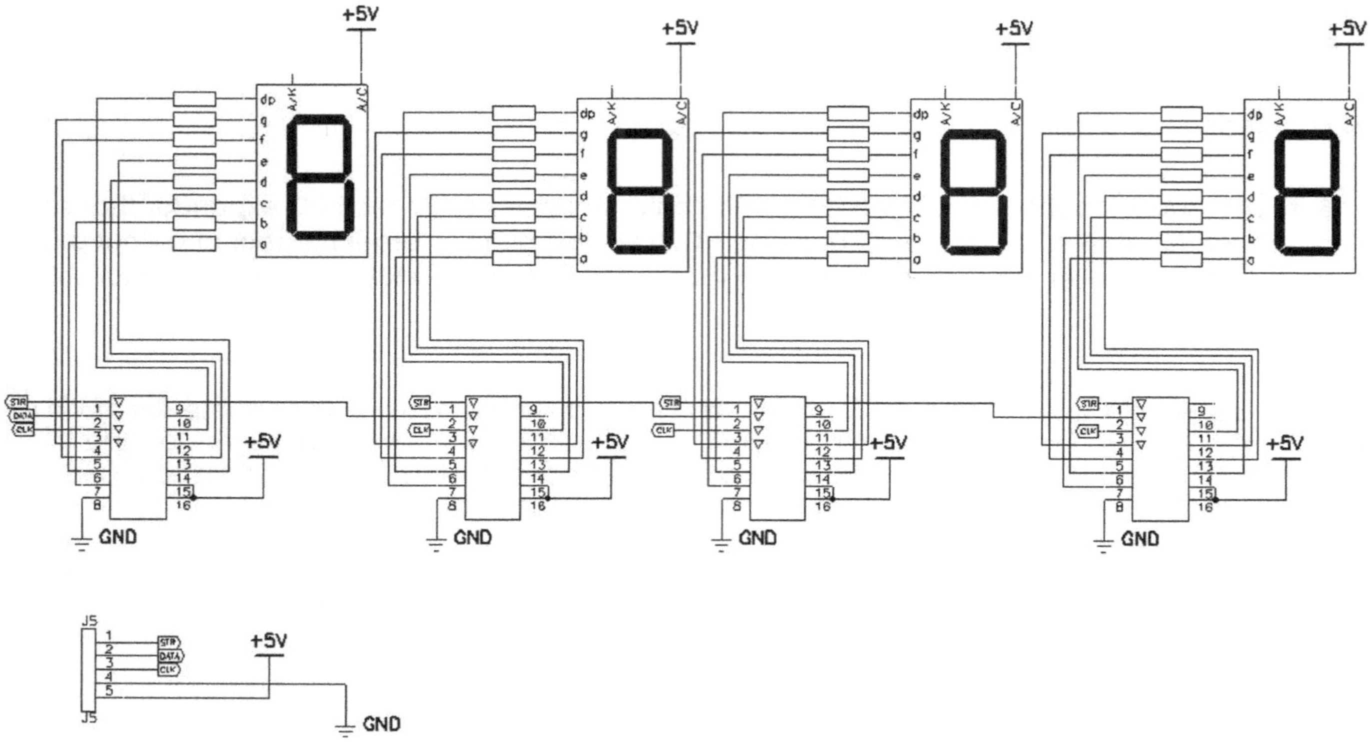

Figure 2: Schematic diagram of LED display

LED display

LED displays are very common in environments where LCD displays don't work so well. For example, in places where we have low ambient light and/or temperature extremes – for example in a car, where the operating temperature can go from very low to very high.

In this section we are going to describe a four-digit LED display, driven by CD4094 shift registers. The CD4094 shift register can be daisy-chained (i.e. several connected in series resulting in many more output pins). In this circuit, we will use four cascaded shift registers, where we connect the output pin Qs of the first shift register to the DATA input pin of the second shift register, and so on.

The basic schematic is very similar as the one shown in Figure 1, except that we have used daisy chaining. I have designed a PCB with four SMD CD4094 and 4 LED displays. For displaying data on the LED displays, I have prepared three different data tables that are needed to correctly display numbers and letters.

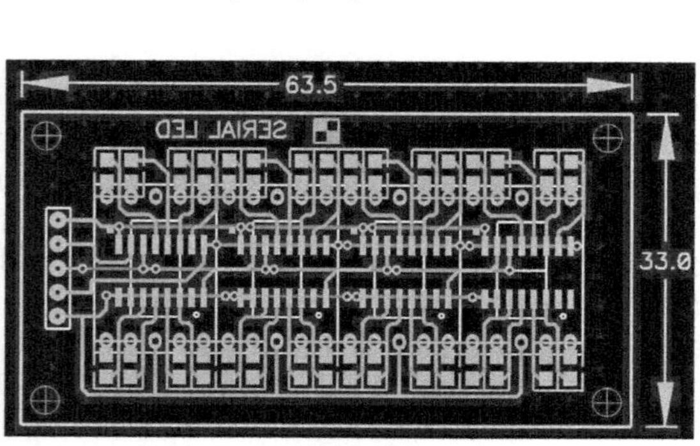

Figure 3: LED display PCB

Why 3 tables?

Most likely you will only need one table for your particular application. Let me explain the purpose of the three data tables.

In the first table, I have defined the basic numbers and some characters, all of which are without a Decimal Point (0, 1, 2, ..., 9, A, b, C, c, d, E, F, U, L, P, H and all segments off).

The second table is the same, but the numbers and characters all have the DP turned On.

In the third table I have prepared data for displaying the same characters, but formatted for an LED digit display that has been mounted "up-side down" (rotated by 180°) This could be done if we want to make a clock display with a colon (:) separating the hours and minutes (see Figure 5). With this "rotated" configuration, we can also display the degree symbol (°).

Let me demonstrate how to display data on LED displays. Of course, we must first define the pins that the microcontroller uses to drive the clock and other shift register pins. We'll assign these pins the names *Strobe, Dat* and *CLK* (using the *Alias* statement).

```
Strobe Alias Portd.2        'to pin 1 CD4094
Dat Alias Portd.3           'to pin 2 CD4094
Clk Alias Portd.4           'to pin 3 CD4094
```

When powering up our circuit, it's possible that the display will show a random pattern due to the undefined state of the shift registers. Therefore, we have to turn off

Figure 4: Test of LED counter on protoboard

Figure 5: Example of a LED clock where the DP serves as the hour/minute separator (:)

all LED segments by writing a value of 255 to all shift registers. As we have four displays, we will need four variables, one for each digit. We'll use variables *N(1), N(2), N(3)* and *N(4)*. After setting those variables to 255, we'll start by calling a subroutine which writes them to the shift registers (*Gosub 4094*).

```
I = 255
N(1) = I              ' rightmost digit (Ones)
N(2) = I
N(3) = I
N(4) = I              'Leftmost digit
                      '(Thousands)
Gosub 4094
```

If you compare the previous example with this one, you will notice that instead of one shift register we now have four, hence the program differs a bit. In the previous example, we had a *For-Next* loop, which set individual bits of a variable. Now, with four variables, we need an additional *For-Next* loop to define the array position of that variable.

```
4094:
  Set Strobe                'enable writing
  For V = 1 To 4            'No. of serial
                            'connected displays
   For C = 0 To 7           'each bit of
                            'variable
     Dat = N(v).c
     Set Clk
    nop
    Reset Clk
   nop
  Next
Next
Reset Strobe                'changes on the
                            'input do not
                            'afect output
Return
```

Dat = N(v).c

Dat is a microcontroller's pin which will have its value defined by bit (c) of the variable *N(v)*.

Additionally, in the program we have to split-up the digits of our variable, (ranging from 0 to 9999), into Ones, Tens, Hundreds and Thousands. Those of you familiar with LED displays will likely remember that we can divide the variable by 1000, 100 and 10 to retrieve the individual digits from the variable. I have chosen another way to retrieve digits from variable.

The "I" variable is first converted to a String (*S = Str (i)*). Next, we compare the value of our number to the values 999, 99, and 9. Depending upon those three comparisons, we call separate subroutines which break up the string s into its thousands, hundreds, tens and ones digits (using the *Mid* statement). Once the string has been broken up into single characters representing each digit, we convert that character into a number, using the *VAL* statement. We use that number with the *Lookup* statement to retrieve the appropriate segment code, for that particular character, from the "dta2" table:

```
  N(4) = Lookup(Thousands , Dta2)
Return
```

Following is an example of one of the four routines that separate out the individual digits from our string, and convert that character into a number:

```
Thousand:
 Ss = Mid(s , Z , 1)
 Thousands = Val(ss)
```

This program provides "leading zero blanking". If you don't want this feature, you can write a similar program which incorporates the *Fusing* statement, which actually results in a shorter program overall.

This procedure retrieves all 4 digits which are then sent serially out to the shift register. On the CD you will find this program titled Test Count2.bas. Also you will find the program Clock.bas, which is a program for a clock that runs on an ATmega32 with a 32,768 kHz crystal connected to PortC.6 and PortC.7. With a little added code, you can make yourself a nice alarm clock which will wake you up in the morning.

Let me emphasize that the subroutine for writing all four digits to the shift registers takes 2,756 processor clock

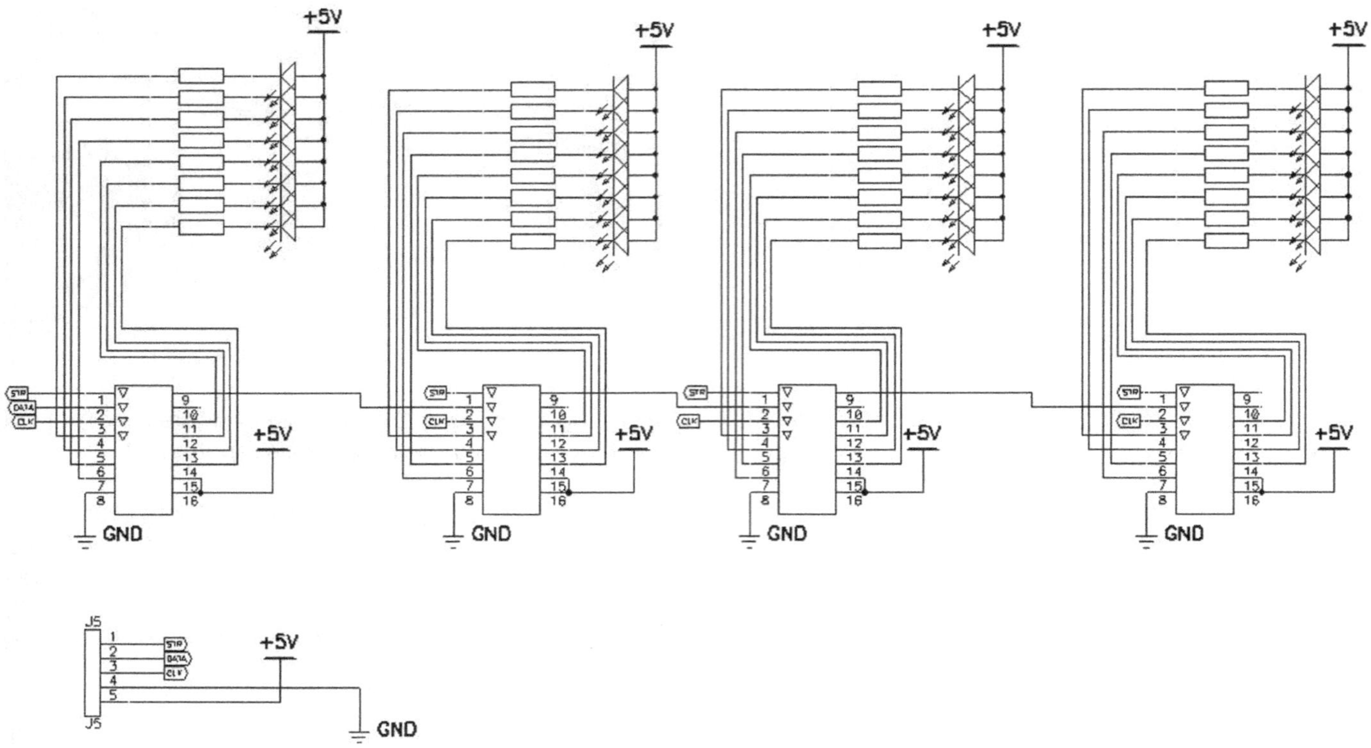

Figure 6: Schematic of dot-bar display

cycles. That number may seem high, but given that the microcontroller runs at 12 MHz, the total write cycle time is 2756/12 or 229.6 μs.

This sample program can be found on download, labelled Test count2.bas. This time can be shortened if we use some inline code to replace the *For-Next* loop

```
4094:
Set Strobe                  'enable input
'  For V = 1 To 4           'number of serial
                            'connected devices
```

```
'  For C = 0 To 7

  Dat = N(1).0
    Set Clk
   Reset Clk
   Dat = N(1).1
    Set Clk
   Reset Clk
    Dat = N(1).2
    Set Clk
   Reset Clk
etc...
```

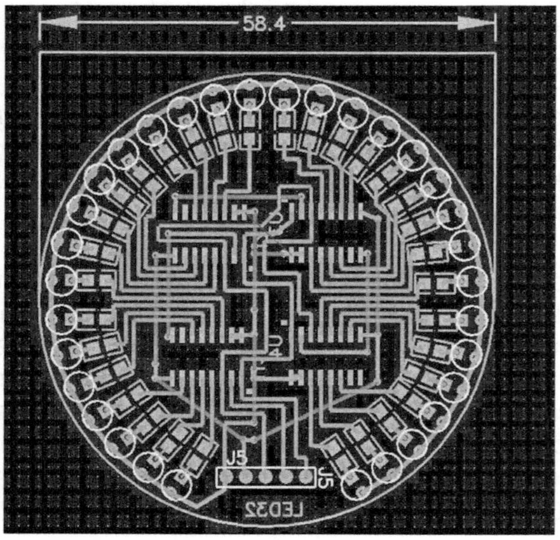

Figure 7: PCB for bar-graph display

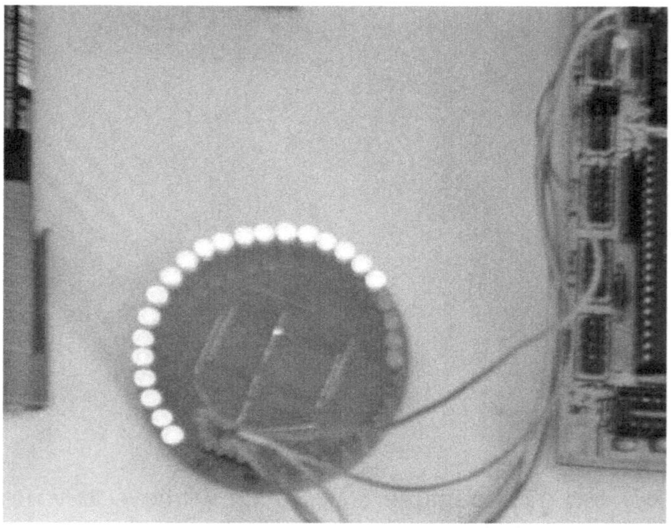

Figure 8: Photo of bar-graph display

Sign	Value	Sign	Value	Sign	Value
0	129	0.	128	'0	1
1	237	1.	236	'1	109
2	67	2.	66	'2	66
3	73	3.	72	'3	72
4	45	4.	44	'4	44
5	25	5.	24	'5	24
6	17	6.	17	'6	16
7	205	7.	204	'7	77
8	1	8.	0	'8	0
9	9	9.	8	'9	8
A	5	A.	4	'A	4
b	49	b.	48	'b	12
C	147	C.	146	'C	19
d	97	d.	96	'd	96
E	19	E.	18	'E	18
F	23	F.	22	'F	22
c	115	U.	160	'P	6
-	127	L.	178	'U	33
U	161	P.	6	'H	36
L	179	H.	36	'L	51
.	254	c.	114	'-	126
P	7			'	127
H	37				
off	255		255		255

Table 1: Variable values for displaying certain characters on LED display (Sign, Value, Sign, Value, Sign, Value)

The same code as shown above should be repeated for *N(2)* to *N(4)*, ending in:

```
Reset Strobe
Return
```

When the program is written in such a way, it will use only 516 processor cycles, which at 12 MHz crystal takes 43 μs. A sample of this can be found in the Test count no for.bas file.

For the sake of comparison, writing 4 bytes of data (*N(1),... N(4)*) to an LCD display takes 13,157 processor cycles, or 3,740 cycles to write four ASCII characters.

The PCB is a double-sided board which can be ordered from our web page.

LED bar-graph display

The schematic diagram is virtually same as the previous one so there is not much to say. Instead of four 7-segment LED displays, we now use LEDs of different colours. The test program has been written for an ATmega32 microcontroller. For entering variables, the *Input* statement was used. This display has the option of displaying data as dot or a bar. Hence I have added an additional variable (B) that

Value	Binary value	Value	Binary value
	Output for Line mode		Output for Dot mode
255	1111 1111	255	1111 1111
127	0111 1111	127	0111 1111
63	0011 1111	191	1011 1111
31	0001 1111	223	1101 1111
15	0000 1111	239	1110 1111
14	0000 0111	254	1111 0111
12	0000 0011	253	1111 1011
8	0000 0001	251	1111 1101
0	0000 0000	247	1111 1110

Table 2: Variable values for displaying on bar-graph display (Value, Binary value, Value, Binary value, Output for Line mode, Output for Dot mode)

defines from which table the data will be read – *Dta* or *Dta2*. The sample program testBargraph.bas provides a sample of both the dot and bar displays. If you send the number 40 to the board (via the BASCOM Terminal program), you will see the dot display. If you send the number 50 then the display will show the bar display.

I have made two tables with all the values needed for the shift register to display those values correctly. One table is meant for displaying the data as a dot and the other one for displaying the data as a bar. This circuit also employs a double-sided PCB, however you can also make it on a single-sided board requiring some jumper wires on the top of the board. The program for the bar-graph is a bit different than the one for the LED display. Here we have to turn off all LEDs higher than the input value (in the case of bar mode). In dot mode we have to turn off all LEDs **before** and **after** the particular LED that is lit. This part of the program is done in the Line1 and the Dot1 subroutines.

The start of the program is similar to the previously-described programs. We just have to turn off LEDs according to which display mode we have chosen. We can display values from 0 to 32. We can also map a range of values which result in a given number of LEDS being lit (i.e. the first LED will light for input values from 0 to 10, the second LED for values from 11 to 21, etc.). If you want faster performance you can modify the program as described in a previous example.

Example program ID	
Name:	Out_port.bas
Microcontroller:	Any AVR microcontroler
Testing circuit:	Figure 1
MiniPin compatibility:	Yes
MegaPin compatibility:	Yes
I/O expansion example	

Example program ID	
Name:	Test count2.bas
Microcontroller:	Any AVR microcontroler
Testing circuit:	Figure 2
MiniPin compatibility:	Yes
MegaPin compatibility:	Yes
Simple counter with LED displays	

Example program ID	
Name:	Test count no for.bas
Microcontroller:	Any AVR microcontroler
Testing circuit:	Figure 2
MiniPin compatibility:	Yes
MegaPin compatibility:	Yes
Same as "Test count2.bas" whithout leading zero blanking	

Example program ID	
Name:	Clock.bas
Microcontroller:	Any AVR microcontroler
Testing circuit:	Figure 2
MiniPin compatibility:	Yes
MegaPin compatibility:	Yes
Simple clock with LED display	

Example program ID	
Name:	Test_Bargraph.bas
Microcontroller:	Any AVR microcontroler
Testing circuit:	Figure 6
MiniPin compatibility:	Yes
MegaPin compatibility:	Yes
Test bargraph program	

Driving motors with AVR

By Vladimir Mitrović

The output connections of MiniPin II and MegaPin development boord are not designed to drive powerful loads: they are directly connected to the I/O pins of the microcontroller and cannot source or sink more than 40 mA. Therefore, we have developed the Power module - a real power extension for both development boord. It uses logic levels at the development board's output connections to control powerful operational amplifiers, which are able to source or sink currents up to 1 A. With one Power module attached, MiniPin II and MegaPin become capable of driving small DC and stepper motors, relays, lamps, heaters and other similar loads.

Power module

The Power module shown in Figure 1 is built around four L272M integrated circuits: IC1-IC4. Each of them contains two powerful operational amplifiers with maximum output currents up to 1 A. These amplifiers are used to switch loads connected to their outputs, to the ground (pin 4) or to the positive power supply voltage (pin 2). The inverting inputs of all amplifiers are connected to LED1, which provides them with a bias voltage of around 1.5 V. Non-inverting inputs are connected, via IDC10 connector PX and appropriate cable, to any I/O connector on MPIN (and from there to the I/O pins of the microcontroller). Logic levels on these pins determine the output states of the power amplifiers:

» logic *Low* ("0") at any pin switches the corresponding output of IC1-IC4 to 0 V;
» logic *High* ("1") at any pin switches the corresponding output of IC1-IC4 to the positive power supply voltage.

NOTE

In all further references in this text related to both development boord, the common name MPIN will be used instead of their separate names MiniPin II and MegaPin.

The Power module is connected to MPIN via a cable, as illustrated in Figure 2. A 10-wire flat cable, with 10-pin IDC10F connectors at both ends, is used. The preferred length of the cable is up to 50 cm, but even longer cables can be used in most applications. Be sure to orient the connectors as shown in Figure 2: equally marked pins should be interconnected (1-1, 2-2, etc.).

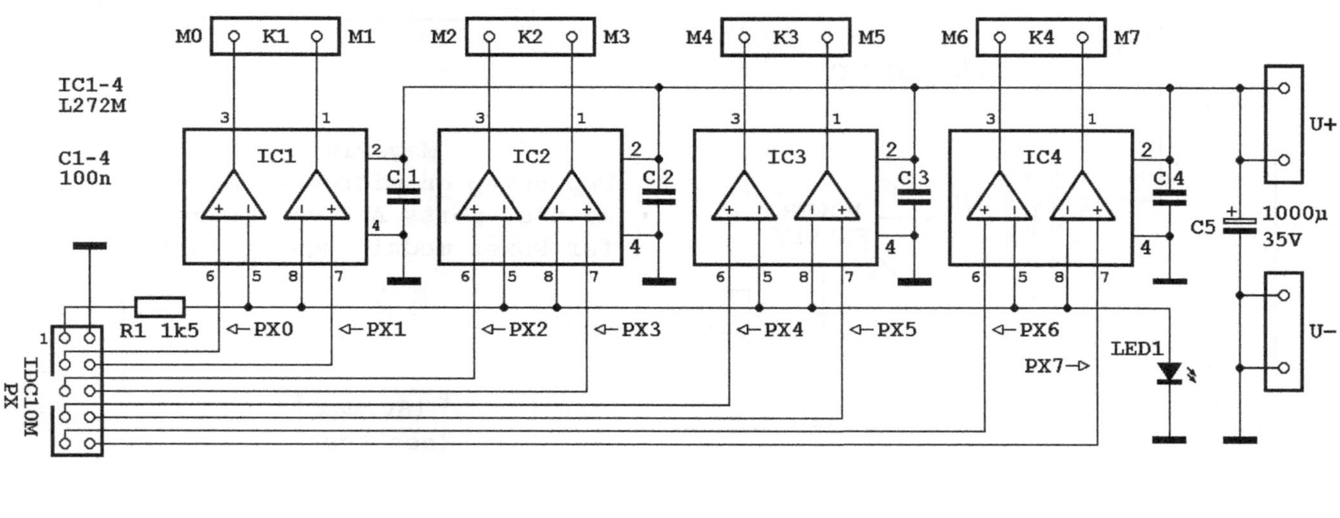

Figure 1: A Power module for MiniPin II and MegaPin development boord

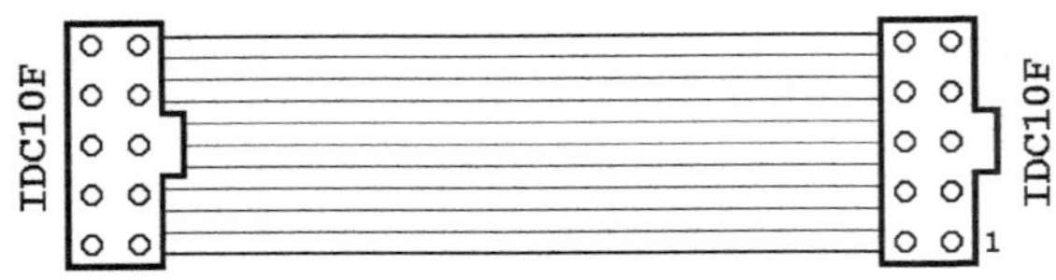

Figure 2: Sketch of the connecting cable

The cable connects the non-inverting inputs of the Power module to the pins of the selected I/O port, as well as the ground planes of both devices, and provides the positive voltage supply from MPIN to the Power module. This voltage (+5 V or +3.3 V) is used only for LED1 - the Power module requires its own power supply. The output voltage of this supply should be selected according to the requirements of the loads connected to the M0-M7 output terminals. You must allow for a 0.5-1.5 voltage drop within driver ICs IC1-IC4, depending upon the load current and the way in which the loads are connected - see the L272M data-sheet. The output voltage should be stable (but it does not have to be regulated) and the power rating depends upon the sum of the maximum currents through all connected loads.

Figure 3 shows how to connect the Power module to MPIN development boord. Although PORTD is used for this connection, any one of PORTA-PORTD connectors on MiniPin II or PORTA-PORTF on MegaPin can be used. Of course, which ports can actually be used depends upon the installed microcontroller and other devices (switches, 1-wire components etc.) that may already be connected to some of the I/O pins. In the following text,

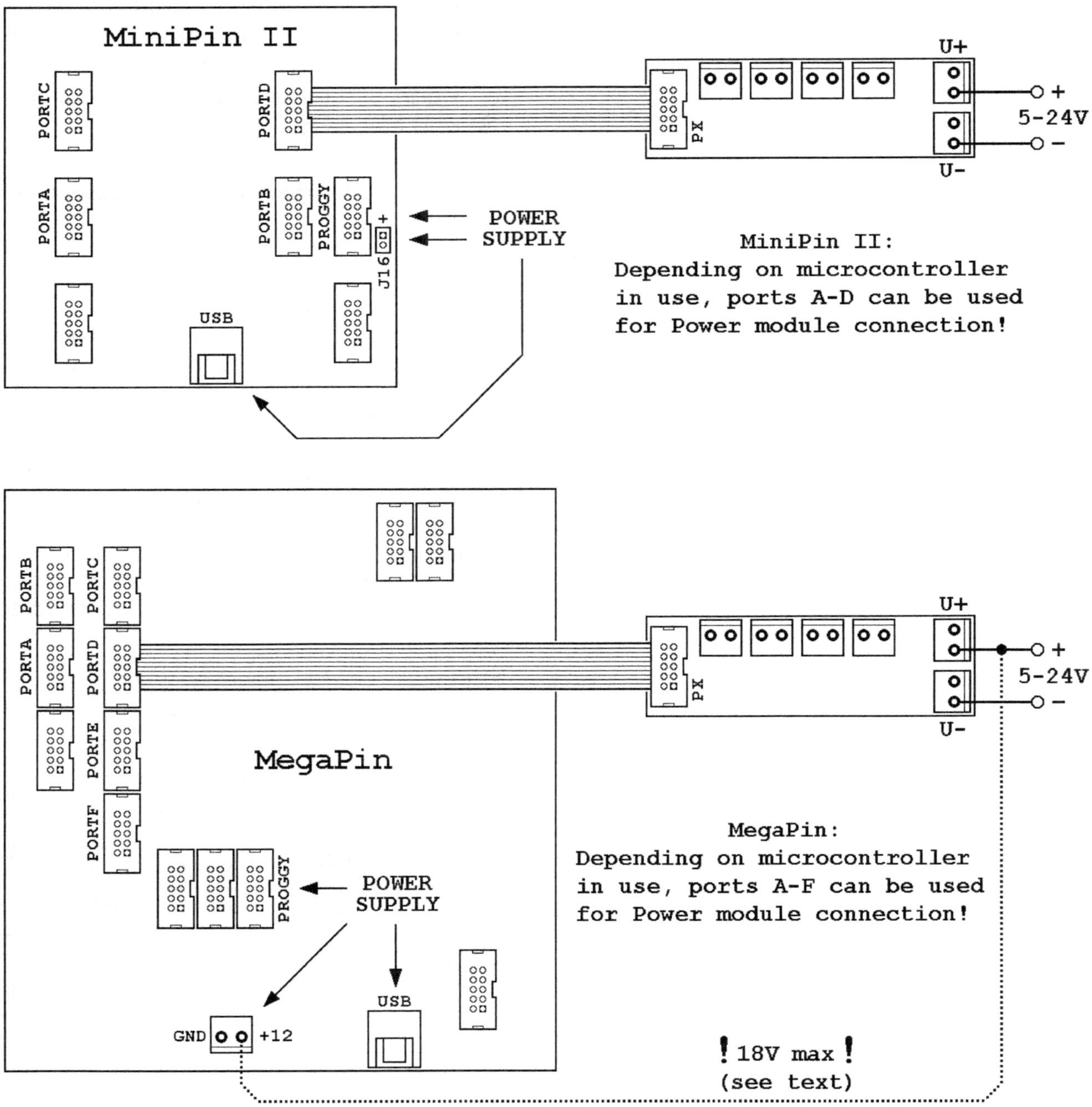

Figure 3: How to connect a Power module to MiniPin II (top) or to MegaPin (bottom)

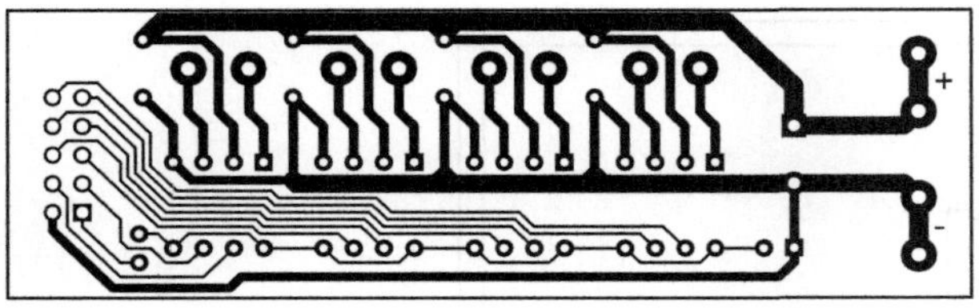

Figure 4a: PCB artwork

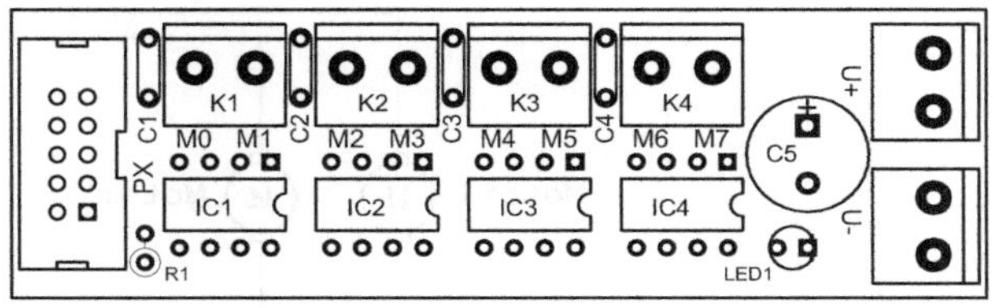

Figure 4b: Component layout

we will assume that PORTD is used, but the same applies to the other I/O ports as well. You can even connect two or more Power modules to one MPIN, as long as you have enough free ports.

As Figure 3 suggests, the MPIN development system should have its own power supply, separate from the power supply used for the Power module. The only exception is shown with a dotted line: in the case of the MegaPin board, it can share the same power supply as the Power module, as long as the power supply voltage doesn't exceed 18 V. The lowest allowable voltage, in this case, depends upon the supply voltage selector on the MegaPin board:

» if it is set to 3.3 V, input voltage can be as low as 5 V and
» if it is set to 5 V, input voltage can be as low as 6 V.

Even short dips in the power supply voltage, below the lowest recommended voltage cited above, can reset the microcontroller!

Construction

The power module is best built on a PCB whose artwork and component layout are shown in Figures 4a and 4b. You can use L2722 devices instead of L272M for IC1-IC4. Both types are recommended for driving inductive loads, including motors, and can withstand non-repetitive peak output currents up to 1.5 A. Nevertheless, avoid short-circuits on their outputs: they have built-in thermal protection, but outputs are not current-limited. High quality sockets are recommended for IC1-IC4 to make replacement easy, in case of a burnout.

The power supply terminals on the PCB are marked as "U+" and "U-". Each of them has connectors with two separate fastening screws and you can use either U+/U- pair to connect the power supply. The remaining two U+/U- connectors can be used for the motor connection.

Examples

The following examples show how to connect various motors to the Power module and how to effectively control them through software. Program examples are written in Bascom-AVR for the ATmega8515 running with an 8 MHz clock. The same examples require minimal program changes when used with most ATtiny and ATmega μCs running with either an 8 MHz or another clock frequency. It's assumed that the Power module is connected to the PORTD connector on MiniPin II or MegaPin development board, as shown in Figure 3. Any other MPIN free port can be used if port references within the program are adequately changed.

DC motor

Figure 5 shows three ways of connecting DC motors to the Power module. Motors Motor1 and Motor2 use only one power output each - with this configuration we can connect up to 8 DC motors to one Power module. With the Motor1 or Motor2 configuration, we can start, stop and control the speed of the motor. Instead of a DC motor, you can connect relays, so-

Label	Description	pcs.
IC1-IC4	L272M (L2722)	4
R1	1,5 kΩ	1
C1-C4	100 nF, ceramic, RM5	4
C5	1000 μF, 35V	1
LED1	LED 3mm, red,*low-current*	1
U+	2-way PCB screw terminal block, red, RM 5mm	1
U-	2-way PCB screw terminal block, blue, RM 5mm	1
K1-K4	2-way PCB screw terminal block, black, RM 5mm	4
PX	IDC10M PCB connector	1
no label	8-pin IC socket	4

Table 1: Component list

Label	Description	pcs.
no label	IDC10F flat cable connector	2
no label	10-pin flat cable	50 cm

Tabele 2: Flat cable component list

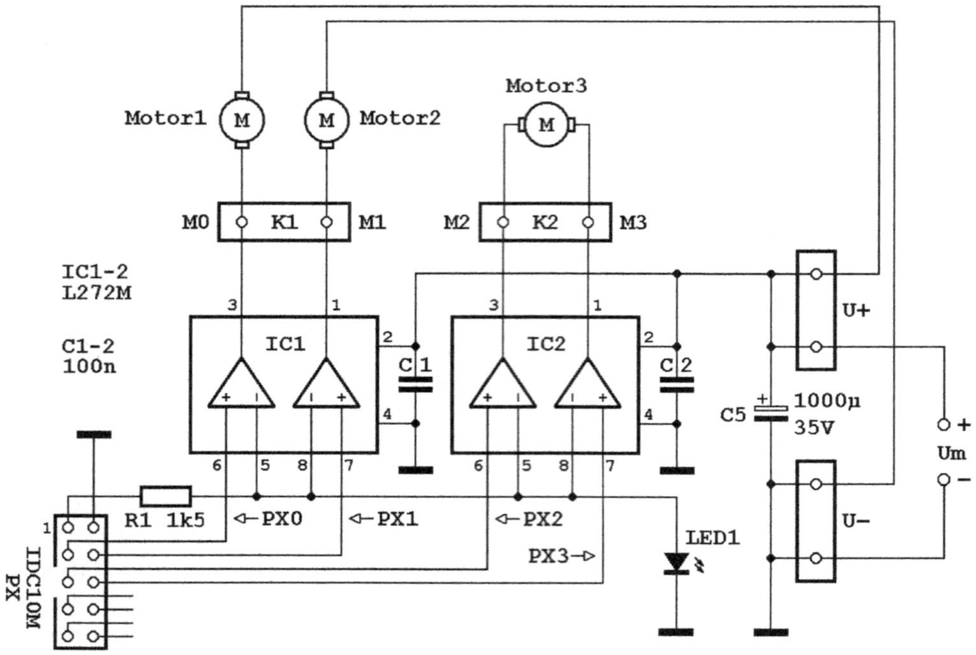

Figure 5: DC motors can be connected to the Power module in several different ways

lenoids, lamps, heaters or other power devices in the same way.

Motor3 uses two power outputs - with this configuration we can connect up to 4 DC motors to the Power module. In addition to being able to start, stop and control the speed of Motor3, we can also control its direction of rotation.

At the beginning of the program, port D has to be configured as output port:

```
Config PORTD = Output     'make PortD an
                          'output port
```

Now we can control motors by applying suitable logic levels to control pins PD0-PD7. The first thing to do is to switch off the power to all motors and other loads connected to K1-K4 terminals. The appropriate commands for the example in Figure 5 are as follows:

```
PORTD.0 = 1                  'stop Motor1
PORTD.1 = 0                  'stop Motor2
PORTD.2 = 0 : PORTD.3 = 0    'stop Motor3
```

The way the motors are controlled depends upon the way they are connected. For example, Motor1 is connected between the M0 output and the + bus of the power supply. This motor is started with a logic *Low* and stopped with a logic *High* at the corresponding microcontroller output pin:

```
PORTD.0 = 0         'start Motor1
Wait 5              'let it run for a while
PORTD.0 = 1         'stop Motor1
```

Motor2 is connected between the M1 output and the - bus of the power supply. This motor is started with a logic *High* and stopped with a logic *Low* at the corresponding output pin:

```
PORTD.1 = 1         'start Motor2
Wait 5              'let it run for a while
PORTD.1 = 0         'stop Motor2
```

Although the statements for motor control are very simple, it's good practice to place them within meaningfully-labelled subroutines. This is particularly useful if we have to control more than one motor. For Motor1 and Motor2 shown in Figure 5 these subroutines would be:

```
'* DC Motor1 subroutines

Motor1_start:               'start Motor1
   PORTD.0 = 0
Return
Motor1_stop:                'stop Motor1
   PORTD.0 = 1
Return

'* DC Motor2 subroutines

Motor2_start:               'start Motor2
   PORTD.1 = 1
Return
Motor2_stop:                'stop Motor2
   PORTD.1 = 0
Return
```

Now we can control motors using easily understandable commands:

```
Gosub Motor1_start          'start Motor1
Wait 5                      'let it run for
```

```
                               'a while
Gosub Motor1_stop              'stop Motor1
```

DC motor – changing the direction of rotation

If we want to control the direction of rotation, we have to connect a DC motor between two power outputs. For example, Motor3 is connected between the M2 and the M3 outputs, as shown in Figure 5. This motor is stopped if both control outputs are at the same logic level and rotates if the control outputs are at different logic levels. The direction of rotation is determined by the logic levels on the outputs (*Low-High* or *High-Low*).

Control subroutines for a motor connected as Motor3 are:

```
'* DC Motor3 subroutines

Motor3_stop:          'stop Motor3
   PORTD.2 = 0
   PORTD.3 = 0
Return

Motor3_left:          'start Motor3,
                      'left rotation
Motor3_ccw:           'start Motor3,
                      'CCW (alternate label)
   PORTD.2 = 1
   PORTD.3 = 0
Return

Motor3_right:         'start Motor3,
                      'right rotation
Motor3_cw:            'start Motor3,
                      'CW (alternate label)
   PORTD.2 = 0
   PORTD.3 = 1
Return
```

Now we can control Motor3 by calling appropriate subroutines:

```
Gosub Motor3_left              'start Motor3,
                               'left rotation
Wait 5                         'let it run
                               'for a while
Gosub Motor3_stop              'stop Motor3
Wait 5
Gosub Motor3_right             'start Motor3,
                               'right rotation
Wait 5                         'let it run
                               'for a while
Gosub Motor3_stop              'stop Motor3
```

DC motor - change of rotation speed

We can effectively control the speed of a DC motor using pulse-width modulation (PWM). In the following example, the voltage across Motor1 is alternatively switched on and off in 10 ms intervals. The average current thru the motor is halved and the motor rotates more slowly:

```
'* DC Motor1 speed control

Dim Dc_i As Byte
For Dc_i = 1 To 250          'speed is
                             'controlled
   Gosub Motor1_start        'by alternative
                             'switching on
   Waitms 10
   Gosub Motor1_stop         'and switching off
   Waitms 10                 'the motor
Next
```

The duration of one cycle (ON + OFF) is 20 ms, which results in a frequency of 50 Hz (i.e., the motor is switched on and off 50 times per second). This value was suitable for all small DC motors that I tested. If the motor being used works improperly (if it jerks or hums), double the switching frequency by shortening the ON and OFF intervals to 5 ms.

The motor speed is controlled by changing the ratio between the ON and OFF periods. For example, if we want to slow down the motor, we should shorten the ON and extend the OFF period. Keep the total cycle time unchanged when changing speed (for example, if you shorten the ON interval to 5 ms, the OFF interval should be 15 ms). Every DC motor has a minimal ON:OFF ratio at which it stops rotating.

The total motor running time equals the execution time of the *For-Next* loop. In the above example, it is 250*20ms=5s. For longer periods, variable *Dc_i* should be dimensioned as Word or Long. Although fully functional, the preceding example has a significant disadvantage: the program cannot perform other functions while controlling the motor. A better solution is to implement a motor control within an interrupt service routine that gets invoked frequently.

```
Dim Motor1_speed As Byte
On Timer0 Tim0_sub
Enable Interrupts
Config Timer0 = Timer , Prescale = 64
```

NOTE

The terms "left" and "right" refer to "counter-clockwise" and "clockwise", respectively. The actual direction of rotation also depends upon the way the motor is connected to the Power module. If the motor rotates in the opposite direction than expected, reverse the connecting wires or complement the logic levels of the control outputs in the program (in this example PORTD.2 and PORTD.3).

```
...
Tim0_sub:
    PORTD.0 = Motor1_speed.0
    Rotate Motor1_speed , Right
Return
```

With an 8 MHz clock, the interrupt service routine *Tim0_sub* executes approximately once every 2 ms. During execution, the subroutine transfers the next bit from the Byte variable *Motor1_speed* to the control pin PD0. Eight iterations are necessary to transfer all bits and, consequently, the cycle will repeat each 8*2 ms, resulting in a 61 Hz pulse frequency (assuming that all "0"s as well as all "1"s are grouped together).

Note: There is a bug in the Bascom-AVR demo, ver. 1.11.9.1 related to the *Config Timer0* statement, when the prescale factor 64 is specified for an ATmega8515. Instead of 64, a 256 prescale factor is set, resulting in a much lower pulse frequency, making the motor jerk and/or hum. If you experience such problems with your version of Bascom-AVR, replace the *Config Timer0* statement with its assembler equivalent:

```
ldi r24,3
!out tccr0,r24
```

The content written to the *Motor1_speed* variable defines the frequency and the duration of the pulses at PD0 and consequently the power output at M0. As Motor1 is switched on by a logic *Low* and switched off by a logic *High*, the average current thru the motor, and therefore its speed, is directly proportional to the number of "0" and "1" bits in the *Motor1_speed* variable (not its value!). For a motor connected like Motor1 shown in Figure 5, more zeroes will result in a higher speed. It doesn't matter how these "0" and "1" bits are arranged within the variable: "00001111", "00110011", "01010101" and other possible permutations will all result in the same speed. Content "11111111" will stop the motor and "00000000" will run it at full speed.

To start the motor, write an appropriate value to the *Motor1_speed* variable and enable the Timer0 interrupt:

```
Motor1_speed = &B11111100    'set the speed
Enable Timer0                'start the motor
```

Once the motor is started, the program can execute whatever statements are needed for other functions, and the motor will continue to rotate at a set speed for as long as the interrupts are enabled. You can change the speed at any time, without stopping Timer0 or disabling its interrupt; just change the value in the *Motor1_speed* variable:

```
Motor1_speed = &B11110000       'change
                                'the speed
```

To stop the motor, write "11111111" to the *Motor1_speed* variable:

```
Motor1_speed = &B11111111       'stop
                                'the motor
```

Although the motor stops, interrupt service routine *Tim0_sub* continues to execute once in every 2 ms. The subroutine lasts about 20 µs and does not slow down the program execution noticeably. However, if this is a problem, Timer0 interrupts should be disabled several ms after the motor stop command:

```
Motor1_speed = &B11111111       'stop
                                'the motor
Waitms 5                        'wait
                                'a moment
Disable Timer0                  'disable
                                'interrupts
```

Using an 8-bit variable *Motor1_speed* allows for 7 different speeds plus stop. If we need a finer resolution, we have to define *Motor1_speed* as a Word variable. In this case, the speed is defined as a 16-bit long binary number:

```
Motor1_speed = &B1111111100000000
```

Now we can define 16 different rotation speeds, but the frequency of current pulses thru the motor is halved to 30.5 Hz (using an 8 MHz clock). If this pulse frequency is too low for the motor in use, it can be easily doubled if we arrange "0"s and "1"s in two approximately equal groups:

```
Motor1_speed = &B1111000011110000
```

This value will result in the same rotation speed, but the pulse frequency will be 61 Hz again.

The same principle is valid for motors connected like Motor2 in Figure 5. The only difference is that the rotation speed is now proportional to the number of binary "1"s in the related variable. It's also possible to control the rotation speed of several motors with almost no overhead; just define one speed-variable per motor and transfer bits from each variable to corresponding control pins, within the same interrupt service routine:

```
Dim Motor1_speed As Byte
Dim Motor2_speed As Byte
...
...
Tim0_sub:
    PORTD.0 = Motor1_speed.0    'Motor1
    Rotate Motor1_speed , Right
    PORTD.1 = Motor2_speed.0    'Motor2
    Rotate Motor2_speed , Right
'add the same procedure for
'the remaining motors here
Return
```

The rotation speeds for the motors are defined by the binary sequences as explained before. Motors can be connected differently (i.e. some like Motor1 and some like Motor2) and the variable types can even be different (Byte type for lower resolution and Word type for higher resolution). The rotation speed of any motor can be changed at any instant and independently of the speeds of other motors. However, we have to be careful with the *Enable Timer0* and *Disable Timer0* statements. I recommend the following sequence:

- write initial values to all *Motor_speed* variables that will stop the motors;
- *Enable Timer0*;
- start and stop motors and change their rotation speed as necessary;
- do not execute *Disable Timer0*.

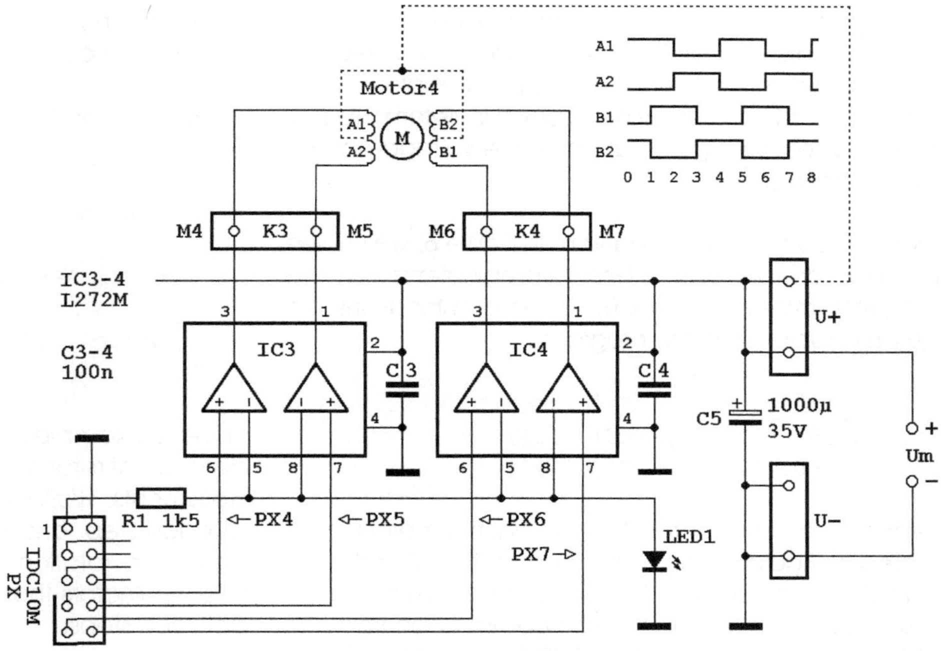

Figure 6: Stepper motors are connected to 4 power outputs. A supply voltage pattern is shown in upper-right corner

DC motor - change the direction of rotation and speed

It's also possible to change the rotation speed for a motor connected like Motor3 shown in Figure 5. In this case we should define two speed-variables, *Motor3a_speed* and *Motor3b_speed*. To make the motor rotate in one direction, write all "0"s to one variable and a speed-related number of "1"s to the other:

```
Motor3a_speed = &B00000000 'define rotation
                           'direction
Motor3b_speed = &B11110000 'set the speed
Enable Timer0              'start the motor
```

The speed is proportional to the number of "1"s in the *Motor3b_speed* - more "1"s means higher speed. The motor will rotate in the other direction if we reverse the variables:

```
Motor3b_speed = &B00000000 'set other
                           'rotation
                           'direction
Motor3a_speed = &B11110000 'set the speed
Enable Timer0              'start the motor
```

Note: *Enable Timer0* is necessary only the first time that the motor is started. If the Timer0 interrupts are enabled, the motor rotates as long as there is a different value in the two speed-control variables. Accordingly, the motor will be stopped as soon as we write the same value to both variables. It is recommended that the stop-values are all "0"s or all "1"s, because this will produce no pulses at the power outputs:

```
Motor3b_speed = &B00000000 'this will
Motor3a_speed = &B00000000 'stop the motor
```

To control the speed of Motor3, *Tim0_sub* should be upgraded with the following statements:

```
Tim0_sub:
   ...                     'for other
                           'motors, if used
   PORTD.2 = Motor3a_speed.0
   Rotate Motor3a_speed , Right
   PORTD.3 = Motor3b_speed.0
   Rotate Motor3b_speed , Right
Return
```

Stepper motor

Stepper motors may be bipolar (two separate coils, four connecting wires) or unipolar (two pairs of coils in a series connection, using six connecting wires). Both types can be connected to the Power module as shown in Figure 6. The difference is that the connections shown using dotted lines do not exist if a bipolar stepper motor is used. As each stepper motor uses four power outputs, the maximum number of stepper motors that one Power module can control is two.

Whether bipolar or unipolar, a stepper motor is driven by applying supply voltages according to the patterns shown in Figure 6 in the upper-right corner.

The motor maintains its current position as long as there is no change in the supply voltages. The motor will advance (step) to the next position when the supply voltages change to an adjacent combination. If supply voltages are changed according to the pattern, from left to right, the motor will rotate in one direction. If supply voltages are changed according to the pattern from right to left, the motor will rotate in the other direction. The motor design determines how many degrees the motor will turn with each step (for example, a step-size of 7.5°or 18°). The rotation speed is determined by the step size and the rate at which the voltage-combinations change.

If we look carefully at the patterns in Figure 6, we will see that there are only four different combinations (i.e., two complete cycles are shown). These combinations are held in a table within the program:

```
Step_table:
Data &B10011111 , &B01011111
Data &B01101111 , &B10101111
```

The table contents match the way that the motor is connected in Figure 6. The four unused bits (3-0 in this example) must be set to "1". To advance the motor to the next step, we have to read a bit combination from the table and set control pins PD7-PD4 accordingly. This is best done within subroutine *New_step*:

```
New_step:
   Step_i = Step_i And &B00000011
                         'only 0-3
                         'is allowed
   Step_aux = Lookup(step_i , Step_table)
   Disable Interrupts    'see explanation
   PORTD = PORTD Or &B11110000
   PORTD = PORTD And Step_aux
   Enable Interrupts     'see explanation
Return
```

The subroutine uses two Byte variables: step counter *Step_i* and auxiliary variable *Step_aux*. Variable *Step_i* is the table index and contains values in the 0-3 range. This is controlled by the first statement within the subroutine. The subroutine fetches the value from the *Step_table* indexed by *Step_i* and transfers it to the control pins PD7-PD4, without affecting the other pins of Port D. The statements that disable and enable interrupts are necessary only if there are other active interrupts that change the PD3-PD0 pins of the PD port (like interrupt service routine *Tim0_sub*, which we used to control the speed of a DC motor). If not, then delete or comment out these statements.

To turn the motor 100 steps in one direction, change *Step_i* in a 0-1-2-3-0... sequence and execute the *New_step* subroutine for each new index value:

```
For Cnt = 1 To 100          'make 100 steps

 Incr Step_i                'prepare the next
                            'step
   Gosub New_step           'move to the next
                            'step
  Waitms 50                 'wait a bit

Next
```

To turn the motor 10 steps in the other direction, change the *Step_i* in a 0-3-2-1-0... sequence:

```
For Cnt = 1 To 10          'make 10 steps in
                           'the other
                           'direction
   Decr Step_i             'prepare the next
                           'step
   Gosub New_step          'move to the next
                           'step
   Waitms 500              'wait a bit
Next
```

In these examples, *Cnt* is an auxiliary counter and the direction of rotation is determined by the *Incr* and *Decr* statements. *Waitms* defines how long the motor stays at each step, and thus the rotation speed. There is a maximum rotation speed for every motor: the small stepper motors that I have tested need at least 2 ms between steps.

At the beginning of the program it's necessary to apply power to the coils according to any of the combinations shown in Figure 6, and thus fix the motor in a certain position:

```
Step_i = 0
Gosub New_step
```

Alternatively, you can put the same voltage at all connection terminals, for example:

```
PORTD.7 = 1
PORTD.6 = 1
PORTD.5 = 1
PORTD.4 = 1
```

If a unipolar stepper motor is connected as shown in Figure 6, it's not a good idea to initially set all connection terminals to 0 V: in this case, current will flow through all coils at once.

Servo motor

A servo motor has three connections: two for the power supply (usually 5 V) and one for control pulses. The control input has a relatively high input resistance and can be driven by any microcontroller output pin. Therefore, no Power module is needed to drive a servo motor and it can be directly connected to any MPIN I/O connector. In the exam-

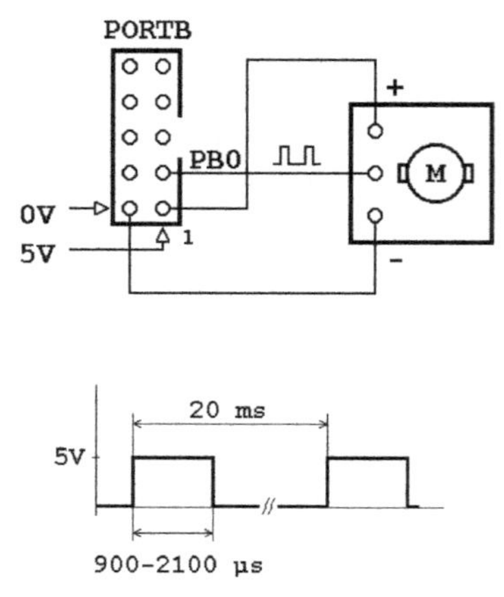

Figure 7: How to connect a servo motor to MiniPin II or MegaPin

ple shown in Figure 7, the control pin PB0 from the PORTB connector is used and the power supply is also taken from pins 1 and 2 of the same connector. This is also an example of how to connect other digitally-controlled devices to MPIN development board.

Figure 7 also shows the shape of the control pulses. The repetition frequency is typically 50 Hz and a positive pulse with the duration of 1500 µs sets the motor in its central position. Changing the pulse duration within the 900-2100 µs range turns the motor up to 90° to the left or right. The values are typical for the HS-311 by Hitec and can differ slightly for other similar servo motors.

Bascom-AVR has an embedded *Config Servos* statement to configure control pins for up to 14 servo motors. Motor position is defined by writing the appropriate value to the associated variable. I have thoroughly tested the *Config Servos* statement and have found several difficulties: some parameters are not automatically adjusted to suit the clock frequency used, and have to be determined experimentally.

Therefore I have written replacement subroutines that use Timer1 and can precisely control one or two servo motors. The subroutines use a value defined by the *$crystal* directive (from the user program this is visible as the constant labelled *_xtal*) to adjust all time-intervals. As a result, these servo routines work properly with clock frequencies from 4 to 24 MHz with no need to experiment with any additional parameters.

The servo subroutines will not be analysed here in greater detail, but we will explain how to use them. At the beginning of the program one should define Word variable *Servo*, define control pins for the two servo motors and call the *Config_servo* subroutine:

```
Dim Servo As Word

Servo1_pin Alias PORTB.0          'Servo1
                                  'control pin
Servo2_pin Alias PORTB.1          'Servo2
                                  'control pin
Gosub Config_servo
```

The *Config_servo* subroutine:

» configures the selected pins as output pins;
» defines and enables Compare1a, Compare1b and Capture1 interrupts;
» calculates and sets initial values in Timer1 registers related to interrupts and
» configures and starts the Timer1.

Upon return from the *Config_servo* subroutine, Timer1 will execute an interrupt subroutine every 20 ms and set both control pins to a logic *High*. Initial values are defined so that both control pins stay at a logic *High* i.e. there are no output pulses. This leaves the servo motors in their previously-held positions. To set a servo motor to a desired position, just write the appropriate value to the *Servo* variable and call the *Servo1* or *Servo2* subroutine:

```
Servo = 1500
Gosub Servo1                      'set servo1 to the
                                  'middle position
Wait 5
For Servo = 900 To 2100
   Gosub Servo2                   'turn servo2 slowly
                                  'from one...
   Waitms 5                       '... to the other
                                  'end position
Next
```

Values in the *Servo* variable correspond to the desired pulse duration in µs. When the desired time interval for any control pin has passed, Timer1 generates an interrupt that sets this port pin to a logic *Low*. The procedures for both pins are mutually independent. The procedure is repeated: every 20 ms both control pins are set and reset again as soon as their given time interval elapses.

The values allowed for the *Servo* variable lie between 1 and 20000, which will generate pulses from 1 µs to 20 ms. This range is much wider than actually required (900-2100 for small servos, but some of them will allow a wider range, for example 500-2500). Be careful: values outside the allowed range for a servo will cause it to try turning beyond its end limits, which is not advisable. Values outside the 1-20000 range will stop pulse production and set the control pin permanently to a logic *High*.

The accuracy of the pulse duration is better than +/- 1 µs. Such an error is totally negligible for servo-motor control. The accuracy is a bit worse with clock frequencies under 8 MHz and with very short pulses (< 5 µs). The accuracy may deteriorate if other interrupt routines are enabled, if they last for more than 1-2 µs.

All the subroutines that control servo motors are visible in the demo program explained below. If you want to use these routines within your program, copy the *Servo_aux* variable definition and *Servo1*, *Servo2*, *Servo12*, *Config_servo*, *C1a_sub*, *C1b_sub* and *T1_sub* subroutines to the end of your program. All interrupt service routines last less than 1 µs and use no registers. You can freely use other interrupts within your program, assuming they are short - if they are not, there will be occasional irregularities in the servo motor operation.

If you intend to use only one servo motor, configure both control pins to the same I/O pin:

```
Servo1_pin Alias PORTB.0          'servo1
                                  'control pin
Servo2_pin Alias PORTB.0          'servo2
                                  'control pin
```

and use only the *Gosub Servo1* subroutine call. Although not used, the *Servo2_pin* definition is necessary during the compilation.

Demo programs

Several demo programs have been written to explain the use of routines introduced above. The programs have been written for an ATmega8515 running with an 8 MHz clock, but the same programs are applicable to most ATtiny and ATmega microcontrollers.

If you want to test a program, do the following:

» program the microcontroller,
» switch off the power supply,
» connect the motor according to the relevant figure and,
» switch the power on again.

Programming the microcontroller with a motor connected to the Power module can cause its uncontrolled operation.

Example program ID	
Name:	Motor1.bas
Microcontroller:	ATmega8515 and most other AVRs
Testing circuit:	Figure 5
MiniPin compatibility:	yes (with appropriate μC), with the Power module
MegaPin compatibility:	yes, with the Power module
The program illustrates the use of routines for a DC motor control (start, stop, speed regulation), if it is connected as Motor1	

Example program ID	
Name:	Motor2.bas
Microcontroller:	ATmega8515 and most other AVRs
Testing circuit:	Figure 5
MiniPin compatibility:	yes (with appropriate μC) , with the Power module
MegaPin compatibility:	yes, with the Power module
The program illustrates the use of routines for a DC motor control (start, stop, speed regulation), if it is connected as Motor2	

Example program ID	
Name:	Motor3.bas
Microcontroller:	ATmega8515 and most other AVRs
Testing circuit:	Figure 5
MiniPin compatibility:	yes (with appropriate μC) , with the Power module
MegaPin compatibility:	yes, with the Power module
The program illustrates the use of routines for a DC motor control (start, stop, speed regulation, rotation direction), if it is connected as Motor3	

Example program ID	
Name:	Motor_step.bas
Microcontroller:	ATmega8515 and most other AVRs
Testing circuit:	Figure 6
MiniPin compatibility:	yes (with appropriate μC) , with the Power module
MegaPin compatibility:	yes, with the Power module
The program illustrates the use of routines for a stepper motor control, if it is connected as Motor4	

Example program ID	
Name:	Motor_servo.bas
Microcontroller:	ATmega8515 and most other AVRs
Testing circuit:	Figure 7
MiniPin compatibility:	yes (with appropriate μC)
MegaPin compatibility:	yes
The program illustrates the use of routines for a servo motor control	

Something about PWM in Bascom-AVR

By Jurij Mikeln

Pulse Width Modulation (PWM) is more or less known to most of us. The PWM principle is widely used in drivers for conventional motors, servo motors, power supplies, driving LEDs, as well as other applications. The newer AVR microcontrollers typically have several built-in PWM hardware units, which facilitate the generation of PWM signals. These hardware PWM units do not slow down the microcontroller's CPU. In this chapter I will show you how to use an AVR MCU to generate PWM signals.

Most AVRs contain PWM hardware, especially the newer ones, which typically have two or more PWM units built-in. A PWM signal is one in which the ratio between a pause and a signal is changing as seen in Figure 1.

Figure 1: A PWM signal

I will not bother to explain the internal structure of a PWM unit within an AVR MCU. For the time being, let me just say that a PWM unit is a part of the Timer circuit. Most AVRs have at least 2 PWMs: one associated with Timer0 and one associated with Timer1. When selecting the microcontroller that we want to use for PWM generation, we have to set the resolution of the PWM that we would like to have: 8, 9 or 10 bits. 8-bit PWM means that our PWM signal is changing within 256 steps, while 512 or 1024 steps are achieved with 9 or 10 bits respectively. Not all AVRs offer more than 8-bit PWM resolution. For everyday use – say to drive an LED or a simple motor, 8-bit PWM is more than enough, while other applications require a higher resolution PWM signal. We will focus on 8-bit PWM.

Programming

Let us start our Bascom-AVR program. First, we have to configure a suitable Timer. If we require 8-bit PWM then we select an 8-bit timer. We can also select a 16-bit timer and configure it as an 8-bit PWM timer as you can see below:

```
Config Timer1 = Pwm , Pwm = 8 ,
Compare A Pwm = Clear Down , Prescale = 1
```

This configuration statement is valid for most AVRs. In this sample we used it with an ATmega16 microcontroller, but program PWM1.bas can also be used with other AVRs. Be aware that AVR timers have Compare outputs designated with the letters A, B and C. If we configure *Compare A Pwm = Clear Down* then we will be using Output Compare 1A (OC1A) as an output pin. In the case of the ATmega16 that corresponds to the PortD.5 pin. It's nearly all done. All that is remaining is to load the PWM counter with the value of a byte variable, as follows:

```
COMPARE1A = N
```

If we now change the value of *N* from 0 to 255 and back to 0 while observing an LED connected to PortD.5, we will see that LED is slowly turning on and then slowly fading out. A simple and wonderful example of driving an LED with PWM!

When Bascom's Config statement is used to configure a timer in PWM mode, it automatically takes care of setting the direction of the Output Compare pin to the Output mode. If you were to do the configuration yourself, using the AVRs timer registers directly, you would have to do this step yourself.

To generate a simple 3-phase PWM signal with ATmega32 you'd have to configure Timers:

```
Config Timer1 = Pwm , Pwm = 8 ,
Compare A Pwm = Clear Down ,
Compare B Pwm = Clear Down , Prescale = 1

Config Timer2 = Pwm ,
Compare Pwm = Clear Down , Prescale = 1
```

and as outputs use the following:

```
COMPARE2 = N
COMPARE1A = N + 85
COMPARE1B = N + 170
```

PWM outputs are on PortD.7, PortD.5 & PortD.4. Watch the LEDs as they gradually turn on while PortD.2 or PortD.3 keypad is pressed.

Let me shortly comment briefly on the above 3 commands, where you see that each PWM has a different *N* value. We have chosen them by simple calculation. If we take 255 and divide that by 3 (because we want to have a 3 phase signal) we get 85, simple isn't it!

It should be possible to generate a 3-phase signal

NOTE

You should note that the AVR is capable of generating several types of PWM signals. A few possibilities are the FAST PWM, and the PHASE-CORRECT PWM. For any given clock frequency, the PWM frequency will depend upon which PWM mode is chosen. The values given above are for the PHASE-CORRECT PWM mode. See the applicable Atmel Datasheet for more details about the different modes.

using these 2 timers, but it would take a lot more complex code than this, and would require interrupt service routines on each timer compare. But as such for driving 3 LEDs we find this simple code to be good enough.

If we change the configuration from *Pwm = 8* to *Pwm = 10* then we would notice that the LED is turning on/off slower than in 8-bit mode. That is logical, because instead of 256 steps there are 1024 steps now. When using PWM resolutions > 8-bits, the variable that you use to load the COMPAREx register must be a word or integer variable, to handle the larger numbers involved. Also note that, in general, PWM resolutions greater than 8-bits can only be handled by the 16-bit timers contained in the AVR MCU.

Depending on the speed of the system clock, we have to choose an appropriate Prescale value. An 8-bit PWM unit basically generates a waveform with a variable "duty-cycle", and with a frequency of 1/510 that of the clock supplying it (1/1020 in the case of a 9-bit PWM, etc.) Since the AVR MCU typically runs with a system clock of 8 MHz or greater, we may want to divide this system clock down (prescale it) before it reaches the PWM unit. A Slower PWM frequency would mean that the attached LED would blink more slowly. You would notice the LED blinking at a *Prescale=1024*, while no blinking would be seen at a *Prescale = 1* (given the same duty cycle of 253/256 (i.e. N=253).

Assuming an 8 MHz MCU system clock, with a *Prescale = 1* the PWM frequency would be 15.686 kHz, while with *Prescale = 8* only 1.960 kHz. At a *Prescale = 1024* the PWM frequency would be only 15.23 Hz. If we were to double the system clock to 16 MHz then we would double the above PWM frequencies.

The above PWM description applies to Timer0 and Timer1 present on most AVR MCUs. However, both the ATmega16 and ATmega 8 also contain a third timer block-Timer 2. Setting up this timer as a PWM block is a bit different:

```
Config Timer2 = Pwm , Async = On ,
Prescale = 1 , Compare B Pwm = Clear Down ,
Clear Timer = 1
PWM2=N
```

Timer 2 allows for a clock which can be externally supplied (i.e. a 32 KHz watch crystal) which explains the extra "Async" parameter. There are many minor differences in the Timer/PWM operation of the various AVR MCUs but the general principle of PWM generation remains the same.

Conclusion

Generation of PWM signals is important for driving BLDC motors, LEDs and other power loads that need smooth, efficient power control. That is done very easily and effectively with Bascom-AVR.

Most AVRs have at least 2 PWMs, some have even more. I have showed you in principle how to use them and what you can expect.

Example program ID	
Name:	PWM1.bas
Microcontroller:	Any AVRs whith PWM
Testing circuit:	/
MiniPin compatibility:	Yes
MegaPin compatibility:	Yes
Simple PWM using hardware PWM in AVR	

Data Displays

57

Data displays are very important in the world of microcontrollers. With modern graphic LCD displays, one can design smart-looking products. But in some cases the »classic« 2x16 alphanumeric LCD or even 7 segment LED display is better-suited. If you have a limited number of I/O pins on your microcontroller, you might even want to connect your LCD via an SPI interface. All this is covered in this chapter.

> **Pick the right display and make sure that your product will stand out!**

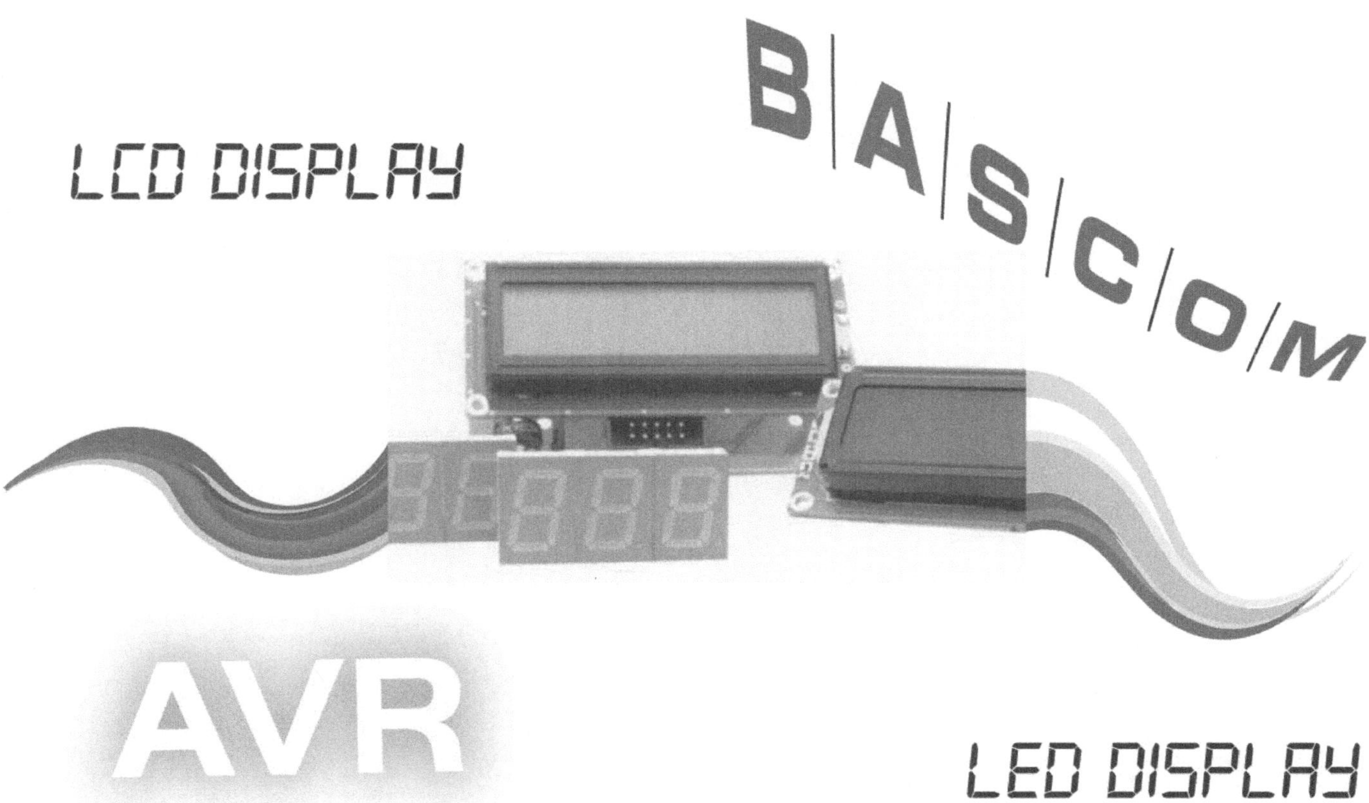

LCD Character Displays

By Jurij Mikeln

Displaying text on an LCD is something that has always attracted newbies to programming. However, this involves many tasks which are less appealing to the newbies. To display data on an LCD, you have to perform 16 tasks if programming in asembler.

Character LCD displays refer to 1x8, 2x8, 2x16, 4x20 and other character LCD modules that are widely available at very affordable prices. When programming in assembly language, it takes 16 steps to display data on LCD. Let me show you some of the steps:

1. after power-up wait at least 15 msec,
2. pins RS and R/W are set to 0,
3. write 0x3 to D7 – D4 ,
4. set and reset pin E,
5. wait 5 msec... etc.

You can trust me when I say that displaying text on a character LCD is one of the easiest tasks when programming with Bascom. You just have to make sure that the configuration (and wiring connections of course!) of the LCD is correct and then it will display data, text or even custom made characters flawlessly. The configuration commands in Bascom are as follows:

```
Config Lcd=16*2        'we will use 2x16 LCD
Config Lcdbus=4        '4-bit data bus will
                       'be used

Config Lcdpin = Pin , Db4 = Portb.4 , _
Db5 = Portb.5 , Db6 = Portb.6 , _
Db7 = Portb.7 , E = Portb.2 , Rs = Portb.1
```

The first statement tells the compiler what type of LCD we are using. In our case we have used the 2x16 LCD. When using the 4x20 LCD, for example, we would write 20*4. You can find all possible LCDs in the Options/Compiler/LCD menu as shown in Figure 1. Note that if using the 2x8 LCD, we should write 16*1a – this is the only case in which the Bascom description does not match the physical layout of the LCD panel.

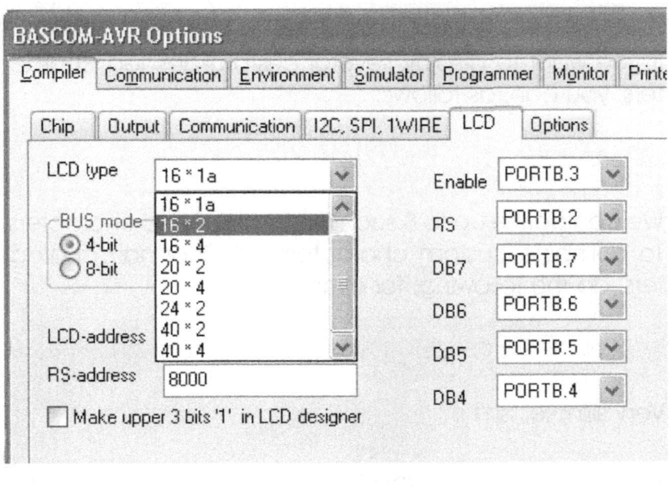

Figure 1: A list of LCDs which can be used with Bascom

As seen in Figure 1 you can also select your LCD in this menu. It is, however, advisable to write the program definitions at the top of your program (just as you would set the microcontroller and other definitions). It's easy to set one type of LCD in the menu and later, when using another LCD, simply forget to change the LCD type. This has happened to me many times. As a result, the program will not work as it should. So, it is good practice to define the LCD type at the top of the program, when programming in Bascom.

The next statement defines the bus mode we use to connect the LCD: 8 or 4 bits. I always use the 4-bit data bus. There are several reasons for that: the 4-bit data bus uses fewer of the microcontrollers' pins and it's nearly as fast as the 8-bit data bus. So far I have not needed the extra speed provided by the 8-bit data format.

Next, you have to define data pins DB7 – DB4, Enable and Rs pins. Assign them according to your hardware. If, by any chance, you have to redesign the hardware, it's easier to change the definition of the pins. You can also define the data pins on different ports, if that is required by your hardware. It's much easier to change the definitions of the data pins within your Bascom program than to change the hardware.

That is all we have to define and now we are ready to display what we want.

Here is the simplest way to display data with only one statement:

```
LCD "Text"; variable1; "  "; variable2
```

It is as simple as that. You will notice that displaying text (or constants, and signs such as +/- etc.) can be done within brackets like "This is test, 123 +/-@". This combination of text, numbers and signs will appear on the LCD exactly as written between the brackets, including spaces. If displaying a variable, then we just write its name instead of *variable1*, *variable2*, as shown in the example statement above. If displaying more than one variable, make sure that you include blank spaces between them, in order to distinguish them on the display.

Of course, let us not forget statements like *CLS* (clear screen), *Cursor On/Off,Blink/Noblink, ShiftLCD* and *Shift-Cursor*. All these statements help us format our display more attractively.

Advanced Display Options

The display routines described so far work, but with some drawbacks. When displaying a lot of data with simple LCD statements, it will quickly make the display unreadable, because variables & characters are simply "thrown" to the LCD one after another. That is not always practical nor does it look good. Fortunately, Bascom-AVR offers many statements which help us to display data more professionally on our LCD panel.

The first set of statements are: *Upperline, Lowerline, Thirdline, Fourthline*. The last two of these apply only to four line LCD panels. Usage is simple:

```
Upperline
LCD "Display data on upper line"
Lowerline
LCD "Display data on lower line"
```

This set of statements works well, but, Bascom-AVR also offers more options than that. It offers precise placement of characters on the LCD with the statement *Locate*, as follows:

```
Locate x,y
LCD "Display data at x position and on y line"
```

Wonderful - now you can display your data very nicely! But the story does not end yet.

Displaying custom-defined characters

Bascom-AVR allows you to display more than just the built-in character set of the LCD panel. It has a built-in LCD designer tool, shown in Figure 2.

The LCD designer tool can be accessed by clicking

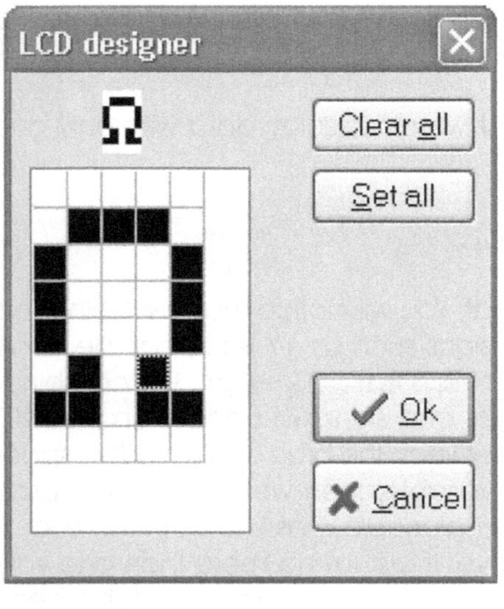

Figure 2: LCD designer tool

Tools, LCD designer , which opens the window seen in Figure 2.

Before you start to create your new character, place the cursor in your program to a new line in the edit window! This is important since Bascom will place the code for the custom-defined character at the current location of the cursor (this is valid for Bascom-AVR versions prior to Ver. 2.0!).

Now you can start clicking and creating your character. When done, click Ok and the LCD designer will generate the code:

```
Deflcdchar [x],32,14,17,17,17,10,27, 32
' replace [x] with number (0-7)
```

As you can see, you should replace [x] with a number from 0 – 7 (corresponding to the 8 custom-defined characters available with these character LCD displays). Let us say that we will use the number 1:

```
Deflcdchar 1,32,14,17,17,17,10,27,32
            ' replace[x] with number (0-7)
```

It is important that a CLS follows the DEFLCDCHAR statement(s). So make sure you place the DEFLCDCHAR statement(s) before the CLS statement, as seen in the Help file:

```
Deflcdchar 1 , 225 , 227 , 226 , 226 ,_
           226 , 242 , 234 , 228
           ' replace[x] with number (0-7)

Deflcdchar 0 , 240 , 224 , 224 , 255 ,_
           254 , 252 , 248 , 240
           ' replace[x] with number (0-7)

Cls
```

To display a custom-defined character use the statement:

```
LCD Chr (1)
```

If you want to display several custom-defined characters, you can, as follows:

```
LCD Chr (1); Chr(2) etc.
```

We can define up to 8 such custom-defined characters. To combine custom characters with "normal" characters, do the following, for example:

```
LCD "Text"; Chr (1); "Text2"; Chr(2) etc.
```

Very simple, isn't it?

Well, the story with displaying with custom characters does not end yet. Did you ever think of using a 2x16 LCD, for example, to display numbers & letters through both lines? Well, the solution is not trivial since we have only 8 custom characters available. With a little help from my friend Matjaž Skubic this is possible. Matjaž has done 8 custom made characters and combined them with those already available. Figure 3 shows how he has done these characters and combined them into larger sized numbers.

With the help of the statement *Locate* we can now design large characters on a 2x16 LCD, as follows:

```
Locate 1,3: LCD chr (2)
Locate 2,3: LCD chr (3)
```

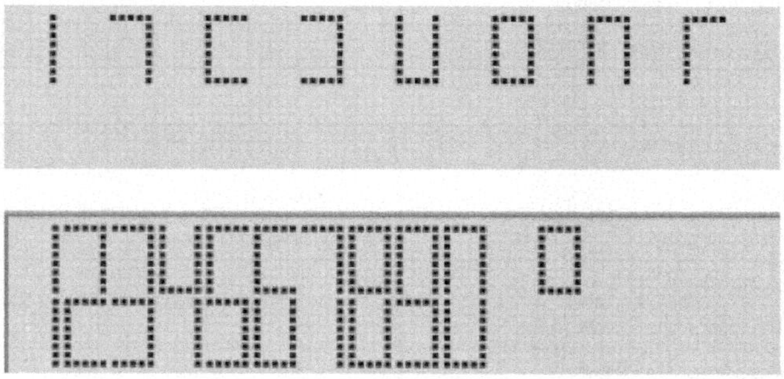

Figure 3: Custom-defined characters make large characters possible

Here are the definitions for standard large characters:

```
'normal
Deflcdchar 0,1,1,1,1,1,1,1,1         ' |
Deflcdchar 1,31,1,1,1,1,1,1,1        ' T
Deflcdchar 2,31,16,16,16,16,16,16,31 ' C
Deflcdchar 3,31,1,1,1,1,1 ,1,31      ' C inv
Deflcdchar 4,17,17,17,17,17,17,17,31 ' U
Deflcdchar 5,31,17,17,17,17,17,17,31 ' O
Deflcdchar 6,31,17,17,17,17,17,17,17 ' n
Deflcdchar 7,31,16,16,16,16,16,16,16 ' L inv
```

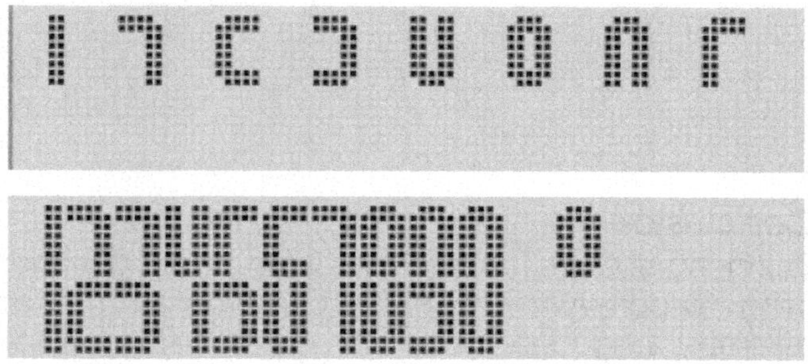

Figure 4: Bold large characters

If you want to create bold large characters, use the following definitions:

```
Deflcdchar 0,3,3,3,3,3,3,3,3              '|
Deflcdchar 1,30,31,3,3,3,3,3,3            'T
Deflcdchar 2,15,31,24,24,24,24,31,15      'C
Deflcdchar 3,30,31,3,3,3,3,31,30          'Cinv
Deflcdchar 4,27,27,27,27,27,27,31,14      'U
Deflcdchar 5,14,31,27,27,27,27,31,14      'O
Deflcdchar 6,14,31,27,27,27,27,27,27      'n
Deflcdchar 7,15,31,24,24,24,24,24,24      'Linv
```

In Figure 4 you can see the bold characters. When defining characters, you can only define 8 custom-defined characters.

For the automatic display of such numbers, we will require a small subroutine to place the characters in their proper positions. There are a couple of steps to be taken:

- change your number (byte, word etc.) to a string,
- calculate the length of the number to be displayed,
- use this length with a For loop, to define how long the display will be,
- for each character, take data from tables Data1 and Data2 (for upper and lower row),
- Send these two binary numbers to the LCD display using the *Chr()* statement.

This is done in the subroutine *Big_disp1*, as follows:

```
Big_disp1:
   St_number = Str(number1)
   Down = Len(st_number)
   For I = 1 To Down
   Z = Mid(st_number , I , 1)
   Zn = Val(z)
   B1 = Lookup(zn , Dta1)
   B2 = Lookup(zn , Dta2)
   Locate 1 , I : Lcd Chr(b1)
   Locate 2 , I : Lcd Chr(b2)
   Next
  ' a degree symbol
  Locate 1 , I : Lcd Chr(223)
  Ix = I + 1
  Locate 1 , Ix : Lcd Chr(2)
Return
```

```
Dta1:                            ' first line
Data 6,0,1,1,4,7,2,1,5,6,6
Dta2:                            ' secondline
Data 4,0,2,3,0,3,4,0,4,3,4
```

Conclusion

Displaying data on LCD modules is fun, especially when using Bascom-AVR. The rather complicated 16 step assembly language procedure is reduced to a few Bascom commands. One can display the complete standard character set as well as 8 custom-defined characters, prepared with the built-in LCD Designer tool. Using custom-defined characters, we have the opportunity to create larger characters, which may improve visibility on some of the smaller LCD panels.

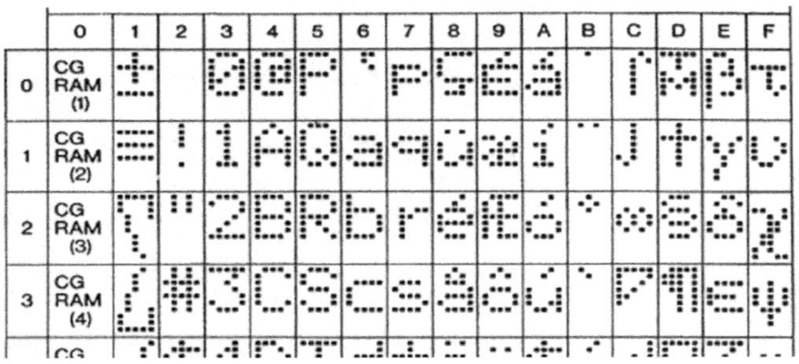

Example program ID	
Name:	BIG_Displ_1.bas
Microcontroller:	Any AVR microcontroler
Testing circuit:	Figure 12
MiniPin compatibility:	Yes
MegaPin compatibility:	Yes
Large characters on 2x16 LCD	

Example program ID	
Name:	BIG_Displ_2.bas
Microcontroller:	Any AVR microcontroler
Testing circuit:	Figure 12
MiniPin compatibility:	Yes
MegaPin compatibility:	Yes
Large characters on 2x16 LCD	

Example program ID	
Name:	LCD 2x16.bas
Microcontroller:	Any AVR microcontroller
Testing circuit:	Figure 12
MiniPin compatibility:	yes
MegaPin compatibility:	yes
Program displays data on 2x16 LCD	

Multiple LCDs on the SPI bus

By Jurij Mikeln

Not long ago, I needed to drive multiple LCDs. There were several possibilities available. I could have used multiple microcontrollers – one for each LCD. Or I could choose a microcontroller with more output ports. Neither of the possibilities seemed economical or technically justified. My colleague Vlado showed to me a nice way to drive LCDs via the SPI bus [1]. Doing so also required a special library [1].

I was very pleased with that method, since it required only three microcontroller pins. A fourth pin was used to drive the LCD's backlight. To test the concept, I fabricated a prototype PCB on our milling machine and the circuit immediately worked as expected. So, could this idea be extended to feeding multiple LCDs from a common SPI bus? Driving multiple LCDs via the SPI bus would seem to be ideal but, as we all know, nothing is as simple as it looks at the start. Specifically, the SPI LCD library was written for a single LCD only. That meant upgrading/changing the library file, which contains a lot of Assembly language. Upgrading the SPI LCD library file took some time, because I don't routinely program in Assembly language. The focus of the library upgrade was to change one internal variable from a constant to a variable accessible by the Bascom program. I won't elaborate on the details of the library file changes which I made: let's focus on the schematic diagram shown in Figure 1.

I have used a common 16x2 LCD module. You will notice that a backlight module is used, driven by transistor Q1. The backlight can be permanently turned on by a means of jumper J1. In this circuit I have used a 74HC164D chip which is a serial to parallel converter. Connector Con1 should be connected to a development board (in my case, the MegaPin board). Using connector Con2 we can set the "address" of our module by connecting pin 6 of Con2 to one of the other pins. An example program, that demonstrates how to use the SPI LCD, follows:

```
Waitms 200
Cls
Lowerline           'all LCD commands work OK
Lcd "TEST LCD"
Waitms 300
#if Test = 0
En_lcd = 2 : Initlcd : Cls : Lcd "LCD"
                    'LCD display on PortA.2
#endif
```

The complete program and its associated library (*multi_lcd-spi.lib*) can be found on our web page. You must place the library file in the LIB directory or the program will not compile. Note that you must first set variable *En_lcd* correctly, before sending the data you wish to display on the LCD. For example if we want to display data on LCD1, then we set the value of to *En_lcd = 1*. It's also important that each time we change the value of the En_lcd variable, we must use the *Initlcd*: *Cls*/statements. Note that if you change ports and *En_lcd*, you will also have to make suitable changes to the library file. Please contact the author for more information.

NOTE

If you decide to use a different port, aside from the library changes outlined above, you would also have to change your Bascom code to reflect the use of a different port.

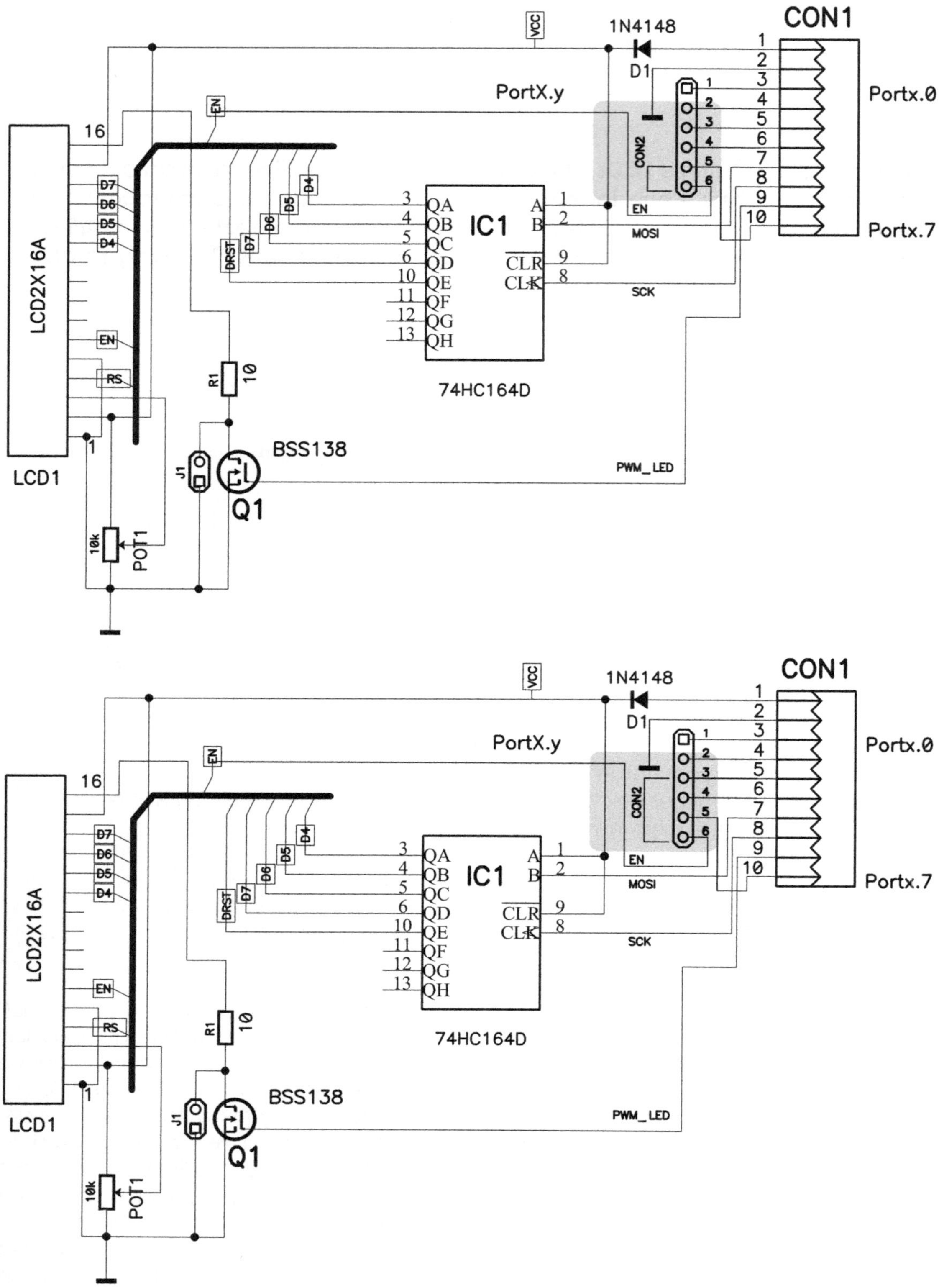

Figure 1: Schematic diagram of two identical SPI LCD modules

On the PCB you will see that it allows the display to be driven also from PortX.3 – which works but not reliably, because PortX.3 is used for Data in at LCD configuration.

Construction

The PCB, shown in Figure 2, is single-sided with SMD components and two jumper wires on the top layer. There is a trimmer potentiometer, for setting LCD contrast and connector Con2 where we set the address of each SPI LCD.

Conclusion

Now, we can use LCDs with 8-pin microcontrollers and any others not having many I/O ports. We only need three pins to drive an LCD display (four if we want to control the backlight as well). I have modified the SPILCD library file, which you can use for non-commercial purpose. I'd like to acknowledge the help of Mark Alberts and Irfan Delalović on this program.

References:

1. http://www.barello.net/

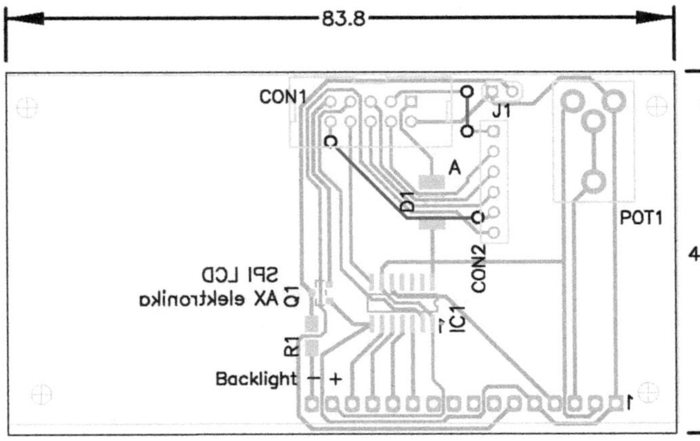

Figure 2: SPI LCD PCB

Example program ID - Library	
Name:	multi_lcd-spi.lib
Microcontroller:	/
Testing circuit:	/
MiniPin compatibility:	/
MegaPin compatibility:	/
Library for use with above	

Example program ID	
Name:	SPI LCD.bas
Microcontroller:	AT MEGA 16
Testing circuit:	Figure 1
MiniPin compatibility:	yes
MegaPin compatibility:	yes
Program to use several SPI LCDs	

Graphical LCD with a touch screen

BY JURIJ MIKELN

Bascom-AVR is very handy "tool". It helps us to use many different electronic components with ease. One such component is a graphical LDC with a touch screen. Due to constantly lower prices of LCDs, it is becoming more and more popular.

Introduction

Most of us are familiar with the graphical LDCs used in our cell phones. Many years ago, the first cell phones used very small 2x16 character LCDs, but quickly cell phone manufacturers started to use graphical LCDs. In the 2000, we obtained a graphical LCD (128x 64 pixels) and Mr. Mitrović published a series of articles in which an AT89C2051 was used to drive the graphical LCD. For that time it was an astonishing project, since the programmer had to calculate the co-ordinates of each pixel on the graphical LCD.

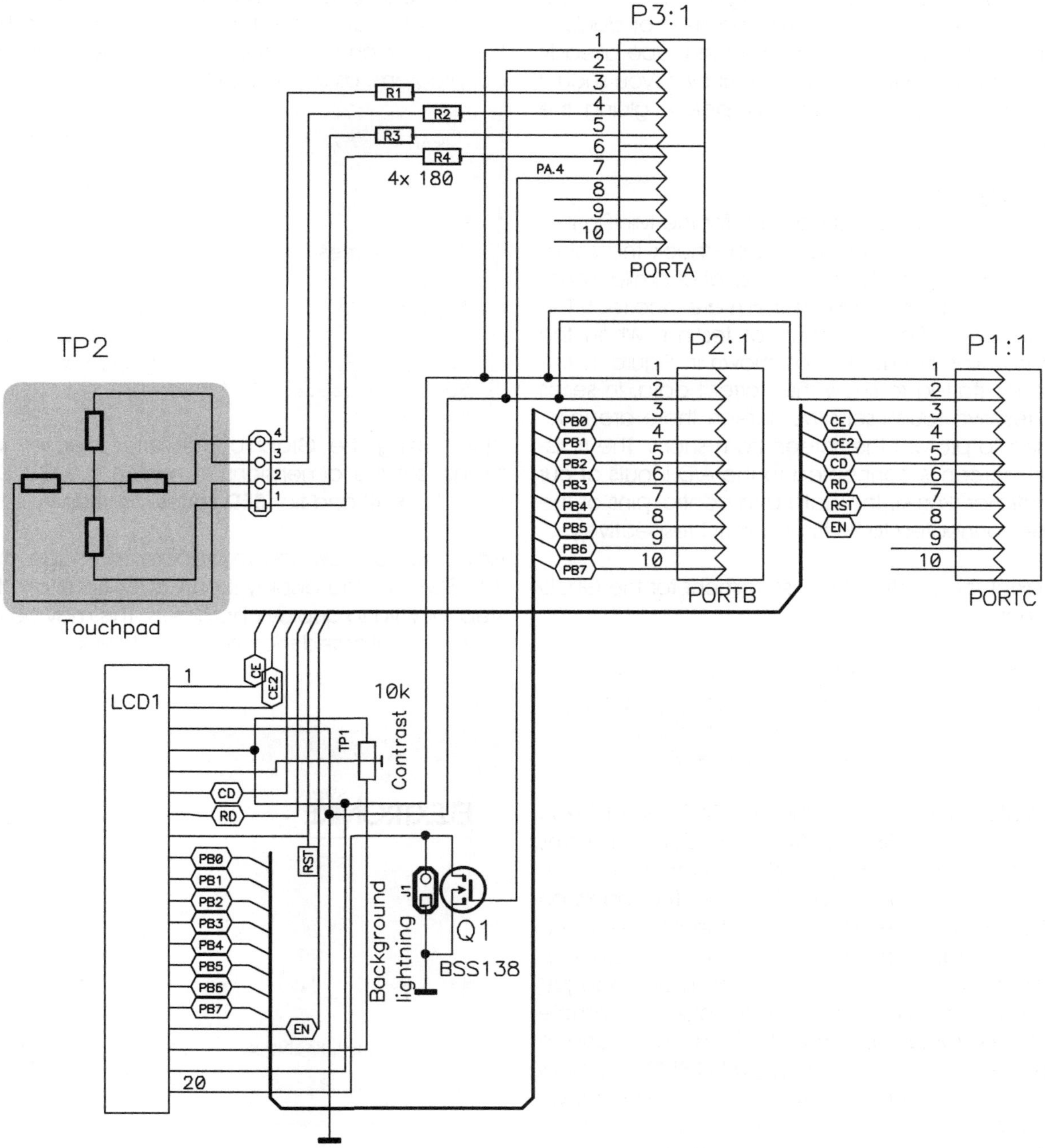

Figure 1: Schematic diagram of GLCD adapter

The situation is very different today. Graphical LCDs (128x 64 pixels) are available for less than 10 Euro. You can add a touch-sensitive screen to it, and can easily use it with the help of Bascom-AVR. We'll use an ATmega16 microcontroller to drive the GLCD. This graphical LCD has 8 Data pins, a few control pins and 4 pins to access the touch screen. The schematic diagram for GLCD adapter can be seen in Figure 1.

Touch-sensitive screens work on the principle of a changing resistance when pressing at a certain point on it. You can visualize the screen as 4 resistors connected as shown in Figure 1. With the microcontroller, we transform the X and Y analogue voltages to digital and with that information we know precisely where on the screen we pressed.

Touch-sensitive screens can be bought separately and can be mounted to a GLCD with the help of double-sided tape. Some screens come with this tape already on them. If you have to do this on your own, you should clean the GLCD screen thoroughly before gluing the touch-screen to it.

GLCD program

If you do not use the GLCD adapter for the MiniPin II or MegaPin development boards, then check the schematics shown in Figure 1. There are a lot of similar schematics on the web, but a lot of them are incorrect. This was established after few hours of testing. When the contrast pot was connected as shown in Figure 1, the GLCD finally started to show the correct data. In series with the resistive touch-sensitive screen there are resistors added to protect the screen from shorts. The resistive touch-screen is connected to the A/D inputs of our microcontroller (PortA), the data and control pins of the GLCD are connected to PortB and PortC respectively.

The syntax of the configuration statement for the GLCD is very simple:

```
Config Graphlcd = 128 * 64sed , _
Dataport = Portb , Controlport = Portc , _
Ce = 0 , Ce2 = 1 , Cd = 2 , Rd = 3 , _
Reset = 5 , Enable = 4 , Mode = 8
```

With this statement we define that the GLCD is a 128x64 pixel panel using the SED controller, we define the pins we are using for Data/Control and a few other pins such as Ce, Ce2, Rd, Reset, Enable & Mode. The labels on the LCD panel don't exactly match the names in the configuration statement, but that shouldn't bother us too much. Bascom-AVR offers us even more than just the Configuration statement. It also includes a simple tool called **Graphic Converter** that can be found in the **Tools** menu. This tool transforms a PC BMP graphical file into a BGF (Bascom-AVR Graphic file). When preparing an image that we want to display on a GLCD, we can draw it using any paint program. When saving your drawing, bear in mind that the image should have a dimension of 128x64 pixels, should be black & white, and

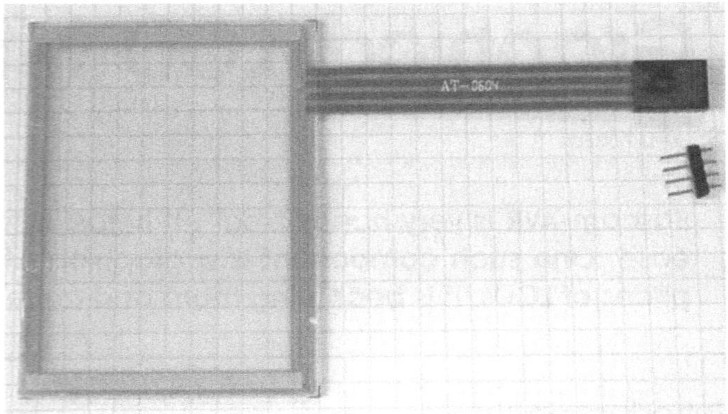

Figure 2: A Touch-sensitive screen that can be glued to a GLCD panel

as mentioned, be saved with the BMP file extension. With the Graphic Converter tool we can convert a BMP to a BGF file, which we can call, much like a subroutine, in our program, as shown below:

```
Showpic 0 , 0 , Logose   'show image with
                         'name Logose
....
End
'Subroutines
....
Logose:                  'here is the file
                         'definition for
                         'image »Logose«
$bgf "logose.bgf"
```

When using the Graphic converter please note two things: set the dimensions to match the GLCD (in our case 128x64) and tick **SED series**, as seen in Figure 3.

Now that we know how to prepare an image, transform it to BGF file and display it on GLCD. Let's take the next step forward to display characters. This may be just a bit more complicated than one might think.

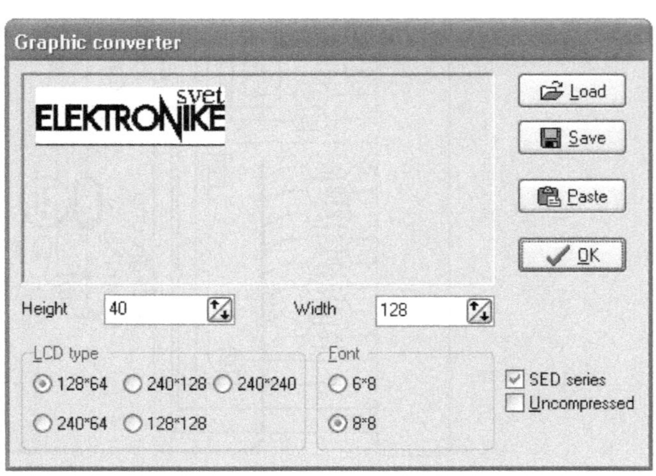

Figure 3: Setting options on the Graphic Converter tool

Namely characters can be as small as 6 pixels or else text can be unreadable.

To display text on a GLCD, use the following command:

```
'Lcdat 4 , 70 , "TEXT"
```

The syntax is as follows:

```
LCDAT y , x , var [ , inv]
```

where the first number is the Y co-ordinate, and the second is the X coordinate on GLCD. The "inv" variable means that the character can be displayed in inverse mode, if we write a 1, and the normal mode if we write a 0. Note that the Y numbers do not correspond to the expected Row position on the GLCD. But it's all logical.

We have defined the font as 8x8 pixels. Actually the character itself is only 7 pixels high. But each character takes up 8 pixels on the screen, in both the X and Y axes. Because we have 64 pixels in the Y axis, we can write 8 lines of characters that are 7 pixels high. One blank pixel is reserved to separate the lines of characters. And yes – with this statement we can only write text in 8 discrete lines, not in-between the lines.

Reading the Touch screen

Bascom-AVR has proven to be an excellent tool for reading touch-screens. It's all done within the Readtouch subroutine:

```
Readtouch:                'read touch
Config Porta.3 = Output   'pin1 (Y1)
Config Porta.1 = Output   ' PIN3 (Y2)
Set Porta.1               'PIN2 (X1)
Reset Porta.3             'PIN4 (X2)
Config Pina.2 = Input     'set as input
Config Pina.0 = Input     '
Waitms 20                 'wait that port
                          'stabilizes
Y = Getadc(0)             'read A/D value
Y = 1024 - Y              'invert it
Config Porta.2 = Output   'repeat same for
                          'X coordinate
Config Porta.0 = Output
Reset Porta.0
Set Porta.2
Config Pina.1 = Input
Config Pina.3 = Input
Waitms 20
X = Getadc(3)
X = 1024 - X
Return
```

In this short subroutine, you can see that each coordinate (X,Y) in sequence is, supplied with a logic 1 and a logic 0 (i.e. roughly 5 volts) after which we read the output voltage on one of the other co-ordinate's pins, with the A/D converter. The two ADC output signals are num-

bers that correspond to the position where we pressed on touch-screen. With the GLCD that you can buy from Svet elektronike[1] magazine, you can press it with fingers and solid objects (but not sharp ones!). To determine the coordinates where we have pressed, I have written a simple program. I draw a coordinate grid on the GLCD and then display the X,Y coordinates where I have pressed the screen. With this information we can make the next step in our program. For this refer to the subroutine *Whichkey*:

```
Whichkey:                        'definition of
                                 'pressed
                                 'coordinate
Select Case X                    'different values
                                 'of X
    Case 300 To 480 : Col = 10
    Case 341 To 486 : Col = 20
    Case 487 To 635 : Col = 30
    Case 636 To 774 : Col = 40
    Case Else Col = 0            'if nothing
                                 'is pressed
End Select                       ' values for
                                 'Y coordinate
Select Case Y                    'different values
                                 'for Y
    Case 200 To 250 : Row = 1
    Case 260 To 290 : Row = 2
    Case 300 To 330 : Row = 3
    Case Else Row = 0
                                 'if nothing
                                 'is pressed
End Select
Key = Col + Row                  'add to get a value
If Key > 0 Then                  'Touchscreen
                                 'is pressed
  Keyarray(keylus) = Key' un-comment
                                 'the following
                                 'for debounce
'  Incr Keylus
'  If Keylus > 3 Then Keylus = 1
'   If Keyarray(1) = Keyarray(2) Then
'    If Keyarray(2) = Keyarray(3) Then
                                 'read 3 times
    'Sound Speaker , 1 , 65000
```

```
                              'beep
        Keypressed = Key
       'Timecount = 0
'     End If
'   End If
  End If
 Return
```

The parts of the subroutine that are commented, are there for the *Debounce* function. If you want to use it, feel free, but I did not use it in my program. Note the interesting use of *Select Case* within the *Whichkey* subroutine. When using a touch-screen, you will get results within a range, as shown in the *Select Case* statements.

Calibration

To achieve the stable performance of a GLCD fitted with a resistive touch-screen it is desirable to calibrate the touch-screen to its GLCD panel and save the calibration results to EEPROM.

The *Calibration* routine can be initiated by pressing PD.3 immediately after releasing the Reset keypad. The practical approach would be to press both the Reset and the PortD.3 keypad. Then release Reset followed by the PortD.3 keypad.

9-point Calibration

First we have to draw on the GLCD, 9 different images representing each of the nine pressed keypads, as well as one blank keyboard, as shown in Figure 4

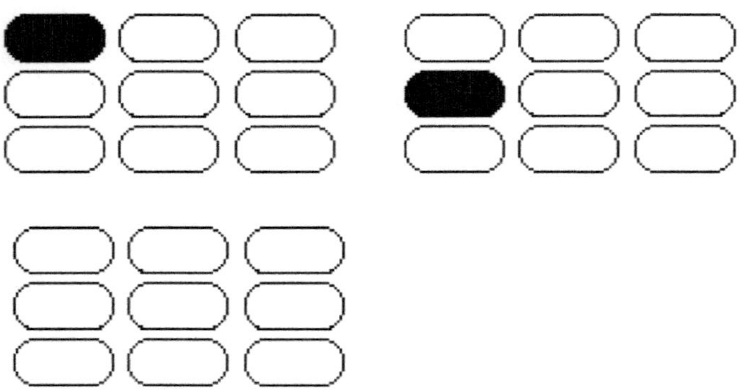

Figure 4: A sample of Images of different pressed keypads as well as a blank keyboard

Next, the calibration program displays each of these images in sequence, indicating where we should press to calibrate that particular keypad. If we press hard enough, we will see the image "OK" as shown in Figure 5 or else the program will keep on flashing the keypad which has yet to be sufficiently pressed.

Program description

At the start of the program, the initialization of the GLCD is performed, as well as the configuration of the A/D converter (needed to transform the analogue signals received from the touch-screen). The definition of variables and functions follow next. The variables *Keypad_x (17)* and *Keypad_y (17)* are defined as ERAM. After that is the program decision whether or not to enter into calibration. In the calibration procedure, the program scans for input from the touch-screen and displays the corresponding image on the GLCD.

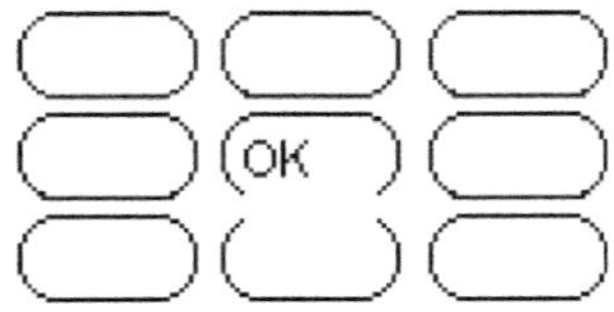

Figure 5: Pressed OK

Function description

Function (*Within_area(byval Ind As Byte) As Byte*) determines whether a keypad was pressed within a determined area. A simple explanation can be seen in Figure 6.

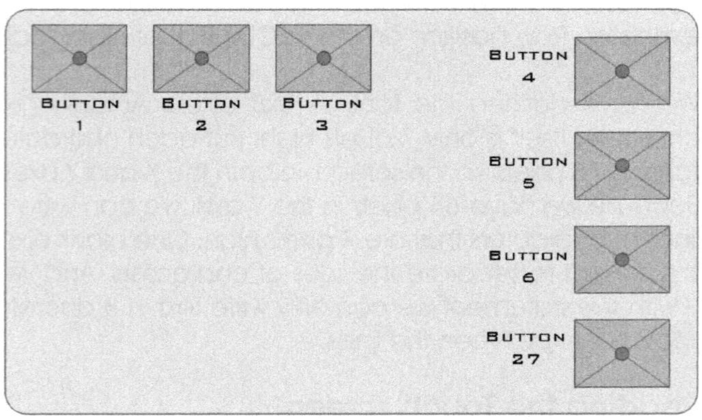

Figure 6: Image of areas covered by function

For each keypad (say Keypad 27), that is shown on the GLCD, we save in the table of X and Y coordinates, the central point where we pressed. To the x coordinate we add and subtract a certain value (preset by our program) – say 35, that represents the coordinate tolerance that we are prepared to accept, when pressing near that saved X co-ordinate. The same is done for the Y coordinate. The function checks to see if the coordinates of a particular screen press correspond to any saved coordinate (+/- the tolerance). If it does, it returns a logical 1, otherwise a logical 0. With respect to that value, we can make decisions later on in the program. The function's value is assigned to a byte, because the function returns a byte value. When calling the function, we define the number of keypads that we wish to check for key presses, within brackets. This number is used to index a memory array where the X and Y coordinates are saved for all of the keypads. Using a simple *For-Next* loop we can determine which particular keypad was pressed.

Subroutine description

The *Calibration* subroutine reads values from the touch screen and saves them to an X,Y matrix for keypads 1 through 9. At the start of the calibration routine, the first keypad is displayed and program waits for the user to press that keypad. At each press of the indicated keypad, we save the values for X and Y.

The *Readtouch* subroutine reads values from the touch screen and performs an A/D conversion within a *For-Next* loop (to take an average of all readings and hence improve results).

The *Pressed_keypad* subroutine displays images of all appropriate keypads on the GLCD along with the saved values. The subroutine works as follows: when pressing the touch-screen, the subroutine detects values for x and y and compares them with the values stored in ERAM. The program calibrates the touch-screen/GLCD combination for 9 keypad positions.

That is time consuming however, considering that calibration values are stored within EEPROM that does prove itself in a very quick performance of GLCD with touch screen.

A new calibration would be needed if an existing touch-screen is replaced with a new one.

Conclusion

A GLCD with touch-screen is very handy device. It's also very important that it is available at an affordable price and that it has full programming support in the Bascom-AVR software and its user community. One can find many Bascom-AVR projects with GLCD + touch screen available on the web. When I started to work with GLCD's, I used the AN148 Application Note by Evert Dekker found at www.mcselec.com. That code worked well, but I wanted to get more reliable readings from the touch-screen, especially for the very small keypads that you can see on our Youtube videos. That was possible only with the introduction of the described function, where we could set tolerance margins around the point where we pressed the touch screen. When using this function, it was easy to calibrate and then to read the touch-screen very reliably.

References:

» [1]: http://www.svet-el.si

Example program ID	
Name:	GLCD_1.BAS
Microcontroller:	ATmega AVRs
Testing circuit:	Figure 1
MiniPin compatibility:	yes
MegaPin compatibility:	yes
Program that draws a table and some lines	

Example program ID	
Name:	GLCD_2.BAS
Microcontroller:	ATmega AVRs
Testing circuit:	Figure 1
MiniPin compatibility:	yes
MegaPin compatibility:	yes
GLCD with fonts that can be placed anywhere on GLCD	

Example program ID	
Name:	GLCD_3.BAS
Microcontroller:	ATmega AVRs
Testing circuit:	Figure 1
MiniPin compatibility:	yes
MegaPin compatibility:	yes
GLCD with the use of a touch panel including simple calibration of the touch panel. Program draws small keypads and uses Touch panel with calibration	

Example program ID	
Name:	GLCD_4.BAS
Microcontroller:	ATmega AVRs
Testing circuit:	Figure 1
MiniPin compatibility:	yes
MegaPin compatibility:	yes
GLCD with improved calibration for the touch panel. Program draws large keypads and uses Touch panel with calibration	

7-segment LED display

By Vladimir Mitrović

Compared to liquid-crystal alpha-numeric displays, 7-segment LED displays are less versatile: their character set is limited to numbers plus several more or less readable letters, they display fewer digits and they consume much more power. However, their digits are much bigger, and they shine brightly in several distinctive colours, making them a perfect choice for some projects. That's why we have developed a 4-character 7-segment display as an add-on module for our MegaPin and MiniPin II development systems.

Figure 1 shows a schematic diagram of the 4-character 7-segment display module. The drive method is a multiplexed one: connecting pins of all segments of the same name (on each of the four digits) are connected together, to minimize the number of connecting wires as well as the number of microcontroller I/O pins needed. In such a design, the digits are activated sequentially, in quick succession. This process is known as multiplexing. The 7-segment display module from Figure 1 can be connected to any two I/O ports on MPIN development systems. Which ports are used depends on the microcontroller being used, as well as what other peripherals (switches, 1-wire components etc.) are already connected to the available I/O pins. Henceforth, we will assume that the display's CON1 connector is connected to PORTB on the MPIN board, while CON2 is connected to PORTD on the MPIN board. Only four lines are needed on the latter port. Note that you can use other I/O ports equally well. You can even connect two or three 7-segment display modules to one MPIN, as long as you have enough free ports.

NOTE

In all further references related to both development systems, a common name, MPIN, will be used instead of their separate names MiniPin II and MegaPin.

A serious drawback of a multiplexed display is that it can keep the microcontroller pretty busy while the display is active. In order to avoid flickering, the whole message should be repeated at least 20 times per second, preferably even more often. To ensure a stable and flicker-free display, we chose a refresh rate of 50 times per second, which requires the microcontroller's attention every 5 ms. (50 Hz = 20 ms period, divided by 4 digits = 5 ms) Every 5 milliseconds the microcontroller must:

- switch-off the currently active digit position,
- activate the appropriate segments corresponding to the pattern needed for the digit in the next position and
- switch-on the following digit.

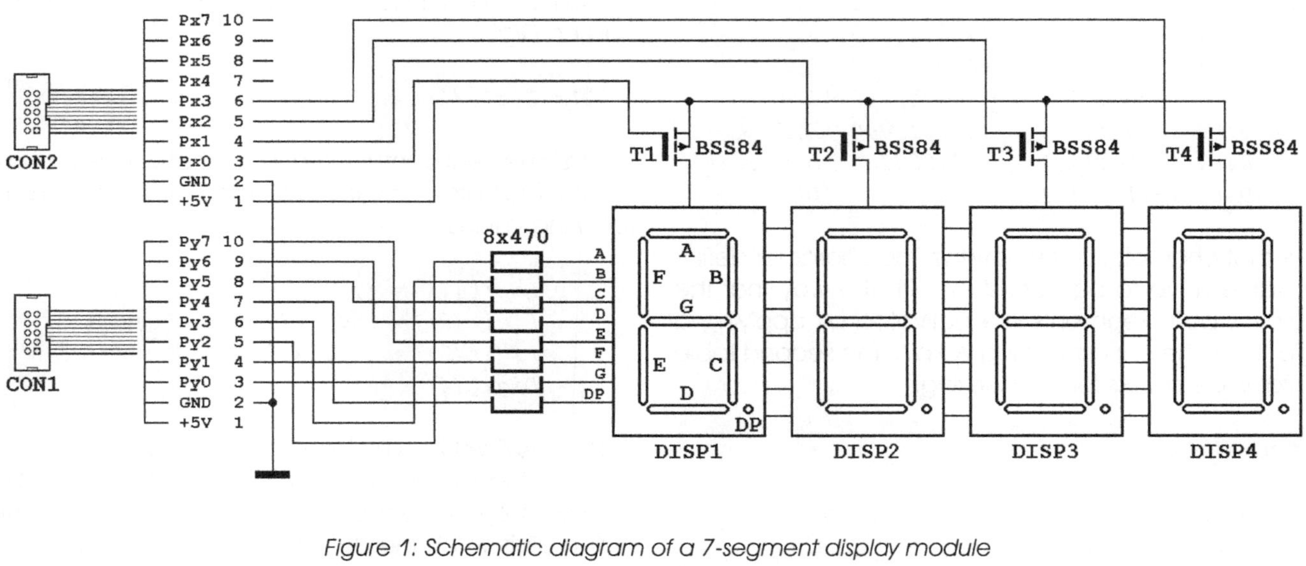

Figure 1: Schematic diagram of a 7-segment display module

NOTE

No external power supply is needed for the display module: it gets a +5 V supply directly from the MPIN development system. If you connect more than one display module to the MPIN, they can share the same port for multiplexing (i.e. PORTD was used above).

The above process takes no more than 20-40 μs. But if the program performs the above actions in a loop, and waits 5 ms before each loop iteration, the program will not be able to do anything else while the message is being displayed. This is not practical, so we will choose a different approach. For this approach, we will use a timer, configured to activate an interrupt every 5 milliseconds. When the interrupt occurs, an interrupt service routine is executed, that prepares the data needed for the following display position. As soon as the next digit is successfully switched on, the program control returns to the main program. During the time between interrupts, the microcontroller can do any other task.

7-segment display routine

The 7-segment display routine is built around two tables, the first of which contains the pattern definitions for all of the characters that the display can show. Besides decimal and hexadecimal digits, a few other characters are defined - blank, all segments on and the decimal point:

```
Table_0f:
    Data &B00010001 , &B11010111 '0,1
    Data &B00110010 , &B10010010 '2,3
    Data &B11010100 , &B10011000 '4,5
    Data &B00011000 , &B11010011 '6,7
    Data &B00010000 , &B10010000 '8,9
    Data &B01010000 , &B00011100 'A,b
    Data &B00111001 , &B00010110 'C,d
    Data &B00111000 , &B01111000 'E,F
    Data &B11111111 , &B00000000 'blank,all
    Data &B11101111              'DP
```

Note that character patterns within the character definition table have to be consistent with the way that the display is built. Segments are activated by applying a logic "0" at the corresponding I/O pin. The second table contains the masks for multiplexing:

```
Table_mux:
    Data &B00001111    'all digits off
    Data &B11111110    '#1 digit on
    Data &B11111101    '#2 digit on
    Data &B11111011    '#3 digit on
    Data &B11110111    '#4 digit on
```

The values in both tables correspond to the schematics shown in Figure 1. Remember: PORTB is used for segment activation while bits 0-3 of PORTD are used for digit multiplexing. Therefore, character definition data from the first table should be fetched and transferred to the PORTB output pins. This is most elegantly done with the *Lookup()* function, which uses the *Disp_aux* variable as an index:

```
Portb = Lookup(disp_aux , Table_0f)
```

For example, if *Disp_aux* = 3, the 4th byte from the table is fetched (the index of the first byte in the table is 0) and the segments that form digit "3" will illuminate. In fact, nothing will illuminate yet - first we have to decide at which position this digit should be displayed. This position data is held by the *Disp_index* variable, which is used as an index into the multiplexing masks table:

```
Portd = Lookup(disp_index , Table_mux)
```

For example, if *Disp_index* = *1*, then pin PD0 will be set *Low* and will activate transistor T1. Given the example in the preceding paragraph, a "3" will be displayed as the first digit. The process described above takes place inside the interrupt service routine *C0a_sub*, which is attached to the Timer/Counter0 Output Compare A interrupt. Timer0 is configured to activate this interrupt every 5 milliseconds, as shown in the following code fragment:

```
On Oc0a C0a_sub
Enable Compare0a
Enable Interrupts
Ocr0a = 156

Timer0 = 0
Config Timer0=Timer,Prescale=256, _
Compare A=Disconnect, _
Compare B=Disconnect, Clear Timer = 1
```

The data to be displayed is stored in a 4-element array named *Digit*:

```
Dim Digit(4) As Byte
```

The first element contains the value that will be shown as the first digit etc. For example, if the array contains the following values

```
Digit(1) = 3,
Digit(2) = 15,
Digit(3) = 10 and
Digit(4) = 0,
```

then "3FA0" will be displayed. The interrupt service routine is actually a bit more complicated than described above. At every interrupt, it must switch off the currently-active digit, fetch the data to be shown at next display position, convert this data to the appropriate pattern, transfer that pattern to PORTB and, finally, switch on the following digit. Also, the procedure must not change the state of the other four pins of PORTD (i.e. the ones NOT used for the digit multiplexing) if they are used for other I/O purposes.

At the very beginning of the interrupt service routine, the *Disp_index* variable is incremented and will point to the next digit to be activated. The value of this variable cycles through the following pattern: 1, 2, 3, 4, 1, ..., which is implemented with the following code fragment:

```
C0a_sub:
   If Disp_index > 3 Then Disp_index = 0
   Incr Disp_index
```

Using the first mask from the multiplexing table, the currently-displayed digit is switched-off:

```
   Disp_aux = Lookup(0 , Table_mux)
   Portd = Portd Or Disp_aux
```

Now, the value of the next digit is fetched from the *Digit* array, and this value is used as an index into the character definition table. The appropriate pattern is copied from the table out to the PORTB output pins, in preparation for displaying the next digit:

```
   Disp_aux = Digit(disp_index)
   Portb = Lookup(disp_aux , Table_0f)
```

Finally, that digit is switched on and the program control returns from the interrupt service routine back to the main loop:

```
   Disp_aux = Lookup(disp_index,Table_mux)
   Portd = Portd And Disp_aux
   Set Disp_flag
Return
```

The purpose of *Disp_flag* will be explained later.

Using the Program

It's recommended that you define the initial values for the digit array before the timer is configured and started. Good practice suggests that all segments of all digits can be switched on for a few seconds and then switched off, to prove that all of the LED display digits are working, as shown in this example:

```
Digit(1) = 17        'switch on all segments
Digit(2) = 17        'of all digits
Digit(3) = 17        'as a validity test
Digit(4) = 17

Timer0 = 0
Config Timer0 = Timer, Prescale = 256, _
Compare A = Disconnect, _
Compare B = Disconnect, Clear Timer = 1
```

```
Wait 1
Digit(1) = 16        'switch off the display
Digit(2) = 16
Digit(3) = 16
Digit(4) = 16
```

Later on in your program, you can change the values in the *Digit* array at any time, thereby changing the message on the display. There is no need to restart the timer - it is active all the time. With an 8 MHz crystal, the execution time of the interrupt service routine is 32 *μs* and it slows down the average program execution speed by 0.64%. This can be totally neglected in most cases.

However, there are situations when even such short interrupt service routine can disturb normal program execution. We can eliminate the problem by introducing a bit-variable labelled *Disp_flag*. As shown before, this flag is set at the end of the display subroutine. The *Disp_flag* can be used within the main program to estimate the remaining time until the next interrupt. If you reset *Disp_flag* and wait until it is set again as in this example,

```
Reset Disp_flag
Bitwait Disp_flag , Set
```

you can be sure that the display subroutine has just been executed and you are at the beginning of a 5 ms interval with no interrupts. Actually, the interval is 32 *μs* shorter, for it takes some time for the interrupt service routine *C0A_sub* to execute. Of course, this "no interrupt interval" applies only to the interrupt service routines used for 7-segment display purposes.

Possible modifications

It's possible to use the 16-bit Timer/Counter1 instead of the 8-bit Timer/Counter0. Values for the Output Compare Register A and the prescale factor should be suitably modified to suit the 16-bit register, as follows:

```
Compare1a = 5000

Timer1 = 0
Config Timer1 = Timer , Prescale = 8 , _
Compare A = Disconnect , Clear Timer = 1
```

The value in the Output Compare Register A should also be adjusted if you intend to use a different crystal than was used here (8 MHz). For example, if a 4 MHz crystal is used, the value in the 8-bit Output Compare Register A should be halved

```
Ocr0a = 78
```

while the appropriate value for 16-bit register A in such a case is:

```
Compare1a = 2500
```

Within the lookup table *Table_0f*, the decimal point is defined as a separate character whose index is 18. Displaying the decimal point as a separate character can look awkward: it looks much better if the decimal point is merged with the preceding character. The simplest way to achieve this is to clear the DP-bit (bit 4, if the display is wired according to Figure 1) before the character pattern is transferred to the PORTB:

```
Disp_aux = Digit(disp_index)
Disp_aux = Lookup(disp_aux , Table_0f)
Portb = Disp_aux And &B11101111
```

In this example, the decimal point will be merged with each digit. Usually, we want to turn it on next to only one specific digit. Therefore we introduce another Byte variable, *Dp_position*. The value of *Dp_position* determines the digit after which the decimal point will be displayed. Values 1 to 4 are allowed, where "1" means "after the first digit" etc. Any other value suppresses the decimal point display in any position.

Within the display subroutine, we have to compare the values in the *Disp_index* and *Dp_position* variables. Only if they are equal, is the decimal point merged with the current digit. The modified display subroutine now looks like this:

```
C0a_sub:
   ...
   Disp_aux = Digit(disp_index)
   Portb = Lookup(disp_aux , Table_0f)
   If Disp_index = Dp_position Then
      Disp_aux = Lookup(18 , Table_0f)
      Portb = Portb And Disp_aux
   End If
   ...
Return
```

Demo programs

Two demo programs have been written to clearly explain the use of the routines introduced above, 7seg_T0.bas and 7seg_T1.bas. Both programs increment the 4-digit number approximately 10 times per second within the main program loop. The decimal point position depends on the first-digit value: if it is a 1, the DP is shown after the first digit, etc. However, the DP is not shown if the first-digit value is outside the 1-4 range. The main loop of both programs looks like this:

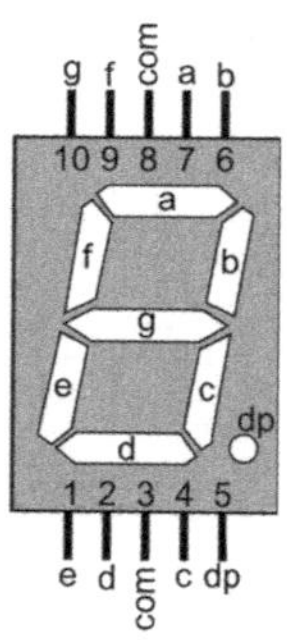


```
Digit(1) = 0
Digit(2) = 0
Digit(3) = 0
Digit(4) = 0
Do
   Waitms 100
   Incr Digit(4)
   If Digit(4) > 9 Then
      Digit(4) = 0
      Incr Digit(3)
   End If
   If Digit(3) > 9 Then
      Digit(3) = 0
      Incr Digit(2)
   End If
   If Digit(2) > 9 Then
      Digit(2) = 0
      Incr Digit(1)
   End If
   If Digit(1) > 9 Then
      Digit(1) = 0
   End If
   Dp_position = Digit(1)
Loop
```

Concurrent with the above process, the previously-described interrupt service routines are used to display the four-digit value on the 7-segment LED display. Although not used in the main program, the *Disp_flag* variable is defined and properly processed within the interrupt service routines. The first program uses the 8-bit Timer/Counter0 and it has been written for the ATtiny2313. The second program uses the 16-bit Timer/Counter1 and is meant for the ATmega8515. Both programs can be used with all AVRs that have compatible timers.

Example program ID	
Name:	7seg_T0.bas
Microcontroller:	ATtiny2313 and other Timer0 compatible AVRs
Testing circuit:	Figure 1
MiniPin compatibility:	yes (with appropriate μC)
MegaPin compatibility:	yes
The program drives 4-digit 7-segment display using Timer/Counter0 related interrupts	

Example program ID	
Name:	7seg_T1.bas
Microcontroller:	ATmega8515 and other Timer1 compatible AVRs
Testing circuit:	Figure 1
MiniPin compatibility:	yes (with appropriate μC)
MegaPin compatibility:	yes
The program drives 4-digit 7-segment display using Timer/Counter1 related interrupts	

Data Measurement

77

Human beings live in an analogue world and feel comfortable there. But this is not so for microcontrollers, which live in a digital world. After successfully measuring data, we have to transform it into digital values. We can do this in many ways, by using smart sensors (and smart programming) to get temperature, air pressure or even a GPS location – all with AVRs.

Get familiar with data measurement using Bascom-AVR!

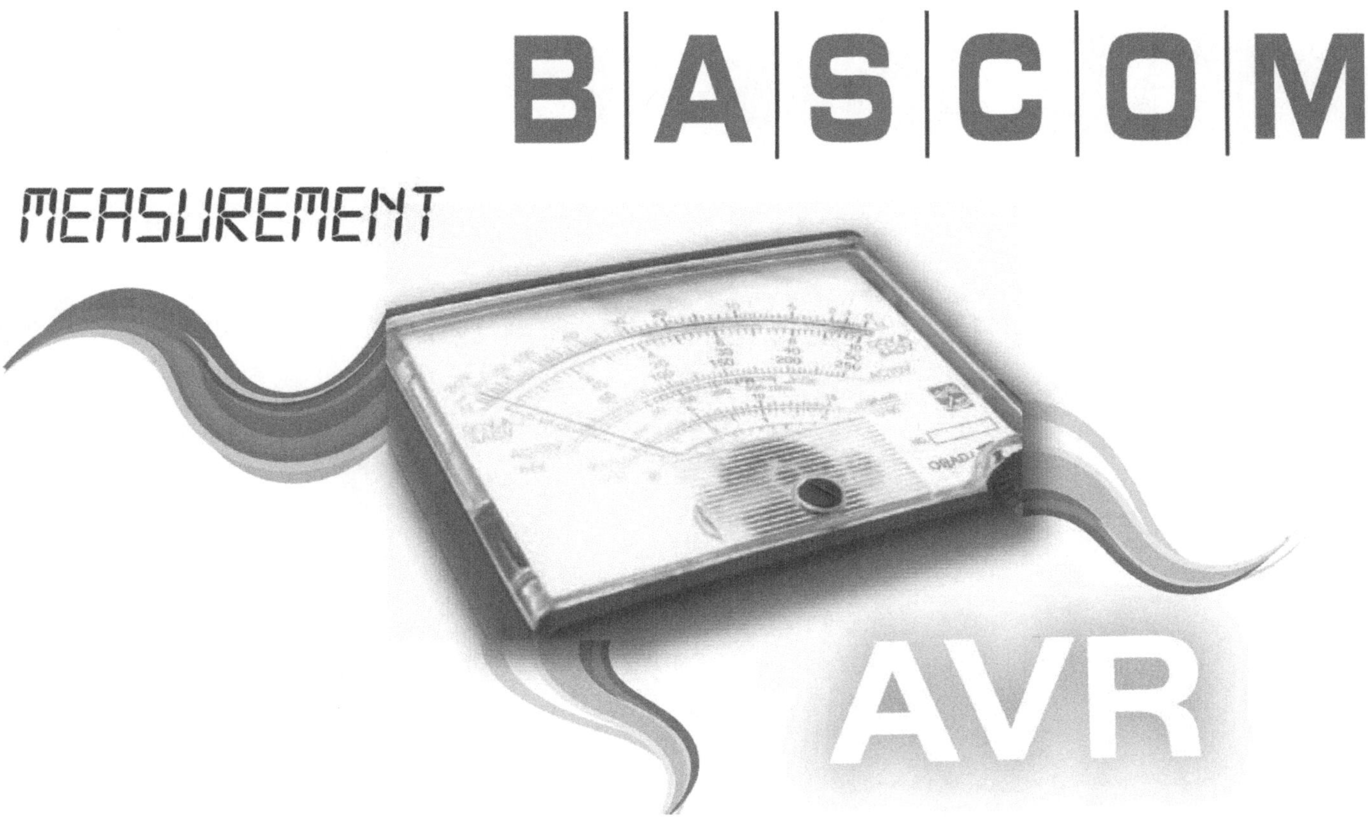

Demystification of 1-Wire® commands

By Jurij Mikeln

Bascom-AVR has a couple of 1-Wire statements available. Many times readers call me about 1-Wire statements. Also, many times during my Bascom seminar lectures, similar questions about 1-Wire statements, like 1wiresearch, 1wirecount, 1wirenext come up. Because I have never studied these statements, I have always replied that "I have never used these statements". One recent hot summer allowed me to rectify the situation. So, here we go: in this chapter you will read all about 1-Wire statements.

Let us briefly see how 1-Wire components perform. In Figure 1 you can see a typical connection of a 1-Wire component.

Although 1-Wire elements can work normally with only 2 pins – one pin is connected to GND and the other communicates with microcontroller, I recommend using the 3-pin configuration as seen in Figure 1. The reason is that addressing a 1-Wire element using only one wire (besides ground) will take more of the processor's time. In the case of long wires, I recommend schematic diagram shown in Figure 2, where you see the protection elements like capacitors and protective diodes.

The most well-known and commonly used 1-Wire element is certainly the DS18S20 thermometer. It's popular because one can connect it to a microcontroller easily, it's reliable and cheap. In addition, the DS18S20 has a digital output and many sensors can be connected in parallel on same wire. Most of you already know the basic 1-Wire commands for reading temperature from one sensor:

```
1wreset
  1wwrite &HCC                  'ignore ROM
  1wwrite &H44                  'convert temp.
  Wait 1
  1wreset                       'reset 1-Wire bus
  1wwrite &HCC                  'ignore ROM
  1wwrite &HBE                  'read Scratchpad
```

```
T = 1wread(2)                 'read 2 bytes
1wreset                       'reset 1-Wire bus
T = T / 2
Cls : Lcd "T =  " ; _
   T ; "C                     'display on LCD
```

Part of this program will display the current temperature that was measured with the DS18S20. Temperature is stored in the variable *T*.

The DS18S20 is being addressed with 1-Wire statements, which instruct the sensor what we want from it. I'll assume that the comments are self explanatory. Only the *Ignore ROM* comment may need some explanation. The DS18S20 has a unique address (ID number) factory-programmed into it which is unique in the World – there are no two sensors with the same ID number! This address is stored within the sensor's ROM. If we do not require this ID information, then we needn't bother reading it, and that's what *Ignore ROM* means. This example can be found in program 1Wire_1.bas.

If, however, there are more 1-Wire sensors on the 1-Wire bus then we

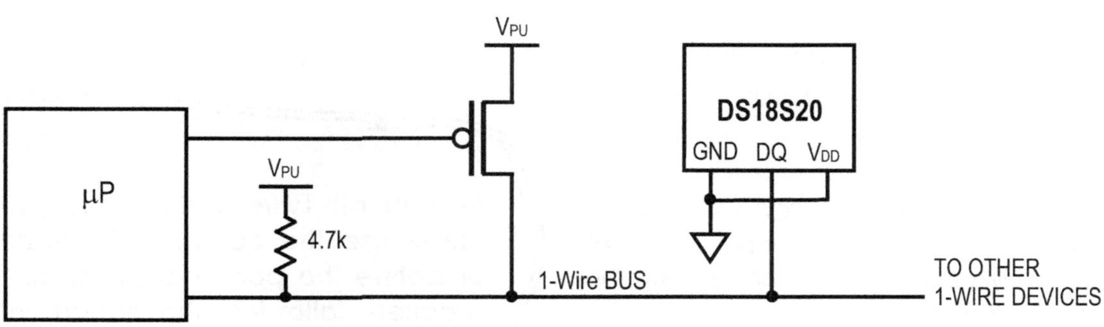

Figure 1: Typical connection of a 1-Wire component

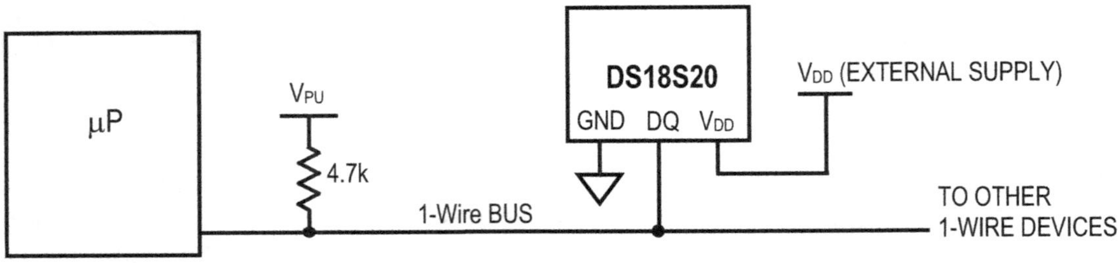

Figure 2: Schematic diagram of 1-Wire (DS18S20) component when wires are long

have to read the IDs of each sensor on the bus, which makes the program a bit longer, but still short enough to be understood.

When reading the sensor's ID, we first have to determine the number of sensors on the 1-Wire bus. The next step is to read their IDs and then the microcontroller can "call" sensors by their names (IDs) and the sensors will individually reply with their temperature information, to the microcontroller.

Reading 1-Wire IDs

There are several Bascom sample programs to read the 1-Wire ID. You can find these programs either on the web or in different magazines. We will introduce you to the statement *1Wiresearch*, which has 2 variants. One is the statement *1Wiresearchfirst*. With this statement, we can search for the first 1-Wire element on the bus. By first element we mean the element with the lowest ID number, and not the element closest to our microcontroller in terms of the wiring.

```
Dim reg_no(8) as byte       ' you must use an
                            'array of bytes
                            '- not a string

Config 1wire = portb.0      'select the port
                            'and pin you
                            'are connecting the
                            '1-wire device to
                            'search first
                            '1-Wire element
Reg_no(1) = 1wsearchfirst()
Cls
Pom = 0
For I = 1 To 8
    Lcd Hex(reg_no(i))      'write HEX code
                            'on LCD
    'Wait 1
Next
```

This part of program loops inside a *FOR-NEXT* loop and displays the sensor's ID No. in a HEX format on LCD display. If you would like the ID No. to display slowly then un-comment the line *Wait 1*.

Next we want to display the ID no. of the next sensor on the 1-Wire bus. We do that with the help of the *1Wiresearchnext()* statement, as follows:

```
Do
'now search for other 1-Wire elements
  Reg_no(1) = 1wsearchnext()
  For I = 1 To 8
     Lcd Hex(reg_no(i)) ; "                   "
                         'display on LCD
     Wait 1
  Next
Loop Until Err = 1
```

The *DO-LOOP* repeats until variable *Err = 1*. That happens when no more (unrecognized) 1-Wire elements are present on the 1-Wire bus. We could, with this program, count the number of 1-Wire elements on a bus. The full program can be found in the 1wire_2.bas program listing. Place sensors to sockets J13, J14 or J15 (MiniPin II) or J23, J24 or J25 (Mega Pin).

Now that we know the ID No. of all of the 1-Wire elements on a bus, it would make sense to store these ID Nos. The most practical place for storing these is in the EEPROM memory within our microcontroller. We do that in program 1Wire_3.bas, where the process of identification remains the same as in the previous program, with the feature of storing IDs to EEPROM added.

```
For I = 1 To 8
   J = I * 10              'define address to
                           'which we write
   Lcd Hex(reg_no(i))
   Writeeeprom Reg_no(i) , J
                           'write first sensor
                           'to EEPROM
```

NOTE

As with all 1wire statements, you must either use the *config 1wire* statement, or define the port and pin used, in the brackets following the statement itself (see the BASCOM-AVR help file)

```
Next
Place sensors to sockets J13, J14 or J15.
                        'search first 1-Wire
                        'element
Reg_no(1) = 1wsearchfirst()
Cls
J=0
For I = 1 To 8
    Lcd Hex(reg_no(i))  'write HEX code
                        'on LCD
   Writeeeprom Reg_no(i) , J
                        'write first sensor
                        'to EEPROM
Incr J
Next
Do
'now search for other 1-Wire elements
  Reg_no(1) = 1wsearchnext()
  For I = 1 To 8
     Lcd Hex(reg_no(i)) ; "          "
                        'display on LCD
   Writeeeprom Reg_no(i) , J
                        'write subsequent
                        'sensors  to EEPROM
   Incr J
  Next
Loop Until Err = 1
```

Note that variable *J* defines the address of the EEPROM byte, to which the individual ID No. byte will be written. If we have more than one 1-Wire sensor on a bus, each subsequent group of ID No. bytes (8 per element) will be written sequentially into the EEPROM memory space.
In cases where we have more than one 1-Wire element on a bus, we can easily determine the number of elements on that bus using the statement *1Wirecount()* without actually "discovering" each one using the *1wsearchnext()* statement outlined above.

```
W = 1Wirecount()
Lcd "No. of sensors = " ; W ; "  "
Wait 2
```

The variable W can be used later in a program, according to our needs.

Multiple sensors on multiple I/O pins

My friend Vilko has called me few times when he was programming in Bascom-AVR and using 1-Wire elements. He told me that he has had problems with 1-Wire temperature sensors which from time to time did not function well. He connected all sensors (a couple in this case) to one 1-Wire bus in parallel and, for no reason at all, the system "hung" completely. Only a reset restored operation. At that time we could find no reason for that strange behaviour. A couple of weeks later, Vilko told me that he had found the reason for the malfunction: it was a faulty sensor which pulled the 1-Wire bus low and hence blocked all 1-Wire elements on the bus. He found that out when he connected each sensor to its own 1-Wire bus. After discovering and changing the faulty 1-Wire element, all worked well!

This story points out the need to put 1-Wire elements on individual microcontroller pins if a truly reliable 1-Wire system is needed.

```
For I = 1 To 8
   1wreset Pinb , K        'set K= PORTB pin
                           'used for the
                           'i-wire bus
   1wwrite &H33 , 1 , Pinb , K
   Ar(1) = 1wread(8 , Pinb , K)

   For A = 1 To 8
     Lcd Hex(ar(a))
   Next

'   Wait 1
Next

Locate 2 , 1
Lcd "Sens. on Portb." ; K ; "       "

Incr K
```

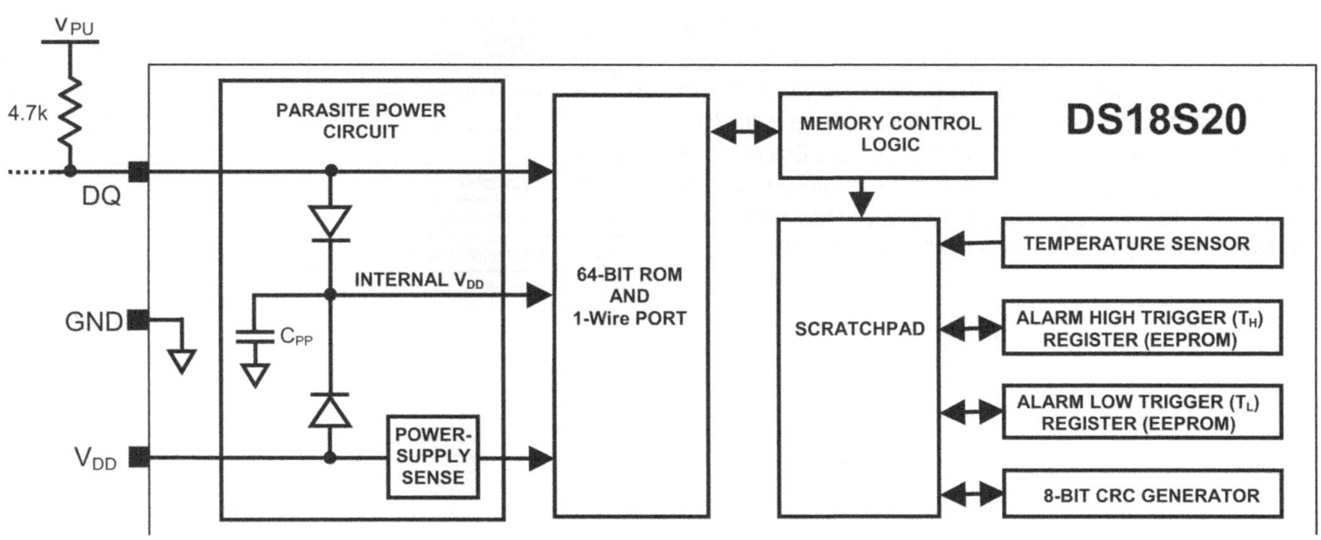

```
If K > 5 Then
   K = 0
End If
```

Program 1Wire_4.bas displays ID Nos of individual elements. Place sensors to sockets J10, J11 or J12 (MiniPin II) or J20, J21 or J22 (MegaPin).

Following is a sample program for measuring temperature with 1-Wire sensors, each connected to its own individual pin on PortC:

```
For K = 0 To 7
   Config 1wire = Portc.k
   1wreset Pinc , K          'reset
   1wwrite &HCC , 1 , Pinc , K
                             'match ROM - choose
                             'DS1820
   1wwrite &HBE , 1 , Pinc , K
                             'READ Scratchpad
   T = 1wread(2 , Pinc , K)
   1wreset Pinc , K
   T1 = T / 2                ' DS1820 sends
                             'temperature X 2
                             'display or store
                             'temperature found
                             'in var
  T1 here
   1wreset Pinc , K
   1wwrite &HCC , 1 , Pinc , K
                             'skip ROM
   1wwrite &H44 , 1 , Pinc , K
                             'convert
                             'temperature

   Wait 1                    'some sensors
                             'require this
                             'Wait 1, or else
                             'they return 85 C
Next
```

The above example can be found in the 1Wire_5.bas program.

Conclusion

1-Wire sensors & other elements are very user-friendly, and are low in price. That may be a reason why they are so popular and wide-spread. An additional advantage of 1-Wire elements arise from their ease of use with Bascom-AVR, brought about by its simple syntax. Enjoy using 1-Wire elements whether it be as temperature sensors or maybe as a security device. Remember that there are no 1-Wire elements in the World with identical ID Nos...

Example program ID	
Name:	1Wire_1.BAS
Microcontroller:	Any AVR microcontroler
Testing circuit:	/
MiniPin compatibility:	yes
MegaPin compatibility:	yes
Single 1-Wire sensor on a bus, temperature is displayed on LCD	

Example program ID	
Name:	1Wire_2.BAS
Microcontroller:	Any AVR microcontroler
Testing circuit:	/
MiniPin compatibility:	yes
MegaPin compatibility:	yes
Program displays 1-Wire ID of two sensors on the bus	

Example program ID	
Name:	1Wire_3.BAS
Microcontroller:	Any AVR microcontroler
Testing circuit:	/
MiniPin compatibility:	yes
MegaPin compatibility:	yes
Same as 1Wire_2.BAS but ID of sensors are stored in EEPROM	

Example program ID	
Name:	1Wire_4.BAS
Microcontroller:	Any AVR microcontroler
Testing circuit:	/
MiniPin compatibility:	yes
MegaPin compatibility:	yes
Multiple 1-Wire sensors, one on each Port	

Example program ID	
Name:	1Wire_5.BAS
Microcontroller:	Any AVR microcontroler
Testing circuit:	/
MiniPin compatibility:	yes
MegaPin compatibility:	yes
Reads multiple 1-Wire sensors, each on its own port	

Using an SD card with the AVR – DOS File System

By Vilko Sustič

If you are designing a device which would, for example, control your house or workshop, protect your home from burglars, water leaks or fire etc., then you need some sort of data logger for later examination of the above-mentioned events. You might want to know who has entered a code on the keypad, when there was a power supply failure, what has caused an alarm to be tripped, etc.

My project involved controlling a central heating system: logging temperatures and controlling an oil burner and pumps. While doing this, I had an unpleasant surprise: the microcontroller would reset itself, on its own, for no apparent reason. Studying the program, I did not find a problem, so I added the capability of logging to an MMC card. I began logging the entry to and the return from all subroutines, as follows:

```
Readtemp:
Print #2 ,   Hex(sph) ;
Hex(spl) ; " E: Readtemp"

. . . .

Print #2 ,   Hex(sph) ; Hex(spl) ; _
    " R: Readtemp T="; temperature
Return
```

I printed the following: (*Hex(sph) ; Hex(spl)*) because I also wanted to know what was happening with the stack as well. I suspected that the problem laid there!

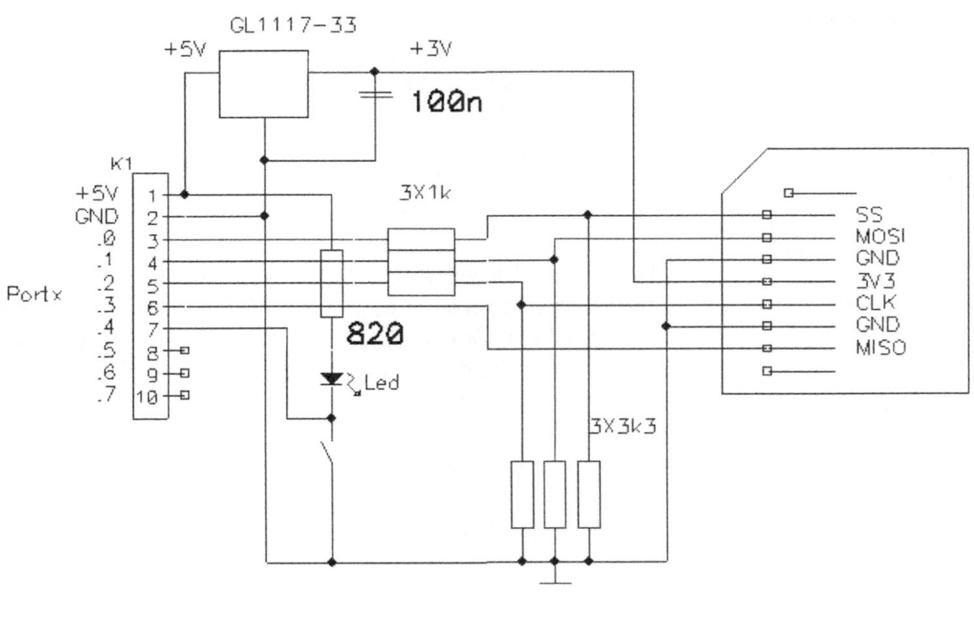

Figure 1: Schematic diagram of MMC card adapter

NOTE

If you decide to use the Micro SD card socket present on the MegaPin board, to try out programs in this chapter, you should carefully read the warning given on page 123 of the MegaPin chapter. This explains a modification you must make to the Megapin board, if your PC is supplying the MegaPin board with 4.5V or less for its Vcc supply.

I used a card similar to the ones used in digital cameras, having a large memory capacity. This made it possible to write to the card for a month or so. To do this, I needed AVR-DOS.

Unfortunately, AVR-DOS requires a lot of RAM memory, so it can only be used with microcontrollers like the ATmega32 or other AVR family members with as much or more RAM.

On the left of Figure 1, you can see the IDC connector which connects to the MiniPin development board, while on the right you see the MMC card socket.

The MMC card requires a 3.3V power supply. However, if our microcontroller operates at 5V, then we need a suitable voltage regulator, such as the GL1117-33. Also, the signals coming from the microcontroller (SS, MOSI, CLK) must be lowered, by

means of a resistor network, to comply with the MMC 3.3 V logic levels. The MISO signal, coming from the MMC card, is at a 3.3V logic level, which our microcontroller already accepts as a logic 1. All 4 signals (MISO, MOSI, CLK & SS) are connected to free microcontroller I/O port pins, which we must later assign within AVR-DOS.

The LED shows when the MMC card is connected to AVR-DOS, which means that we must not take it out of its socket when the LED is lit. The Switch is read by the microcontroller program. If we press it, the program performs a CLOSE FILE statement, turns the LED turns off, and we can then eject the MMC card safely from its socket.

Utilizing an MMC card with AVR-DOS

First, we have to define in AVR-DOS, the port connections to the MMC card. The file named Config_MMC.bas should be included in your program, using the *$Include* statement. Before doing so, it must be modified slightly. The file has two sections: HW and SW. You choose either a hardware or a software SPI connection by setting the value of *Const Cmmc_soft*. In this case, I am using a Software SPI connection so:

```
Const Cmmc_soft = 1
```

After that, you must edit the following section to match the port pins you are using:

```
#if Cmmc_soft = 0          'Hardware SPI
                           'configuration
                           'goes here
```

In the section of the file shown below, we define the pins used for the Software SPI connection:

```
#else
' Config here SPI pins, if not using HW SPI
' --- Start of Section for Soft-SPI ---

   ' Chip Select Pin  => Pin 1 of MMC/SD
   Config Pina.0 = Output
   Mmc_cs Alias Porta.0
   Set Mmc_cs

   ' MOSI - Pin  => Pin 2 of MMC/SD
   Config Pina.1 = Output
   Set Pina.1
   Mmc_portmosi Alias Porta
   Bmmc_mosi Alias 1

   ' MISO - Pin  => Pin 7 of MMC/SD
   Config Pina.3 = Input
   Mmc_portmiso Alias Pina
   Bmmc_miso Alias 3

   ' SCK - Pin   => Pin 1 of MMC/SD
   Config Pina.2 = Output
   Set Pina.2
   Mmc_portsck Alias Porta
   Bmmc_sck Alias 2

' --- End of Section for Soft-SPI ---
```

The characters shown in bold should be changed to match the MMC card connection in our circuit. As you can see, PinA.0 is chip select, PinA.1 is MOSI, PinA.2 is SCK, PinA.3 is MISO, which matches Figure1, the schematic diagram - assuming that we connect MMC adapter to MiniPin PortA.

Once we have edited the Config_MMC.bas file to match our circuit, and saved it the disk, we can proceed. Using another *$include* command we add the Config_AVR-DOS.BAS code to our program:

```
$include "Config_AVR-DOS.BAS"
```

The first thing that AVR-DOS has to do is to initialize the MMC card:

```
Gbdriveerror = Driveinit()
```

The variable *Gbdriveerror* has already been defined in the included .bas files and you do not need to define it again. We do, however, have to constantly check it, to see if everything is OK:

```
If Gbdriveerror <> 0 Then  Print _
   "Napaka Config " ; Gbdriveerror
```

The error codes can be found in the Help file. If there are no errors, we can proceed to use the other AVR-DOS statements that are available:

```
INITFILESYSTEM , OPEN , CLOSE, FLUSH ,
PRINT, LINE INPUT, LOC, LOF , EOF ,
FREEFILE , FILEATTR , SEEK , BSAVE ,
BLOAD , KILL , DISKFREE , DISKSIZE , GET ,
PUT ,FILEDATE , FILETIME , FILEDATETIME ,
DIR , WRITE , INPUT , FILELEN
```

In this chapter, we will only use those statements that are necessary to write a file to the MMC card. These are: *Initfilesystem*, *Open*, *Close* and *Print*. The *Initfilesystem* is first function that we must call and we check to see if it was successful or not.

```
I = Initfilesystem(1)     'init file system

If I <> 0 Then
   Print                  'Init filesystem
                          'error', I
   End
End if
```

> **NOTE**
>
> **The AVR-DOS File System was written by Jozef Franz** Vögel to be used for non-commercial purposes. If you need it for commercial purposes, contact Mr. Vögel for a special licence.
> The file system works with Compact - FLASH cards, and is intended for data logging in embedded systems.

Now, we can open a file on our MMC card, which appears as a DOS disc.

```
Open "Data.txt" For Append As #9
                              'create file in MMC
```

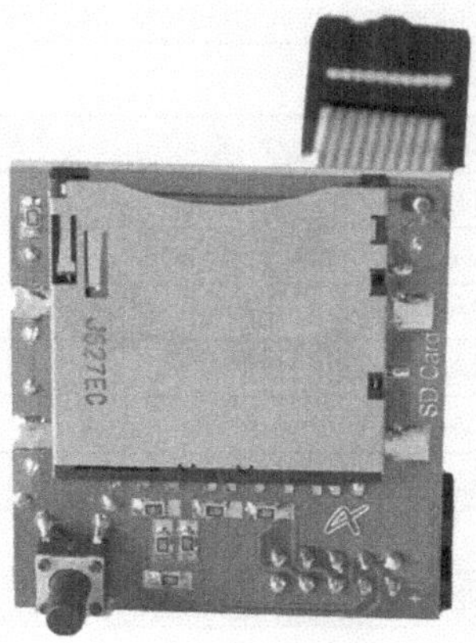

The first parameter of the Open statement is the DOS filename – this file name can be changed to suit our needs. We can specify it in our program, for example, by using a String variable, and assigning the desired file name to it.

Once the file is open, we can use the *Print* statement to write anything to the open file. You should note that after you have finished writing data, the file must be closed using a *Close* statement. If, while writing to a file, the microcontroller "hangs" due to a software bug, then the file on the MMC card cannot be accessed.

When the program has finished writing to the file, and closes it with the *Close* statement, we can safely eject the MMC card from its socket. If we then insert it into a MMC reader on our PC, it will appear as a removable disc. We will see our file in the directory, and can open it with Notepad, Wordpad or any other MS Windows text editing program.

If, for example, the microcontroller is monitoring meteorological parameters like temperature, humidity, wind direction and speed etc. then we can use the *Print* statement to format files in such a way that they are suitable to be read by MS Excel, which can also make nice graphs from the data.

Software description

Besides the previously-mentioned *Driveinit*, *Initfilesystem*, *Open* and other AVR-DOS statements, the file Test6.bas includes a Timer interrupt service routine. This is activated every 500 miliseconds, and sets the *Tiflag* flag variable.

```
Timer1_isr:
Load Timer1 , Timer1reload
   Incr Ticntr
   Set Tiflag
Return
```

Within the main program loop, we monitor whether this flag is set, and if so, we increment counter I and write it to both the MMC and an auxiliary serial port (using a software UART).

```
Do
  If Tiflag = 1 Then
     Print #9 , I
     Print #2 , I
     Incr I
     Reset Tiflag
  End If
```

In the main loop we take care of the flashing LED:

```
Fawrite = I.0
```

and scan for activity on the MMC switch shown in Figure 1:

```
Debounce Keypad , 0 , Keypadsr , Sr
Config Keypad = Output
```

If the switch was pressed, then we write a message to both the UART & MMC and set counter I to a value which represents the end of the task:

```
Keypadsr:
     Print #2 , "keypad end"
     Print #9 , "keypad"
     I = 50
Return
```

The previous statement *Config Keypad = Output* deserves further explanation. In this program, Keypad is an alias to Portx.4 (where x is the Minipin port that the circuit is connected to).This is connected to the switch shown in Figure 1. Portx.4 serves a dual purpose: as an input, it can be read by the *Debounce* statement, as shown above. However it can also be configured as an output- in which case it can light the LED, when it is set to a logic low level.

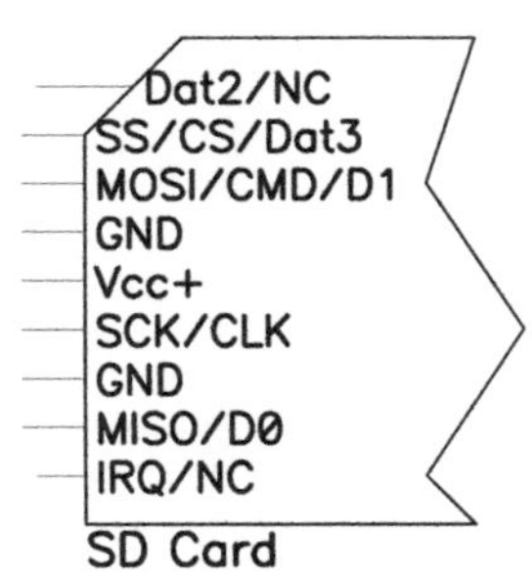

Conclusion

Writing data and event - logging to an MMC card has proven to be an excellent tool for monitoring what is happening within a program, as well as for debugging. It's also very handy for logging events like when an alarm was tripped, who has entered a code via the keyboard, or for logging temperature and other parameters over long periods of time. This data can be saved in such a way that MS Excel or other spreadsheet programs can read the file.

Unfortunately, AVR-DOS requires a significant amount of RAM: you can see this if you examine the Bascom-AVR Report file (using Program/Show Result in the Bascom-AVR menu bar). This will limit your choice of AVR micro-controllers to those with sufficient RAM resources.

Example program ID	
Name:	Test_SD_B_Write_HW-UART.bas
Microcontroller:	ATmega32
Testing circuit:	Figure 1
MiniPin compatibility:	yes
MegaPin compatibility:	yes
Program tests SD memory card on SD card adapter; does writing to the card	

Example program ID	
Name:	Config_MMC.bas
Microcontroller:	ATmega32
Testing circuit:	Figure 1
MiniPin compatibility:	yes
MegaPin compatibility:	yes
Configures SD card	

Example program ID	
Name:	Test_SD_B_Read_HW-UART.bas
Microcontroller:	ATmega32
Testing circuit:	Figure 1
MiniPin compatibility:	yes
MegaPin compatibility:	yes
Program tests SD memory card on SD card adapter; does reading from the card	

Example program ID	
Name:	CONFIG_AVR-DOS.bas
Microcontroller:	ATmega32
Testing circuit:	Figure 1
MiniPin compatibility:	yes
MegaPin compatibility:	yes
Configures AVR-DOS. Note: this file cannot be used for commercial purposes. Contact author in that case	

Measuring analogue values

By Jurij Mikeln

As we all know, microcontrollers are digital devices, i.e. they "live" in a binary world of zeros and ones. While microcontrollers live happily within their digital world, humans tend to operate better within an analogue world. Most measurements in our world are analogue. If we want to measure them with microcontrollers, we must convert them to digital. There are many techniques for doing this, I will show you the techniques that Bascom-AVR supports.

Introduction

Those of us who are involved in electronics generally want to measure analogue values such as voltage, current, resistance and other electronics parameters. When microcontrollers firstly appeared, they did not have A/D (analogue to digital) converters built-in, so engineers had to figure out that problem. Today, we are lucky: most AVR microcontrollers contain a 10-bit A/D converter, only a few do not. However they usually have at least a built-in comparator which can also be handy for making an A/D conversion.

In this chapter I will show you some program examples that are widely used and suitable for most of our measurements.

AVR internal registers

If you look at an AVRs datasheet, you'll see many internal functional blocks. In Figure 1, you can see the internal circuitry of the A/D converter.

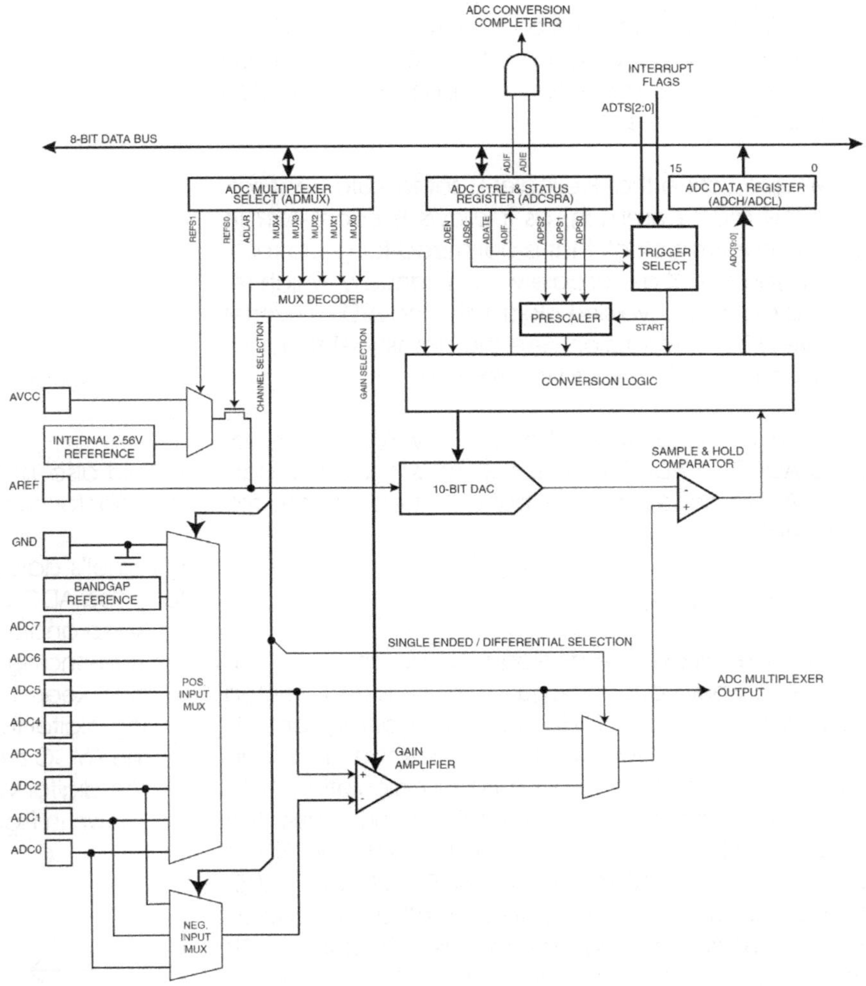

Figure 1: The internal registers of the A/D converter

There are a couple of things that are important to know when dealing with A/Ds. The first is the number of bits of resolution that we get from the A/D conversion. What does this mean? Well, say we have a voltage of 5 Volts, and we interpret (in electronics, we use the word "sample") it to 8 bits, then one bit corresponds to 0.0195 Volts ($5/2^8 = 5/256$), say 20 milivolts. If the same voltage is sampled to 10 bits, then the resolution is not 20 mV but 0.00488 Volts ($5/2^{10} = 5/1024$), say 5 mV, which is 4-times better than the 8-bit A/D conversion. This tells us that the resolution is important: probably the most important factor in A/D conversion. Since the A/D converters contained in AVRs are 10-bit ones, the resolution is fixed. If better resolution is needed, then we can do the following: use an external A/D converter with better resolution or use another reference voltage. You can see in Figure 1 that AVRs have an internal reference voltage of 2.56 Volts. This reference voltage can be used if we measure voltages that do not exceed 2.5 Volts. We can also use AVcc (5V) as the reference voltage. In any case, we must define the reference voltage as a part of the **Config Adc** statement, in our program, as follows:

```
Config Adc = Single , Prescaler = Auto ,_
Reference = Avcc
```

In the above case, the reference voltage is AVcc. If we want to use the internal 2.56 V reference, then we must write the configuration as follows:

```
Config Adc = Single , Prescaler = Auto ,_
Reference = INTERNAL
```

So what is the big deal about the internal or external reference voltage? Well, to begin with, the internal 2.56V reference is intended for sampling analogue voltages that are no higher than 2.5V. Second, is the matter of resolution again. We could have used AVcc as a reference voltage when measuring 2.5V but let's remember when using a 5V reference, the resolution is 4 mV. With a 2.56 V reference, the resolution is 2 mV ($2/2^{10} = 5/1024$), which is twice as good as the 5V reference. When you need millivolt resolution then it's important which reference source you select!

You will also notice that Prescaler is set to Auto. That setting is the most common, as it allows Bascom-AVR to pick a conversion clock that is optimized for good resolution. If you select a prescale value manually, which results in a higher conversion clock rate, the A/D converter will have a lower resolution. See the datasheet for more details on the ADC clock rate selection.

Most AVR microcontrollers have many A/D inputs, labelled ADC0 to ADC7 (and sometimes higher). In Bascom-AVR we access these input channels with the following statement:

```
W = Getadc(channel)
```

Basically, we retrieve the analogue value and store it in variable W, where our analogue voltage is represented by values in the range of 0 to 1024.This scale is probably not too practical. If we want to display the analogue voltage on an LCD we need a bit of calculation. Let's say that we have obtained W= 980. In our case, the reference voltage is 5V so we have to divide the ADC's Full-scale value of 1024 by 5 (1024/5= 204.8 = 205) and then divide the 980 A/D result by that 205 factor. So, the measured analogue voltage is 980 / 205 = 4.78 Volts. That's all what it takes to perform A/D conversion using Bascom-AVR! Simple, isn't it?

Practical experience and circuits

Let me share with you few experiences and some practical circuits in the field of A/D conversion. One very important fact when designing A/D conversion circuits is to use a reverse-biased Shottky diode at the A/D input, connected to + Vcc. This Schottky diode will protect the microcontroller from too large analogue signal, in case we hook up something incorrectly, or an external component fails. You can use a Zener diode connected from A/D input to GND but you may find that the Zener diode affects the measured results too much, especially when measured the voltage is near the Zener diode's breakdown or "knee" voltage. Also, if there is a chance of negative voltages appearing at the A/D input, you should also include a reverse-biased Schottky diode to ground, for protection.

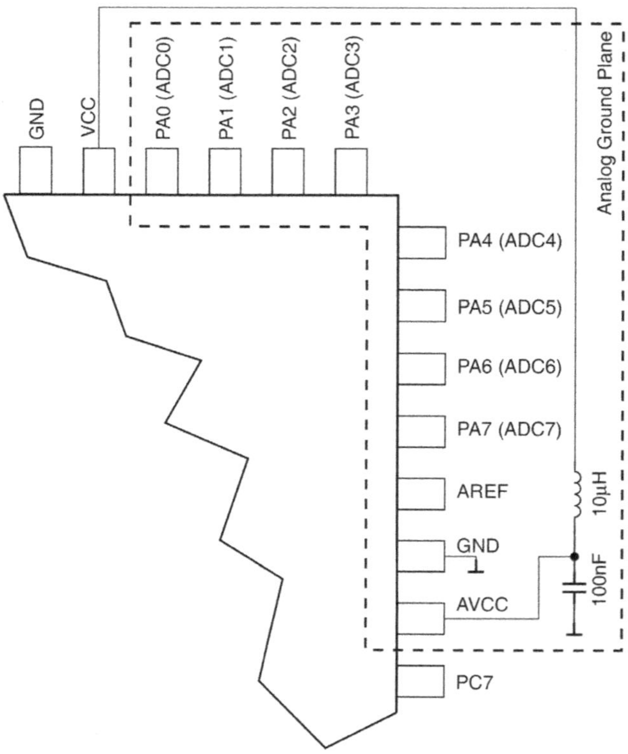

Figure 2: Suggested ADC power connections

In Atmel's datasheet for AVRs you can find suggestions for good ADC power connections:

1. Keep analog signal paths as short as possible. Make sure analog tracks run over the analog ground plane, and keep them well away from high-speed switching digital tracks,
2. the AVCC pin on the device should be connected to the digital VCC supply voltage via an LC network as shown in Figure 2,

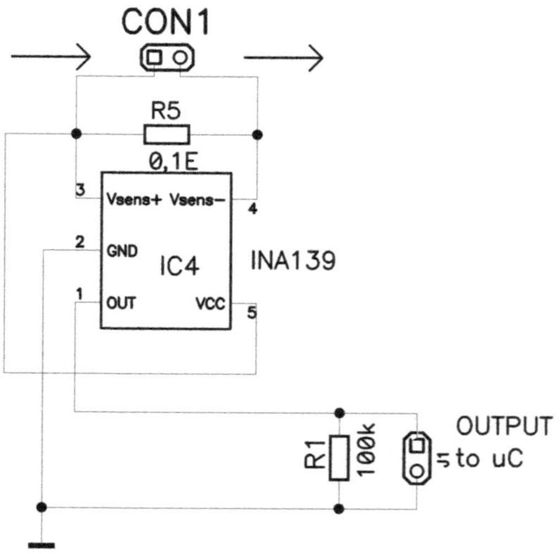

Figure 3: Measuring current with an INA139

3. use the ADC noise canceller function to reduce induced noise from the CPU,
4. if any near-by ADC port pins are used as digital outputs, it is essential that these do not change state while a conversion is in progress.

Not long ago, I had to measure electrical current within a PWM power supply project. When designing the PWM power supply, we had several options available to perform the output current measurement. We were considering the new Hall-Effect sensors by Allegro, but at that time they weren't available (and not very affordable either). Later we have found a practical (and cheap) solution by using an INA139 IC, as shown in Figure 3.

Current measurement is performed using shunt resistor R5. The current flowing through R5 gives a voltage drop across it but this voltage drop is very small, at low current levels. At 100 mA current, the voltage drop across R5 is only 10 mV, which is too low for an accurate A/D conversion. To achieve a reliable A/D conversion, we have to amplify it. Here is where the INA139 comes in very handy because it amplifies the voltage across R5 with a gain which we can set simply by selecting the value of external resistor R1. In this case, with resistor R1=100k, we set an amplification factor of 100. So, with 100 mA current flowing through R5, the output voltage from the INA139 is a full 1.0 Volt, which is a respectable voltage that can be easily converted to a digital value.

When converting analogue voltages to digital, there is always a certain degree of noise present, plus errors and other un-wanted factors. Usually, these present themselves as instability in the least-significant digit, when displaying the data. The last digit may drift a bit over time, but we don't expect it to quickly change its value. How do we avoid that? It's good practice when performing A/D conversions, to sample more than just one sample. It really depends on the application, but if you sample 50 samples and take the average of the 50 of them, you will receive a more stable result in which the last digit is more or less constant.

A/D conversion with MiniPin II and MegaPin

A sample of A/D conversion code, written in Bascom-AVR, can be easily demonstrated on the MiniPin II and MegaPin development boards. Both boards have a built-in trimpot which can be used to generate a variable analogue voltage that can be sampled with our microcontroller. Let's set up the MiniPin II /MegaPin as shown in the Figure 4.

We have connected PortA.0 (ADC0) to the trimpot, as shown in Figure 4, but you can connect it to any ADC pin. Now, if we start our microcontroller program and change the setting of the trimpot, we can see that the measured voltage on the LCD is changing accordingly.

Actually, the normal function of the trimpot on the MiniPin II & MegaPin board is to serve as an adjustable external reference voltage, which is enabled by placing a jumper at AREF Enable (J8 at MiniPin II or J19 at MegaPin). However, in this case we have used it as the source of a variable analogue voltage.

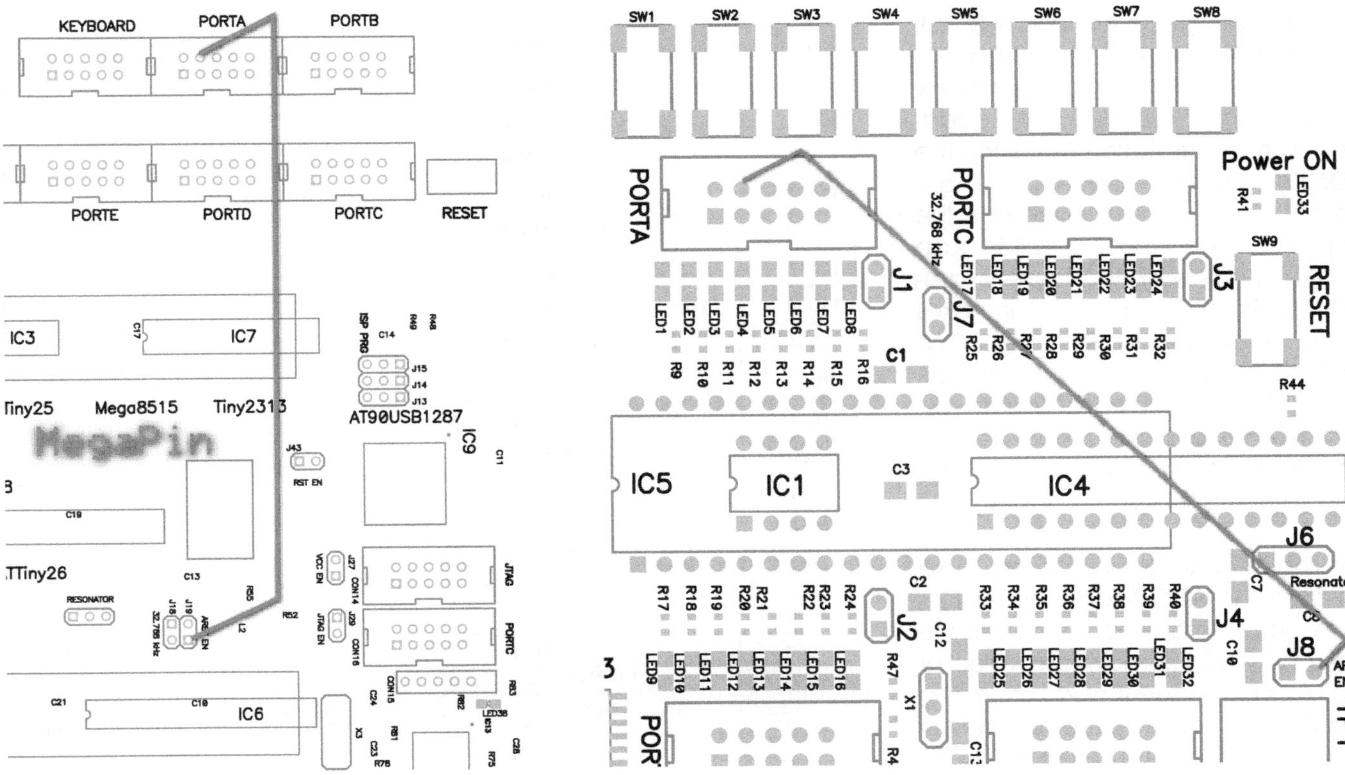

Figure 4: Connecting the ADC input to the trimpot on the MiniPin II and MegaPin

With TP1, the user can set AREF from nearly 5V down to 2.5 Volts. The External AREF is handy when performing analogue to digital conversions on voltages between 2.5 and 5.0 Volts. AVRs have a built- 2.56V reference source, as well as allowing you to select AVcc as a reference (usually 5V). Using a 5V reference, the resolution of the 10-bit A/D conversion is 4.88 milivolts. If we are performing A/D conversions with an input voltage <= 3.0 V, then we can see that the 5V reference does not provide optimal resolution. If we used TP1 to set a reference voltage of 3.0 V, we can achieve a resolution of 2.93 milivolts, which is nearly twice as good as that obtained with a 5.0 V reference.

Differential A/D conversion

The Bascom-AVR A/D conversion statements mentioned earlier are what's needed in conjunction with the simple circuit shown in Figure 3. However, it is different story when measuring differential voltages, i.e. those from a strain gauge. A strain gauge is a device consisting of four special resistors bonded to an aluminium plate. It is usually used to measure force i.e. weight.

Let's take a look at Figure 7. Because of the very low signals produced by the strain gauge (in the low millivolts), as well as the fact that these small signals are "riding" on a voltage roughly equal to Vcc/2, we must use a good-quality **Instrumentation Amplifier.** The AD620 is one such amplifier, having a very low input offset voltage and the high common-mode rejection ratio (CMRR) necessary to properly amplify the Strain Gauge signal. It makes sense to set the gain of the AD620 as high as possible. However, we can also get some additional gain by using the internal Gain Amplifier which is part of the AVR's A/D convertor block, and selecting a Gain=10 setting.

Looking at Figure 6, we can see Table 84 from the ADC section of Atmel's ATmega32 datasheet. Looking at the entry for MUX 4..0 having a value of 01001, we can see that we are telling the ADC to measure the differential voltage between ADC0 and ADC1, using a Gain of 10. This would be a good choice for this application.

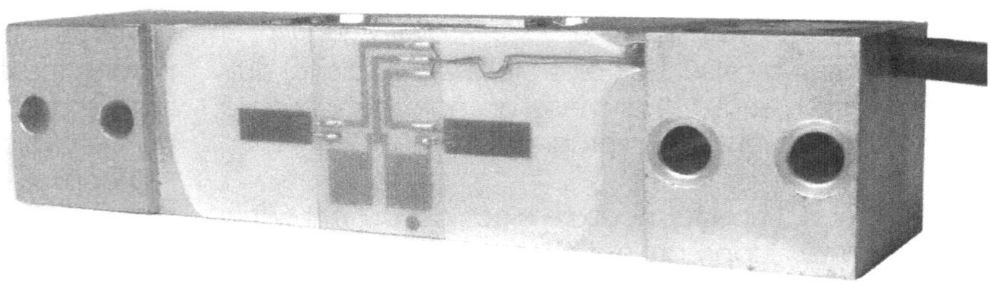

Figure 5: Photo of a strain gauge

MUX4..0	Single Ended Input	Positive Differential Input	Negative Differential Input	Gain
00000	ADC0			
00001	ADC1			
00010	ADC2			
00011	ADC3	N/A		
00100	ADC4			
00101	ADC5			
00110	ADC6			
00111	ADC7			
01000		ADC0	ADC0	10x
01001		ADC1	ADC0	10x
01010[1]		ADC0	ADC0	200x
01011[1]		ADC1	ADC0	200x
01100		ADC2	ADC2	10x
01101		ADC3	ADC2	10x
01110[1]		ADC2	ADC2	200x
01111[1]		ADC3	ADC2	200x
10000		ADC0	ADC1	1x
10001		ADC1	ADC1	1x
10010	N/A	ADC2	ADC1	1x
10011		ADC3	ADC1	1x
10100		ADC4	ADC1	1x
10101		ADC5	ADC1	1x
10110		ADC6	ADC1	1x
10111		ADC7	ADC1	1x
11000		ADC0	ADC2	1x
11001		ADC1	ADC2	1x
11010		ADC2	ADC2	1x
11011		ADC3	ADC2	1x
11100		ADC4	ADC2	1x
11101		ADC5	ADC2	1x
11110	1.22 V (V_{BG})	N/A		
11111	0 V (GND)			

01000		ADC0	ADC0	10x
01001		ADC1	ADC0	10x
01010[1]		ADC0	ADC0	200x

Figure 6: Table 84 from Atmel's data sheet for ATmega32

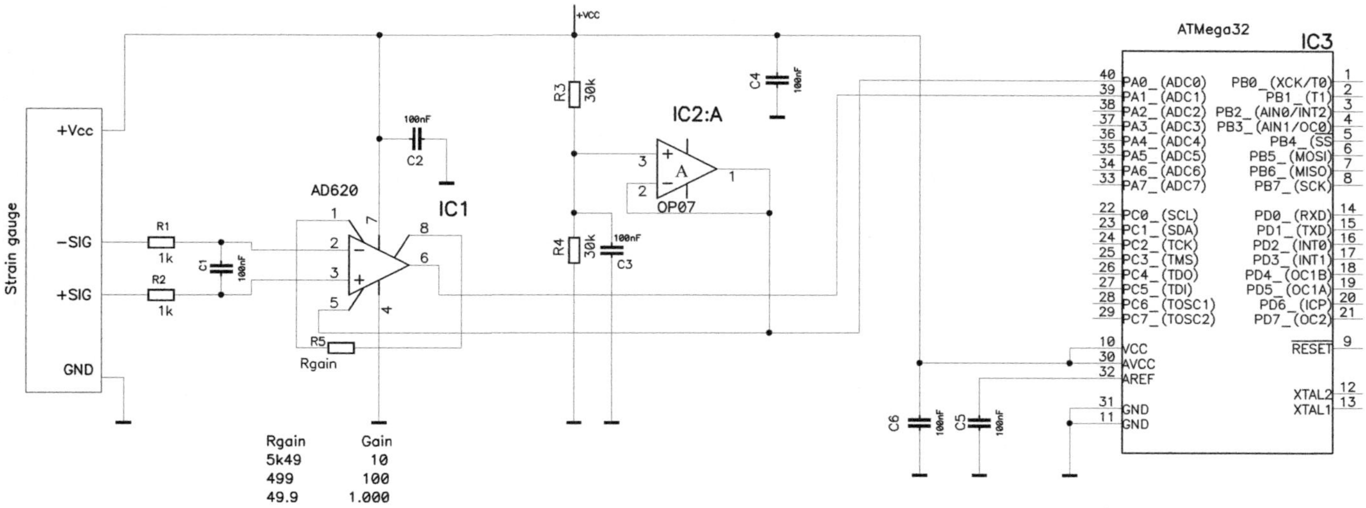

Figure 7: Circuit for the differential measurement of analogue signals

How do we define in our program to use this setting? We use the following statement:

```
W = Getadc(channel, offset)
```

Now, what does the "offset" mean? In the Bascom-AVR Help file it is defined as "An optional numeric variable of constant that specifies gain or mode" (*not related to the input offset voltage of the Gain Amplifier, as mentioned above*). We use the MUX4.0 value which we chose above, for this offset setting, or:

```
W = Getadc(0 , 9)
```

Going back to Figure 6, observant readers will notice that you can set up the ADC MUX to select ADC0/ADC0, What's the sense in this? These settings allow us to take ADC reading with the input to the Gain Amplifier shorted together. The resulting reading is a measure of the input offset voltage of the Gain Amplifier, and can be stored and subtracted from our actual readings later on, to improve the accuracy of our readings. Atmel themselves admit that this gain amplifier is not particularly accurate, especially at the 200X gain setting, so you may want to consider incorporating some form of zero offset correction in your program.

In Figure7, several R_{GAIN} values are shown for common Gain settings. To set other gains, use the following formula:

$$\textbf{Gain} = (49{,}400 / R_{GAIN}) + 1$$

You would set this gain to properly handle the Full-Scale output of your chosen Strain Gauge. For the AVR's A/D convertor, the formula that applies to differential measurement is as follows:

$$ADC = \frac{(V_{POS}-V_{NEG}) * GAIN * 512}{V_{REF}}$$

The result ranges from -512 to + 511 and is represented in the two's-complement format. You can find out if a result is positive or negative by reading the MSB of the result (bit ADC9 in register ADCH). If this bit is one, the result is negative, and if this bit is zero, the result is positive.

Conclusion

We have shown how to transform analogue signals into digital. Bascom-AVR is very helpful in that respect. Besides knowing how to write program routines, it's also good to know some of the details of the hardware. In the datasheets, you'll find some tips on how to improve A/D converter accuracy. Unfortunately, Bascom-AVR does not support all of the possibilities, but it's not too difficult to add a few Assembly language statements, if needed. Just bear in mind that the **Config ADC** statement starts the ADC automatically! This is important if you are trying to optimize for low-power performance. In that case you can use the **START ADC** and **STOP ADC** statements to shut down the ADC when it is not actually being used.

Example program ID	
Name:	USB-ADC_UK.bas
Microcontroller:	All AVRs with ADC
Testing circuit:	use dev. board and Bascom-AVR Terminal program
MiniPin compatibility:	yes
MegaPin compatibility:	yes
Program that acquires analogue voltages and communicates through USB to the PC. Open Terminal window and typeon PC keyboardto see how program corresponds.	

Using a pressure sensor

By Vlado Berend

I obtained an HP03M pressure sensor manufactured by HopeRF. This great sensor contains a built-in A/D converter. It features an I²C bus, which makes communication with a microcontroller very easy.

HopeRF offers many pressure sensors, besides the HP03M that I received. They also offer some with a built-in compass. Figure 1 shows the internal structure of the HP03M sensor.

Some features of the HP03M pressure sensor:

- power supply voltage: 2.2 V to 3.6 V,
- stand-by current: 1 μA, 500 μA during conversion,
- air pressure measurement range: 300 – 1,000 hPa,
- error in pressure measurement: +/- 1 hPa,
- temperature range: - 20°C to + 60 C,
- error in temperature measurement: +/- 0.8 °C,
- built in 16-bit A/D converter,
- conversion time: 32 cycles.

I became interested in this sensor due to its I²C communication bus. Most available pressure sensors generate a voltage output proportional to pressure. This requires the addition of both a high resolution A/D converter and a very stable reference voltage. Most pressure sensors do not have a built-in temperature sensor, so we would have to add it, if we want to measure altitude by measuring air pressure and temperature.

The HP03M sensor has power supply pins, I²C pins and two additional ones: MCLK (clock) and XCLR (reset).The XCLR pin resets the A/D converter when set low. It must be held high during a conversion (which typically takes 40 milliseconds). For normal operation, the sensor's A/D converter requires a 32 KHz external clock. The HP03M also contains a built-in EEPROM, where factory constants are stored.

This EEPROM is read the same way as one would read a 24C02 EEPROM. By this I mean that the I²C Read address is the same (A1 hex). The sensor's EEPROM stores 11 parameters that are needed for accurate calculation of air pressure and temperature. The memory map of these coefficients is shown in Table (EEPROM - stored coefficients needed for accurate calculations).

Coefficient	EEPROM ADDRESS
C1 (MSB:LSB)	(16:17)
C2 (MSB:LSB)	(18:19)
C3 (MSB:LSB)	(20:21)
C4 (MSB:LSB)	(22:23)
C5 (MSB:LSB)	(24:25)
C6 (MSB:LSB)	(26:27)
C7 (MSB:LSB)	(28:29)
A	(30)
B	(31)
C	(32)
D	(33)

We will read two parameters from the sensor:

- D1: pressure
- D2: temperature

These values are not direct representations of pressure

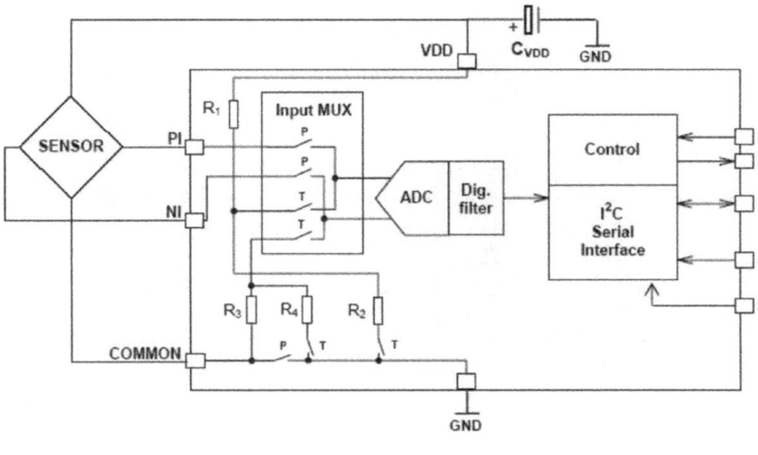

Figure 1: Block diagram of HP03M

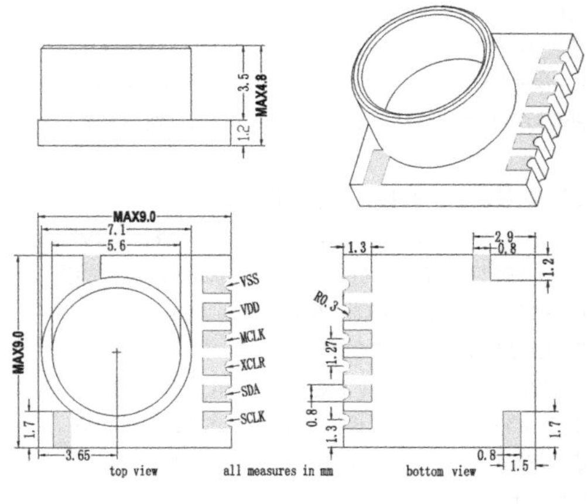

Figure 2: HP03M dimensions

and temperature, but values that are used, along with the EEPROM constants, in calculating the actual pressure and temperature.

There are two I²C addresses that are used to communicate with the HP03M's sensors:

- EE hex to write to the sensor,
- EF hex to read from the sensor.

Flow diagram to read air pressure is as follows:

S	11101110	A	11111111	A	11110000	A	P	D	S	11101110		
A	11111101	A	S	11101111	A	MSB	A	LSB	N	P		

Flow diagram to read temperature is as follows:

S	11101110	A	11111111	A	11110000	A	P	D	S	11101110		
A	11111101	A	S	11101111	A	MSB	A	LSB	N	P		

- S I2C Start
- A ACK
- P I2C Stop
- N NCK
- D pause 40 ms
- MSB result higher byte
- LSB result lower byte

Let me point out that Bascom-AVR knows *ACK* command only at reading telegram on I2C bus but not at writing. Why has HopeRF included *ACK* also at writing it is not known to me.

The sensor's manufacturer has issued some warnings:

- before starting an A/D conversion, set XCLR to a logical 1, to take the device out of the Reset state,
- after power-up, you should ignore the first data reading and use only subsequent ones.

Figure 3 shows a schematic diagram of the sensor connected to the microcontroller. For the prototype, I soldered the sensor to a DIL8 socket, which I then soldered to the protoboard. For the A/D convertor's clock we would normally use an external 32.768 kHz crystal oscillator. Instead, I decided to generate that using a PWM signal from the microcontroller.

The Bascom program

At the start of the program, we have to define the microcontroller being used, the crystal frequency and the baud rate (for communication). Since a PWM signal will be used for generating the 32.768 KHz clock source, we define Timer1 as a PWM generator and the OC1A pin as the PWM output pin. The OCR1A value that is needed to generate this frequency is calculated with this simple formula:

$$OCR1A=(F_{crystal}/(2*32768))-1$$

Variable N represents the prescale factor (1, 8, 32, 64, 128, 256, or 1024. Timer1 configuration looks like this:

```
Config Timer1 = Timer , Prescale = 1 , _
Compare A = Toggle , Clear Timer = 1
Start Timer1
Ocr1a = 182                    'F=32.768 kHz
Oc1a_pin Alias Portb.1         'PWM output signal
                               'connect to pin MCLK
Config Oc1a_pin = Output
```

Let's continue with the definitions of the other pins that are used: SCL, SDA and XCLR, all of which should be immediately set to a low level. According to the datasheet, the HP03M has a max. I²C clock frequency of 100 kHz. Since I was using this particular sensor, I had to introduce an I²C delay:

```
    Config I2cdelay = 15
```

Note that the HM03MA has a max. I²C clock frequency of 500 kHz, and therefore does not need this statement.

Next, the variables and constants, needed to calculate the result, are dimensioned/declared. There are a couple of constants needed for the calculations. I decided to define them in advance, as follows.

```
Const K1 = 32                  '2^5
Const K2 = 16384               '2^14
Const K3 = 65536               '2^16
Const K4 = 1024                '2^10
Const K5 = 67108864            '2^26
Const Adresw = &HA0            'EEPROM WRITE
                               'ADDRESS
Const Adresr = &HA1            'EEPROM READ
                               'ADDRESS
```

We also have to define the LCD display parameters, if we use it for debugging. Similarly, we can also use the

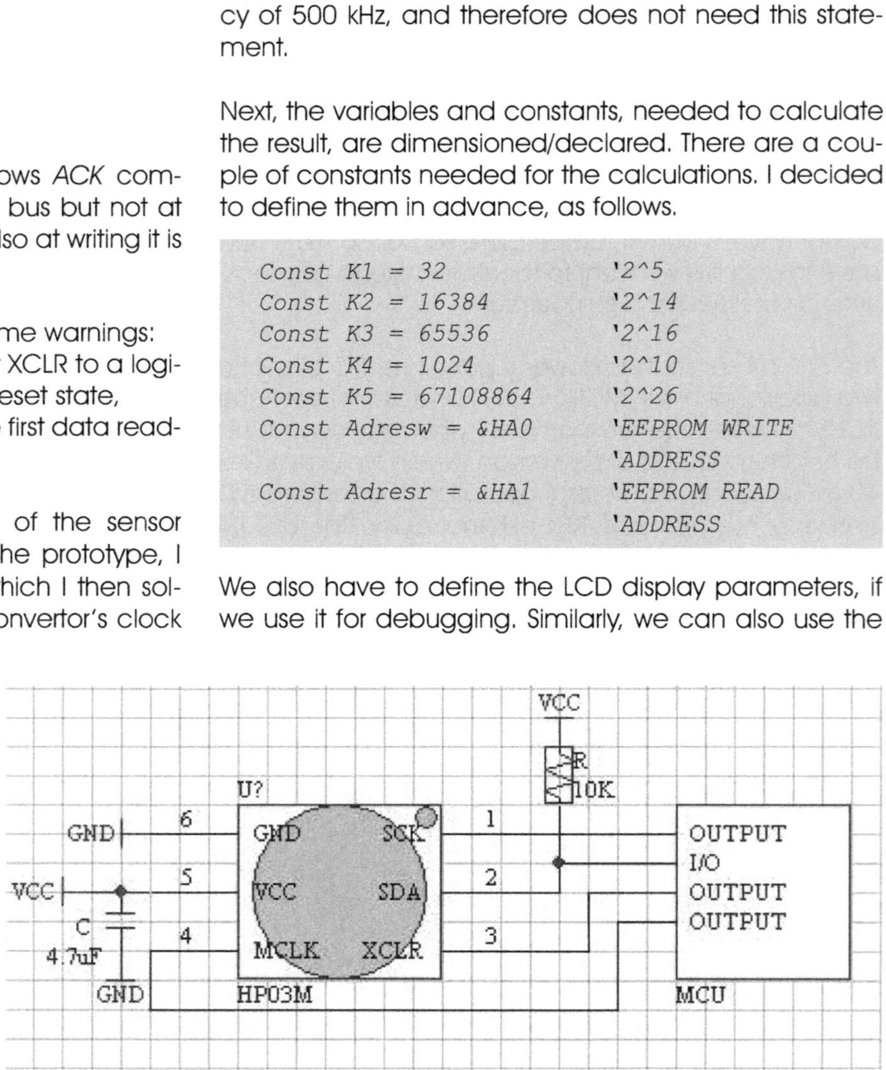

Figure 3: Typical application circuit.

```
T=250+dUT*C6/K3
OFF=(C2+(C4-2048)*dUT/K2)*4
SENS=C1+C3*dUT/K4
X=SENS*(D1-7168)*K2-OFF
P=X*10/K4+C7

IF  T>450 T2=3*C6*(450-T)^2/K5      P2=3*T2*(P-3500)/K2
IF  T<0   T2=11*C6*(0-T)^2/K5       P2=3*T2*(P-3500)/K2
IF 0=<T=<450 T2=0                   P2=0
P=P-P2
T=T-T2
```

Table 1

```
D2>=C5   dUT=D2-C5-((D2-C5)/2^7)*((D2-C5)/2^7)*A/2^C
D2<C5    dUT=D2-C5-((D2-C5)/2^7)*((D2-C5)/2^7)*B/2^C
OFF = (C2+(C4-1024)*dUT/2^14)*4
SENS = C1+C3*dUT/2^10
X = SENS*(D1-7168)/2^14-OFF
P=X*10/2^5+C7
T=250+dUT*C6/2^16-dUT/2^D
```

Table 2

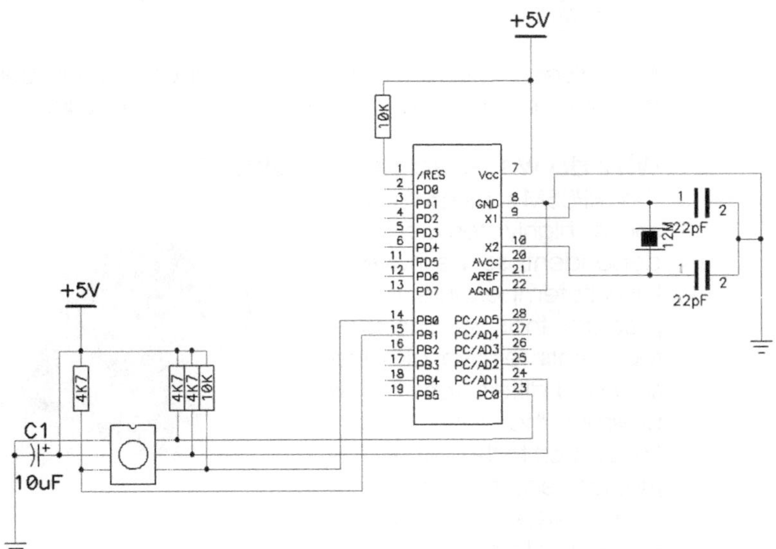

Figure 4: Schematic diagram showing the ATmega8 microcontroller and the HP03M sensor

ATmega8's serial port, for monitoring, using Bascom-AVR's terminal emulator.

```
Config Lcdpin = Pin , Db4 = Portd.4 ,_
Db5 = Portd.5 , Db6 = Portd.6 ,_
Db7 = Portd.7 , E = Portd.3 , Rs = Portd.2
Config Lcd = 16 * 2
```

As mentioned before, the values returned by the HP03M do not represent the actual values of temperature and air pressure. We must calculate them using the D1 and D2 values returned by the device, in conjunction with the calibration coefficients that are stored in the EEPROM. The Formulae for these calculations used in our program are as follows:

- for sensor HP03M see table 1.
- and formulae for sensor HP03MA see table 2.

There is not much difference in the formulae for sensor HP03M and HP-03MA, because the HP03M device also has constants A, B, C & D that are documented in the datasheet.

One difference between these sensors is the rated power supply voltage. The HP03M requires 5V while the HP03MA only 3.6 Volts.

Before doing any calculations, we must read the constants from the EEPROM. Constants C1 to C7 are Word type, which means that we will have to form a word variable out of two bytes. We'll do that using the Makeint (C_LSB, C_MSB) statement. We have to be careful not to mix up the MSB and LSB, because we read both bytes at once, in the *Read_eeprom* subroutine.

Parameters A, B, C and D are Byte type and do not need to be converted.

```
Adres = 16
   Gosub Read_eeprom
C1 = Makeint(c_lsb , C_msb)out of _
two bytes we make one Word

Read_eeprom:
  I2cstart
  I2cwbyte Adresw
  I2cwbyte Adres
  I2cstart
  I2cwbyte Adresr
  I2crbyte C_msb , Ack
  I2crbyte C_lsb , Nack
  I2cstop
  Waitms 20
Return
```

The *Read_eeprom* subroutine is called repeatedly until all constants in the sensor's EEPROM are retrieved. In early versions of my program, I read each value twice, just to be sure that the values were correct. Later, I removed this, as it was unnecessary. The program executes a main loop, reading the values of D1 and D2. Based upon the value of these variables, we calculate temperature and air pressure. Using these two measurements, we can also calculate altitude, if necessary.

```
  Gosub Read_pressure      'gosub to read air
```

```
                        'pressure
  Gosub Read_temperature 'gosub to read
                         'temperature
  D2 = Makeint(c_lsb , C_msb)

 Beri_tlak:
  Xclr = 1
  Waitms 4
  I2cstart
  I2cwbyte &HEE
  I2cwbyte &HFF
  I2cwbyte &HF0
  I2cstop
  Waitms 40
  I2cstart
  I2cwbyte &HEE
  I2cwbyte &HFD
  I2cstart
  I2cwbyte &HEF
  I2crbyte C_msb , Ack
  I2crbyte C_lsb , Nack
  I2cstop
  D1 = Makeint(c_lsb , C_msb)
  Xclr = 0
  Waitms 4
  Xclr = 1
  Waitms 4

  I2cstart
  I2cwbyte &HEE
  I2cwbyte &HFF
  I2cwbyte &HF0
  I2cstop
  Waitms 40
  I2cstart
  I2cwbyte &HEE
  I2cwbyte &HFD
  I2cstart
  I2cwbyte &HEF
  I2crbyte C_msb , Ack
  I2crbyte C_lsb , Nack
  I2cstop
  D1 = Makeint(c_lsb , C_msb)
  Xclr = 0
  Waitms 4
  Return

 Read_temperature:
  Waitms 4
  Xclr = 1
  Waitms 4                      'sensor's reset
  I2cstart
  I2cwbyte &HEE
  I2cwbyte &HFF
  I2cwbyte &HE8
  I2cstop
  Waitms 40
  I2cstart
  I2cwbyte &HEE
  I2cwbyte &HFD
  I2cstart
  I2cwbyte &HEF
  I2crbyte C_msb , Ack
  I2crbyte C_lsb , Nack
  I2cstop
  Xclr = 0
  Waitms 4
  Xclr = 1
  Waitms 4
  I2cstart                 'repeat reading
                           'because we accept
                           'second reading
  I2cwbyte &HEE
  I2cwbyte &HFF
  I2cwbyte &HE8
  I2cstop
  Waitms 40
  I2cstart
  I2cwbyte &HEE
  I2cwbyte &HFD
  I2cstart
  I2cwbyte &HEF
  I2crbyte C_msb , Ack
  I2crbyte C_lsb , Nack
  I2cstop
  Xclr = 0
  Waitms 4
  Return
```

The values we read for D1 and D2 will be used in our formulae to calculate temperature and air pressure.

Why do we need temperature?

The HP03M's pressure sensor is highly temperature-dependent, so we have to know its temperature. The air pressure that we measure represents relative air pressure and differs from the air pressure that weather stations report to the public. The publicly-reported air pressure however is referenced to sea level (i.e. absolute air pressure 1,023 hPa).

To calculate the absolute air pressure, we must know the current altitude. This formula is rather complicated as it involves logarithms, so I decided to use a simpler formula by Laplace, which is valid for altitudes up to 500m above sea level.

In the formula, we need to know the change of altitude for an air pressure change of 1 hPa. This can be calculated from the formula:

```
Hp = 8000/P_sea * (0.004 * T + 1)
```

The **highlighted section below** seems to match this formula, if *N= P_sea*. But that doesn't seem right, as N is the measured air pressure, presumably NOT at sea level. This makes *Auxillary(1) = Hp*.

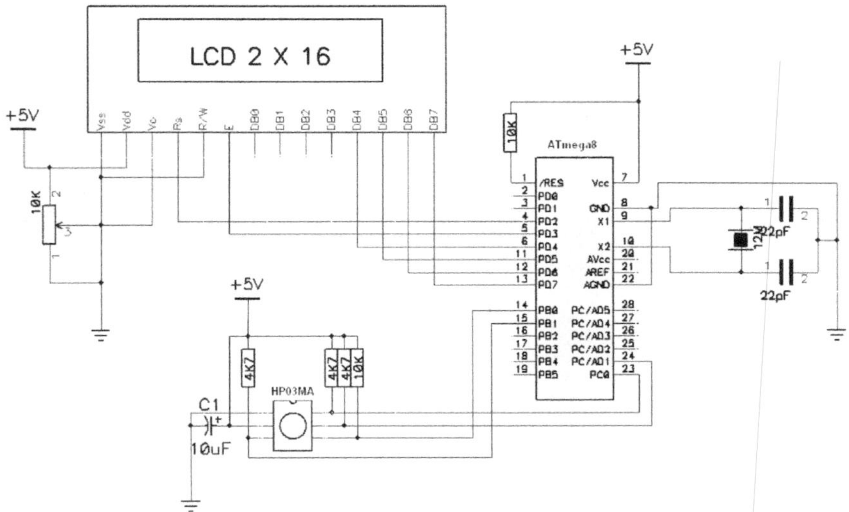

Figure 5: Schematic of the test circuit using an ATmega8

Hp is the altitude difference for a change of air pressure of 1 hPa, 8000 is a constant based on air density and gravity, T is the current temperature, 0,004 = a constant.

```
Aa = 8000 / N          'where N is the
                       'measured air
                       'pressure
Bb = 0.004 * T3        'where T3 is the
                       'measured
                       'temperature
Bb = Bb + 1
Auxillary (1) = Aa * Bb

Pabs = Hnm / Auxillary (1)
                       'The altitude of
                       'my town is 280m
Pabs = N + Pabs
```

When comparing the calculated results from my microcontroller pressure sensing circuit and those observed on a simple weather station, I see difference of +/- 0.2 hPa, which is very good considering data that I get from a simple weather station.

Can we calculate altitude?

Yes, it is possible. To do so, we must have a known altitude. Using this, we can calibrate the measurement. While searching for data on the web, I found a useful table. On the basis of this, we can calculate altitude with respect to the measured air pressure. In most cases, what we really need is information regarding altitude change, So, I added a Boolean (bit) variable that is reset after the current altitude is measured. This becomes the reference altitude and all further altitudes that are measured are compared with it.

Conclusion

I consider this sensor to be very useful in various areas of electronics. It can be used to build a home made weather station. It can also be used to measure the altitude of a rocket or airplane model, to store the highest altitude reached, or as a data logger. The goal of this article was not to build an accurate altimeter. It was to interface the sensor correctly, and to make a program that can serve as a template for other users who are building pressure measuring devices, like a weather station, an altimeter, etc.

Figure 6: Photo of test circuit

Example program ID	
Name:	HP03MA.bas
Microcontroller:	Any AVR microcontroler
Testing circuit:	Figure 4
MiniPin compatibility:	/
MegaPin compatibility:	/
Program demonstrates use of HP03MA, air pressure sensor	

GPS modules, their description and use

By Jurij Mikeln

The abbreviation GPS is known to virtually all of us. Amongst those who have an electronics background, it's been known for many years. Within the general public it's only been common knowledge for the last 10 years due to the existence of low-cost GPS devices and smart phones with GPS built in. In this chapter, I will introduce to you two GPS modules that are representative of the GPS market. Also, I'll show you some Bascom examples and other interesting programs.

GPS modules came to my attention a few years ago, when our company purchased a few GPS01 modules from HopeRF [1]. A few weeks later, we purchased another GPS module, the FGPMMOPA6B by Global Top [2]. They differ one from each other by the chipset that is used. The GPS01 is based on the Skytraq Venus6 chipset while the FGPMMOPA6B is based upon the Mediatek MT3329 chipset.

To the average GPS user, which module you use doesn't make much difference, as both modules work well. Technical details matter to those of us who want to include these modules in our devices. For everyday use, we need a GPS location update every second, while for advanced use, such as for airplane navigation, we need location updates every 1/10th of a second. To achieve this, we have to set our GPS module accordingly. This, and much more will be covered in this chapter.

All those abbreviations

First, let me explain a common delusion held by some novice GPS users: when they ask me how strong the GPS transmitter is. A GPS module never transmits signals - it only receives them from the GPS satellites! For that, it only needs open sky.

There are many abbreviations within the GPS world. Let me start with the abbreviation GPS, which stands for Global Positioning System, which is well-known. Then we have NMEA, WAAS, HDOP and many others, which may not be known by everyone. I will introduce you to some of the most common ones:

- ***NMEA*** stands for National Marine Electronics Association. GPS modules can communicate with the host system (or microcontroller) in binary or via the NMEA01823 protocol. All GPS devices that are sold in volume use the NMEA protocol. In most GPS modules, the output protocol can be set during programming.
- ***WAAS*** stands for Wide Area Augmentation System, which consists of approximately 25 reference stations (called Wide Area Augmentation System Stations) that receive the GPS signal on the ground. These stations analyze those GPS signals and send corrected data to geostationary Inmarsat satellites, which send this data back to Earth on the GPS L1 frequency. WAAS signals are received by our GPS module. In Europe, you can receive WAAS satellites No. 33, 37 and 44, while in the USA satellites No. 35 & 47 can be received. There are places on the internet to look if you would like to know more about this subject [3].
- ***SBAS*** stands for Satellite-Based Augmentation System. Several countries have implemented their own satellite-based augmentation systems. Europe has the European Geostationary Navigation Overlay Service (EGNOS) which covers Western Europe and beyond. USA has its Wide Area Augmentation System (WAAS). Japan is covered by its Multi-functional Satellite Augmentation System (MSAS). India has launched its own SBAS programme named GPS and GEO Augmented Navigation (GAGAN) to cover the Indian subcontinent. SBAS systems are essential for applications where accuracy and integrity are critical. In particular, they are indispensable for all applications where people's lives are at stake or for which some form of legal or commercial guarantee is required.
- For example, ***SBAS*** make it possible to improve and extend the scope of GPS applications in areas such as precision farming, the guidance of agricultural machinery, on-road vehicle fleet management, and oil exploration (for the positioning of platforms at sea) or for scientific applications such as geodesy (source [4].
- ***EGNOS*** stands for European GEO-.stationary Navigation Overlay System which is satellite supported system to improve GPS and GLONASS navigation

Figure 1: Photo of GPS01 and FGPMMOPA6B GPS modules

systems. Earth stations receive GPS signals and send a correction factor via geostationary satellites to users. With these correction factors, an accuracy of 1.5 meters can be achieved.

» ***GLONASS*** is the Russian version of GPS system.
» ***DGPS*** stands for Differential GPS. DGPS is a system of Earth-based stations that transmit location data to augment the GPS signals. The accuracy of DGPS is below 1 meter - in some cases within a range of a few centimetres.
» ***AGPS*** stands for Assisted GPS, which is a system that enables the quick display of coordinates when the GPS module is first powered-up, by helping to obtain a faster "time to first fix" (TTFF). AGPS acquires and stores information about the location of satellites via an almanac. For smart phones, the satellite almanac is provided via the cellular network, so this information does not need to be downloaded via satellite. To store that information when we turn the GPS module off, we need a backup battery on the GPS module.
» ***HDOP*** stands for Horizontal Dilution Of Precision which means the accuracy of the calculated coordinate which the GPS module constantly calculates. HDOP is expressed in meters and it is lower if the number of satellites being received with the GPS module is higher.

Of course there are many more GPS abbreviations but these are sufficient for us. One can find very good reading resources about GPS satellites and their theory at [5].

GPS01 and FGPMMOPA6B GPS modules

Let's look at the technical details of the above-mentioned GPS modules, as illustrated in Figure 1. One difference is immediately evident: the FGPMMOPA6B has a built-in GPS antenna while the GPS01 needs an external GPS antenna.

Both modules are relatively small and ready to use with few external components. See the block diagram for the GPS01 and for the FGPMMOPA6B in Figure 2 and Figure 3 respectively.

From these block diagrams, one can see that GPS modules are no "Boogies" that we should be afraid of. As with all communication devices, they have Rx and Tx pins, power supply pins and a few additional pins. Referring to Figure 2, the pins are as follows:

» VBAT: connect a backup battery to that pin, to ensure quick startup of the GPS module,
» RXD0, TXD0: are communication pins. Location data comes out of the module via TXD0, and data is transmitted into the module (for setting parameters, etc.) via RXD0,
» P1PPS: (1 pulse per second) is output pin where the GPS module generates an accurate 1 second pulse. This pulse is very accurate and can be used as a time-base in devices like frequency counters,
» GPIO: general I/O pin reserved for GPS status,
» NRST: an external reset signal needed only if the power supply voltage rises too slowly,
» most of the other pins are connected to GND or left unconnected (NC).

Referring to Figure 3, the pins on the FGPMMOPA6B are defined as follows:

» D+ and D-: USB input/output, which can be connected to a PC directly,
» VBACKUP: Connect a backup battery to this pin, to

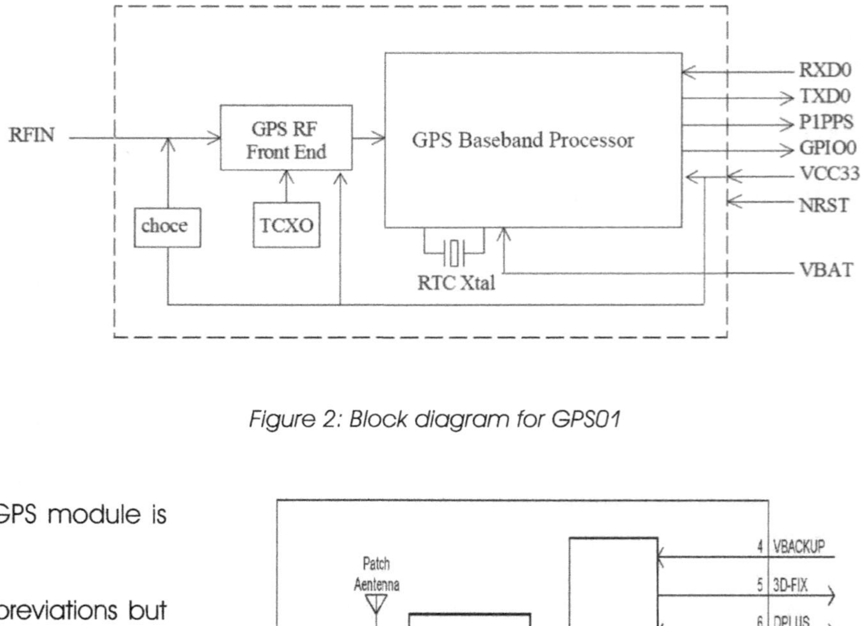

Figure 2: Block diagram for GPS01

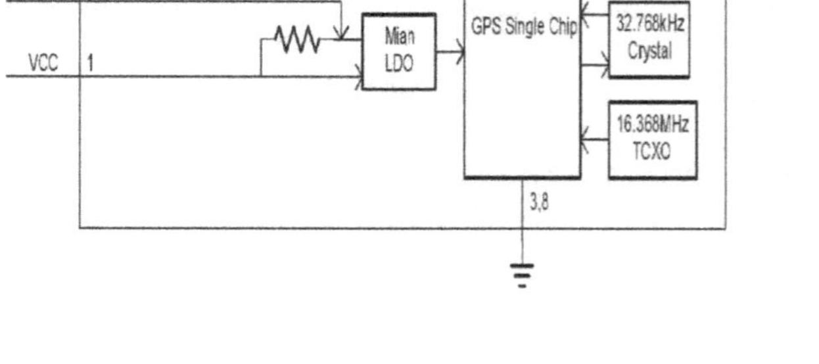

Figure 3: Block diagram for the FGPMMOPA6B

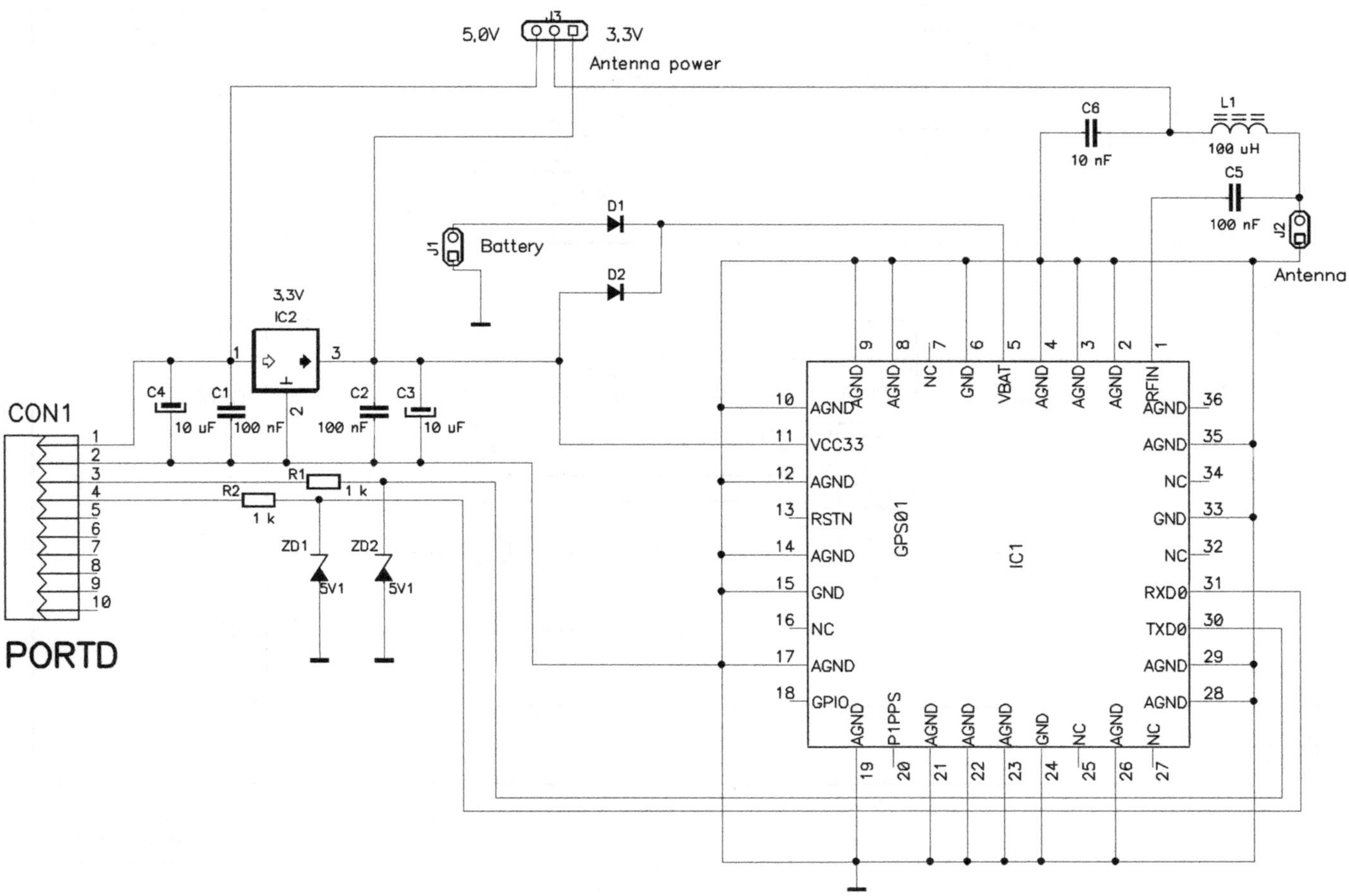

Figure 4: Connection of the GPS01 to MegaPin / MiniPin II

ensure the quick start-up of the GPS module,

- 3D-FIX: this pin generates a 1 sec pulse if the GPS module is receiving enough GPS signals (minimum 4) to perform 3D navigation,
- TXD, RXD: are communication pins. Data comes out of the module via TXD, and data is sent to the module (for setting parameters, etc.) via RXD,
- ENABLE: leave this pin unconnected. If you tie it to GND it will disable the GPS module,
- typical schematic diagrams for both GPS modules can be seen in Figure 4 & 5.

GPS output signals

GPS modules constantly send data messages. Every second (providing the refresh rate is 1 second) we receive a stream of data which, at first sight, looks like a jungle of letters and numbers, as shown in Table 1.

Of course, we can configure what data the GPS module should send to our microcontroller (or our PC) and how frequently it should do that. We can configure the GPS module by means of a microcontroller or with a suitable PC program. It's been proven that using a PC program is much more reliable and user-friendly than writing our own routines to configure a GPS module. One such a program is Skytrack, intended for GPS modules incorporating the Skytrack chip-set. The Skytrack program can be seen in Figure 6.

$GPGGA,	154034,4604.3850,N,01428.8644,E,1,05,02.3,00313.8,M,044.1,M,,	*40
$GPGSA,	A,3,11,17,20,23,28,,,,,,,,02.9,02.3,01.7*01	
$GPGSV,	3,1,12,01,62,106,00,11,83,263,41,14,31,047,00,17,17,319,41	*79
$GPGSV,	3,2,12,19,24,175,33,20,49,259,46,22,00,066,00,23,11,198,34	*73
$GPGSV,	3,3,12,25,11,127,00,28,08,274,36,31,13,106,00,37,,,00	*4C
$GPRMC,	154034,A,4604.3850,N,01428.8644,E,000.0,114.2,290107,,,A	*75
$GPGGA,	154035,4604.3850,N,01428.8644,E,1,05,02.3,00313.7,M,044.1,M,,	*4E
$GPGSA,	A,3,11,17,20,23,28,,,,,,,,02.9,02.3,01.7	*01
$GPGSV,	3,1,11,01,62,106,00,11,83,262,41,14,31,047,00,17,17,319,41	*7B
$GPGSV,	3,2,11,19,24,175,27,20,49,259,46,22,00,066,00,23,11,198,34	*75
$GPGSV,	3,3,11,25,11,127,00,28,08,274,36,31,13,106,00,,,,	*4B

Table 1: Typical GPS data received from a GPS module

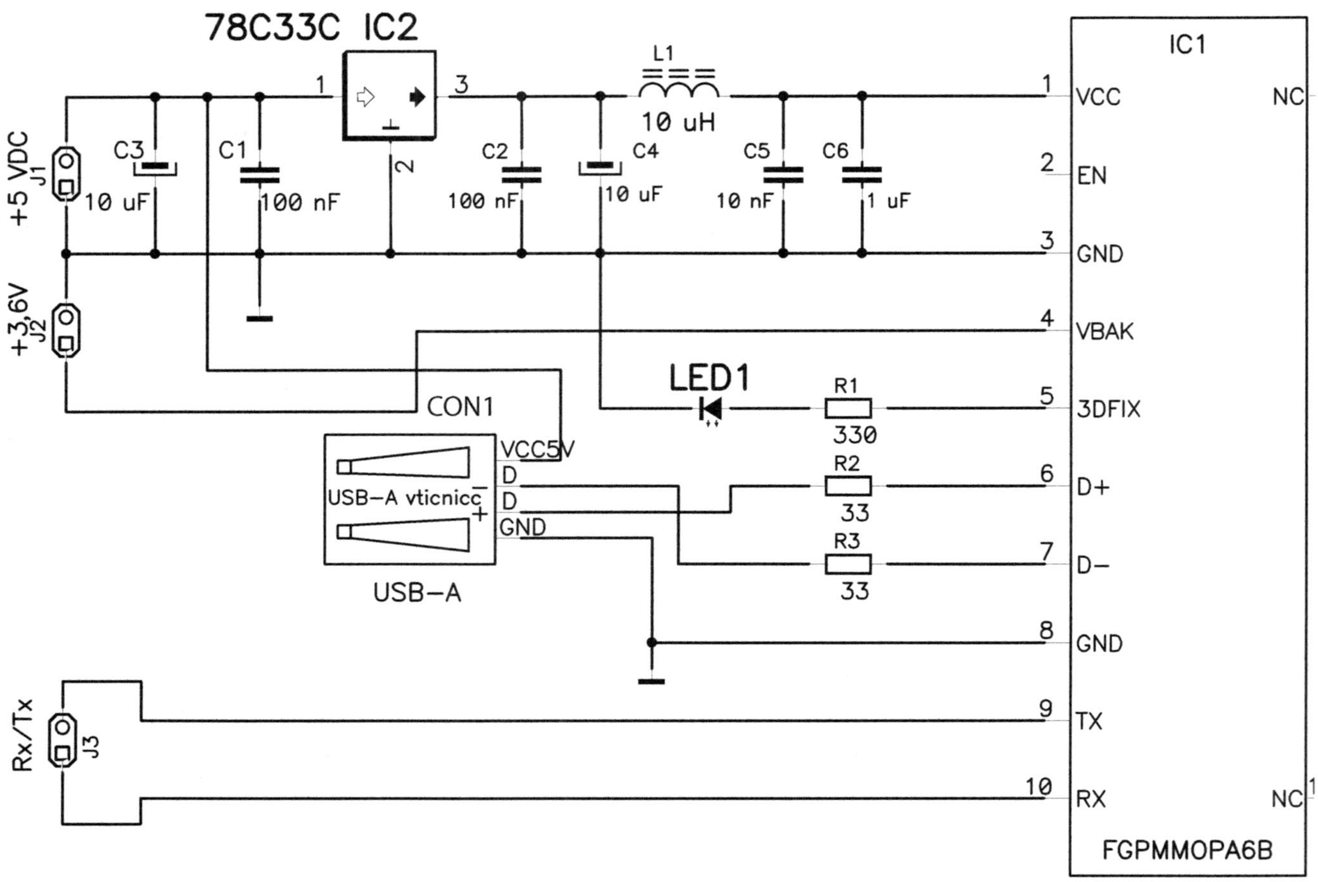

Figure 5: Connection of the FGPMMOPA6B to USB

MiniGPS is a suitable program for setting parameters of Mediatek chipset GPS modules, and can be seen in Figure 7.

Both programs can be used for receiving streams of data transmitted from GPS modules, however, only a compatible one is suitable for setting the GPS module parameters. That is, one cannot set Skytrack GPS module parameters with the MiniGPS program (intended for Mediatek GPS modules) and vice versa.

Getting involved with Bascom

Well now the Bascom party begins. At first sight, Table 1 can be worrisome, because data is being sent constantly at a fast rate – especially if the GPS module is configured to send data every 1/10th of a second. Well, it may look complicated, but if you look closely, you will see a distinctive data pattern hiding within Table 1. For a start, here are some explanations of various data blocks.

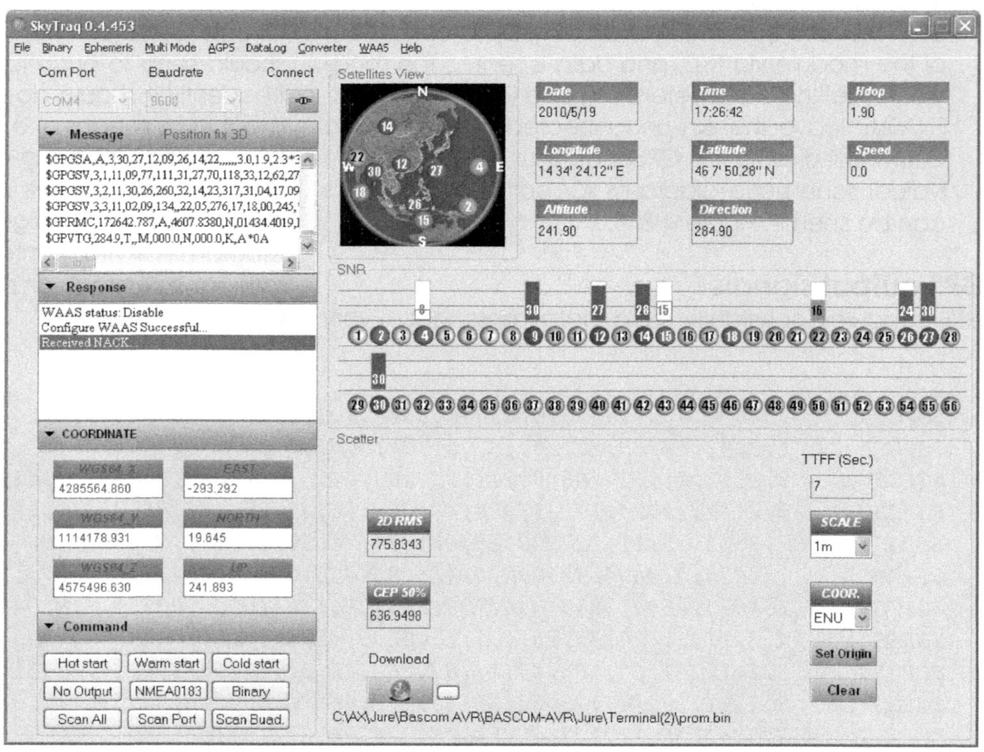

Figure 6: The Skytrack program can be used with the GPS01 module

```
$GPRMC              identification of telegram
154034              UTC time: 15 hours,
                    40 minutes, 34 seconds
"the telegram is valid"
4604.3850,N         Latitude: 46 degrees and
                    4.3850 minutes North
01428.8644,E        Longitude: 14 degrees and
                    28.8644 minutes East
000.0               speed 0.0 in knots
114.2               compass direction
                    of current travel with
                    respect to North
290107      date 29.01.2007
*75         checksum
```

A more detailed explanation can be found at [6].

There are many ways to parse suitable data from the $GPRMC telegram. One very interesting way can be found at [8], where the author made a GPS/GSM two-way communication device to find a lost (or stolen) car. Another somewhat simpler way can be found at [7], which was successfully used with our GPS modules.

A suitable program can be found on our web page, labelled GPS01.bas where we perform all the basic commands needed by the GPS module, and receive data back from the GPS module. All data fields are displayed on a GLCD for easy viewing (much more data can be displayed on a GLCD than on a 2x16 character LCD).

The same program but using a 2x16 LCD is labelled GPS_2x16_LCD.bas.

This program is just a backbone for communicating with the GPS module that you are using in your devices. It offers complete configuration of the GPS module, whereby we can set GGA & VTG ON or OFF, the Baudrate, Car/Pedestrian mode, Update rate and WAAS.

You will notice that most of the program has been purposely well-commented. For example, let us say we want to change the Baudrate from 9,600 Bd to 19,200 Bd. GPS modules are factory programmed at 9,600 Bd, hence Bascom should be initially configured to that, using the statement $Baud = 9600:

```
'$baud = 4800
$baud = 9600
'$baud = 19200
'$baud = 38400
'$baud = 57600
'$baud = 115200
```

Next, we have to send the GPS module a certain set of commands at the default Baudrate. If we elect to change the GPS module's Baudrate, we have to change the microcontroller's baudrate too, otherwise the microcontroller will no longer communicate with the GPS module. The following lines describe the sequence of bytes we must send to the module, to increase its Baudrate to 19,200.

```
'*19200
Print Chr(&Ha0) ; Chr(&Ha1) ;_
Chr(&H00) ; Chr(&H04) ; Chr(&H05) ;_
Chr(&H00) ; Chr(&H02) ; Chr(&H00) ;_
Chr(&H07) ; Chr(&H0d) ; Chr(&H0a)
Baud = 19200
```

You will notice that the last statement used is not *$Baud = 19200,* but *Baud=19200*! This is important as it instructs the compiler to use this Baudrate onwards. See Bascom Help for more information about this.

Now that we have successfully changed the Baudrate of both our GPS module and microcontroller, we can start performing data acquisition and interpretation. We do that using the Do loop where we parse the data as follows:

```
Gps = Waitkey()
If Gps <> "$" Then Goto Startloop
Gps = Waitkey()
If Gps <> "G" Then Goto Startloop
Gps = Waitkey()
If Gps <> "P" Then Goto Startloop
etc.
```

With these simple commands we can parse data from the data stream that the GPS module is sending us. Later, we display that data (time, longitude, latitude, valid data, No. of satellites receiving, HDOP and altitude in meters) on the LCD.

Construction

We have designed two PCBs: one for the GPS01 and one for the FGPMMOPA6B. Both can be connected to MegaPin, while the FGPMMOPA6B PCB can also be connected to a PC's USB port directly. As mentioned, FGPMMOPA6B has an embedded USB interface, which makes it very handy to use with a PC. The PCB for the FGPMMOPA6B is double-sided while the PCB for the GPS01 is single sided with one short jumper wire connected and another wire that can connect to a backup battery. On the GPS01 PCB, we can select 3.3 or 5.0 Volts to supply an external powered antenna while the FGPMMOPA6B PCB has a built-in 3.3 Volt regulator. The backup battery is soldered to J2 with two wires.

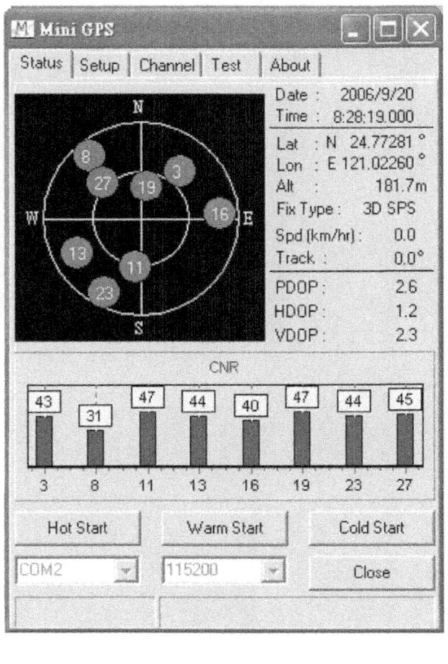

Figure 7: The MiniGPS program can configure parameters of the FGPMMOPA6B

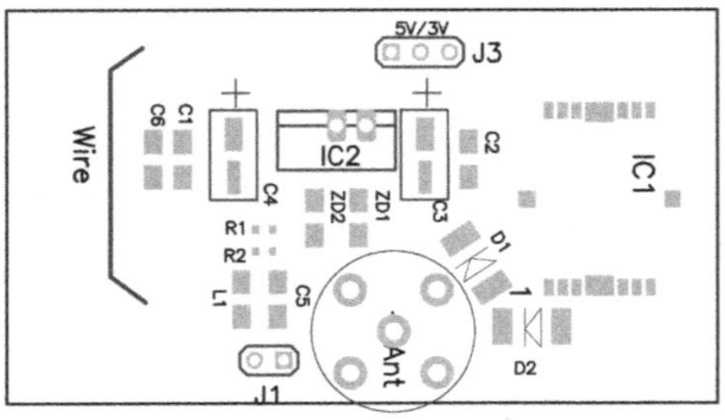

Figure 8: GPS01 PCB

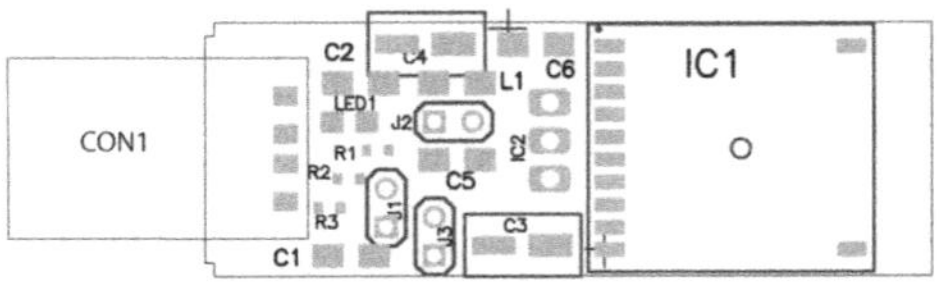

Figure 9: FGPMMOPA6B PCB

Conclusion

GPS modules nowadays are very affordable, which, for many years wasn't true. Today, we can buy a GPS module, add solid state gyroscopes, microcontroller, web camera, transceiver, remote control etc. and make a tricopter that can fly very well [9]. Note that all software for this tricopter was done using Bascom-AVR! To make a tricopter fly is not an easy task, but receiving signals from GPS is. The programs and hardware presented here work on the MegaPin board only. If we were to use a software UART within our Bascom program, and receive GPS module data on any other pin than PD.0, then we could also use these programs on the MiniPin II board too.

References:
1. http://www.hoperf.com/
2. http://www.gtop-tech.com/jsf/index.jsf
3. http://www.kowoma.de/en/gps/waas_egnos.htm
4. http://egnos-portal.gsa.europa.eu/discover-egnos/about-egnos/what-is-sbas-
5. http://lea.hamradio.si/~s53mv/navsats/theory.html
6. http://www.werple.net.au/~gnb/gps/nmea.html
7. http://avr.15.forumer.com/a/serial-gps-nmea0183-decoder-bascom_post512.html
8. Svet elektronike No. 147, Author Vilko Sustič
9. http://www.mcselec.com/index.php?option=com_content&task=view&id=263&Itemid=57

Example program ID	
Name:	GPS01.bas
Microcontroller:	AT MEGA 16
Testing circuit:	Figure 4
MiniPin compatibility:	possible, see text
MegaPin compatibility:	yes
GPS data displayed on graphic LCD	

Example program ID	
Name:	GPS_2x16_LCD.bas
Microcontroller:	AT MEGA 16
Testing circuit:	Figure 5
MiniPin compatibility:	possible, see text
MegaPin compatibility:	yes
GPS data displayed on LCD 2x16	

Development tools 105

Having programmed microcontrollers for many years, we have become regular users of development boards. There are many available on the market. Some expensive ones attempt to achieve universality by handling many different MCU models and including many different peripherals on-board. Others are nothing more than a »break-out« board for a specific MCU device.

In contrast, we have designed optimal development boards, that will meet most of your requirements while writing/testing your AVR programs. These boards emerged from extensive usage in our daily work, so there are very good reasons why our tools are designed as illustrated in this chapter.

Use smart tools when writing your Bascom-AVR programs!

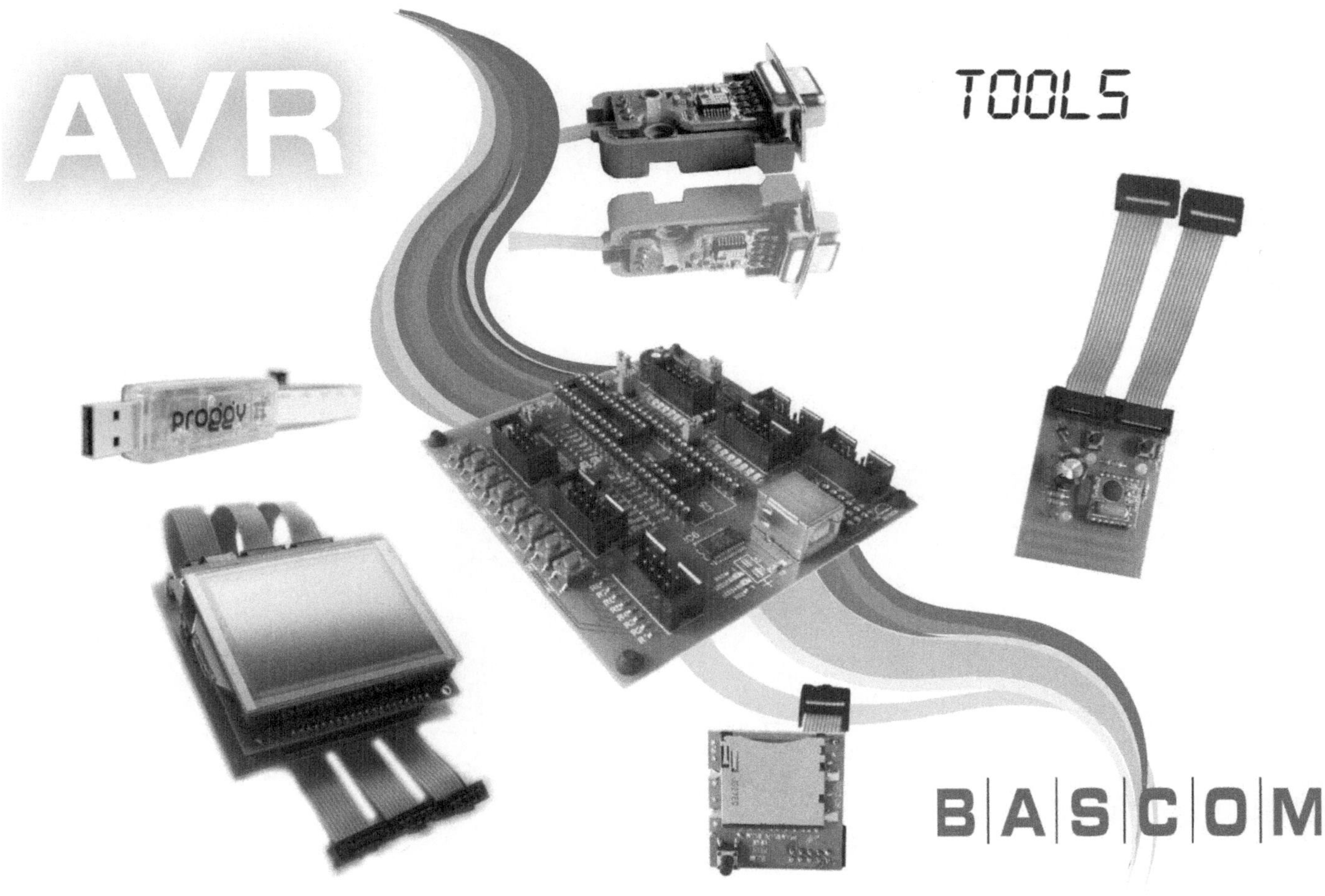

MiniPin II development board

By Jurij Mikeln

MiniPin II is a smaller brother of MegaPin. Smaller, but still very user friendly and versatile development board, where programs for AVRs may be tested and evaluated.

Key MiniPin II features:

1. supports all AVR microcontrollers in 8-pin, 28-pin & 40 pin DIL packages (except ATmega8515, 8535, i.e. older AVRs),
2. 6 built-in sockets for 1-Wire DS18S20 temperature sensors, which can be connected to any I/O Port,
3. 8 LEDs on each of four I/O ports (PortA, PortB, PortC & PortD),
4. IDC I/O connectors on four ports: (PortA, PortB, PortC, PortD),
5. built-in 250 mA fuse to protect USB from short circuit on board,
6. built-in USB communication to UART (not on MiniPin II B version!),
7. built-in external oscillator circuit to clock microcontroller from an external quartz crystal,
8. built-in 3-pin socket for ceramic resonator,
9. built-in 2-pin socket for 32,768 kHz quartz crystal,
10. built-in adjustable reference voltage for the AVRs ADC,
11. built-in keyswitch array which can be connected to any I/O Port,
12. built-in Power-ON LED,
13. built-in serial communication Tx/Rx LEDs.

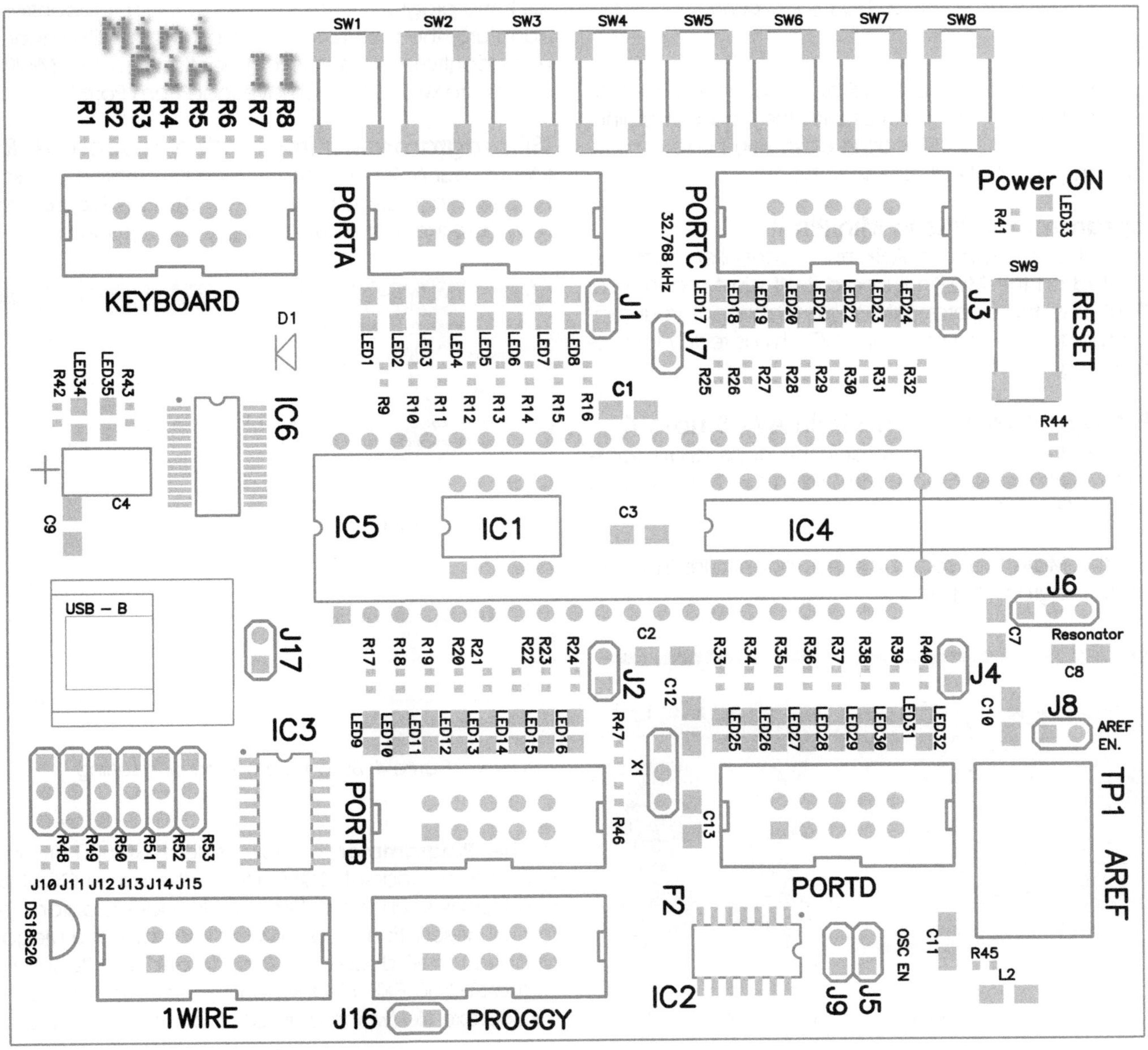

Connecting your programmer to the MiniPin II board.

When connecting your programmer to the MiniPin II board, be sure that you connect the programmer's socket to the socket labelled "PROGGY", as shown in Figure1. If you don't own a Proggy programmer, make sure that you connect it's signals to the MiniPin II board, as follows:

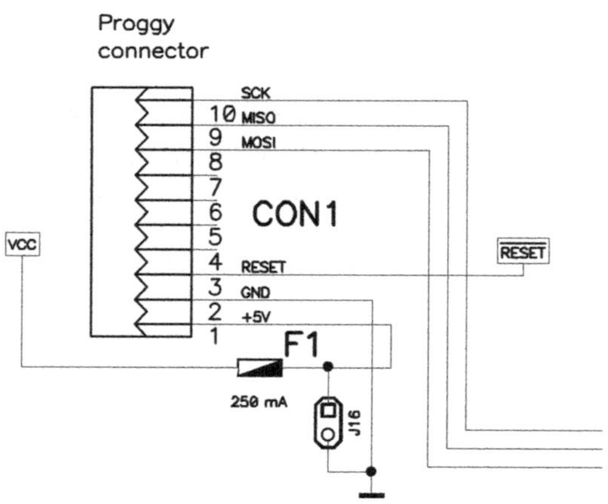

Figure 1: SPI Signals on Proggy IDC connector

The MiniPin II board is powered by the programmer and it has a 250 mA fuse in series with the Vcc power line, to protect your PC's USB port in case you have a short-circuit on your MiniPin II extension board.

Programming AVRs in MiniPin II

MiniPin II can program AVR microcontrollers that are mounted on the MiniPin II board itself - just mount your AVR chip in the appropriate socket, connect your programmer to MiniPin II and your AVR chip is ready for programming.

ISP programming from within AVR Studio 4

Mount your AVR microcontroller in the appropriate socket and click the AVR icon from within the AVR Studio 4 program (Figure2).

Using the **Main** tab, select the microcontroller that you want to program (Figure 3).

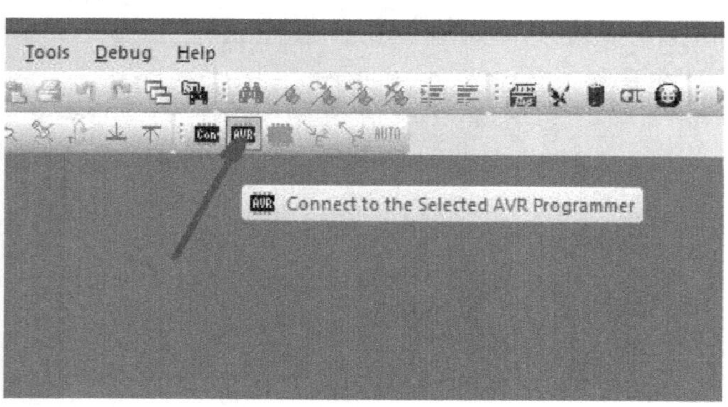

Figure 2: Connect to Programmer icon

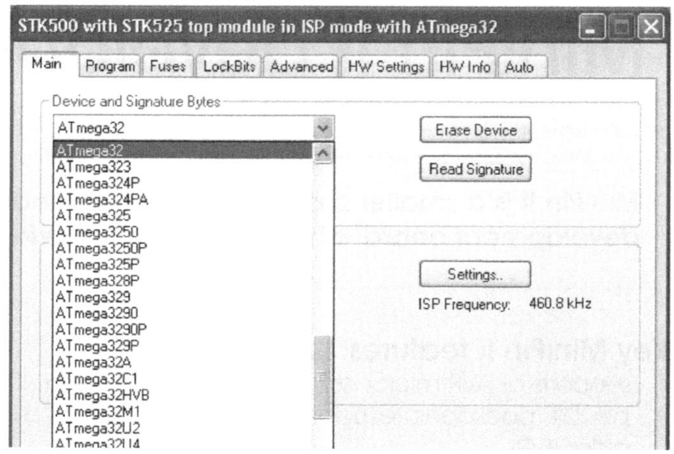

Figure 3: Select microcontroller

To insure that communication is OK, and that you have selected the correct microcontroller, press the **Read Signature button.** If the read signature corresponds to the microcontroller you are programming, then you may proceed with programming. If the signature doesn't match, then select the correct microcontroller from the list. If the program can't even read the microcontroller's signature, then there is something wrong with either the microcontroller, or some connections on the MiniPin II board are wrong (i.e. remove load from PortB).

ISP programming from within Bascom-AVR

Mount your AVR microcontroller in an appropriate socket, and within Bascom-AVR select **Options/Programmer**. A window like that shown in Figure 4 will pop-up.

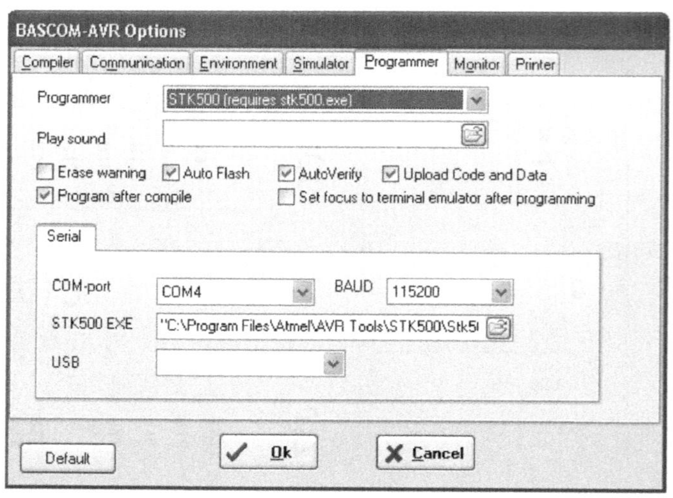

Figure 4: Bascom programming setting

In the **Programmer** window, select STK500 (requires stk500.exe), and set **COM-port** to the same COM port number as seen in the Device Manager program (see the full description regarding this subject in the MegaPin chapter). Then double-click the **folder** icon (to the right of the STK500 EXE window) and select the path to your STK500.exe file (which is usually the same as that shown in Figure 4). Set the Baud rate to 57,600. Click OK and your Bascom-AVR settings are all done.

ISP programming in Bascom-AVR – the STK500 Native driver

Figure 5 shows the proper settings for programming using the **STK500 native driver**.

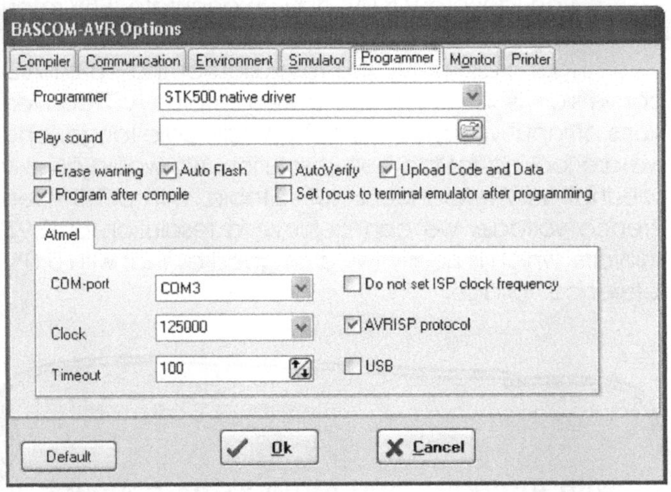

Figure 5: STK500 native programmer settings

1-Wire® sensors

The MiniPin II board has circuitry built-in to allow the use of popular DS18S20 temperature sensors. Please note that three sensors (J10-J12) are individually connected to their own I/O pin while those connected to J13 – J15 share the same I/O pin. For easier programming, sockets are labelled as follows: J10 connects to PortX.0, J 11 connects to PortX.1 etc. All data lines are pulled up to Vcc by 4k7 resistors. Connect CON5 to any I/O port (PortA, PortB, PortC, PortD) with a flat cable and you can now measure temperature with your sensor(s). For a Bascom sample program, please refer to "Bascom-AVR sample programs for use with MiniPin II" at the end of this chapter.

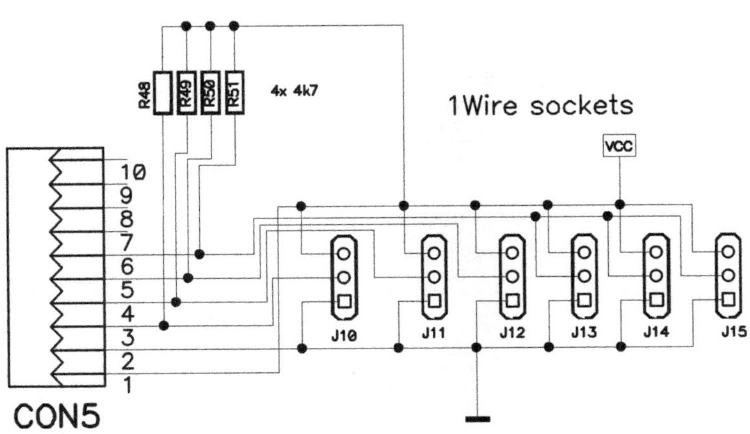

Figure 6: 1-Wire connections

Keyboard

The MiniPin II board has 8 keyswitches built-in, with protection resistors and a connector which allows the user to connect the keyswitches to any free I/O Port connector on MiniPin II.

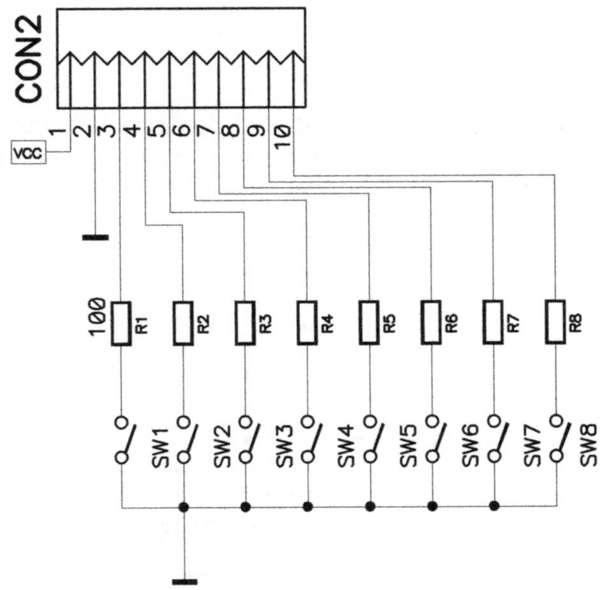

Figure 7

To use the keyswitches, connect CON2 to any I/O port (PortA, PortB, PortC, PortD) with a flat cable.

External Crystal oscillator

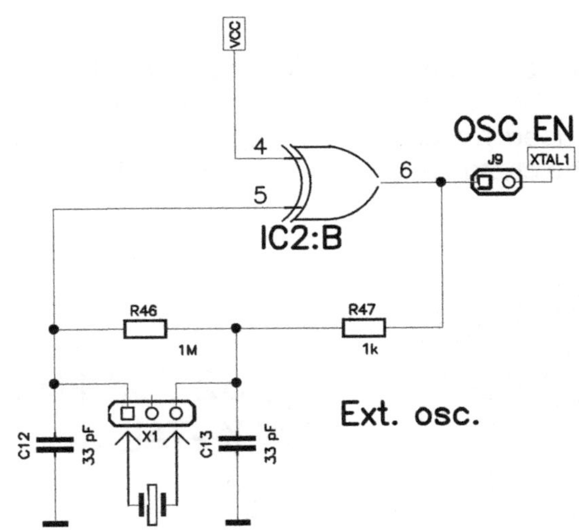

Figure 8

MiniPin II has a built-in External oscillator, where you can mount any crystal from below 1 MHz to up to 16 MHz. The External oscillator can be enabled with jumper J9. When using it with 8-pin AVRs you must also place a jumper at J5.

The external oscillator is very handy to have "on-board" when a microcontroller has its fuse bits

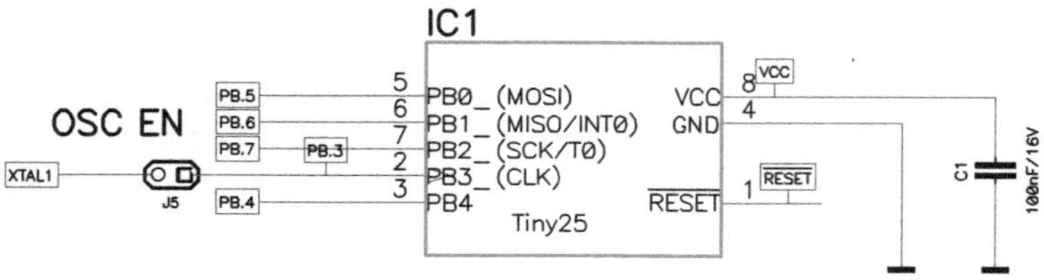

Figure 9

set (usually) accidently to External Oscillator. With the external oscillator enabled (and a crystal placed in socket X2) we can restore a wrongly-programmed AVR.

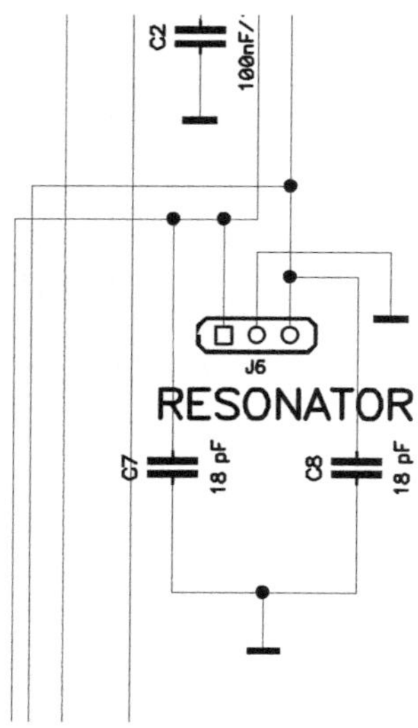

Figure 10

Use of a resonator or Quartz crystal

The MiniPin II board can also use a resonator or XTAL, if it is placed in socket J6. The capacitors needed for use with the crystal are pre-placed on the PCB.

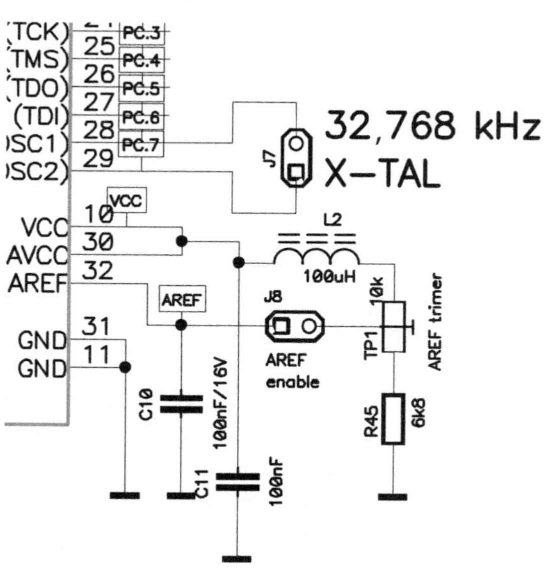

Figure 11

AREF and 32,768 kHz XTAL

The MiniPin II board has a built-in external reference voltage, which can be enabled with jumper J8 (AREF Enable). With the TP1 trimpot, the user can set AREF from nearly 5V down to 2.5 Volts. An external AREF is handy when performing analog to digital conversion (A/D) on voltages between 2.5 and 5.0 Volts. Most AVRs have both a built in Vcc (generally 5.0V) and an accurate 2.5V reference voltage. Using the Vcc reference voltage (generally 5.0V), the resolution of the 10-bit A/D conversion is 4.88 milivolts. If we perform A/D conversions of input voltages in the 3.0 V full-scale range, and we are looking for the best resolution, we would quickly see that a 5V reference is not suitable. With a 3.0 V reference voltage, we can achieve a resolution of 2.93 milivolts, which is nearly twice as good as that with 5.0 V reference voltage.

NOTE

With ATmega8 and ATmega168 connect a 32,768 kHz crystal to socket J6 and set fuse bits to "Ext. Low freq. crystal"!

A 32,768 kHz (watch) crystal is very handy with AVRs that have a Timer2 which can operate in asynchronous mode. With a little Bascom code and 32,768 kHz watch crystal (see RTC chapter), we can make a Real Time Clock with actual date & time and not using too many microcontroller resources. RTC (Real Time Clock) clock routines can also wake-up the AVR microcontroller while in the Powersave mode, thus conserving battery power.

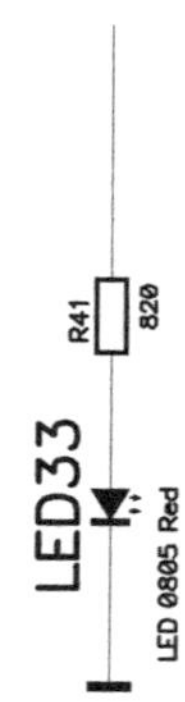

Figure 12

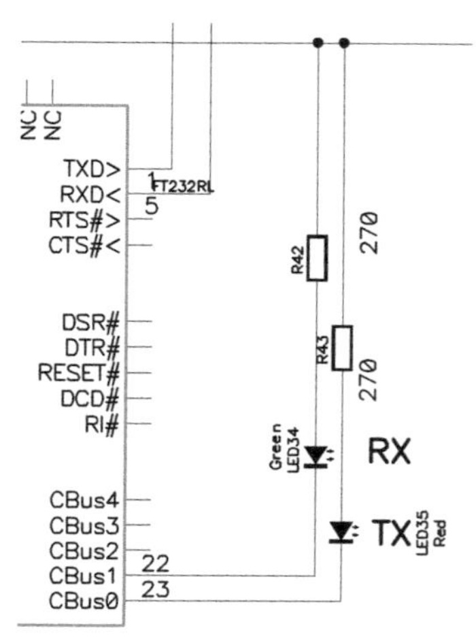

Figure 13

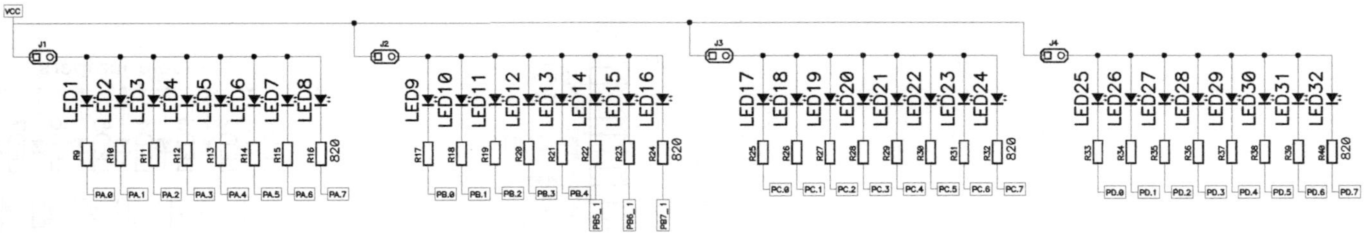

Figure 14

LED signalization

The MiniPin II board features many LEDs:

» Power supply OK,
» Rx/Tx communication,
» 8 LEDs on all four I/O Ports.

Communications

The MiniPin II board supports the following communications methods:

Serial bi-directional communications:
bi-directional communication between the target microcontroller and the USB port using an FT232RL USB bridge.

1-Wire

Place a DS18S20 in any of the sockets J10 to J15, connect CON5 with a flat cable to any Port connector (CON3, CON4, CON6, CON7). Socket J10 corresponds to PortX.0, J11 corresponds to PortX.1 etc. See the 1-Wire sensor section earlier in the chapter for more details.

Example program ID	
Name:	1Wire_1.BAS
Microcontroller:	Any AVR microcontroler
Testing circuit:	Figure 16
MiniPin compatibility:	yes
MegaPin compatibility:	yes
Single 1-Wire sensor on a bus, temperature is displayed on LCD	

Example program ID	
Name:	1Wire_2.BAS
Microcontroller:	Any AVR microcontroler
Testing circuit:	Figure 6
MiniPin compatibility:	yes
MegaPin compatibility:	yes
Program displays 1-Wire ID of two sensors on the bus	

Example program ID	
Name:	1Wire_3.BAS
Microcontroller:	Any AVR microcontroler
Testing circuit:	Figure 6
MiniPin compatibility:	yes
MegaPin compatibility:	yes
Same as 1Wire_2.BAS but ID of sensors are stored in EEPROM	

Example program ID	
Name:	1Wire_4.BAS
Microcontroller:	Any AVR microcontroler
Testing circuit:	Figure 6
MiniPin compatibility:	yes
MegaPin compatibility:	yes
Multiple 1-Wire sensors, one on each Port	

Example program ID	
Name:	For_loop.BAS
Microcontroller:	Any AVR microcontroler
Testing circuit:	/
MiniPin compatibility:	yes
MegaPin compatibility:	yes
Simple FOR-Next loop for testing LEDs on all ports	

Example program ID	
Name:	GLCD_1.BAS
Microcontroller:	ATmega AVRs
Testing circuit:	Figure 1, page 67 (GLCD chapter)
MiniPin compatibility:	yes
MegaPin compatibility:	yes
Use of graphical LCD with table drawn on LCD and 8x8 font	

Example program ID	
Name:	GLCD_2.BAS
Microcontroller:	ATmega AVRs
Testing circuit:	Figure 1, page 67 (GLCD chapter)
MiniPin compatibility:	yes
MegaPin compatibility:	yes
GLCD with fonts that can be placed anywhere on GLCD	

Example program ID	
Name:	GLCD_3.BAS
Microcontroller:	ATmega AVRs
Testing circuit:	Figure 1, page 67 (GLCD chapter)
MiniPin compatibility:	yes
MegaPin compatibility:	yes
GLCD with the use of a touch panel including simple calibration of the touch panel	

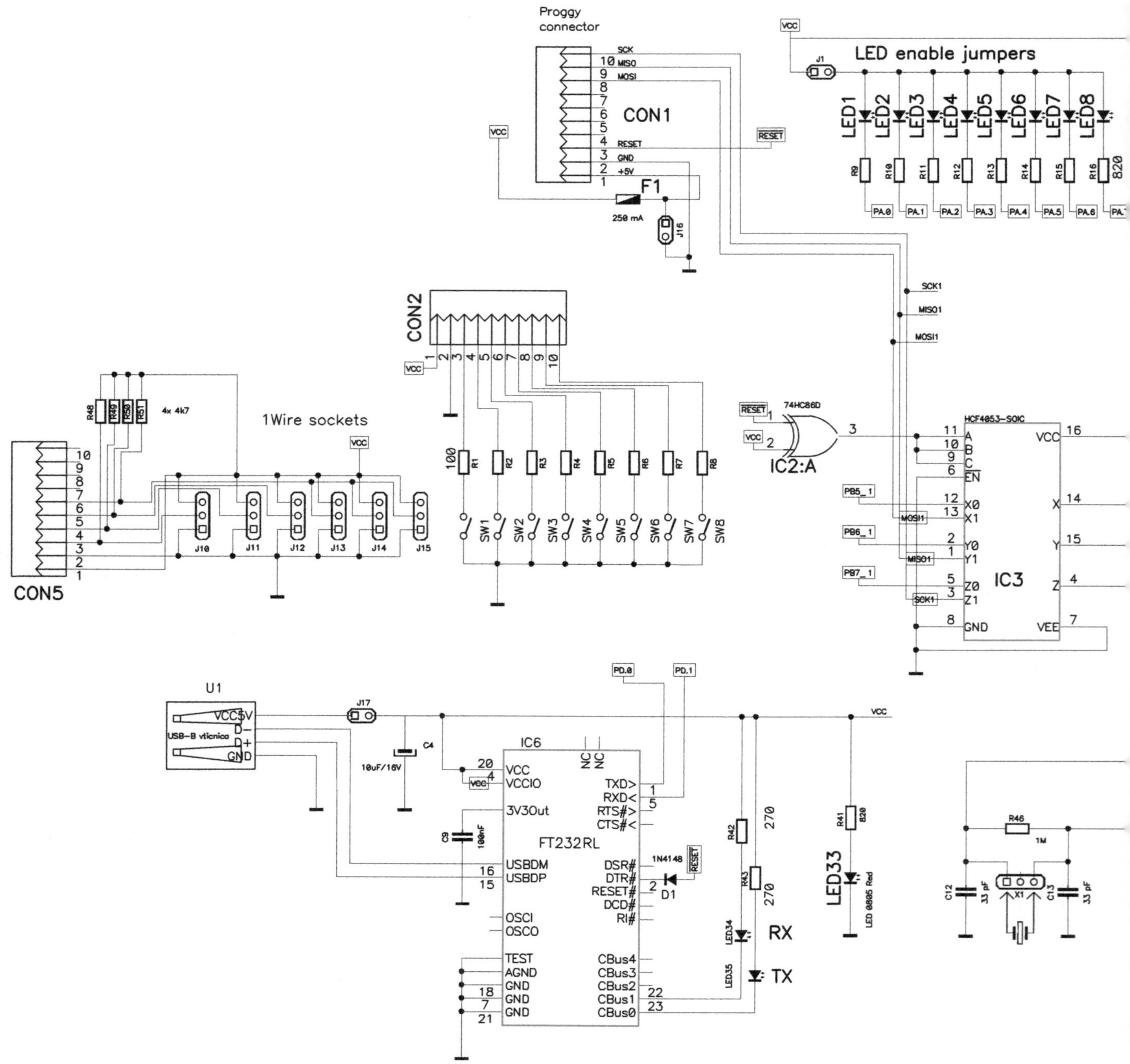
Proggy connector
CON1
SCK
MISO
MOSI
RESET
GND
+5V
F1
250 mA
J16
VCC
LED enable jumpers
J1
LED1
LED2
LED3
LED4
LED5
LED6
LED7
LED8
R9
R10
R11
R12
R13
R14
R15
R16
820
PA.0
PA.1
PA.2
PA.3
PA.4
PA.5
PA.6
SCK1
MISO1
MOSI1
CON2
R48
R49
R50
R51
4x 4k7
1Wire sockets
CON5
J10
J11
J12
J13
J14
J15
100
R1
R2
R3
R4
R5
R6
R7
R8
SW1
SW2
SW3
SW4
SW5
SW6
SW7
SW8
74HC86D
IC2:A
HCF4053-SOIC
IC3
PB5_1
PB6_1
PB7_1
VCC
GND
VEE
U1
USB-B vticnica
VCC5V
D-
D+
GND
J17
C4
10uF/16V
IC6
FT232RL
PD.0
PD.1
VCCIO
3V3Out
C9
100nF
USBDM
USBDP
OSCI
OSCO
TEST
AGND
TXD>
RXD<
RTS#>
CTS#<
DSR#
DTR#
RESET#
DCD#
RI#
CBus4
CBus3
CBus2
CBus1
CBus0
NC
1N4148
D1
R42
R43
270
LED34
LED35
RX
TX
R41
820
LED33
LED 0805 Red
R46
1M
C12
C13
33 pF
X1

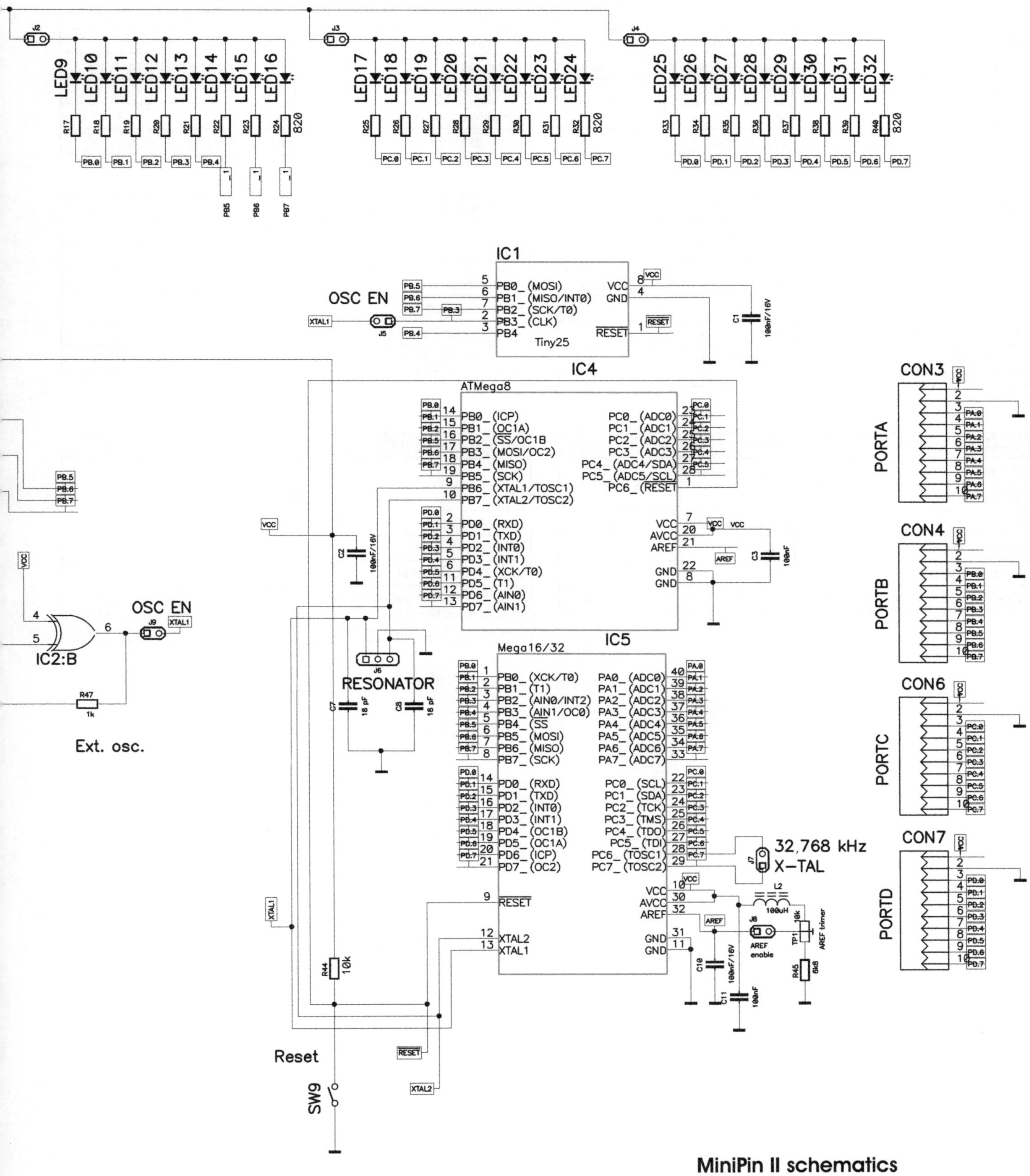

MiniPin II schematics

Example program ID	
Name:	GLCD_4.BAS
Microcontroller:	ATmega AVRs
Testing circuit:	Figure 1, page 67 (GLCD chapter)
MiniPin compatibility:	yes
MegaPin compatibility:	yes
GLCD with improved calibration for the touch panel	

Example program ID	
Name:	LCD8x2.bas
Microcontroller:	Any AVR microcontroler
Testing circuit:	Figure 1, page 67 (GLCD chapter)
MiniPin compatibility:	yes
MegaPin compatibility:	yes
Simple program to display characters on blue 8x2 LCD, including PWM for controlling backlight	

Example program ID	
Name:	Megaclock.bas
Microcontroller:	ATmega AVRs
Testing circuit:	Figure 1, page 67 (GLCD chapter)
MiniPin compatibility:	yes
MegaPin compatibility:	yes
Clock with 32,768 kHz XTAL and 8x2 LCD	

Example program ID	
Name:	Megaclock1.bas
Microcontroller:	ATmega AVRs
Testing circuit:	Figure 1, page 67 (GLCD chapter)
MiniPin compatibility:	yes
MegaPin compatibility:	yes
Same as Megaclock.bas with simple routines to set hour/min/sec	

Example program ID	
Name:	PWM1.bas
Microcontroller:	ATmega AVRs
Testing circuit:	/
MiniPin compatibility:	yes
MegaPin compatibility:	yes
Simple PWM routine using the hardware PWM in the AVR MCU	

Example program ID	
Name:	USB-ADC2.bas
Microcontroller:	AVRs with ADC
Testing circuit:	/
MiniPin compatibility:	yes
MegaPin compatibility:	yes
Acquires an analogue voltage and converts it with the A/D, then transmits it to both the USB and to LCD. You can see the value of the voltage in the Terminal window within Bascom-AVR	

MegaPin development board

By Jurij Mikeln

MegaPin is a modern development board built upon the experience of many microcontroller programmers. It's user-friendly, very compact and yet offers many possibilities in developing microcontroller programs.

Key features:

» supports 8-pin, 20-pin, 28-pin and 40-pin DIL AVRs,
» supports AT90USB1287 USB AVR microcontroller,
» built-in fast USB 2.0 programmer,
» in-circuit programming of target microcontroller,
» supports JTAG programming/debugging*,
» powered from USB or 12V DC,
» protection from wrong polarity,
» power supply for target microcontroller is 3,3 or 5 V,
» power-on LED,
» programmed OK LED,
» built in UART<>USB communication,
» 4x8 LEDs to indicate status of I/O ports,
» 6x 1-Wire® DS18S20 sockets,
» built-in MicroSD memory card socket,
» 8 independent buttons which can be connected to any I/O port,
» built-in protection resistors on each button,
» built-in crystal oscillator (crystal not mounted),
» built-in socket for 32,768 kHz RTC quartz crystal for ATmega 8/16/32,
» built-in socket for ceramic resonator,
» built-in trimmer for setting external AREF voltage,
» built-in socket for STK200 input/output,
» expansion sockets for PortA, PortB, PortB, PortD, PortE, PortF,
» RESET button.
» JTAG not supported whit MegaPin B

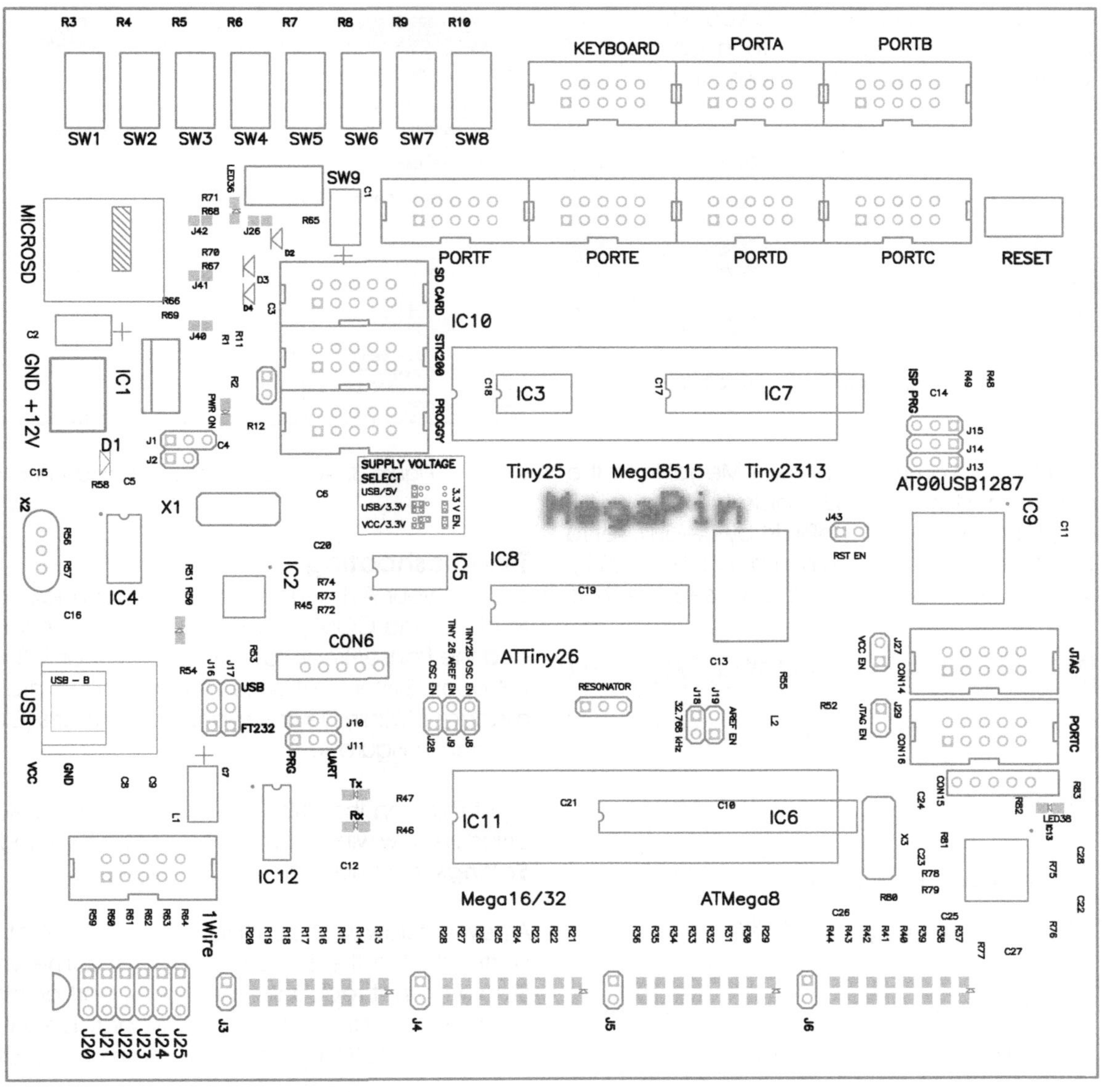

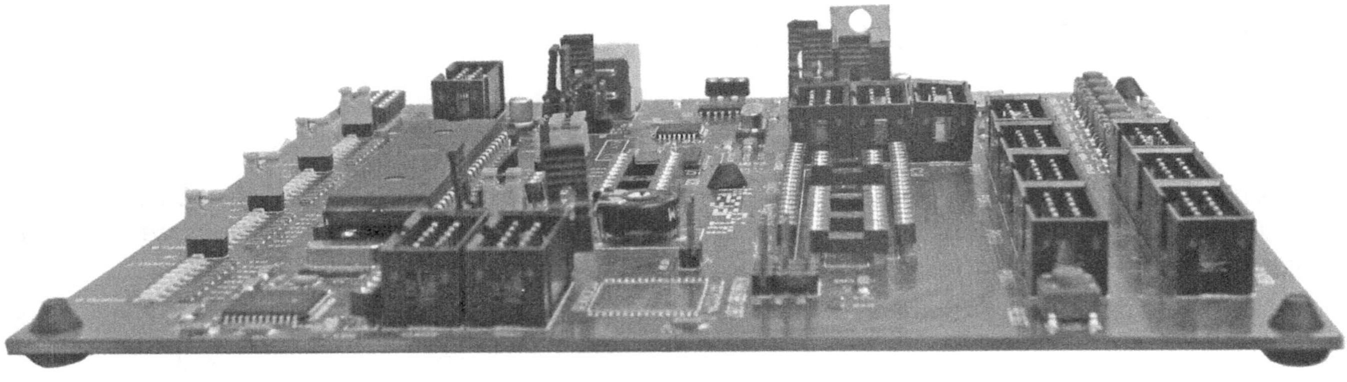

The MegaPin development board for AVR microcontrollers supports all 8-pin, 20-pin, 28-pin and 40-pin DIL AVRs, including with AT90USB1287 USB AVR. MegaPin features jumpers which select the USB connection: using either the built-in FT232RL chip or directly to an AT90USB1287, which includes its own USB port. With the help of Bascom's USB Add-on Library, one can make their own USB chips. In case you need your own VID or PID numbers, you can order them from the MCS company.

The Initial connection of MegaPin to USB

The first time you connect MegaPin to your PC system, it will likely inform you that you have to install drivers. If this is the case, you can install them from the FTDI driver folder.

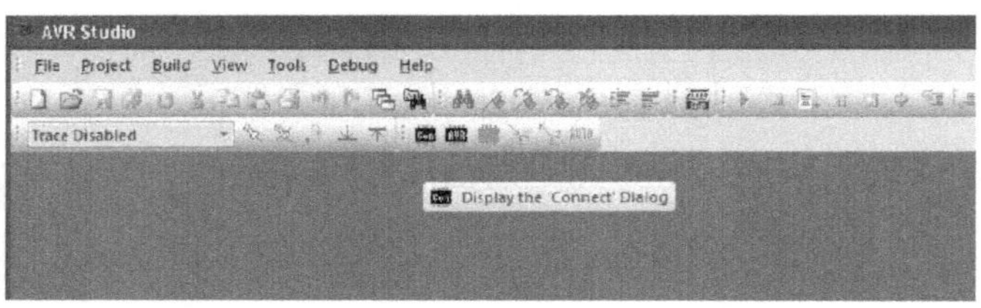

Figure 1: Connecting MegaPin to AVR Studio 4

When Setup finishes, you may connect MegaPin to the PC's USB port via a standard USB cable (such as a USB printer cable, for example). MegaPin is, by default, set to use the FTDI USB chip FT232RL (with jumpers J16 & J17). When you plug in the USB cable, you will see the Rx & Tx LEDs flash a few times. This indicates that the FTDI USB chip has successfully connected MegaPin to the PC's USB port.

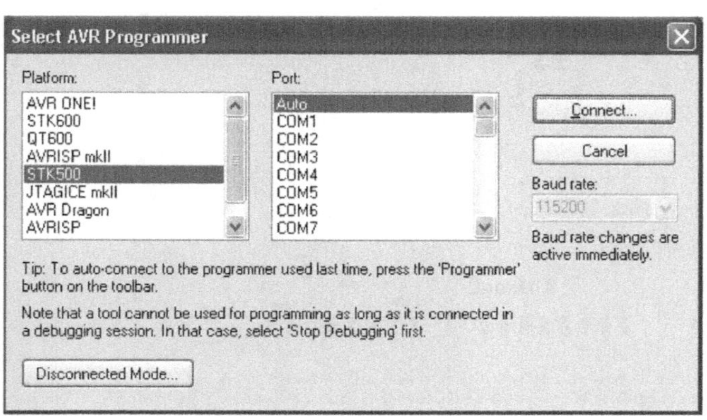

Figure 2: Select platform

Connect MegaPin with AVR Studio 4 as you would normally do, by pressing the CON button (see Figure 1). A new window will open, see Figure 2.

Select STK500, leave Port on "Auto" and press "Connect" button. The Rx & Tx LEDs should flash quickly and the AVR Studio window should appear as seen in Figure 3.

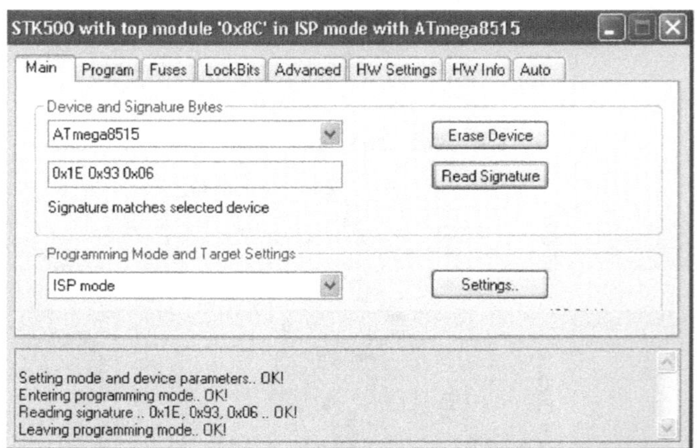

Figure 3: AVR Studio programming window

Troubleshooting

In case your AVR Studio does not connect, you'll have to check the COM port. Press and hold the Window key and the Pause/Break key on your keyboard. This shortcut will open System- choose Hardware and press Device manager. Within Device manager find Ports (COM & LPT) as seen in Figure 4.

Right-Click on the USB Serial Port entry and select "Properties". A new window will open (Figure 5). Select the ***Port Settings*** tab and within click "Advanced".

A new window will open (Figure 6). While all of the COM ports listed in the List Box are valid, some versions of Studio do not recognize any COM port above 9. Therefore select an available COM port below 9. When doing this, MS Windows® may inform you that the port

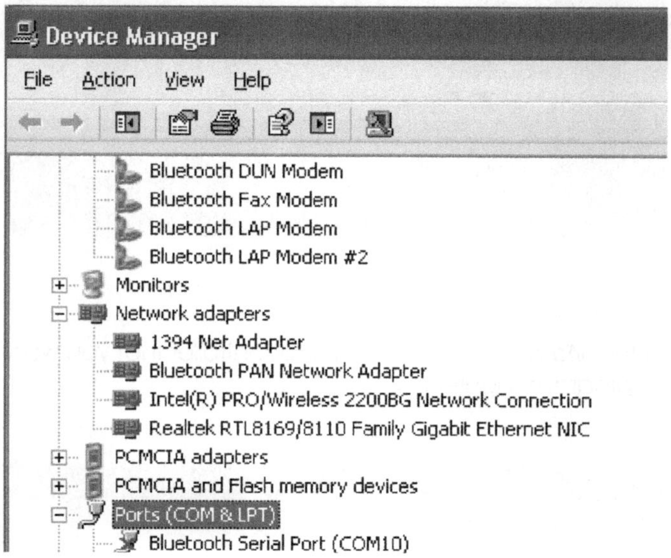

Figure 4: Device manager

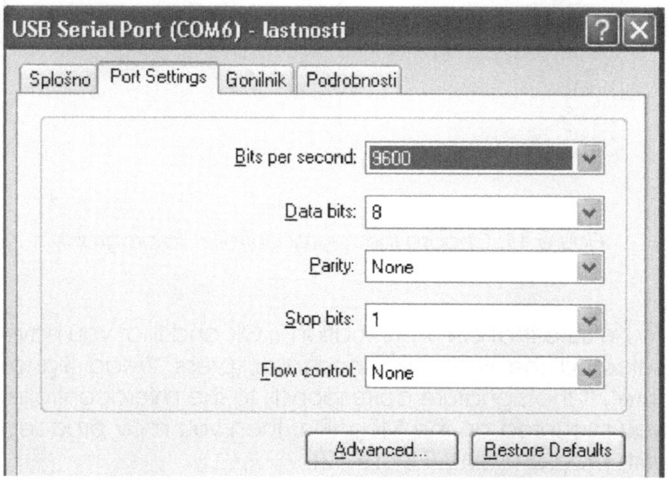

Figure 5: USB Port settings

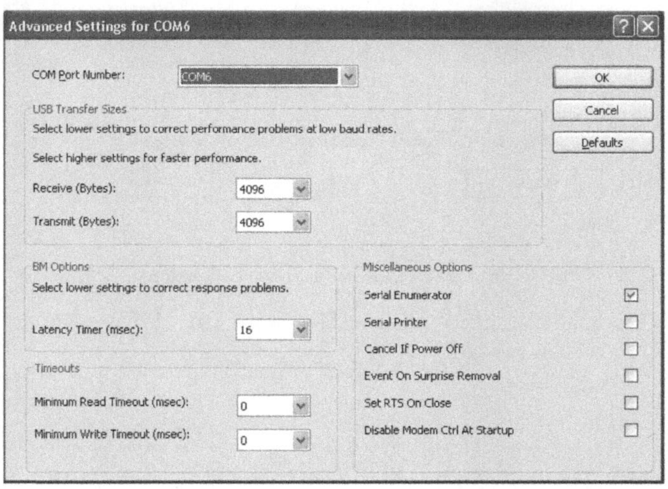

Figure 6: Set COM port

you have chosen is already in use, even though you may think it is not. This happens because MS Windows® "remembers" what COM port it has assigned to

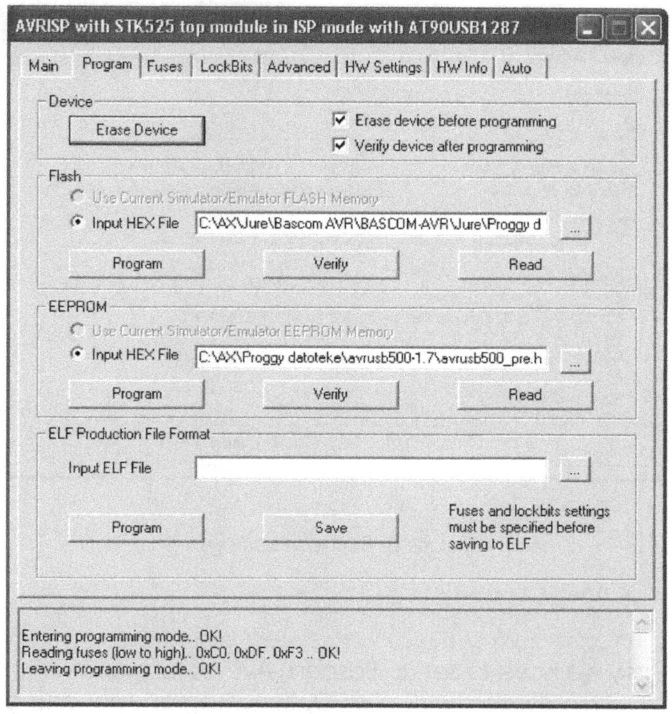

Figure 7: AVR Studio programming window

any USB-COM port bridge devices you have connected in the past, even though they are not currently plugged in, and which may no longer be used.

MegaPin use

When AVR Studio connects to MegaPin a new window will appear (Figure 7).

Within this window we can program the microcontroller and set Fuse and Lock bits. More details follow in the Programming chapter.

Programming

MegaPin has two built-in programmers and can function as an ISP or a JTAG programmer. If the user wants to use an AT90USB1287 USB AVR, it can be programmed on MegaPin with Atmel's FLIP™ program too. Here are the available programming modes:

a. programming directly from Bascom-AVR,
b. programming from AVR Studio,
c. programming with the FLIP™ program,
d. programming with an external Proggy II programmer,
e. programming with STK200 compatible programmer via parallel port,
f. programming via the JTAG interface.

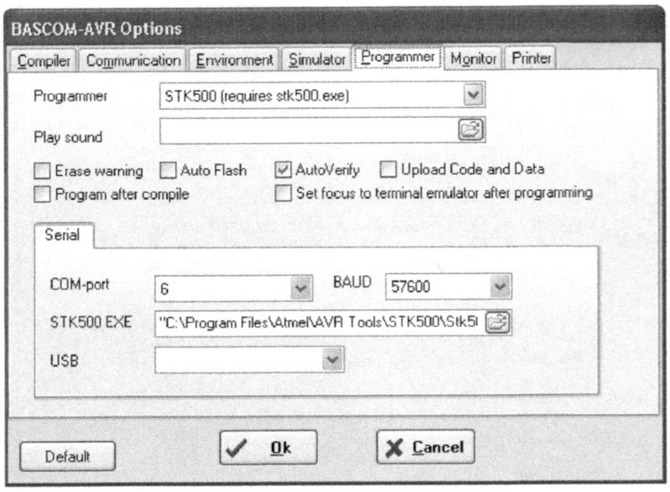

Figure 8: Bascom settings

a. Programming directly from Bascom-AVR

Firstly we have to set-up Bascom-AVR as follows:

» within Bascom-AVR click Options/Programmer and a new window (Figure 8) will open.

» In the ***Programmer*** selection window, choose STK500, as seen in the Figure 8. Set COM-port to same value that you saw in Device manager, as described earlier. In the next line, click the file folder icon and choose the path where the STK500.exe file is located on your PC. Normally it's at: C:\Program Files\Atmel\AVR Tools\STK500. The BAUD value should not be changed! Click OK and Bascom is ready for programming.

When you want to program from Bascom simply right-click and the window shown in Figure 9 will appear. Click Program and Bascom will automatically program the microcontroller.

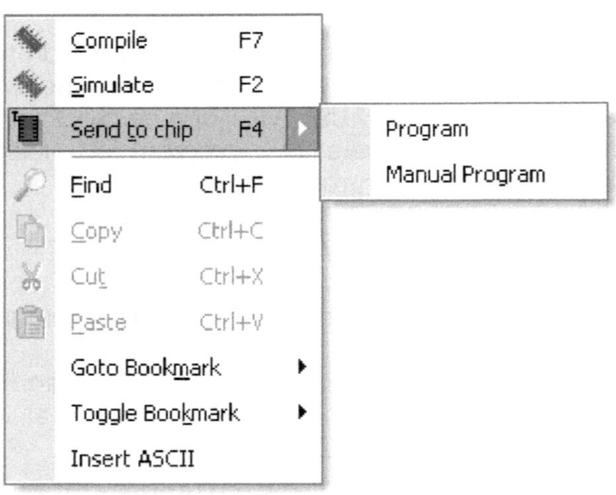

Figure 9: Right-clicking in Bascom-AVR shows this window

b. Programming from AVR Studio 4

Set J16 & J17 to FT232 position, set J10 & J11 to PRG position, place the AVR microcontroller in the appropriate socket and click the AVR icon as shown in Figure 10.

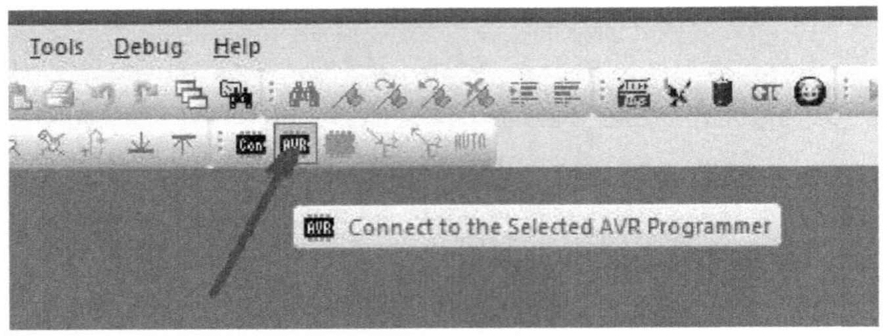

Figure 10: Connecting to AVR Studio 4

In the ***Main*** tab select the microcontroller that you want to program (Figure 11).

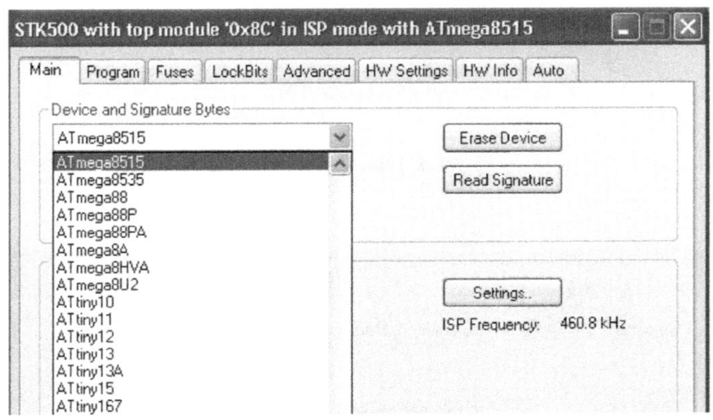

Figure 11: Choose the microcontroller to program

To be sure that communication is OK and that you have selected the right microcontroller, press "Read Signature". If the signature corresponds to the microcontroller you mounted on the MegaPin, then you may proceed with programming (Figure 12).

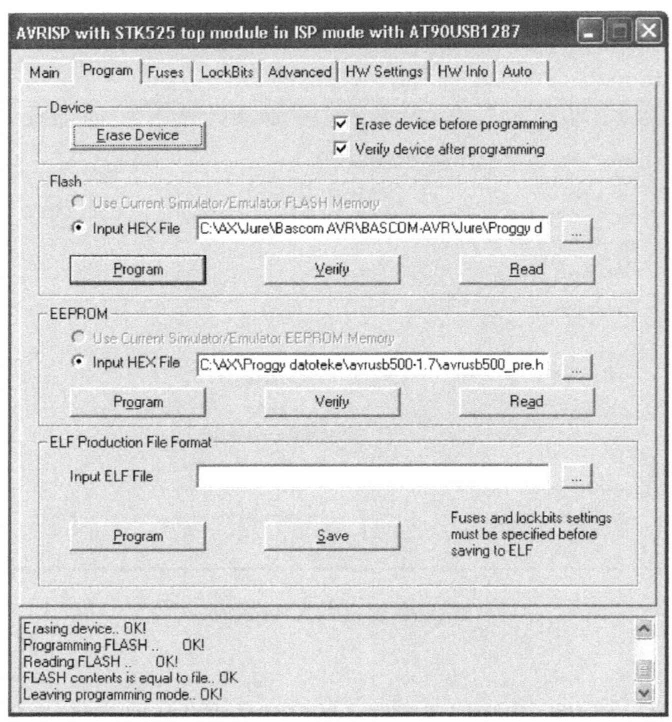

Figure 12: AVR Studio 4 programming window

If the signature does ***not*** match the selected device, select the correct device from the list.

Click on the button with 3 dots (...) (see Figure 12) to select the file containing the program that we want to program into the microcontroller and then click ***Program***. In the lower part of the window you will see a message that microcontroller was correctly programmed.

If you want to restore the Bootloader program, download it from Atmel's web page or write an email to AX elektronika and we will send it to you via email free of charge. When programming the Bootloader, set BOOTSZ Fuse bits to the highest possible value.

In the same ***Program*** tab you can also program the EEPROM and ELF production files.

To set Fuse bits, click tab ***Fuses***. You will see a window as shown in Figure 13.

The Fuse bits set the working mode of the microcontroller in the following ways:

- BODLEVEL: sets voltage for Brownout reset-a. Several voltages can be selected,
- HWBE: Hardware boot enable,
- OCDEN: On Chip Debug Enable: enables debugging on a chip,

ATTENTION

When programming AVR USB microcontrollers within AVR Studio, you will erase the USB Bootloader program!

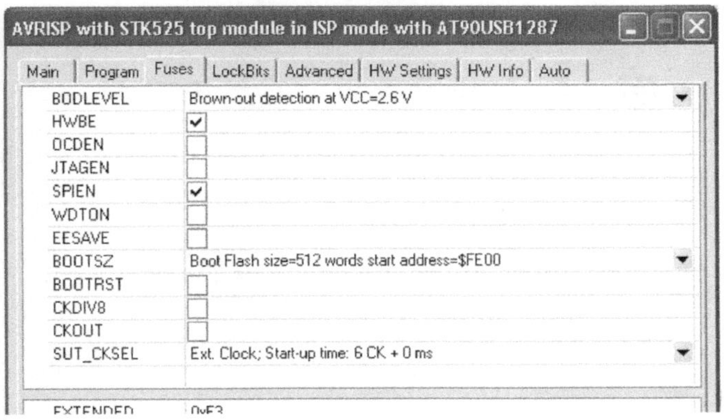

Figure 13: AVR Studio 4 fusebits window

- JTAGEN: enable JTAG interface,
- SPIEN: enables the SPI interface. ***(ATTENTION! This tick should not be removed under any circumstances!*** If you will remove it you will disable the SPI ISP programming mode of the microcontroller!)
- WDTON: enable Watchdog timer,
- EESAVE: leaves the EEPROM content intact during microcontroller programming,
- BOOTSZ: sets aside memory space intended for the Bootloader,
- BOOTRST: enable boot reset vector,
- CKDIV8: enables system clock divide by 8,
- CKOUT: enables clock generation on PORTC.7,
- SUT_CKSEL: choose system clock source (RC internal, RC external, external oscillator ...).

Lockbits tab

Within this tab are options allowing you to lock the microcontroller by clicking LB (see Figure 14).

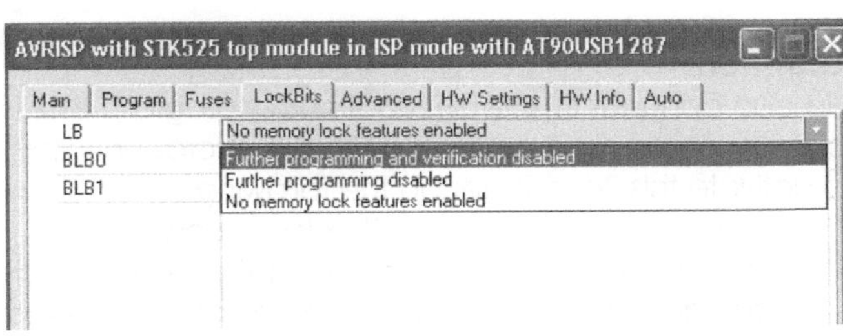

Figure 14: AVR Studio 4 lockbits window

Choose »Further programming and verification disabled«. By clicking the ***Program*** button we have locked the microcontroller's program memory from being observed by other individuals, using a programmer.

c. Programming with FLIP™

The FLIP™ Program can be downloaded from Atmel's web page. FLIP is simple program interface allowing the programming of Atmel microcontrollers with embedded USB or CAN interfaces (see Figure 15).

If you press the USB connection icon (or CTRL+U) a new window opens, and FLIP connects to your microcontroller (see Figure 16).

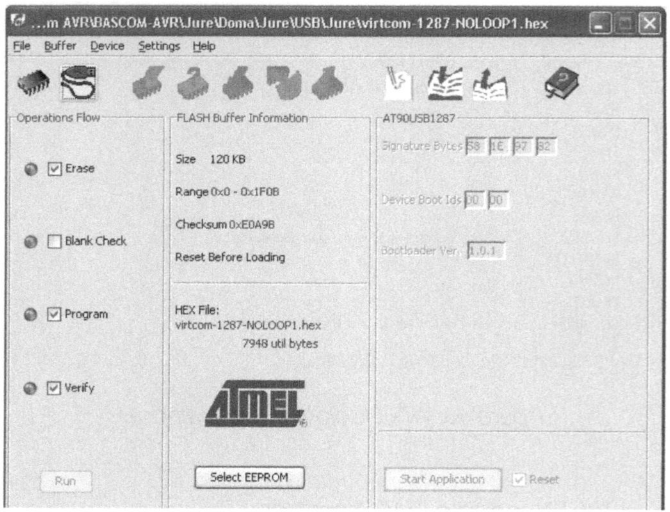

Figure 15: FLIP window

NOTE

Fuse and Lock bits cannot be programmed with Flip!

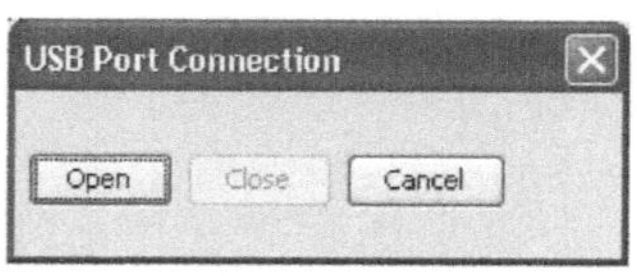

Figure 16: Connect to FLIP

Attention!

Flip can connect to the USB Bootloader program that is factory programmed into all AVR USB microcontrollers. To activate this Bootloader do the following:

- Connect a switch from PORTE.2 to ground,
- Press both the PORTE.2 switch and the Reset switch together, and then release the Reset switch followed by the PORTE.2 switch.

The above procedure starts the USB Bootloader within the AT90USB1287. Now you can click ***Open*** and start using Flip for programming. Click ***File*** and choose the program to be programmed into the microcontroller. Then click ***Run*** which starts the programming process. After programming is complete, click ***Start application*** (with Reset ticked). That will reset the microcontroller and start running your program in the target microcontroller.

NOTE

In order for the AT90USB1287 to perform correctly, it needs an 8 MHz quartz crystal (for the USB port), which should be placed at footprint X2. Also connect a jumper at J28.

NOTE

When programming the AT90USB1287 with the Flip programmer, the AT90USB1287 USB Bootloader is not erased!

ISP programmer for the AT90USB1287

Jumper position:

- Set J16 & J17 to USB position,
- close J43,
- set J10 & J11 to PRG position,
- J13, J14 & J15 to ISP position,

click AVR button within Studio 4. The AT90USB1287 AVR microcontroller must have been previously soldered to the MegaPin board. In tab Main select micro controller AT90USB1287 (see Figure 11).

To insure that communication is OK and that you have selected the correct microcontroller press Read Signature. If the signature read matches the AT90USB1287 then you may proceed with programming. If it doesn't, then double-check that the AT90USB1287 is soldered in correctly, and check to make sure jumpers J16 & J17 are set to USB (the settings of J10 & J11 don't matter).

NOTE

If your PC does not already have a USB driver for AVR USB microcontrollers, you can find it in the FLIP/Driver folder.

Important!

If you program the AT90USB1287 with ISP, you will erase the factory programmed USB Bootloader, which means you can't program the microcontroller using the USB Bootloader! However, you can always restore the USB Bootloader to the AT90USB1287 using the ISP programmer. The USB Bootloader firmware can be found on Atmel's web page.

USB programmer for the AT90USB1287

On the MegaPin board, set J16 & J17 to USB position, (the settings of J10 & J11 do not matter). The AT90USB1287 AVR microcontroller should already be mounted on the MegaPin board. From within AVR studio 4, click the FLIP button. A new window will open (see Figure 15). Click the Icon showing a USB cable or press Ctrl + U to open Connect window (see Figure 16).

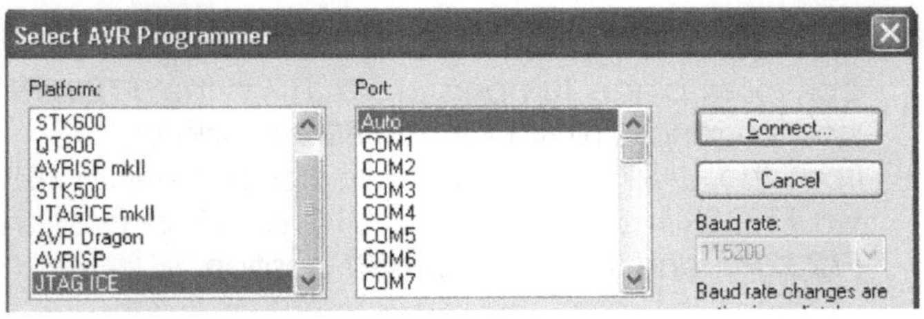

Figure 17: Connect AVR Studio 4 to MegaPin JTAG programmer

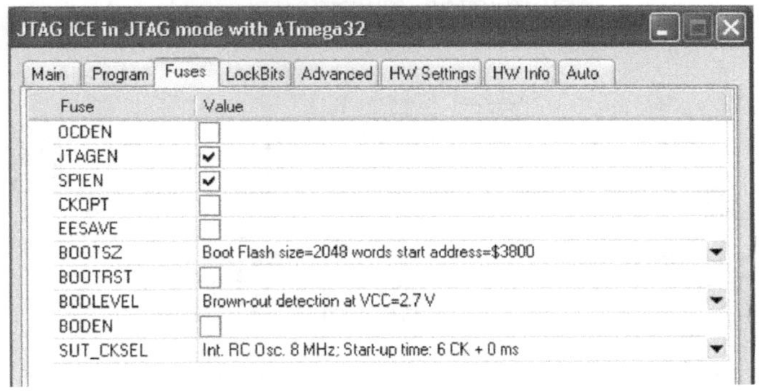

Figure 18: JTAG ICE programmer

d. Programming devices with external Proggy II

Programming with an external Proggy II programmer is simple: just connect the Proggy II IDC connector to CON4 (PROGGY), start AVR Studio 4 and follow the procedure described earlier by using Studio 4 or Bascom-AVR program.

e. Programming devices with STK200 interface

MegaPin can program external boards that are equipped with an STK200 interface. Connect a 10-pin IDC flat cable female connector to STK200 connector (CON3) on MegaPin, while other end of the cable should be connected to target board. You can now start programming!

f. Programming devices with Proggy II

MegaPin has built-in Proggy II support. Connect a 10-pin IDC flat cable female connector to the PROGGY connector on MegaPin, and connect the other end of the cable to the target board. You can now start programming!

g. Programming devices with JTAG interface

To enable JTAG programming of AVR devices connect jumpers JTAG EN and VCC EN, disconnect jumper J11, connect PORTC of your AVR device with socket CON16 (PORTC) using the supplied flat cable. Next click the ***CON*** icon in AVR Studio 4. See Figure 1, and Select ***JTAG ICE*** on the left and ***Auto*** on the right.

Now click "Connect", RX & Tx LEDs will blink few times and quickly you will see similar programming interface as you may know from ISP programming (see Figure 18).

NOTE

The target microcontroller must have its JTAG fuse programmed, as shown. If this is not the case you will see window shown in Figure 19.

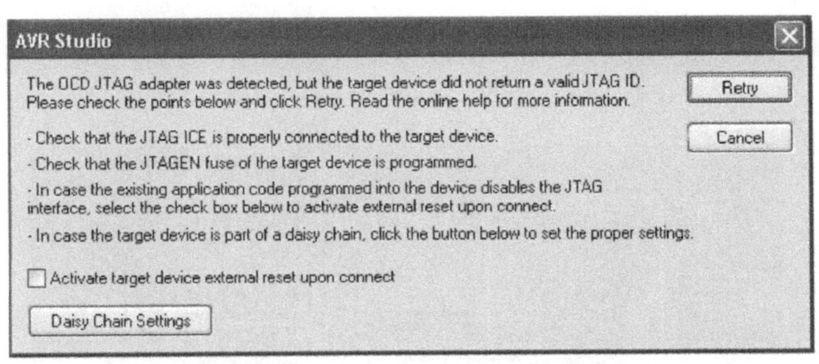

Figure 19: This window also opens also if we did not connect PORTC and CON16 using the supplied cable

Power supply options

The MegaPin board has several options to supply the target microcontroller (see Figure 20) with different voltages and supports several different input voltage sources:

- USB as the power supply
  - The MegaPin board can be powered from USB directly. The Target microcontroller can be powered with either 5V or 3.3V. For details see Table 1,
- 12 V DC as the power supply
  - The MegaPin board can be powered from an external 12V power supply. The target microcontroller can be powered with either 5V or 3.3V. For details see Table 1.

Meaning of status LEDs

The MegaPin board features several status LEDs:

- Power supply OK,

Power source /Jumper	J1	J2	J7	Target Vcc (V)
USB	Shorted pins 1 of both jumpers together		open	5 V
USB	pin 1,2	pin 1,2	short	3.3 V
12 VDC	pin 2,3	pin 1,2	open	5 V
12 VDC	pin 2,3	pin 1,2	short	3.3 V

Table 1: Jumper positions for different supply and target voltages. Pin 1 is square shaped

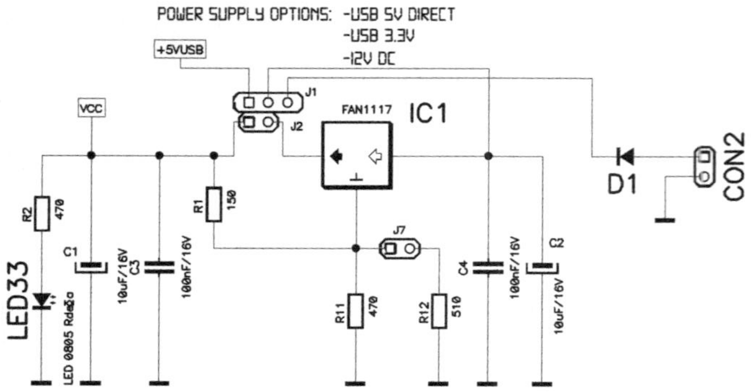

Figure 20: MegaPin has built-in protection against the application of the wrong polarity on CON2

» from USB through the FT232RL to the target microcontroller: place Jumpers J16 & J17 in the ***FT232RL*** position, and J10 & 11 to the ***PRG*** position,

» from the UART of the target microcontroller to USB via FT232RL: place Jumpers J16 & J17 in position ***FT232RL***, and J10 & 11 to ***UART*** position.

Serial-USB using the AT90USB1287

Serial via AT90USB1287 to USB:

» place Jumpers J16 & J17 in position ***USB*** (J10 & 11 do not matter).

1-Wire sensors

» Place a DS18S20 in any of the sockets J20 to J25,

» microcontroller programmed successfully,

» Rx/Tx communication,

» MicroSD card removed,

» 8 LEDs on four I/O Ports.

Communication

The MegaPin board features several communication modes:

» serial-USB using a FT232RL bridge,

» serial-USB using the AT90USB1287,

» 1-Wire®

» JTAG using the built-in JTAG interface.

Serial-USB using a FT232RL bridge

Serial communication via the FT232RL flows in two directions (Figure 21):

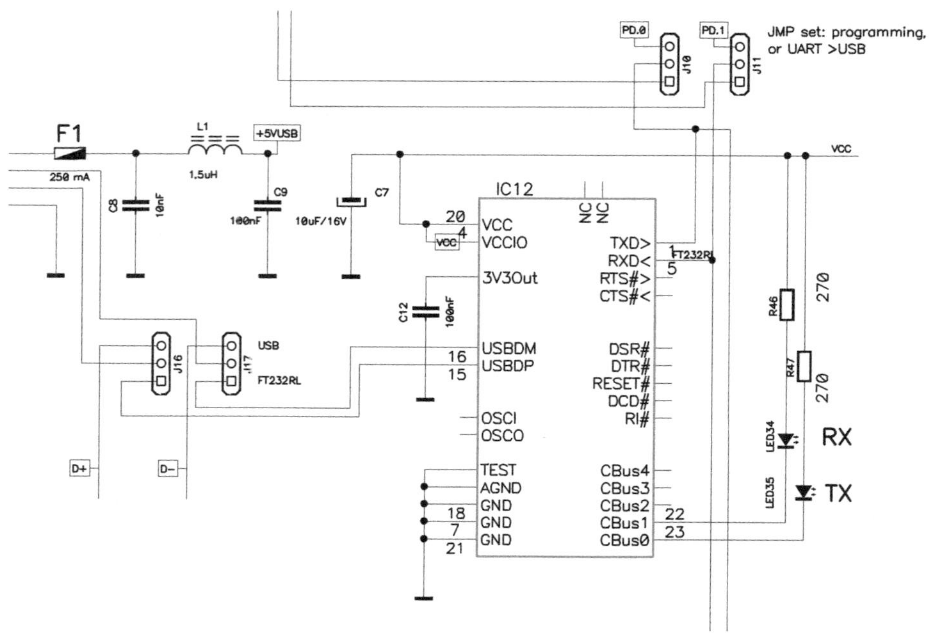

Figure 21: Communication circuit on MegaPin

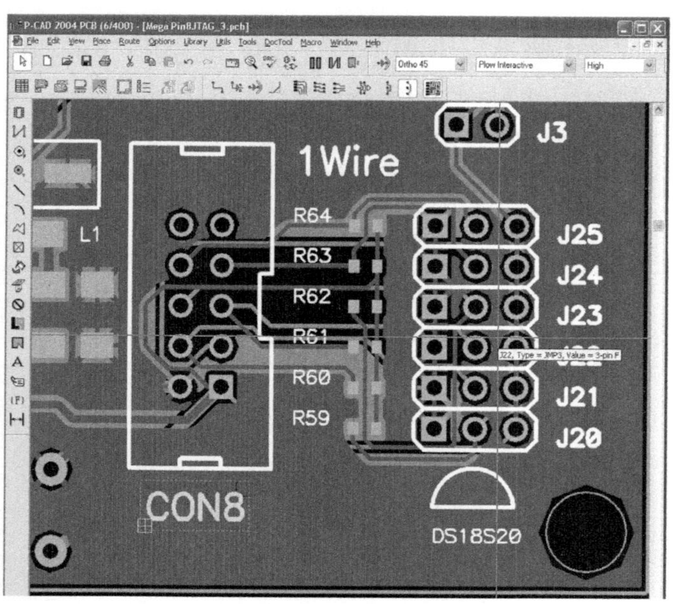

Figure 22: Correct placement of DS18S20 on the MegaPin board

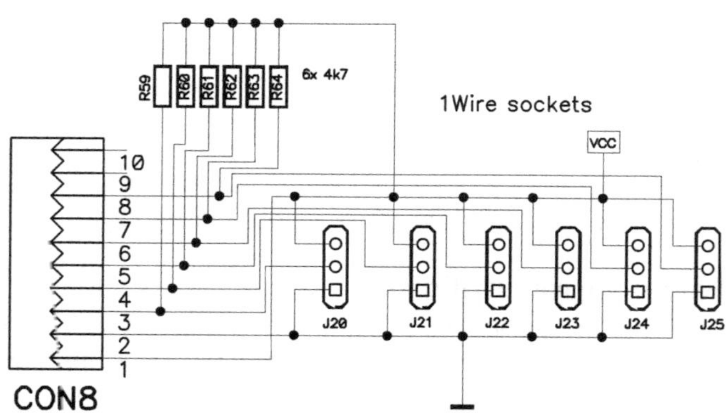

Figure 23: 1-Wire sensor circuitry on MegaPin

connect CON8 with a flat cable to any Port connector (CON5, CON7, CON10, CON11, CON12, CON13), see Figure 22. Socket J20 corresponds to PortX.0, J21 corresponds to PortX.1 etc.

MegaFin has sockets and circuitry built-in for the popular DS18S20 temperature sensors (Figure 23). Please note that each sensor socket is attached to its own I/O port pin. For easier programming, sockets are numbered as follows: J20 corresponds to PortX.0, J21 corresponds to PortX.1 etc. All sockets have 4k7 pull-up resistors. Connect CON8 to any I/O port (PortA, PortB, PortC, PortD, PortE, PortF) with flat cable and measure temperature with your sensor.

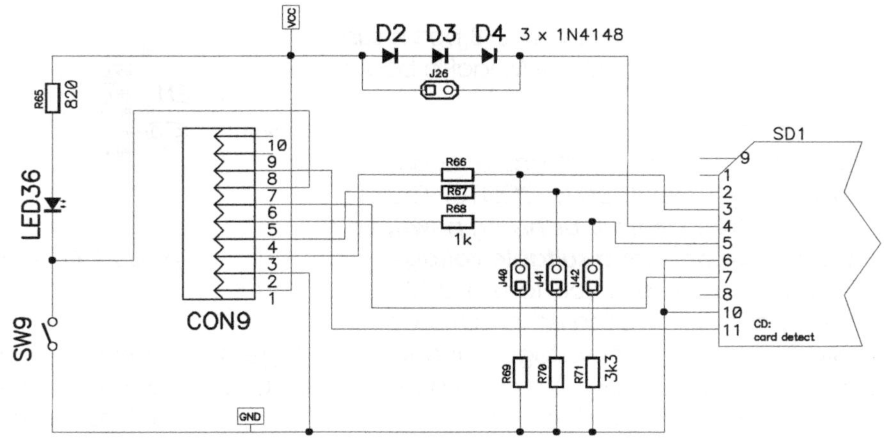

Figure 24: SD card socket on MegaPin

MicroSD card

The MegaPin board has a built-in MicroSD memory card socket. MicroSD memory cards all operate at 3.3V only, so please read this section carefully to make sure you use the MicroSD memory card correctly.

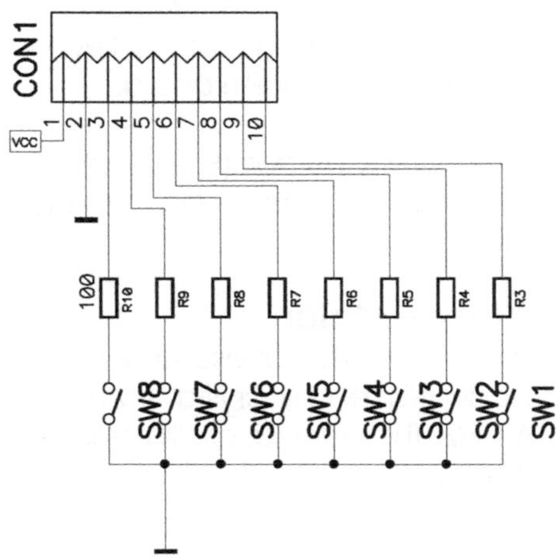

Figure 25: Keyboard on MegaPin

Possible problems

The part of the circuit shown in Figure 24, which supplies power to the Micro SD card socket, can result in problems accessing the SD card, if the following three conditions are all present:

» the MegaPin board is running with a Vcc of 5V,
» that 5V is supplied by the USB port (i.e. not an external power source),
» your PC is supplying 4.5V or less to the MegaPin board, via its USB host port. This voltage may vary somewhat over the time, depending upon several factors such as how many USB devices are plugged into your PC, the length and quality of the USB cable, etc.

If the above conditions are present, and you are experiencing SD card access problems, short out diode D2, by soldering a short jumper wire across its two terminals. Make sure that you don't bridge any adjacent component leads when you solder this wire in place.

Diode D2 can be located in the PCB component layout drawing, Figure 24 near jumper J26.

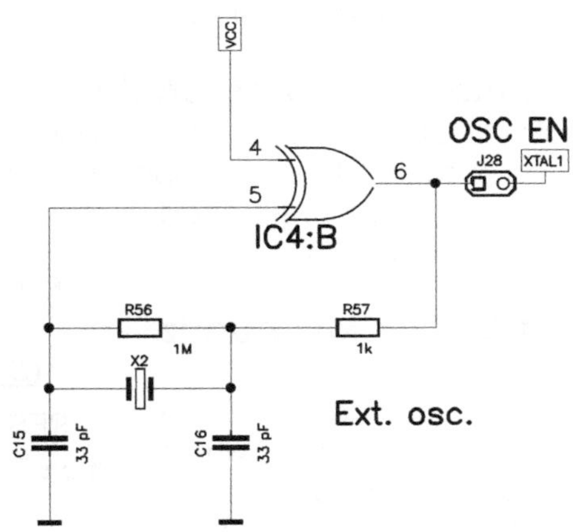

Figure 26: External oscillator on MegaPin

WARNING

All mentioned Jumpers (J26, J49, J41 and J42) are just PCB footprints so they need to have wires soldered in place.

Don't do this procedure if your USB port is supplying the normal 5.0V to the MegaPin board!

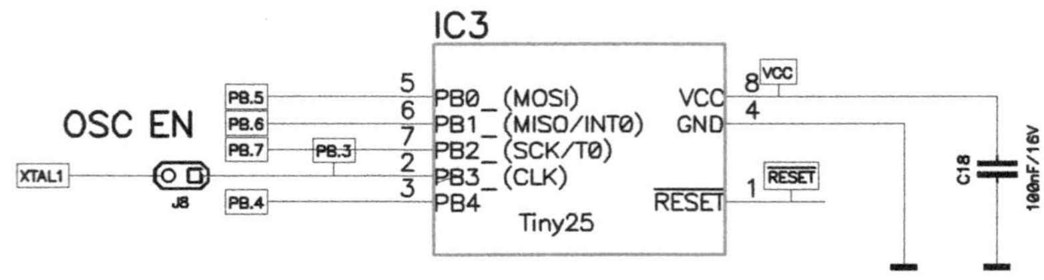

Figure 27: External oscillator connection to 8-pin AVRs

Keyboard

Connect CON9 with a flat cable to any Port connector (CON5, CON7, CON10, CON11, CON12, CON13). ***Before applying power you must choose and set a suitable voltage***. The MegaPin board allows you to use a MicroSD memory card when using either a 5.0 V or 3.3 V target Microcontroller voltage. If the target voltage is 5.0 V, then leave jumper J26 open and close jumpers J40, J41 and J42 (default setting).

If the target voltage is 3.3V then close jumper J26 and leave J40, J41 and J42 open, as seen in Figure 24.

The MegaPin board has a built-in 8 switch keyboard (see Figure 25) with protective resistors and a connector which allows the user to connect the keyboard to any free connector on the MegaPin board.

Connect CON1 to any I/O port (PortA, PortB, PortC, PortD, PortE, PortF) with a flat cable and use the keyboard where needed.

External Xtal oscillator

MegaPin has built-in External oscillator (see Figure 26), where you can place any crystal from below 1 MHz to up to 16 MHz. The external oscillator is enabled with jumper J28. When using it with 8-pin AVRs also enable jumper J8 (see Figure 27).

The external oscillator is very handy to have "onboard" when a microcontroller has its fuse bits set (usually) accidently to External Oscillator. With the external oscillator enabled (and a crystal placed in socket X2) we can restore a wrongly-programmed AVR.

Use of resonator or Quartz crystal

The MegaPin board can also use a resonator or XTAL, if it is placed in socket J12. The capacitors needed for use with the crystal are pre-placed on the PCB (see Figure 28).

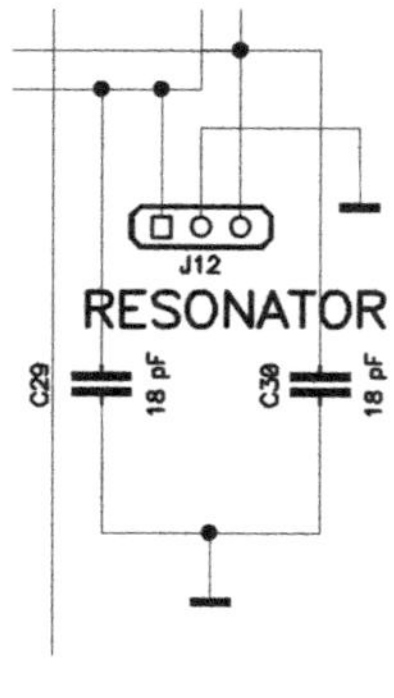

Figure 28: Resonator and Crystal circuitry with suitable capacitors pre-placed on board

AREF and 32,768 kHz quartz crystal

The MegaPin board has a built-in external reference voltage, which can be enabled with jumper J19 (AREF Enable). With the TP1 trimpot, the user can set AREF from nearly 5V down to 2.5 Volts. An external AREF is handy when performing analog to digital conversion (A/D) on voltages between 2.5 and 5.0 Volts. Most AVRs have both a built in Vcc (generally 5.0V) and an accurate 2.5V reference voltage. Using the Vcc reference voltage (generally 5.0V), the resolution of the 10-bit A/D conversion is 4.88 milivolts. If we perform A/D conversions of input voltages in the 3.0 V full-scale range, and we are looking for the best resolution, we would quickly see that a 5V reference is not suitable. With a 3.0 V reference voltage, we can achieve a resolution of 2.93 milivolts, which is nearly twice as good as that with 5.0 V reference voltage (see Figure 29).

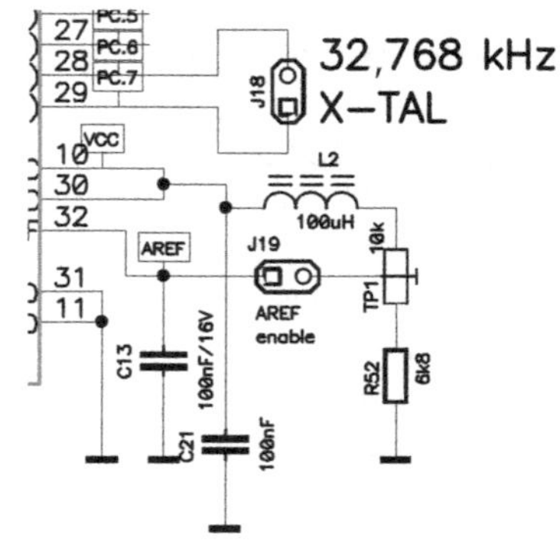

Figure 29: AREF & 32,768 kHz crystal

A 32,768 kHz (watch) crystal is very handy with AVRs that have a Timer2 which can operate in asynchronous mode. With a little Bascom code and 32,768 kHz watch crystal, we can make a Real Time Clock with actual date & time and not using too many microcontroller resources. RTC (Real Time Clock) clock routines can also wake-up the AVR microcontroller while in the Powersave mode, thus conserving battery power.

NOTE

With ATmega8 or ATmega168 you can connect a 32,768 kHz crystal to socket J12 and set fuse bits to "Ext. Low freq. crystal"!

Input & Outputs on MegaPin

MegaPin features:

- supports all AVR microcontrollers in 8-pin, 20-pin, 28-pin & 40 pin DIL packages + AT90USB1287,
- 6 built-in sockets for 1-Wire DS18S20 temperature sensors, that can be connected to any I/O Port,
- built in socket for Micro SD card that can be connected to any I/O Port via CON9,
- circuitry enabling the SD card to operate at either 3.3 or 5.0 target voltage ,
- 8 LEDs on four I/O ports: PortA, PortB, PortC & PortD,
- 6 I/O connectors for ports: (PortA, PortB, PortC, PortD, PortE & PortF),

- built-in voltage regulator. Output voltage is selectable for 5V or 3.3V supply voltage,
- can be powered from USB directly or from 12V DC,
- built-in 250 mA fuse to protect USB from short circuit on board,
- built-in 2.0 USB fast serial programmer compatible wih STK500 - programmer works directly from AVR Studio 4,
- pre-placed components for JTAG ICE programmer/ debugger,
- built-in options to to use the same board for programming and for connection of the microcontroller's UART to the PC via USB. If the user wants to send data via μC's serial port it can be done through USB without reconnecting the USB cable to another socket,
- built-in oscillator circuit to clock the microcontroller from an external quartz crystal,
- built-in 3-pin socket for ceramic resonator,
- built-in 2-pin socket for 32.768 kHz quartz crystal,
- built-in adjustable external reference voltage for the internal ADC in AVR,
- built-in SMD pads for 90USB1287 micro controller (which has a USB port built- in). Just solder the 90USB1287 on the MegaPin board and you can start using it. It can be programmed via ISP, JTAG or USB FLIP SW,
- built-in 8-button keyboard that can be connected to any I/O Port,
- built-in STK200 ISP programming socket for customers who want to have compatibility with STK200,
- built-in protection against wrong polarity of the 12V DC power supply voltage,
- built-in Power-ON LED,
- built-in serial communication Tx/Rx LEDs.

Example program ID	
Name:	1Wire_1.BAS
Microcontroller:	Any AVR microcontroler
Testing circuit:	Figure 23
MiniPin compatibility:	yes
MegaPin compatibility:	yes
Single 1-Wire sensor on a bus, temperature is displayed on LCD	

Example program ID	
Name:	1Wire_2.BAS
Microcontroller:	Any AVR microcontroler
Testing circuit:	Figure 23
MiniPin compatibility:	yes
MegaPin compatibility:	yes
Program displays 1-Wire ID of two sensors on the bus	

Example program ID	
Name:	1Wire_3.BAS
Microcontroller:	Any AVR microcontroler
Testing circuit:	Figure 23
MiniPin compatibility:	yes
MegaPin compatibility:	yes
Same as 1Wire_2.BAS but ID of sensors are stored in EEPROM	

Example program ID	
Name:	1Wire_4.BAS
Microcontroller:	Any AVR microcontroler
Testing circuit:	Figure 23
MiniPin compatibility:	yes
MegaPin compatibility:	yes
Multiple 1-Wire sensors, one on each Port	

Example program ID	
Name:	For_loop.BAS
Microcontroller:	Any AVR microcontroler
Testing circuit:	/
MiniPin compatibility:	yes
MegaPin compatibility:	yes
Simple FOR-Next loop for testing LEDs on all ports	

Example program ID	
Name:	GLCD_1.BAS
Microcontroller:	ATmega AVRs
Testing circuit:	Figure 1, page 67 (GLCD chapter)
MiniPin compatibility:	yes
MegaPin compatibility:	yes
Use of graphical LCD with table drawn on LCD and 8x8 font	

Example program ID	
Name:	GLCD_2.BAS
Microcontroller:	ATmega AVRs
Testing circuit:	Figure 1, page 67 (GLCD chapter)
MiniPin compatibility:	yes
MegaPin compatibility:	yes
GLCD with fonts that can be placed anywhere on GLCD	

Example program ID	
Name:	GLCD_3.BAS
Microcontroller:	ATmega AVRs
Testing circuit:	Figure 1, page 67 (GLCD chapter)
MiniPin compatibility:	yes
MegaPin compatibility:	yes
GLCD with the use of a touch panel including simple calibration of the touch panel	

Example program ID	
Name:	GLCD_4.BAS
Microcontroller:	ATmega AVRs
Testing circuit:	Figure 1, page 67 (GLCD chapter)
MiniPin compatibility:	yes
MegaPin compatibility:	yes
GLCD with improved calibration for the touch panel	

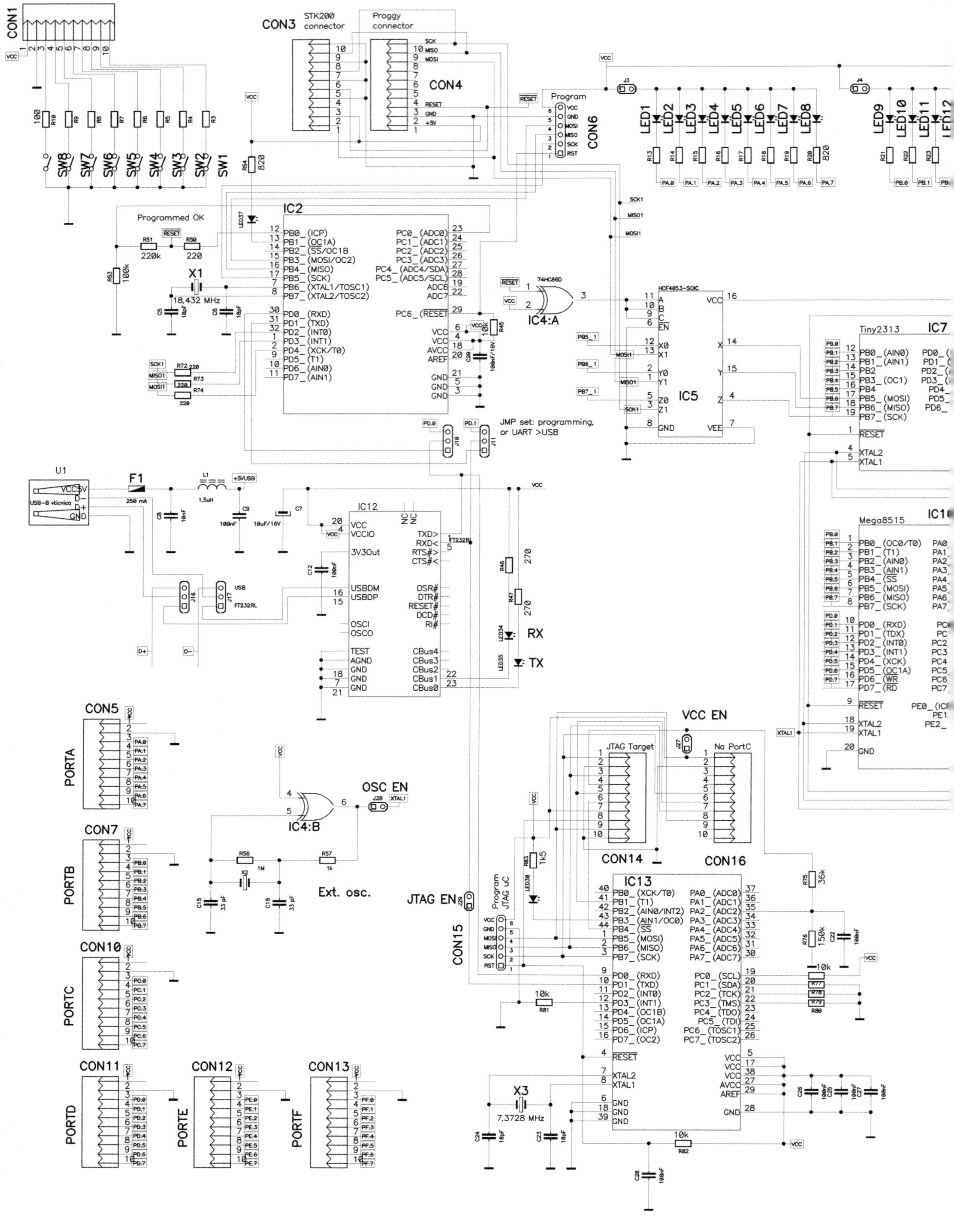

CON1
CON3 STK200 connector
Proggy connector
CON4
Program
CON6
IC2
Programmed OK
X1
18,432 MHz
IC4:A
74HC86D
HCF4053-SOIC
IC5
Tiny2313
IC7
Mega8515
JMP set: programming, or UART >USB
U1
USB-B vticnica
F1
250 mA
1,5uH
IC12
FT232RL
RX
TX
CON5
PORTA
CON7
PORTB
CON10
PORTC
CON11
PORTD
CON12
PORTE
CON13
PORTF
OSC EN
IC4:B
Ext. osc.
JTAG EN
CON15
Program JTAG uC
VCC EN
JTAG Target
Na PortC
CON14
CON16
IC13
X3
7,3728 MHz

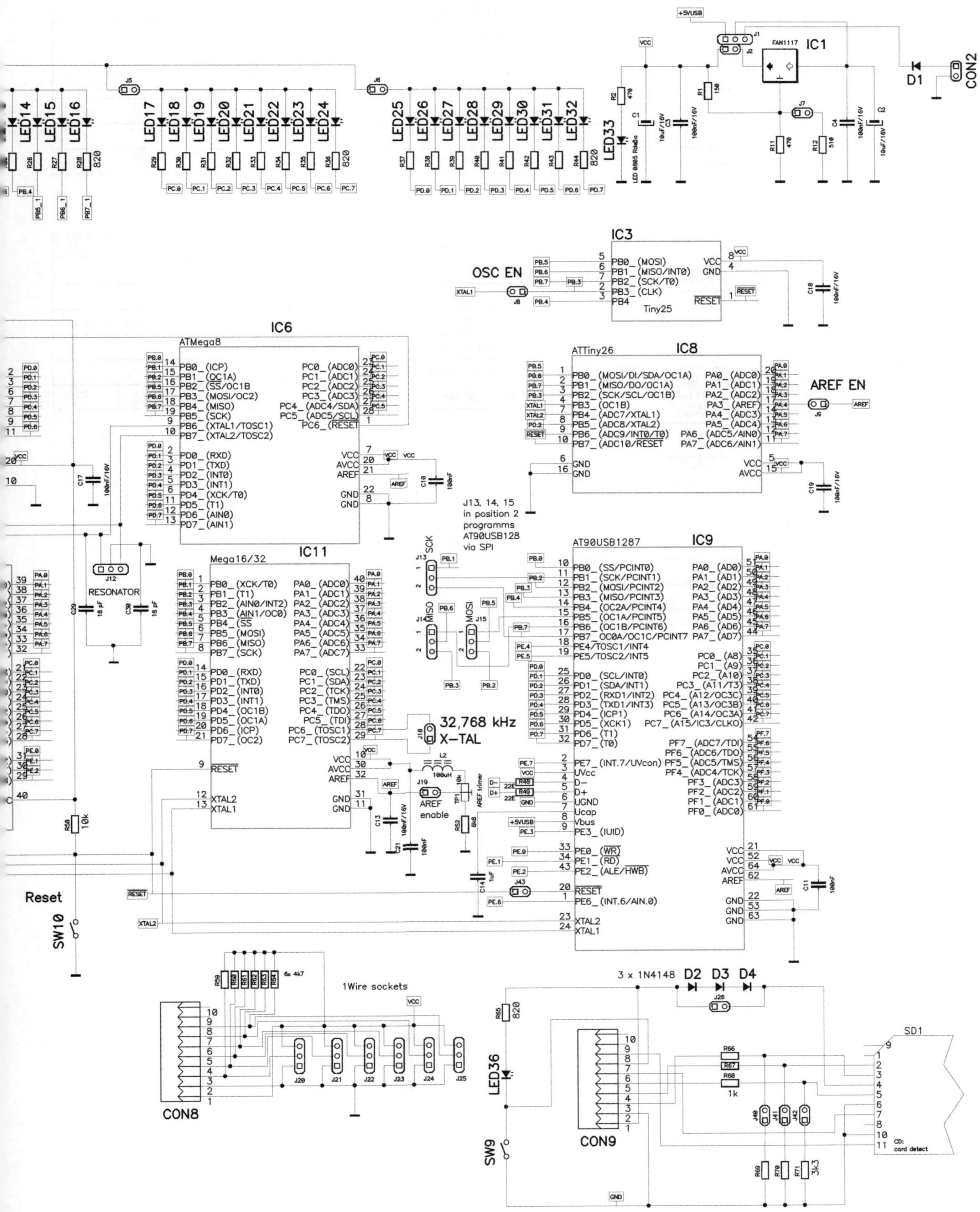

MegaPin schematics

Example program ID	
Name:	LCD8x2.bas
Microcontroller:	Any AVR microcontroler
Testing circuit:	Figure 1, page 67 (GLCD chapter)
MiniPin compatibility:	yes
MegaPin compatibility:	yes
Simple program to display characters on blue 8x2 LCD, including PWM for controlling backlight	

Example program ID	
Name:	USB-ADC2.bas
Microcontroller:	Any AVR whith UART
Testing circuit:	/
MiniPin compatibility:	yes
MegaPin compatibility:	yes
Acquires analogue voltages and converts it with the A/D, then transmits using the USB port and displays it on the LCD. You can see the transmitted voltage value in the Terminal window within Bascom-AVR	

Example program ID	
Name:	PWM1.bas
Microcontroller:	ATmega AVRs
Testing circuit:	/
MiniPin compatibility:	Yes
MegaPin compatibility:	Yes
Simple PWM using hardware PWM in AVR	

Example program ID	
Name:	Megaclock.bas
Microcontroller:	ATmega AVRs
Testing circuit:	Figure 1, page 67 (GLCD chapter)
MiniPin compatibility:	yes
MegaPin compatibility:	yes
Clock with 32,768 kHz XTAL and 8x2 LCD	

Example program ID	
Name:	Megaclock1.bas
Microcontroller:	ATmega AVRs
Testing circuit:	Figure 1, page 67 (GLCD chapter)
MiniPin compatibility:	yes
MegaPin compatibility:	yes
Same as Megaclock.bas with simple routines to set hour/min/sec	

Proggy II, an in-system programmer for AVR microcontrollers

By Jurij Mikeln

At AX elektronika, we have made many programmers, both for 89C/89Sxx51 and AVRs. To tell the truth, we have sold many more AVR programmers - which is no coincidence. AVRs are more popular than their 89C/89Sxx51 counterparts. It was about time to replace the old Proggy-AVR's nice blue but somehow bulky programer.

Proggy-AVR has been very popular for the last five years or so. It had a nice blue enclosure which made it attractive and distinctive from other programmers (that often had no enclosure at all). Now we are making a renovated, faster AVR programmer that is both less expensive and smaller. No wonder we expect it to be well accepted within the AVR programmer's community.

Schematic diagram

The schematic diagram shown in Figure 1 can be divided into two parts: the FT232RL USB interface circuitry and the ATmega8 microcontroller circuitry.

In the schematic diagram, you can see that we have replaced the FT232BL, manufactured by FTDI [1] with the more modern FT232RL (which needs fewer support components and offers more functionality). One such feature is a clock output pin. The FT232RL can generate different clock signals. We can use such a clock signal to unlock an incorrectly-programmed AVR chip. This is a handy feature because one doesn't always have a clock source available. We have added two LEDs to indicate Rx and Tx signals. This is handy to quickly see whether or not the programmer is alive and programming.

The second part of the schematic diagram is the ATmega8 microcontroller. The ATmega8 handles all of the signals for communications with the PC host, via FT232RL chip and also generates all the signals necessary to program the target microcontroller.

Surrounding the ATmega8 you can see two connectors: CON1 is meant for the factory programming of the ATmega8 microcontroller, while CON2 represents the ISP connector that serves to program the AVR microcontroller on the target board. You'll notice there is also a CLK12 pin, coming from the clock signal that the FT232RL generates.

Beside the Rx and Tx LEDs, there is also a LED which indicates whether the target microcontroller was programmed correctly: if the LED blinks after programming, it means that the target microcontroller was not programmed correctly. If the LED lights steadily the target microcontroller was programmed correctly.

The programmer also has three built-in protective resistors on the MISO, MOSI & SCK lines which protect both the target and host microcontrollers. Note that an 18.432 MHz crystal was used in this circuit, although ATmega8 is specified to only work at up to 16 MHz. That is true in harsh environments with extremely low or high temperatures. But, that is not likely with this programmer, so this higher frequency clock is perfectly satisfactory.

PCB and soldering

When designing the PCB we wanted it to be small - and fit into a "nice" translucent USB stick enclosure as shown in Figure 6. Hence, we designed a double-sided PCB that fits nicely into such a USB enclosure. The PCB is shown in Figures 2 through 4.

Due to the relatively small enclosure, we had to use small components: typically 0603 SMD components. Also we

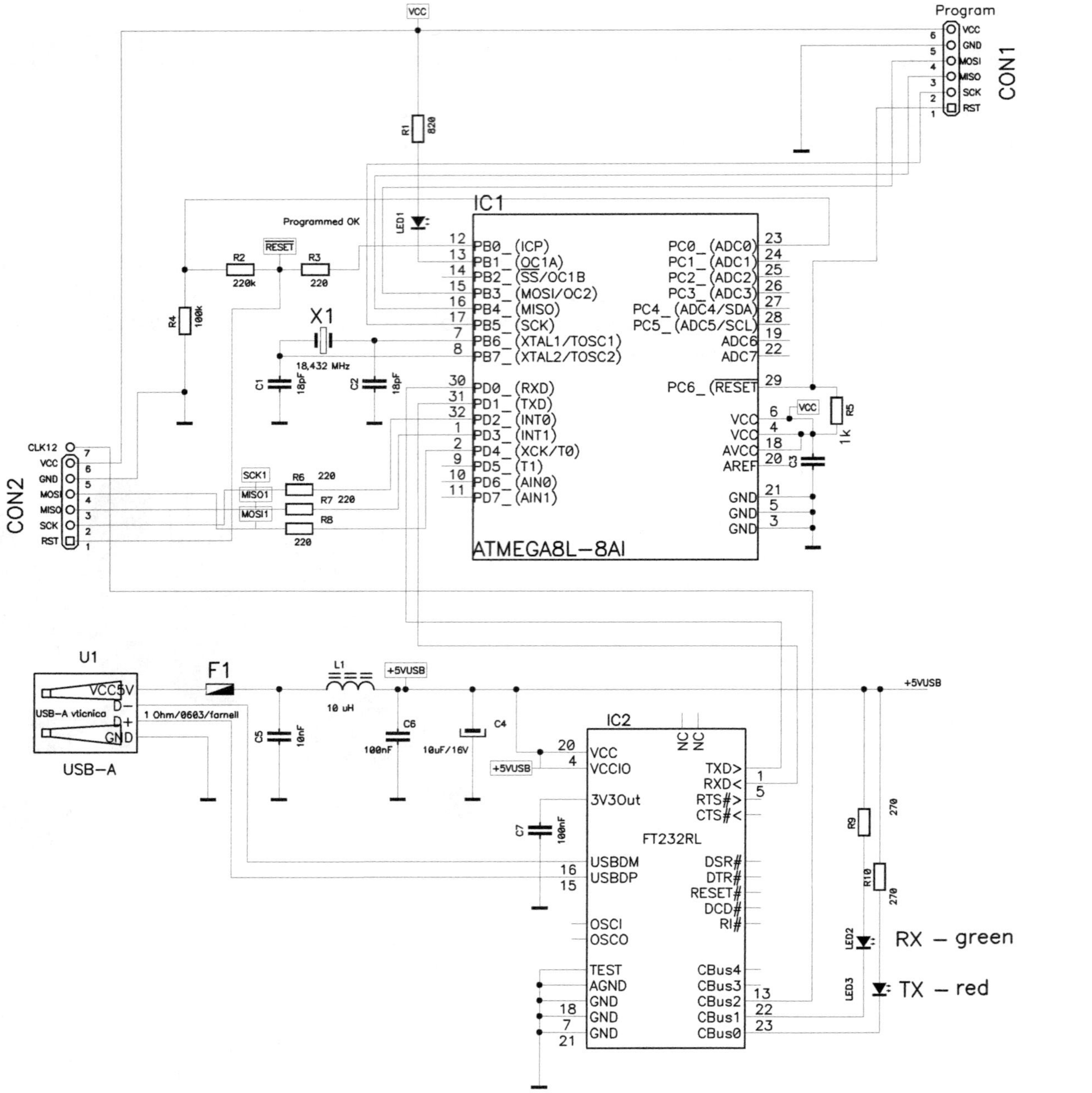

Figure 1: The Schematic diagram of Proggy II

used an SMD crystal with a low profile. A standard profile crystal would not have fit into such a small enclosure. The FT232RL we used is not the smallest one FTDI makes, but it's in an SMD case which can be hand-soldered. There is also an FT232RL in a QFN case, which is virtually impossible to hand-solder.

When soldering, use a good soldering iron with a very fine tip to enable you to solder theFT232RL and 0603 parts. When soldering, I strongly suggest you do so under a suitable stereo microscope. If you're not confident soldering such a small components under a microscope, leave that task to the professionals.

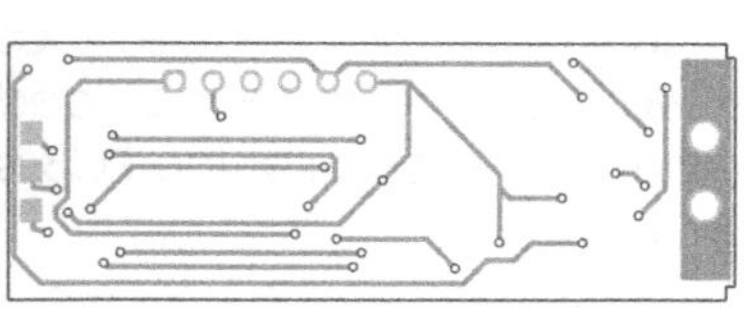

Figure 2: PCB layout, solder side

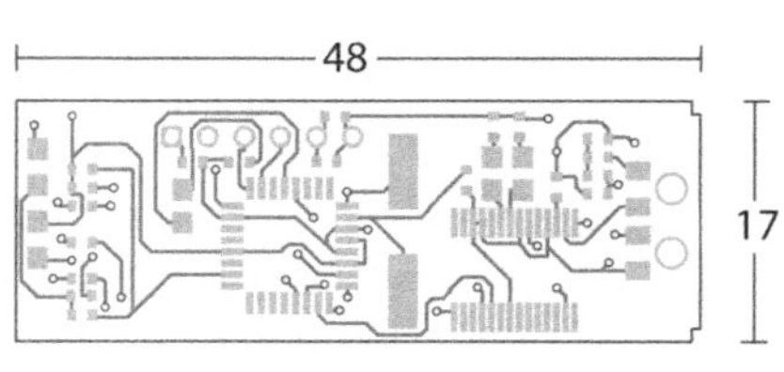

Figure 3: PCB layout, top side

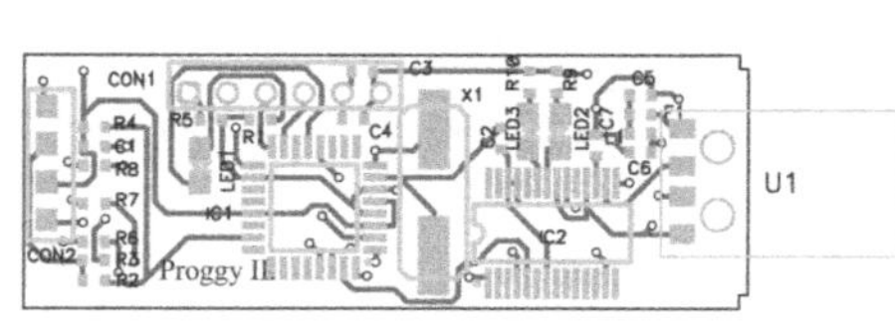

Figure 4: PCB layout, top silk side

Solder the two ICs first, followed by the smaller parts, like the 0603 resistors and capacitors, then the LEDs. Make sure that the LEDs are properly oriented. You can check this with a multimeter on the diode - check range, by connecting the positive terminal of the multimeter to one LED's pin and the negative terminal to the other. If the LED glows then the anode is the one connected to the positive terminal of the multimeter. Finally, you can solder the crystal and connector U1. As mentioned, CON1 is meant for factory programming - you need not mount this component.

All components are placed on the top side, including USB connector U1. The programming connector (CON2) consists of 6 wires (one more if you need the CLK signal). All these wires are part of a 10-pin flat cable, which is terminated with an IDC male connector. The CON2 wiring is shown in Figure 5.

When all the soldering is done, check the PCB under a microscope, or magnifying glass, for short circuits, noting especially the FT232RL chip. Note that pins 25 and 26 are shorted together, which is normal, but if any other pins are shorted you should remove that solder bridge with desoldering wick.

Before testing, you must program an ATmega8 using the ISP firmware, which can be downloaded from our web page. If you do not have programming capability already, you can always contact our distributor to purchase a pre-programmed ATmega8.

At this stage, the Proggy II programmer is ready to start programming AVR devices. Optionally, you can elect to "customize" the FT232RL with Proggy II firmware. This can be done using the free MPROG software that can be downloaded from FTDI's web page. This customizes the various USB device descriptors to make the Proggy II identify itself as such, and not an FTDI USB-serial bridge. The programming procedure follows, see Figure 7.

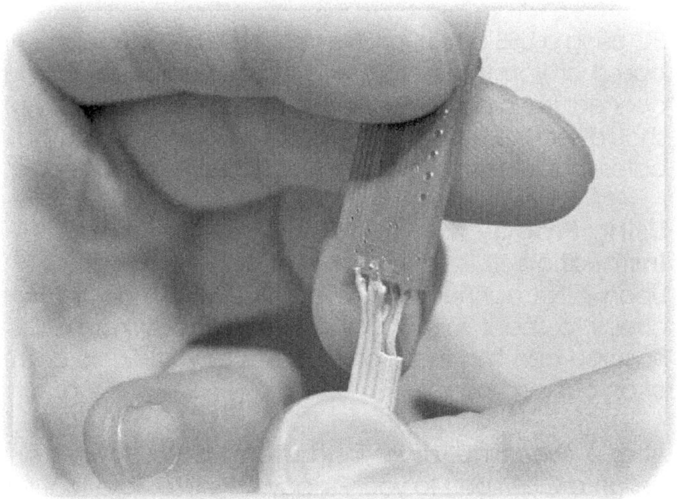

Figure 5: Detail of CON2 soldering

Figure 6: A suitable enclosure for Proggy II

When initially programming the FTDI chip, click F5 or Devices/Scan and parse.

The window will fill with data from the empty chip. Now load the template (for example for Proggy II) by clicking File/Open template. Chose the Proggy II template and click ***Device Program***. You will see the data being programmed into FT232RL chip.

You are now ready to connect your programmer to your

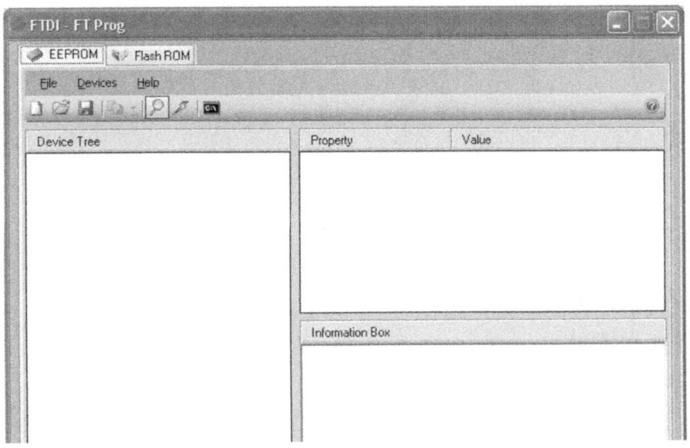

Figure 7: F-PROG programmer for the FT232RL chip

PC using a USB cable, and to your MiniPin II development board or your target microcontroller board. When you connect the programmer to the USB port on your PC, you should see the Rx and Tx LEDs blink few times, which indicates that USB communication has been established.

Using Proggy II

Installation

Upon initial connection to your PC, MS Windows® will check to see if suitable drivers are already installed. If not, you can find them on web-site (www.ftdichip.com) or on our web page.

After a successful driver installation MS Windows®, will assign a COM port to your Proggy II. Please note that for proper software operation, it ***must*** be in the range from 1 to 9. If it's not, then you should change it using Device manager.

NOTE

For a detailed description of the process of changing a COM port's assigned number, see the chapter on the MegaPin development board.

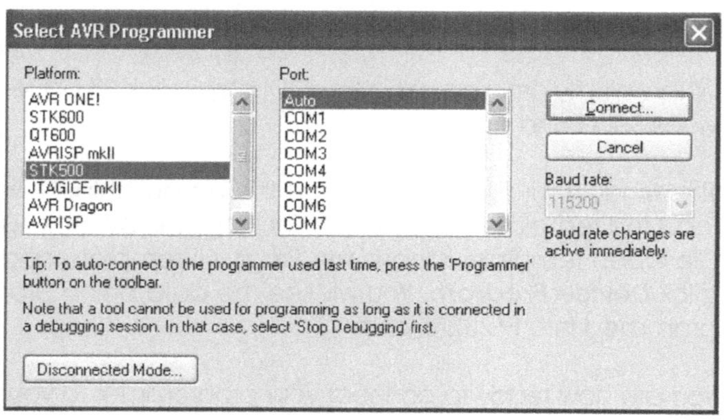

Figure 8: Choose COM port

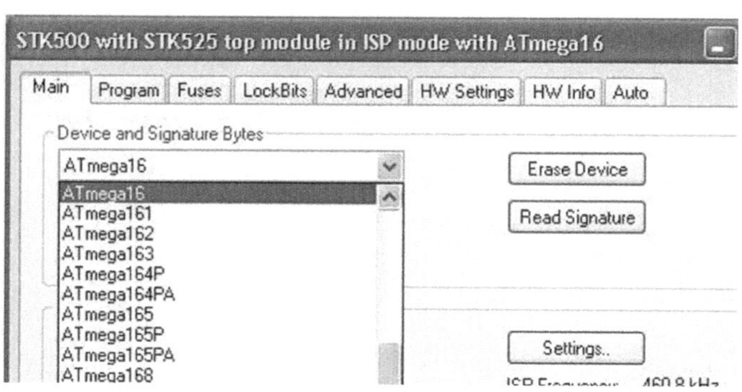

Figure 9: Choose device

Programming

Programming is simple. Start AVR Studio (Ver. 4 or lower) and click the icon ***Con***, set the COM port to AUTO, choose STK500 or AVRISP and click ***Connect***.

Figure 10: Proggy II

Then click Program and choose the device that you wish to program. To test the connection between Proggy II and the microcontroller you may click ***Fuses***, to see if the programmer reads the fuses correctly. If all is OK, you'll see how the fuses are set. If not, you should change the ISP frequency to a lower value. Keep dropping the frequency until you get valid connection.

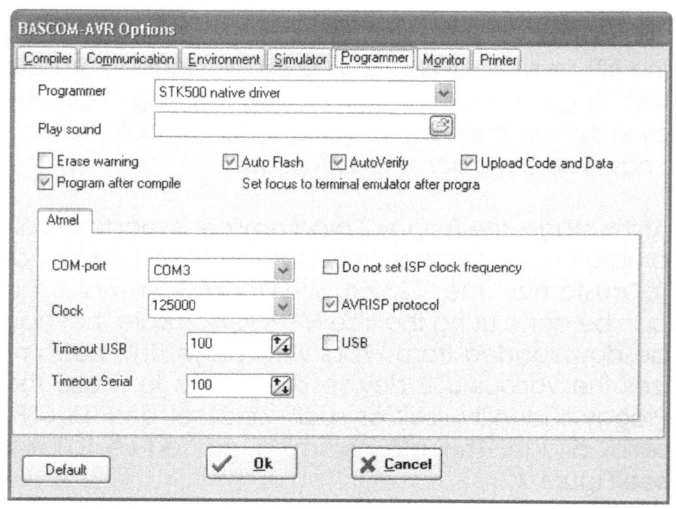

Figure 11: Set up Bascom to use the STK500 native driver

Alternatively, for use with Bascom-AVR, you can set the programmer to ***STK500 Native driver*** as shown in Figure 11.

Note that you must check off all of the boxes shown in Figure 11, and set the COM port to the value you found using Device manager, and then click OK. Although Proggy II is connected to USB do not tick the USB window (since Proggy II is using the FT232RL in serial port emulation mode)!

Programming with the STK500 native driver is similar to programming within the AVR Studio program. You can also set the fuse bits as shown in Figure 12.

You can check the EEPROM's content, erase the microcontroller and do everything that can be done within AVR Studio, except that you cannot program ELF files. Elf files (***E***xecutable and ***L***inkable ***F***ormat) are special files, produced by some compilers, which contain the image data for Flash, EEPROM and Fuse bits, all in one file

Conclusion

The Proggy II programmer is a simple, but effective ISP programmer for AVR microcontrollers. It's STK500 compatible so it works very well with Bascom-AVR and AVR Studio ver. 4 or lower. Proggy II can also power target device like MiniPin II or any other microcontroller board providing that it does not draw more than 150 mA.

For protection of the USB port on your PC there is a fuse built into Proggy II. This fuse has done its job many times many times when I overloaded it!

Enjoy programming with your Proggy II!

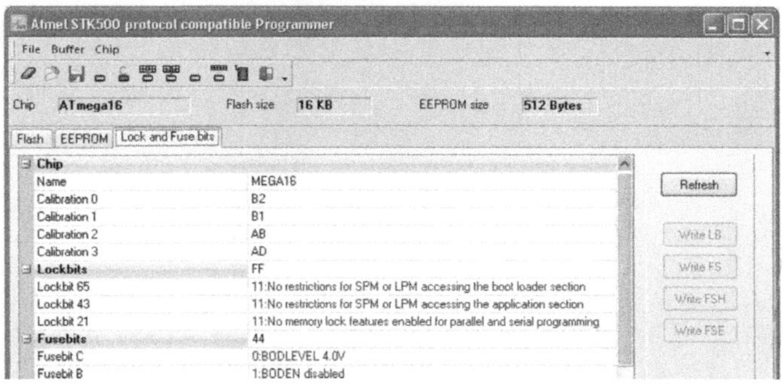

Figure 12: Setting Fuse bits from within the STK500 native driver

Links

1. Future Technology Devices International LTD., URL: www.ftdichip.com
2. http://www2.atmel.com - ATMEL AVR studio

Debugging Bascom programs in AVR Studio

By Jurij Mikeln

Debugging is a procedure, where we trace program flow with the help of suitable software and/or hardware. While tracing program flow, we can find annoying "bugs" inside our program. If we do not have suitable debugging hardware we can use a simulator, like the one included in Bascom-AVR. We can also find problems by displaying some "debugging data" on an LCD display or in a terminal window, if we send data out to the RS232 or USB port. I will show you how you can debug Bascom programs with a help of the AVR Studio 4 program and the MegaPin development board.

As mentioned, we can debug in many ways. Generally we use a principle of displaying "debugging information" on an LCD display or terminal window. The data displayed can determine whether or not our program is performing properly.

That is a quite usable procedure if no debugging tools are on hand, however, this procedure is sometimes not good enough. In such cases, we have to look "inside" the microcontroller to find those nasty bugs that may be elusive. Atmel has provided many free software tools that, in conjunction with suitable hardware, work very well. A good example is Atmel's JTAG ICE, which we'll demonstrate in conjunction with the MegaPin development board (which has proven to be a real multi-purpose development board!)

What do we need?

To debug using the AVR Studio 4 program, some device preparation (hardware & software) needs to be done. For hardware, you will need a JTAG ICE unit, the source of which can be found on the web. Alternately, you can use the JTAG ICE included on the MegaPin board. One must use an AVR device that supports JTAG, such as the ATmega16, ATmega32, to name a few. Also, we must enable JTAG operation with the appropriate Fuse bit, as shown in Figure 1. Note that all AVRs with JTAG available come factory-programmed with the JTAG Fuse bit enabled.

The JTAG Fuse bit can be turned on with the SPI program-

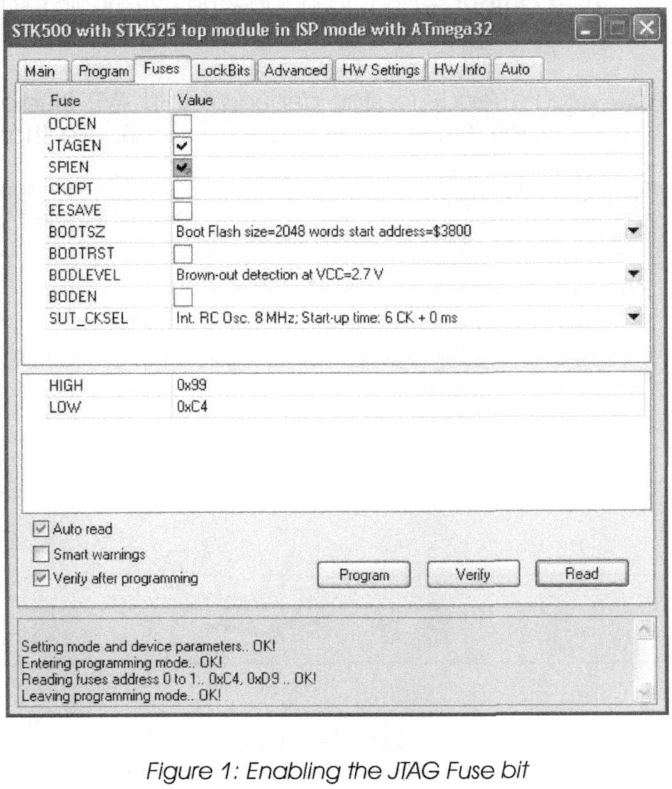

Figure 1: Enabling the JTAG Fuse bit

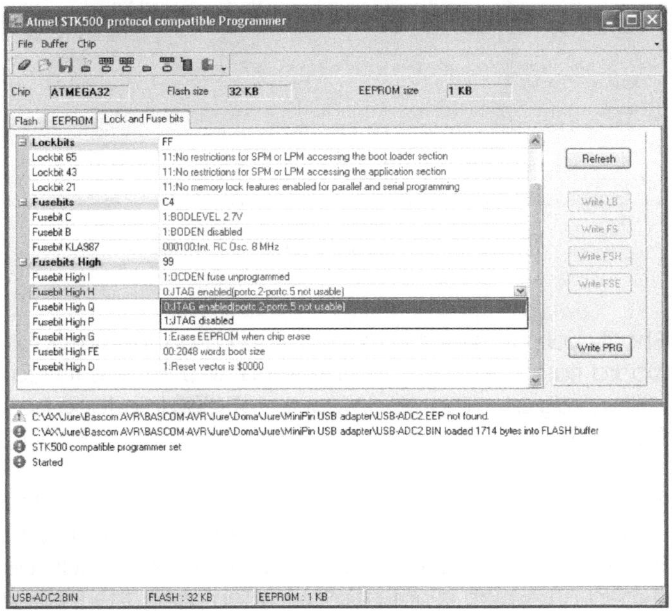

Figure 2: Setting the Fuse bit within the STK500 native programmer window

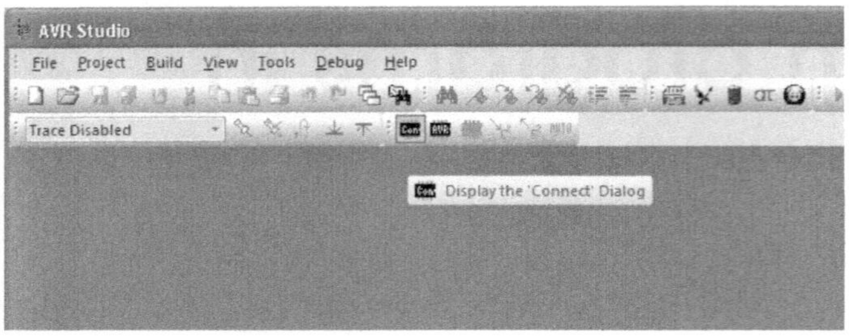

Figure 3: Press the **Conn** *icon to connect to JTAG ICE*

mer built-in to the MegaPin board, or we can use the STK500 programmer, in conjunction with Studio 4. We can also accomplish this from Bascom-AVR using the STK500 native programmer, as shown in Figure 2. Note that you do not need to turn on the OCDEN Fuse bit.

Once the JTAG Fuse bit has been programmed, we can continue by connecting the JTAG ICE interface to PortC via a 10-pin flat cable. The communication pins Rx and Tx of the ATmega16, should be connected to Tx and Rx of the FT232RL USB bridge device. All this is done on the MegaPin board by connecting PortC to socket CON16 with a 10-pin flat cable, and connecting jumpers J27 and J29 (VCC EN & JTAG EN) and, finally, disconnecting jumper J11. Now open AVR Studio 4 and press the **Conn** icon as shown in Figure 3.

You will see the window shown in Figure 4, where we can select the platform on the left, while on the right, we select the COM port (we suggest leaving it on Auto.)

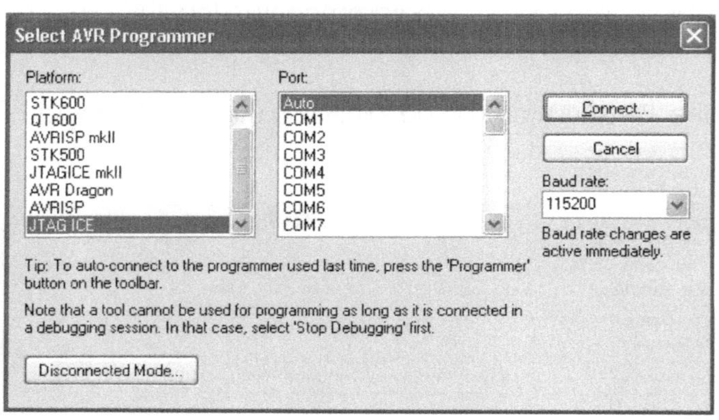

Figure 4: Connect to JTAG ICE window

Shortly you will see the Rx and Tx LEDs on the MegaPin board flash few times and after that you will see the familiar programming window of the STK500 interface (see Figure 5).

There are not much difference between the SPI and the JTAG software interfaces. One difference is that within the JTAG interface window, the SPI Fuse bit can be turned off, which is not possible when using the STK500 interface. Note that using the JTAG interface we can restore an AVR microcontroller whose Fuse bits were incorrectly programmed.

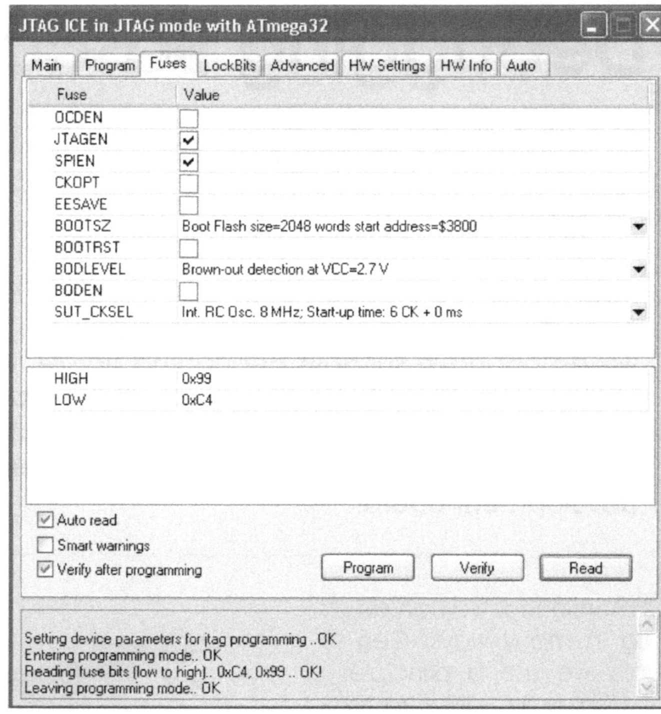

Figure 5: JTAG ICE interface window

AVR Studio 4

AVR Studio 4 is free software, provided by Atmel (www.atmel.com), which can be freely downloaded from Atmel's web site. I suggest that you download version 4 because prior versions had various bugs. Users of the Proggy-AVR programmer are already familiar with AVR studio, but not necessarily the functionality that I will present here. I suggest that you introduce yourself to debugging by using a simple program, which you know well. Make sure that within Bascom-AVR, you set the **Compiler Output** settings to include the AVR Studio OBJ file, by checking off the box, as shown in Figure 6.

Now we are ready to start debugging. In AVR Studio 4, click **Open Project** and choose the OBJ file that

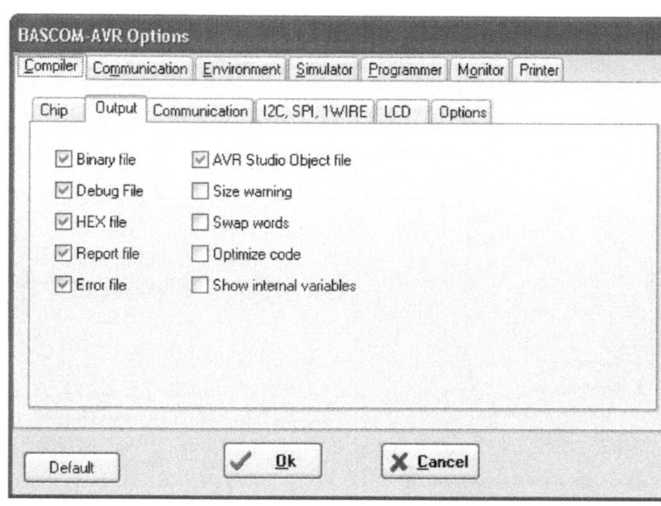

Figure 6: Setting the **Compiler output** *file settings within Bascom-AVR to include the AVR Studio Object file*

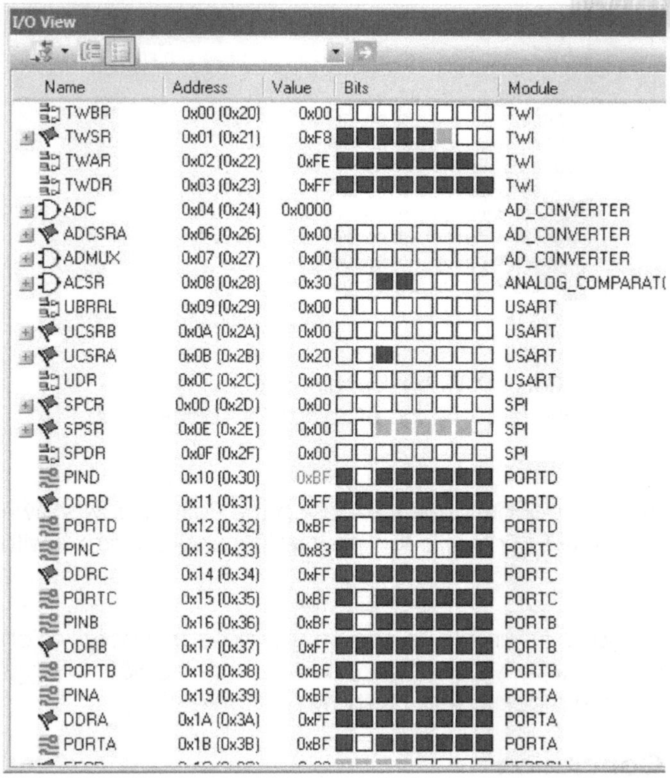

Figure 7: The I/O View window

Bascom-AVR has generated for the program you wish to debug. Then, AVR Studio will prompt you whether you want it to make an AVR Studio Project file. Click OK, and a lot of new windows will open. Normally your program is loaded into the microcontroller automatically. We can also start it manually by clicking the **Start Debugging** button. The Main window now displays the Bascom-AVR program Listing. For easier debugging, I suggest that you also open **I/O View** (Alt+5). Here you can monitor and change registers within the AVR microcontroller. If you are seeing the internals of the AVR microcontroller for the first time, do not worry about it at this point. If you are more familiar with AVRs you will be able to use the I/O View information more readily. Most of you know the PORT and PIN registers (see Figure 7), which you will see in I/O View as well. You have also heard about the DDR registers. In time, you will get familiar with many registers.

Somewhere in the middle of our program I suggest that you place a Breakpoint(s). Now you can start debugging by pressing **RUN** (or F5) and "show time" can begin! First, we will look at the PORT registers. Let's chose PORTD. We can see that on PortD.6 there is a blank window which means that PortD.6 is at logical 0 (which turns the LED on, due to the way it is connected to the power supply). If you now click on that empty window, the LED will turn off, because PortD.6 is now at logical 1. You can also change values of the DDRD register. You will probably remember that using the DDRD register, we set whether an I/O pin is an input, an output or 3-state (high impedance). You can review this by referring to Table 1.

Now it's time to try a practical example of debugging. Click on the DDRD register block corresponding to a PORTD pin which has the LED is turned on. The DDRD will change colour and the LED will turn off, as defined in Table 1. We can go one step further and press a keypad on the keyboard (which we have connected to PORTD via a flat cable). We will notice that LED does not turn on. Now click again on one DDRD register's pin, press keypad and LED will turn on.

With the AVR in output mode, and set for a logic "1", the LED might light if the switch were closed, as the current sourced by the port (~ 25-40 mA) would be overridden by the low condition caused by the switch being pushed (and the 100 ohm current limiting resistor). However, a beginner would never figure this out without more explanation than what is included above. Also, it would not represent a normal use of an I/O port.

Step by step...

Let us go a bit further with debugging. We have seen how to set Breakpoints, where program flow stops. We can also debug a program in a "step-by-step" manner. Let me show you simple example:

But, if U is a byte variable then the *Shift U, Right, 8* statement shifts the U variable eight times in the right direction, resulting in U=0.

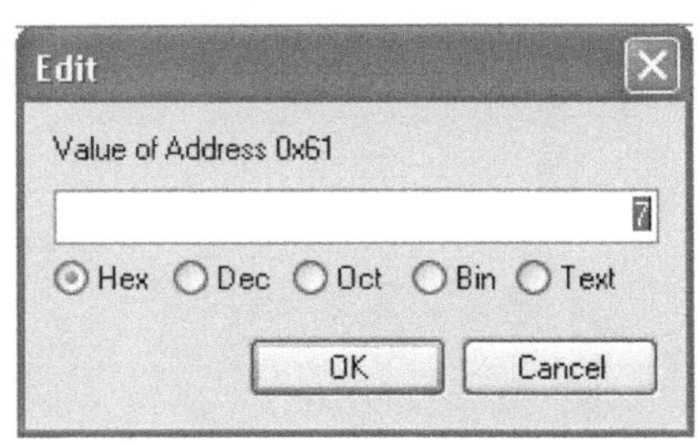

Figure 8: Window for changing a variable's value

DDR Dn	PORT Dn	I/O	Pull up	Comment
0	0	Input	No	3-state (Hi -Z)
0	1	Input	Yes	PBn will source current if ext. pulled low.
1	0	Input	No	Push-Pull Zero Output
1	1	Input	No	Push-Pull One Output

Table 1: The DDRDn register and its effect on I/O pins

```
For J = 1 To 46
   U = Not T
      Eight_bit = U
      Portd = Eight_bit
      Shift U , Right , 8
      Eight_bit = U
      Portc = Eight_bit
      Shift U , Right , 8
      Eight_bit = U
      Portb = Eight_bit
      Shift U , Right , 8
      Eight_bit = U
      Porta = Eight_bit
      Waitms 120
      Shift T , Left , 1
      F = F + 1
      If F < 9 Then
      T = T Or 1
      End If
 Next J
```

Let us say that we want to see how the above *For-Next* loop performs. We can do that, by setting a Breakpoint at the *For J=1 to 46"* statement. Then we set the cursor to the next line and click **{} Run to cursor** (Ctrl + F10). You will notice that an arrow within the debugging window will jump to the place where the cursor is, and values inside the I/O window will change.

Advanced debugging

Advanced users can change the value of variables in the program. Click **View/Memory** (Alt + 4), and at the dropdown menu choose **Data**. Now you can see and change the value of variable(s) (Note that the values are in HEX format). To do this, you must know the address of the variable within the AVR's data memory. How do we establish that? It's easy: in the Bascom-AVR report file (click on **Program/See result**) you can see a variable's name and its address. With that knowledge, you can change only the variable that you want to change. To

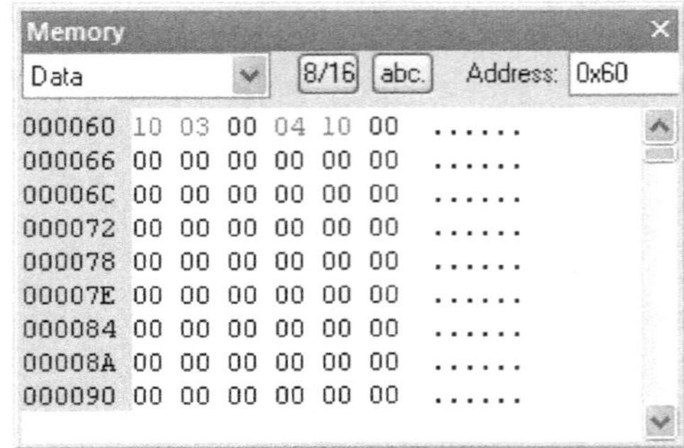

Figure 9: When variables change, it is signified by a change of colour from black to red

do that, double click it, exposing the Edit window shown in Figure 8. Enter it's the new value and confirm it with an OK.

Actually, it's simple to see, in the data memory, which variable(s) have changed, because their colour changes from black to red, as shown in Figure 9.

Conclusion

AVR Studio 4, in conjunction with the MegaPin development tool and JTAG ICE debugger is a winning combination. In this chapter we have shown you how to work with these tools to control and debug your program on real microcontroller. These techniques are intended for advanced programmers and those who wish to broaden their programming knowledge.

Example program ID	
Name:	Test MegaPin.bas
Microcontroller:	ATmega AVRs
Testing circuit:	/
MiniPin compatibility:	yes
MegaPin compatibility:	yes
Program tests all ports on MegaPin or MiniPin II	

Let's explore Bascom-AVR

By Vladimir Mitrović

Have you ever wondered what your program looks like when Bascom-AVR translates it into a form understandable to a microcontroller? Well, it's not difficult to find out - just open the .hex file of your program and look at these sequences of hexadecimal numbers. They seem quite obscure, don't they? It is hard to believe that these "random strings of numbers" could mean anything to anybody... But no, they are not random, and yes, they make a microcontroller act in just the way you have foreseen in your program!

There is a simple tool that can convert such incomprehensible object code into a more understandable symbolic language, namely assembly language or assembler. That tool is called a disassembler: it is a computer program that reads in a .hex file containing the AVR program code and outputs assembly code which can be fed into an AVR assembler. It is not our intention here to actually re-assemble the code; we will instead use the disassembled program to analyze Bascom-AVR statements, as its mnemonics are easier to understand than a series of numbers.

I usually use the Revava disassembler for this purpose. It has been released under the GNU Public License (freeware), so you can download it free of charge from various internet sites, either as C++ source code or as an executable (.exe) file. No installation is necessary: just copy revava.exe to the folder where your .hex files are located and it's ready for use. You can use other similar programs for this purpose, but their output can differ from the examples presented here.

Figure 1 shows an example of disassembling the object code in the Asm_1.hex file into assembler source code. This object code is the result of the compilation of an "empty" Bascom-AVR program, containing only the *End* statement. Despite this, Bascom-AVR has generated some code.

Revava is executed from a DOS prompt:

```
>revava Asm_1.hex -o Asm_1.txt -e
```

Asm_1.hex:	the name of input .hex file
-o:	set output file name
Asm_1.txt:	the name of output file
-e:	use Intel byte order

The most common options are -o and -e, but you can get a listing of all possibilities if you execute Revava without any option. The generated assembler code is shown in the lower part of Figure 1 (it's slightly modified "by hand" to make it easier to read). To understand it, you will need an elementary knowledge of programming in assembler and a familiarity with AVR assembler mnemonics. Some information can be found in Bascom-AVR's Help topics "Assembler mnemonics" and "Mixing ASM and BASIC". It's also useful to study the "Language Fundamentals" chapter.

Before examining the generated code, let's look at its structure. The revava output file contains assembler mnemonics where they exist and *dc.W* declarations where no mnemonic matches the data. The comment field for each assembly instruction contains the program address from the object code and the destination address for branches, calls, jumps, etc. In the case of multiple assembly instructions that assemble to the same op-code, all choices are presented in a group, with all but the first choice commented out. For example:

```
brbc   1, -6        ; 0054, Dest: 0050
;brne  -6           ; 0054, Dest: 0050

clr    r6           ; 0056
;eor   r6, r6       ; 0056
```

In this example, *brbc* and *brne* as well as *clr* and *eor* would generate the same opcode. Revava cannot know which instruction was originally written and offers both possibilities. Besides being commented out, these alternatives share the same address locations as the original ("0054" and "0056" in this example). You can just choose the one that is more meaningful to you. I have deleted all multiple choices from the example shown in Figure 1 to make it easier to read.

Now let's explore the code Bascom-AVR has generated for an empty program!

The first instruction of every program is a jump to the first "real" program instruction. In this example, its address is "0026" hexadecimal. The interrupt vectors have fixed locations between this jump and the first "real" instruction. Each interrupt vector is a jump to the associated interrupt service routine. Since there are no interrupts in this program, all interrupt vectors are merely returns (*reti*). The number of interrupt vectors depends upon which microcontroller is configured in the original Bascom-AVR program. The ATtiny2313 has been used in this example; it has 18 interrupt vectors in total, only 6 of which are shown in Figure 1, to make the listing shorter.

The Bascom-AVR compiler generates a few initialization and clean-up procedures that are performed before executing the first instruction of your program. Hardware and software stack pointers, as well as a temporary data storage pointer, are set up initially. A set of instructions that configure the Watchdog timer follows. The initial value of the MCUSR register is saved to the R0 register and can be retrieved later in the program, to establish whether the microcontroller has been reset by the Watchdog or due to some other cause.

The next compiler-generated routine is a loop that clears the contents of the entire SRAM. If you want to preserve the SRAM contents at start-up (i.e. this can be of interest if the reset was generated by the Watchdog), you can remove this clean-up routine by adding the *$noramclear* directive to your program. Bear in mind, however, that without the initial clearing of SRAM, the initial values of all variables will be undefined. If this can cause ambiguity in your program, you should set the initial values of critical variables, at the beginning of the program, yourself.

The last initialization routine clears the R6 register, which is internally used for the storage of several flags. For example, the error flag is stored here.

What follows next in the program is the code that you have actually written: I've highlighted this part in grey in Figure 1. In this example, the Bascom-AVR program contained only the *End* statement, which has been compiled as a disable interrupts instruction (*cli*), followed by an endless loop (*rjmp -2*). In a "normal" Bascom-AVR program, which contains a sequence of statements followed by the *End* statement, these statements would be translated and placed here, just before the shaded area. If the Bascom-AVR program contains some tables, subroutines or other code that is situated beyond the *End* statement, the compiler would place the corresponding compiled code below the shaded area. In short, the Bascom-AVR compiler respects the structure of your program and will insert its own routines before or after, but not within your program code.

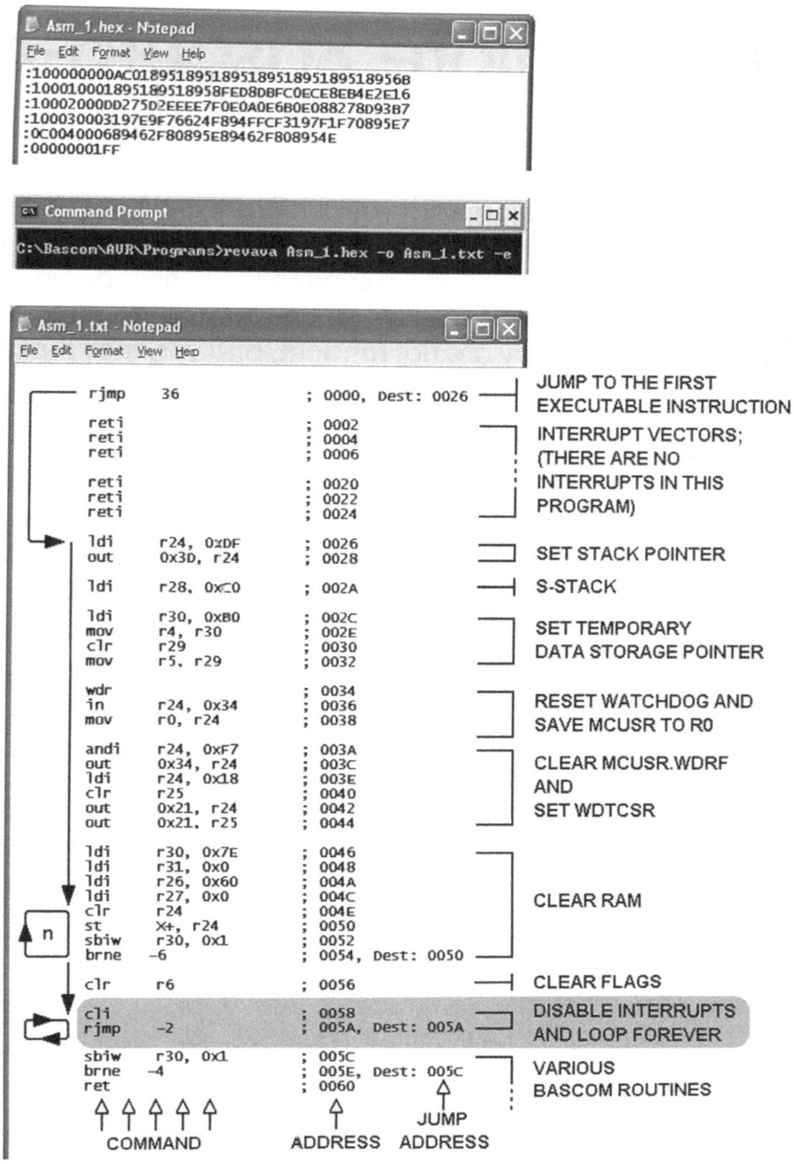

Figure 1: An example of disassembling Asm_1.hex into assembler source code

Actually, there is some code below the shaded area even in this example. These routines are never used by the program and are therefore surplus (or I cannot figure out their meaning). However, many Bascom-AVR statements generate their own subroutines which the

NOTE

Which initialization routines are included and their exact structures depend on which microcontroller has been configured.

Besides the *$noramclear* directive, some other directives such as *$noinit* or similar *$no...* directives affect the initialization part of the program.

You can use the *$initmicro* directive to add your own initialization routines to your program. This directive will call a label named *_INIT_MICRO* just after the most important initialization is performed. See Bascom-AVR help for details.

compiler places in this zone. For example, when you use *Wait 1* in your program, it will compile in two parts:

- parameter settings and a subroutine call are placed where you have written your *Wait 1* but
- the subroutine that actually delays program execution for one or more seconds is situated somewhere beyond your program code.

1st analysis: Wait and Waitms

Wait and *Waitms* statements are good starting examples for a Bascom-AVR program analysis. If you want to analyse these or any other statements, surround them with a few assembler *nop* instructions:

```
$crystal = 8000000
$regfile = "ATtiny2313.dat"
...
...
nop
nop
nop
nop
Wait 1
nop
nop
nop
nop
Waitms 1
nop
nop
nop
nop
End
```

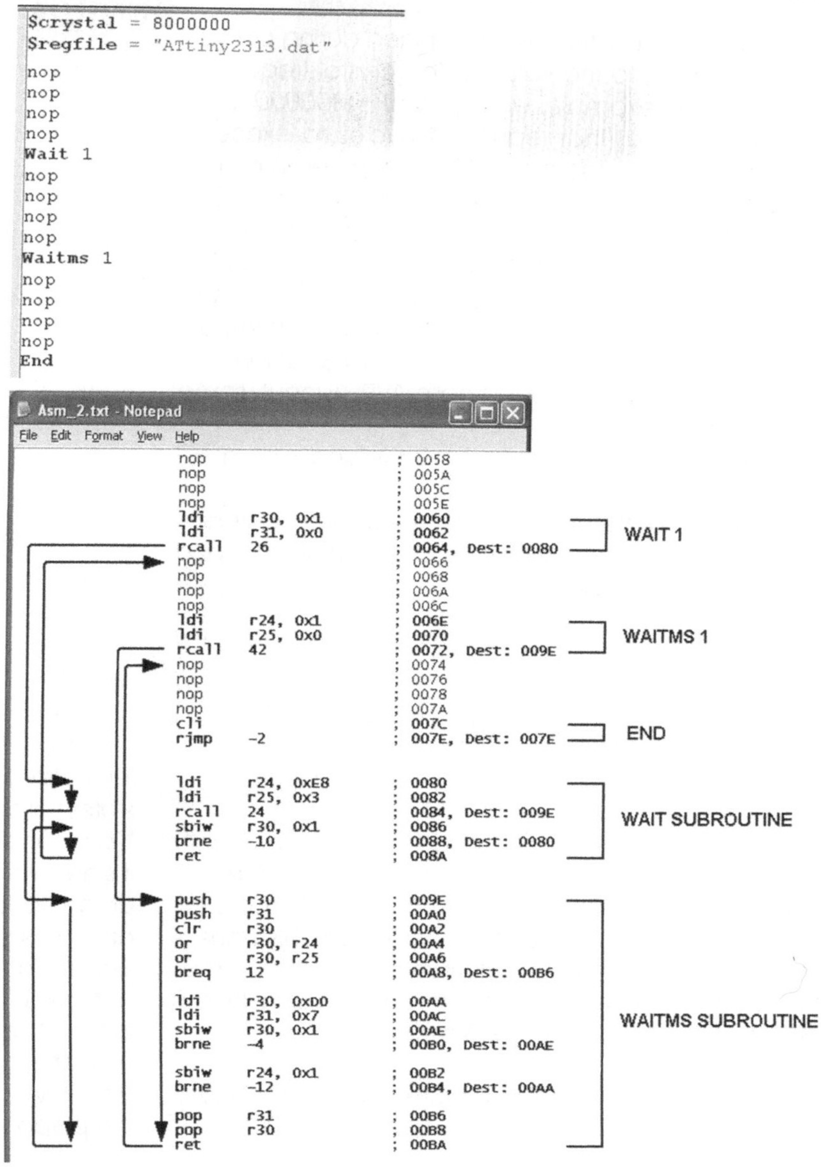

Figure 2: Analysis of Wait and Waitms statements

This will help when you look for specific routines in the associated assembler code: i.e. if you want to analyse a specific statement or a logical unit within a complex program. An example from Figure 2 shows that *Wait 1* has been translated into:

```
ldi    r30, 0x1   ; 0060
ldi    r31, 0x0   ; 0062
rcall  26         ; 0064, Dest: 0080
```

Register pair R30:R31 is used to transfer the desired wait interval (here, 1 second) to the subroutine that starts at address "0080".

Similarly, *Waitms 1* has been translated into the following code:

```
ldi    r24, 0x1   ; 006E
ldi    r25, 0x0   ; 0070
rcall  42         ; 0072, Dest: 009E
```

Waitms uses another register pair, R24:R25, to transfer a desired wait interval (here, 1 ms) to the subroutine that starts at address "009E". Many Bascom-AVR statements are translated in the same way: appropriate values are loaded into corresponding registers, at the program location where the statement itself occurs, and then a subroutine call is executed. As mentioned before, these subroutines are usually placed somewhere beyond the end of the user code. This approach allows for efficient use of memory resources because any (potentially) extensive routines are added to the program just once, no matter how often these routines are called in the program.

The *Waitms* subroutine from Figure 2 is actually a loop that executes for an appropriate number of times to achieve a 1 ms delay:

```
ldi    r30, 0xD0    ; 00AA
ldi    r31, 0x7     ; 00AC
sbiw   r30, 0x1     ; 00AE
brne   -4           ; 00B0, Dest: 00AE
```

The number of repetitions is determined during compilation according to the value of the crystal frequency directive. In this example, with *$crystal = 8000000*, the loop *sbiw + brne* (that requires 4 cycles to execute) executes in 0.5 μs. Therefore, 2000 loop iterations are necessary to obtain a 1 ms delay. 2000 equals "7D0" hexadecimal - that value is loaded to register pair R30:R31. You can check the duration of this routine yourself if you write it in a Bascom-AVR program and execute it in the simulator. I must point out that the assembler code obtained from the Revava disassembler cannot be compiled by Bascom-AVR without some slight modifications:

» hexadecimal values should be prefixed with a "$" rather than a "0x".
» it is much better if you replace relative addresses in jump and branch instructions with jumps and branches to labels:

```
ldi     r30,$D0
ldi     r31,$7
1ms_loop:
sbiw    r30,$1
brne    1ms_loop
```

The simulator shows that this code executes in exactly 1.000125 ms. Register pair R24:R25 contains the parameter from the *Waitms* statement. It is a 1 in this example, but it would be 100 for *Waitms 100*. This value is used as a counter which determines how many times the delay routine will be executed, resulting in delays from approximately 1 to 65535 ms.

If you now look at the *Wait* subroutine, you will see that it actually calls *Waitms* (*Waitms* is located at "009E"):

```
ldi     r24, 0xE8  ; 0080
ldi     r25, 0x3   ; 0082
rcall   24         ; 0084, Dest: 009E
```

The Hexadecimal value „3E8" (= 1000), stored to register pair R24:R25, is resulting in a basic delay that lasts for approximately 1 second. This basic 1 second delay routine is executed the number of times specified in the R30:R31 register-pair, resulting in a range of delays from 1 to 65535 seconds.

It is interesting how the *Wait* subroutine calls *Waitms* to obtain the basic 1 s delay. This is very common in analysing Bascom-AVR code that you will find that even seemingly-unrelated statements often call each other internally. In this way, the flash memory space is used efficiently, but it can make program analysis difficult.

2nd analysis: Timer/counter statements

Figure 3 shows disassembled Timer/Counter1-related statements *Config*, *Start* and *Stop*:

```
$crystal = 8000000
$regfile = "ATtiny2313.dat"
...
...
nop
nop
nop
nop
Config Timer1 = Timer , Prescale = 8 , _
   Clear Timer = 1 , Compare A = Toggle
nop
nop
Stop Timer1
nop
nop
Start Timer1
nop
nop
nop
nop
End
```

They are translated into several assembler instructions without any subroutine call and hence seem to be easily-understood. But, to understand what they actually do, you should have a good knowledge of microcontroller registers. For example, the *Config Timer1* statement stores some values to I/O registers located at addresses "0x2F" and "0x2E". To find the names of these registers, it's necessary to look in the datasheet of the related microcontroller. You'll find the list of all I/O registers, their addresses, structures and links to pages with their detailed description, in the chapter called "Register Summary". Here you'll find that registers TCCR1A and TCCR1B are located at these addresses and that their descriptions exist on pages 108 and 111 (for the ATtiny2313 datasheet, Rev. 2543I–AVR–04/06). These descriptions explain the purpose of each register bit in detail.

It's not our intent now to explore what the actual values in these registers mean. Let's just say that the values of the three least significant bits of the TCCR1B register, namely CS12, CS11 and CS10, select the clock source. If they are different from "000", which is true for every *Config Timer* statement, then the timer will be started simultaneously. Remember: the *Config Timer* statement not only configures, but also starts the timer. The timer mode itself is determined by other bits in these two registers.

The next statement being analysed in this example is *Stop Timer1*. It simply clears the CS12, CS11 and CS10 bits from the TCCR1B register and thus stops the timer, regardless of its mode of operation. To re-start the timer, the *Start Timer1* statement restores the value in the TCCR1B register to the value that was previously set in the configuration statement. The value in the TCCR1A register is not affected by *Start* and *Stop* commands. This works perfectly and you can stop and restart the timer many times in the program, unless you choose to reconfigure it. If you do reconfigure the timer during program execution, it's possible that a subsequent Start timer statement "doesn't know" how to restart the timer properly. I encountered this problem early in my

Bascom-AVR odyssey and I have discovered its cause by disassembling the same statements seen in this example. To avoid such problems in complex programs, I usually repeat the *Config Timer* statement instead using *Start*, when I want to restart the timer.

You can analyse other similar hardware-related statements in the same way: for example the configuration of external interrupts, the Watchdog and I/O pins (*Config INTx*, *Config Watchdog*, *Config Pinx.y*), setting the system clock division factor (*Config Clockdiv*), configuring the A/D converter (*Config ADC*), enabling and disabling of interrupts etc. These statements affect other registers, but you can analyse them in the same way. Note: Some configuration statements (for example, *Config Debounce* or *Config 1wire*) produce no executable code; they only affect the way that the associated Bascom-AVR routines are compiled.

```
$crystal = 8000000
$regfile = "ATtiny2313.dat"

nop
nop
nop
nop
Config TIMER1 = Timer , Prescale = 8 , Clear Timer = 1 , Compare A = Toggle
nop
nop
Stop TIMER1
nop
nop
Start TIMER1
nop
nop
nop
nop
End
```

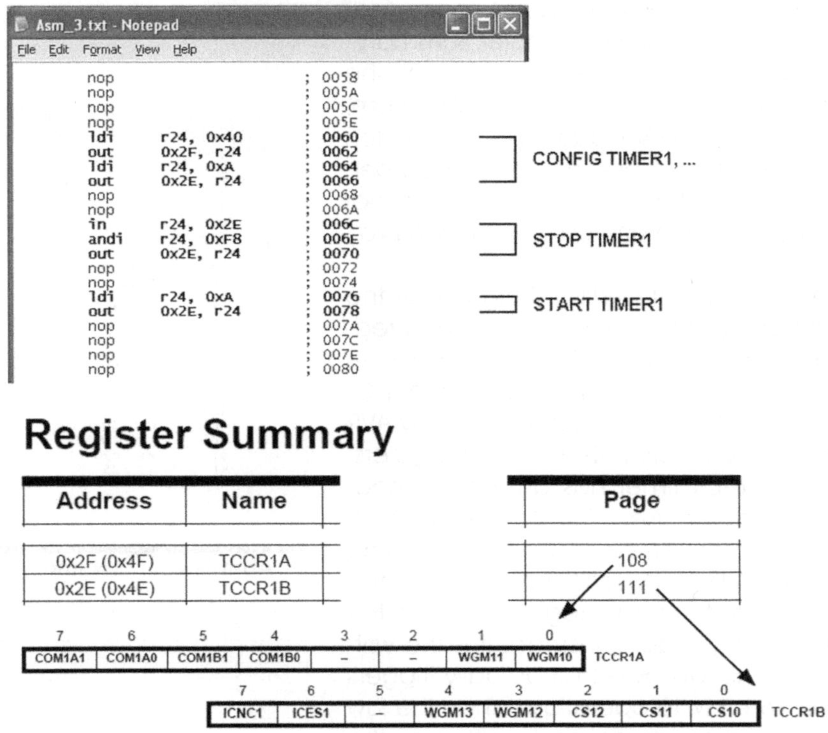

Figure 3: Analysis of Timer/Counter1-related statements

3rd analysis: Addressing registers and variables

It is interesting to explore in more detail how Bascom-AVR addresses registers from the I/O memory address space and variables that are located in the internal SRAM. We'll do it by disassembling this simple program:

```
$crystal = 8000000
$regfile = "ATtiny2313.dat"

Dim V_byte As Byte
Dim V_word As Word
nop
nop
nop
nop
Counter0 = 100
nop
nop
Counter1 = 100
nop
nop
V_byte = 100
nop
nop
V_word = 100
nop
nop
nop
nop
End
```

The same value, "100" ("64" hexadecimal) is written to 8- and 16-bit registers and to a Byte and Word variable.

The disassembled program is shown in Figure 4. What is referred to as "Counter0" in Bascom-AVR is actually the 8-bit Timer/Counter0 register TCNT0. Storing a value to Counter0 results in the following two steps:

- the value is first transferred to the R24 register (in this example it is a constant, but the value could instead be loaded from a variable);
- the value in the R24 register is then transferred to the TCNT0 register using the assembler instruction *out*.

We have seen the same procedure in the previous section: only the register names and addresses were different. A somewhat different situation arises if we try to store some value to Counter1. What is referred to as "Counter1" in Bascom-AVR are registers TCNT1H and TCNT1L. These two registers act as a unique 16-bit counter, but the microcontroller and the assembler treat them as separate entities. The disassembled code shows how the Bascom-AVR compiler has prepared the required value "100" in registers R25 and R24 and then transfers their contents into registers TCNT1H and TCNT1L.

Two things are of special interest here. In this example, the Bascom-AVR compiler uses assembler *sts* instructions to transfer the values to the registers, instead of the previously used *out*. Both instructions are valid and lead to the same result, so don't be puzzled when you see the compiler using one instruction or the other. Note, however, that different addresses should be used; the *out* instruction "sees" the TCNT1H register as part of the I/O memory space (address "0x2D"), while *sts* "sees" it as part of the internal SRAM space (address "0x4D"). In the "Register Summary" chapter, both addresses of all of the registers are given. To differentiate them, the internal SRAM addresses are written in brackets. The only difference between *out* and *sts* (from this perspective) is that *out* executes in one cycle and *sts* in two.

The second interesting thing is that the higher register of all microcontroller register pairs (here, TCNT1H) should always be written before the lower one (TCNT1L). This is determined by the way AVR microcontrollers write to 16-bit registers: Each 16-bit timer has an 8-bit temporary register used for storing the high byte of the 16-bit register-pair. Writing the high byte doesn't actually store the value into the target register, but into this temporary register instead. It is the writing of the low byte that actually triggers the 16-bit write operation. When the low byte of a 16-bit register is written by the CPU, the high byte, previously stored in the temporary register, and the low byte, are both copied into the 16-bit register in the same clock cycle. The same is true for reading, but the sequence is opposite: you should read the low byte first, at which time the high byte will be transferred to the temporary register in the same cycle. When reading the high byte, you will get the value from the temporary register. Note that the Bascom-AVR compiler always takes care of these details.

```
$crystal = 8000000
$regfile = "ATtiny2313.dat"
Dim V_byte As Byte , V_word As Word

nop
nop
nop
nop
V_byte = 100
nop
nop
V_word = 100
nop
nop
COUNTER0 = 100
nop
nop
Counter1 = 100
nop
nop
nop
nop
End
```

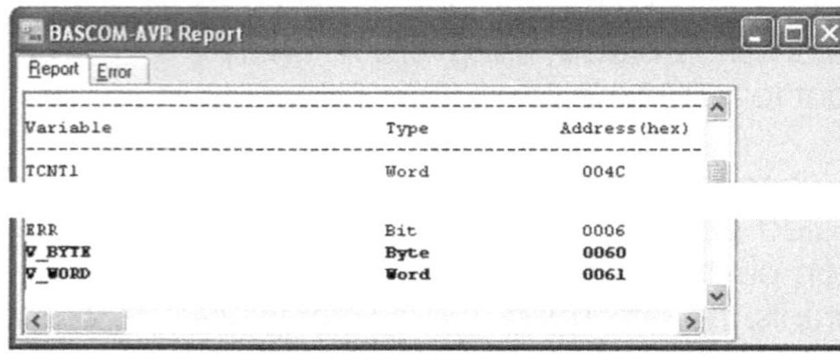

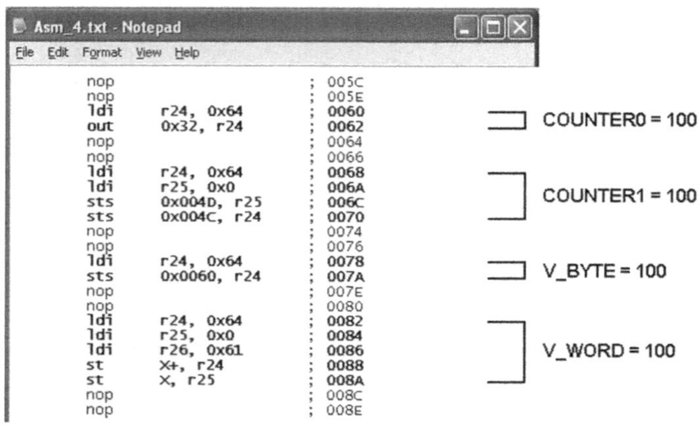

Address	Name		Page
0x32 (0x52)	TCNT0	Timer/Counter0 (8-bit)	81
0x2D (0x4D)	TCNT1H	Timer/Counter1 – Counter Register High Byte	112
0x2C (0x4C)	TCNT1L	Timer/Counter1 – Counter Register Low Byte	112

Figure 4: Addressing registers and variables

Variables are located in the internal SRAM address space, which starts at location "60" hexadecimal (in the case of the ATtiny2013). Two variables are defined in the example program: the Byte variable *V_byte* and the Word variable *V_word*. Bascom-AVR has placed them at the addresses "60" and "61:62", respectively. This can be seen from the Bascom-AVR report window, also shown in Figure 4. The Bascom-AVR compiler uses direct and indirect addressing to access variables. In this example, *V_byte* is addressed directly, with the *sts* instruction:

```
ldi    r24, 0x64     ; 0078
sts    0x0060, r24   ; 007A
```

Bascom-AVR usually uses indirect addressing for Word, Integer, Long and other variables needing more than 1-byte. In our example, *V_word* is addressed indirectly using the contents of the X register:

```
ldi    r24, 0x64     ; 0082
ldi    r25, 0x0      ; 0084
ldi    r26, 0x61     ; 0086
st     x+, r24       ; 0088
st     x, r25        ; 008A
```

The X register is actually register pair R26:R27. Note that here, only register R26 (the lower byte of the X-register) is loaded with the address. This is the case with the ATtiny2313 and other microcontrollers which contain 128 or fewer bytes of internal SRAM. If you write a program for a microcontroller with more SRAM, R27 will also be used for indexing purposes. For example, the same statement for the ATtiny4313 would be compiled this way:

```
ldi    r24, 0x64     ; 0082
```

```
ldi     r25, 0x0        ; 0084
ldi     r26, 0x61       ; 0086
ldi     r27, 0x0        ; 0088
st      x+, r24         ; 008A
st      x, r25          ; 008C
```

4th analysis: Interrupts

Let's look at this simple program that counts pulses at the PD3 input pin using external interrupts:

```
$crystal = 8000000
$regfile = "ATtiny2313.dat"

Dim Pulse_counter As Byte

Config Pind.3 = Input
Config Int1 = Falling
On Int1 Int1_sub
Enable Interrupts
Enable Int1

Do
'   do whatever
Loop
End

Int1_sub:
   Incr Pulse_counter
Return
```

The compiled and disassembled program is shown in Figure 5 (only those parts of the disassembled code that are relevant to this discussion are shown). Near the top of the program, you can see the INT1 interrupt vector, which is actually a jump to the first executable instruction of the associated interrupt service routine. This interrupt vector has been generated as a result of the *On Int1 Int1_sub* statement. The interrupt service routine, although consisting of only one *Incr* statement followed by a *Return*, has been translated into a quite extensive list of code. The *Incr* and *Return* instructions make up the small bold part of that code. The rest is a sequence of assembler *push* and *pop* instructions that save the contents of almost all of the registers on the stack at the beginning of the subroutine, and retrieve them all before returning from the interrupt. The Bascom-AVR compiler does that as a precaution: it doesn't know which registers will be altered in the interrupt service routine and hence it saves/restores all registers that might be changed.

The result of this precaution is not only the extensive code, but also the fact that the execution lasts longer - 116 cycles in this example. Compare this to 10 cycles that are necessary to execute *Incr* and *Return*! Of course, you can use the *nosave* option in the *On INT1* statement and thus prevent the compiler from generating *push*es and *pop*s, but then you have to save/restore the used registers yourself.

Optimising Bascom-AVR with assembler

Now we are prepared to do something really exceptional: to optimise the code generated by Bascom-AVR by replacing some critical Bascom statements or routines with several assembler instructions. The *Incr* statement from our last example uses only two registers, R24 and R26. It is necessary to save and restore only their contents, plus the contents of status register SREG. Even better, if we use direct addressing instead of the indirect addressing originally used, we can realize the *Incr* statement using only one register. An optimized pulse-counting program looks like this example (only modified parts have been shown):

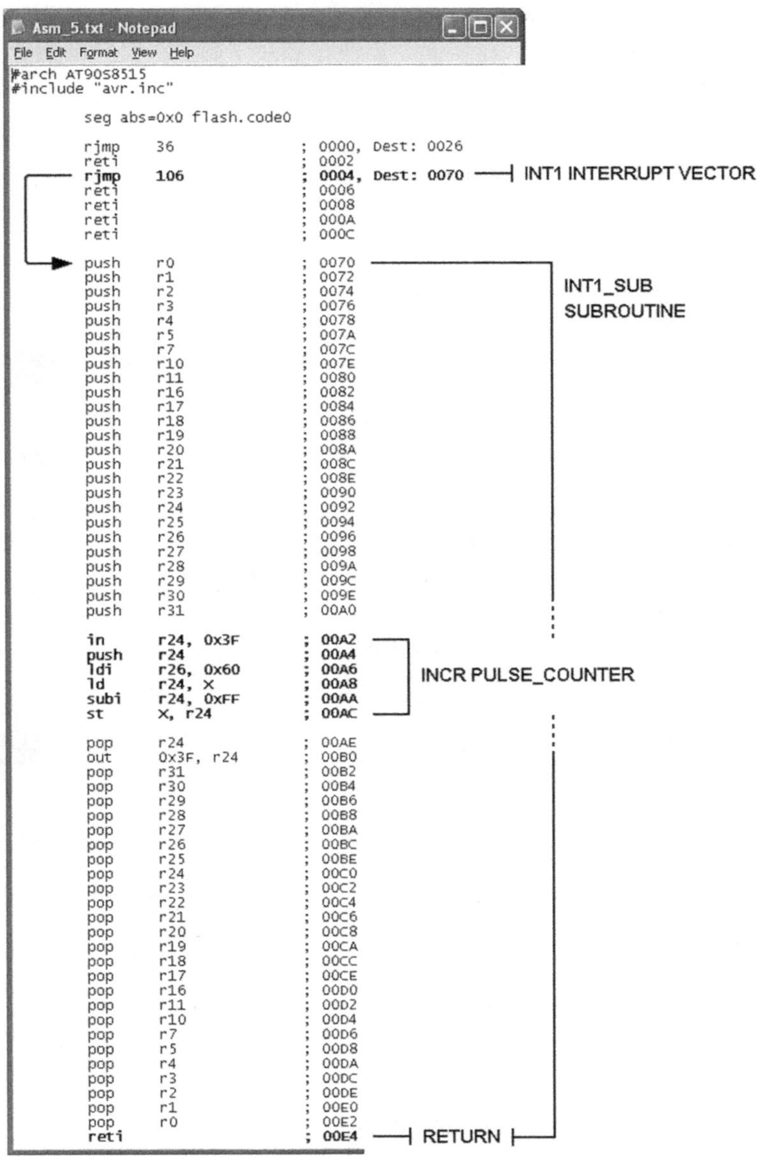

```
Asm_5.txt - Notepad
File Edit Format View Help
#arch AT90S8515
#include "avr.inc"

        seg abs=0x0 flash.code0

        rjmp    36              ; 0000, Dest: 0026
        reti                    ; 0002
        rjmp    106             ; 0004, Dest: 0070
        reti                    ; 0006
        reti                    ; 0008
        reti                    ; 000A
        reti                    ; 000C

        push    r0              ; 0070
        push    r1              ; 0072
        push    r2              ; 0074
        push    r3              ; 0076
        push    r4              ; 0078
        push    r5              ; 007A
        push    r7              ; 007C
        push    r10             ; 007E
        push    r11             ; 0080
        push    r16             ; 0082
        push    r17             ; 0084
        push    r18             ; 0086
        push    r19             ; 0088
        push    r20             ; 008A
        push    r21             ; 008C
        push    r22             ; 008E
        push    r23             ; 0090
        push    r24             ; 0092
        push    r25             ; 0094
        push    r26             ; 0096
        push    r27             ; 0098
        push    r28             ; 009A
        push    r29             ; 009C
        push    r30             ; 009E
        push    r31             ; 00A0

        in      r24, 0x3F       ; 00A2
        push    r24             ; 00A4
        ldi     r26, 0x60       ; 00A6
        ld      r24, X          ; 00A8
        subi    r24, 0xFF       ; 00AA
        st      X, r24          ; 00AC

        pop     r24             ; 00AE
        out     0x3F, r24       ; 00B0
        pop     r31             ; 00B2
        pop     r30             ; 00B4
        pop     r29             ; 00B6
        pop     r28             ; 00B8
        pop     r27             ; 00BA
        pop     r26             ; 00BC
        pop     r25             ; 00BE
        pop     r24             ; 00C0
        pop     r23             ; 00C2
        pop     r22             ; 00C4
        pop     r21             ; 00C6
        pop     r20             ; 00C8
        pop     r19             ; 00CA
        pop     r18             ; 00CC
        pop     r17             ; 00CE
        pop     r16             ; 00D0
        pop     r11             ; 00D2
        pop     r10             ; 00D4
        pop     r7              ; 00D6
        pop     r5              ; 00D8
        pop     r4              ; 00DA
        pop     r3              ; 00DC
        pop     r2              ; 00DE
        pop     r1              ; 00E0
        pop     r0              ; 00E2
        reti                    ; 00E4
```


Figure 5: An external interrupt service routine disassembled

```
On Intl Intl_sub Nosave

Intl_sub:
    push r24                 'save R24
    in r24 , sreg            'save SREG
    push r24
    lds r24 , {pulse_counter}
                             'Incr Pulse_counter
     inc r24
     sts {pulse_counter},r24
     pop r24
     !out sreg , r24         'restore SREG
     pop r24                 'restore R24
Return
```

Besides being visually much shorter, it executes in only 19 cycles - it is more than 6 times faster than the original program!

Similar optimization can be done with a pulse counting routine using a Word variable. BascomAVR increments a Word variable using the following routine (the code has been obtained by disassembling):

```
ldi     r26, 0x60  ; 00A6
rcall   56         ; 00A8, _
                     Dest: 00E2
...
...
ld      r30, X+    ; 00E2
ld      r31, X     ; 00E4
subi    r30, 0xFF  ; 00E6
sbci    r31, 0xFF  ; 00E8
st      X, r31     ; 00EA
st      -X, r30    ; 00EC
ret                ; 00EE
```

It uses three registers (or four with AVRs containing more than 128B of SRAM), indirect addressing and calls a subroutine - a lot can be optimized here! An optimized routine that uses direct addressing and can increment a Word variable using only one register, looks like this:

```
lds r24,{pulse_counter}
                   'Incr
                   'Pulse_counter
subi r24,$ff
sts {pulse_counter},r24
lds r24,{pulse_counter+1}
sbci r24,$ff
sts {pulse_counter+1},r24
```

If you are puzzled by the subtraction instructions that are used to increment the value, look at the AVR instruction set. There is no single *add* instruction that could add a register value, a constant and the carry bit, but the *sbci* does just that (you have to use the complement of the number that you want to add; in this instance, "$FF"). Maybe this routine doesn't seem significantly shorter than the original one. However, it is more economical if used within an interrupt service routine, because only registers R24 and SREG have to be saved and restored. Examples of optimized interrupt service routines that increment Byte and Word variables are shown in Figure 6.

Interrupt service routines are a good subject for optimizing - we want them to be as simple and as quick as possible. You can optimize them according to the following steps:

» disassemble the BascomAVR program;
» locate the code that belongs to the interrupt subroutine (it is not difficult to find it because it is surrounded with a bunch of *push*es and *pop*s);
» if you have more than one interrupt subroutine in your program, consult the interrupt vectors to locate the right one;

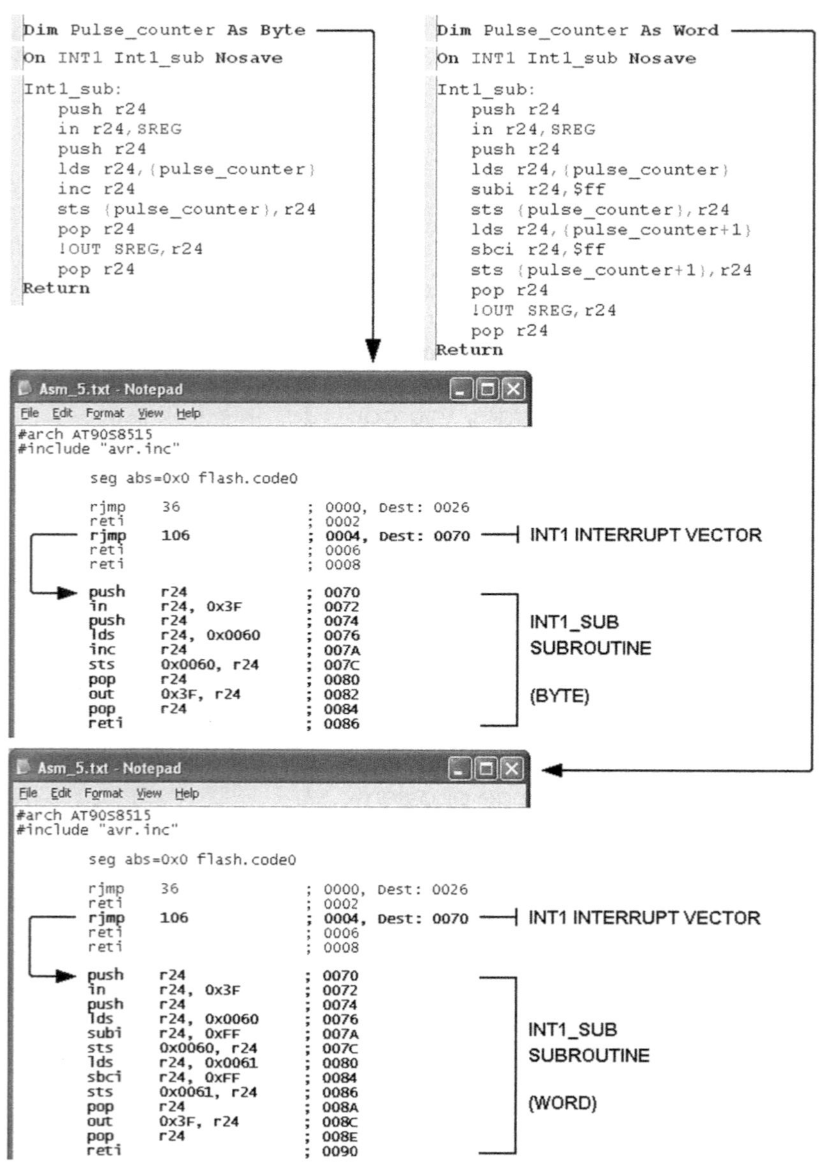

Figure 6: Optimised external interrupt service routines

- notice which registers are used by the interrupt subroutine and other subroutines it may call;
- add the *nosave* option to the *On interrupt* statement;
- add *push* instructions for any register used (don't forget SREG!) at the beginning of the interrupt subroutine;
- add *pop* instructions in the reverse order for the same registers before return;
- recompile the program.

Such modification does not require assembler programming skills – it's enough if you can recognize register-oriented instructions and write *push*es and *pop*s for all the used registers. An example in Figure 6 shows how to do this for R24 and SREG registers (don't forget to take care of the latter!). A possible further step is to replace the critical Bascom-AVR statements with assembler instructions. The advantages of this replacement are that your code might be shorter than the original and that it is no longer version-dependent (the way that a given Bascom-AVR statement is compiled can be different with different versions of the Bascom-AVR program). Both can be very useful not only in interrupt service routines, but also whenever you need full control of the generated code. However, this requires a good knowledge of assembler programming and the microcontroller itself.

TIPS

For further reading:

Bascom-AVR help, chapters "Language Fundamentals", "Assembler mnemonics" and "Mixing ASM and BASIC";

The AVR instruction set, can be downloaded from the web site www.atmel.com;

The datasheet of the microcontroller in use, can be downloaded from the web site www.atmel.com.

High-voltage Programmer for AVR Microcontrollers

By Vladimir Mitrović

We usually use ISP programmers for AVR microcontrollers because they offer all the functions that an ordinary user needs. However, there are situations in which such programmers are not helpful: for example, if *Serial programming enable fuse* (SPIEN) is disabled or if *External reset disable fuse* (RSTDISBL) is programmed. Although you cannot disable SPIEN in serial programming mode yourself, you may affect some other fuses and disable further serial programming. After that, you may throw the microcontroller away... or use this simple and low-cost parallel and serial high-voltage programmer that will revive it in a minute.

The programmer whose schematic is shown in Figure 1 can read and program the fuses and erase the lock bits for most new AVR microcontrollers (note: it is not intended to program flash and EEPROM memory). It is designed as an extension to MiniPin II and MegaPin development systems, to which it is connected via three 10-pin flat cables.

NOTE

In all further references related to both development boards, the common name MPIN will be used instead of their separate names, MiniPin II and MegaPin.

These 3 cables are connected to ports A, C and D of the MPIN development boards. The 4th port, port B, is used for driving a 16x2 LCD display. The electronic circuit of the programmer is powered by +5 V, taken from the PORTD of the MPIN. It consists of a DC/DC converter (T1, L2 and D1) that raises this voltage to 18-20 V, a 12 V voltage regulator IC1 and two electronic switches (IC2 and T2).

DC/DC converter works at 32 kHz. It is driven by the PD5 pin of the microcontroller contained on the MPIN development systems. The microcontroller keeps PD5 at a logic *Low* most of the time, which switches off transistor T1 and the DC/DC converter minimizing the power consumption. 100 ms before a programming session starts, the microcontroller starts to produce pulses on the PD5 pin. These pulses wake-up the DC/DC converter and the voltage across C3 rises to 18-20 V. The exact value de-

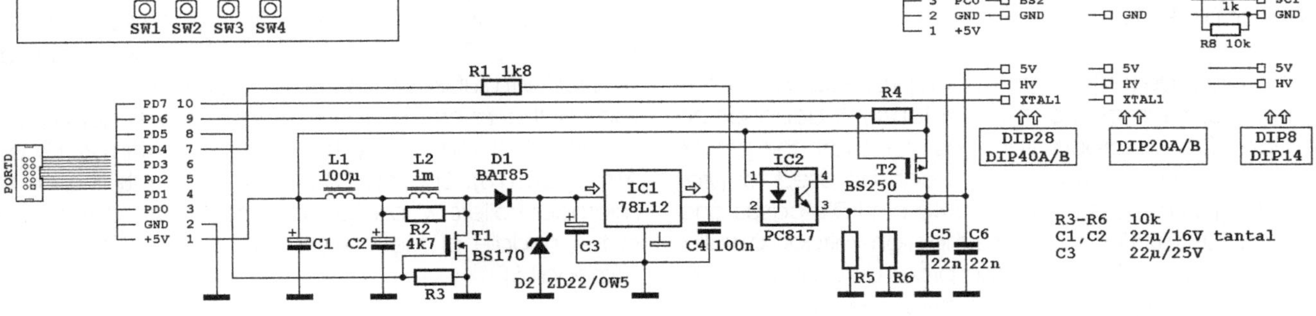

Figure 1: Simple high-voltage programmer for AVR microcontrollers

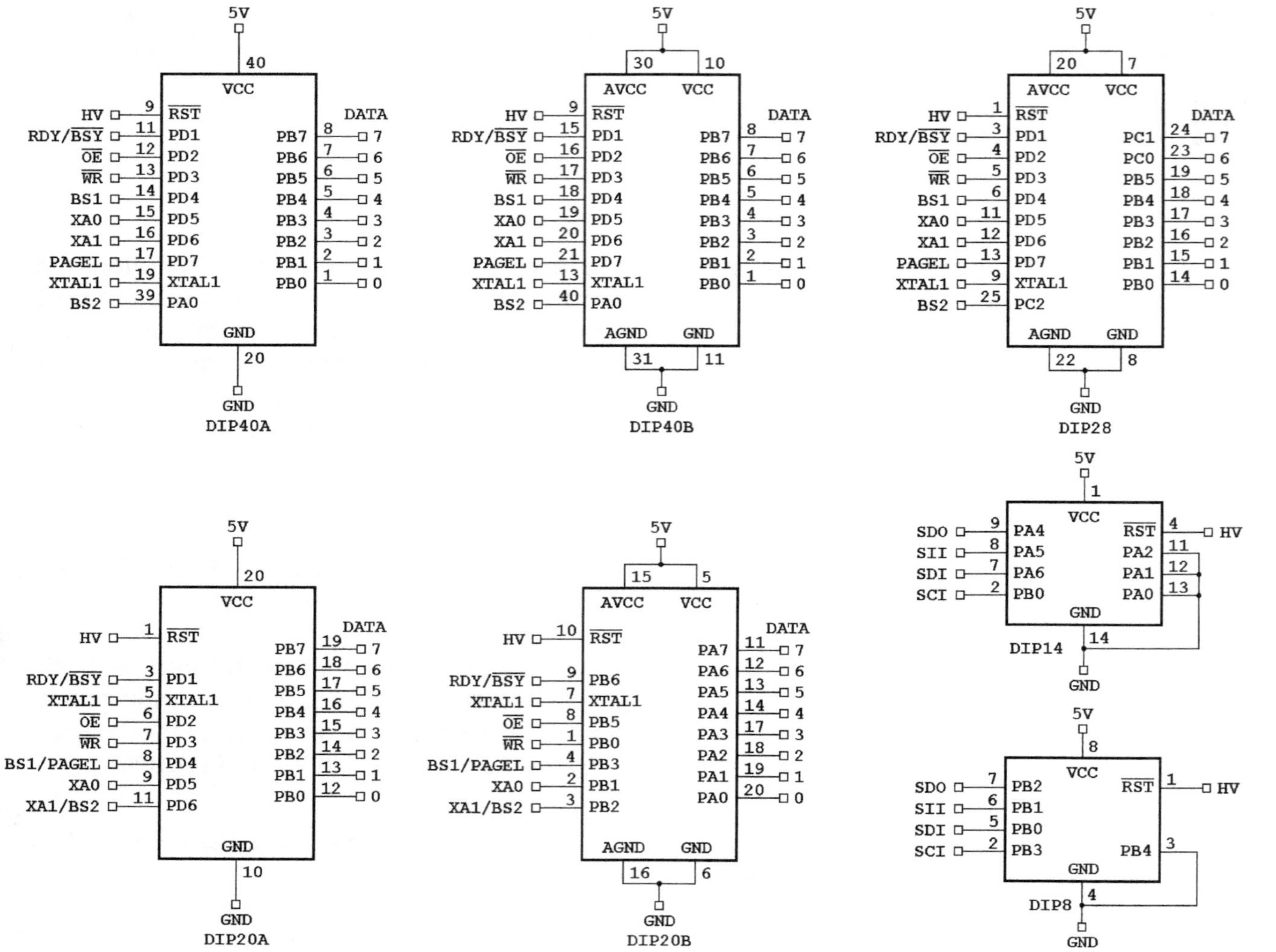

Figure 2: Control signals and pinouts for typical AVR microcontrollers

pends on L2, which has a pretty high tolerance. Zener diode D2 prevents the voltage across C3 exceeding 22 V. This voltage is regulated to 12 V by IC1 and is used as a high voltage source during the programming session. IC2 and T2 are electronic switches that apply either high voltage or the standard 5 V to the microcontroller being programmed.

Besides control signals for the DC/DC converter, the microcontroller produces a number of control and data signals needed during programming. These signals are present at ports A and C (for which all pins are used) as well as at pin PD7.

The high-voltage (HV) programming procedure is not the same for all members of the AVR family. It depends on the type of the microcontroller, as well as on the pinout and the number of I/O pins that can be used for programming. ATmegas in 28- and 40-pin PDIP cases and ATtinys in 20-pin PDIP cases use the high-voltage parallel programming method, but the procedure and control signals for ATmegas and ATtinys are somewhat different. ATtinys in 8- and 14-pin PDIP cases use the serial high-voltage programming method. Which signals are necessary for each category is shown on the right side of the Figure 1.

Figure 2 shows the control and data signals and pinouts for typical AVR microcontrollers. Most contemporary AVR microcontrollers belong to one of these categories. All of this is summarized in Table 1, in which the microcontrollers are classified into seven groups. All microcontrollers within the same group are pin-compatible with each other and share a common programming procedure.

20-pin microcontrollers are produced with two different pinouts and the same holds true for 40-pin microcontrollers. In Figure 2 and in Table 1, these pinouts are marked with suffixes A and B. Sockets DIP20A and DIP40A match the microcontrollers whose power supply pins are located diagonally (for example, ATtiny2313 and ATmega8515). Sockets DIP20B and DIP40B match the microcontrollers whose power supply pins are located in the middle of the case (for example, ATtiny26 and ATmega16).

The programmer is best built on the PCB whose component layout is shown in Figure 3, while Figure 4 shows a

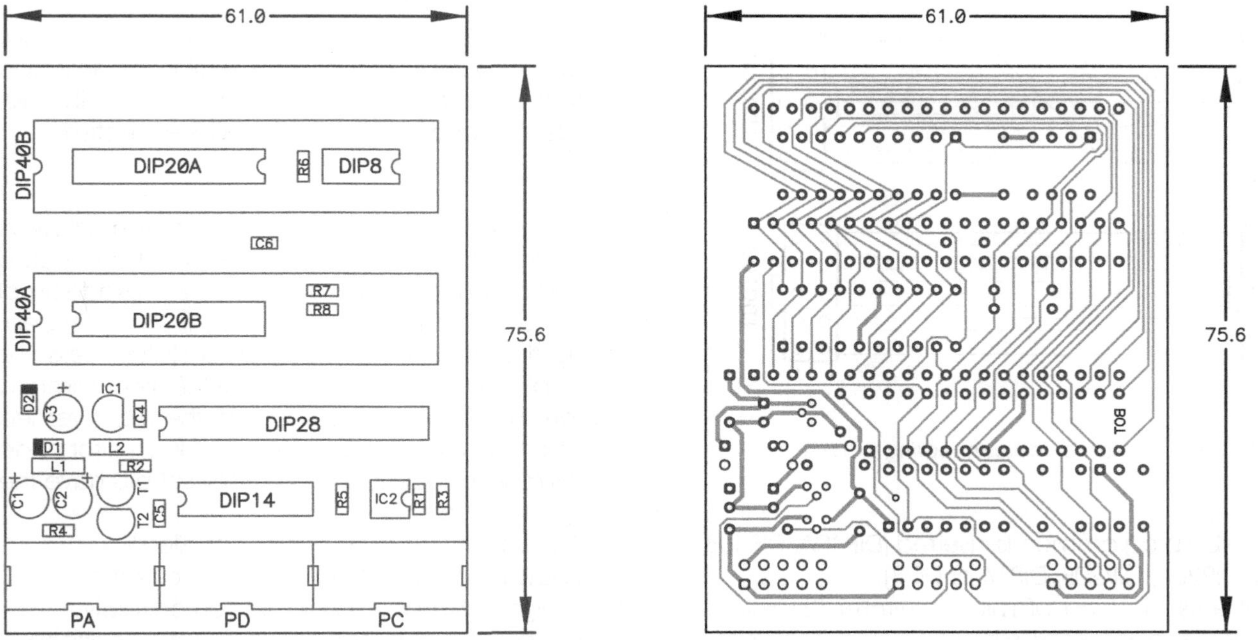

Figure 3: Component layout: note that not all sockets are oriented the same way

photo of the prototype. The microcontroller to be programmed should be inserted in one of the seven DIP sockets of the programmer. Be careful: not all sockets are oriented in the same way!

How to use the programmer

The programmer is designed as an extension to the MPIN development boards, with an ATmega8515 or ATmega8535 used as the control microcontroller. The ATmega should be programmed with the HV_AVR_programmer.bas program and it should run using the internal 8 MHz RC clock, CKSEL3-0 = "0100". This is not the default setting, so be sure to set the proper CKSEL values when programming the microcontroller. Push-buttons SW1 to SW4 should be connected to the PD0 through PD3 input pins, respectively. These push-buttons, together with the LCD display connected to PORTB, enable an interactive communication with the control microcontroller's program.

NOTE

Instead of MPIN, you can control the programmer with an ATmega8515 or similar microcontroller mounted on a similar development system or even a standalone microcontroller unit. Be sure to use the same ports and modify the connecting cables if necessary. The LCD display configuration statement within the Bascom program should correspond to the way that the display is connected to PORTB.

The programmer is connected to MPIN via three identical cables, the sketch of which is shown in Figure 5. 10-wire flat cables with 10-pin IDC10F connectors at both ends are used. Equally marked pins should be interconnected (1-1, 2-2, etc.) - be sure to orient the connectors as shown in Figure 5. The preferable cable length is 20-50 cm. Connect the cables to the ports according to Figure 1.

As soon as the program starts, it will display a message which explains the purpose of push-buttons SW1-SW4:

» **SW1** selects one of 7 sockets in which the microcon-

Figure 4: Photo of the programmer

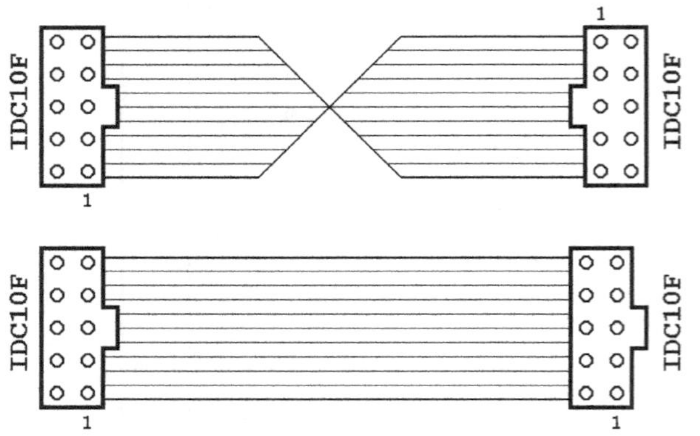

Figure 5: Sketch of the connecting cables

troller to be programmed is inserted (DIP40A, DIP40B, DIP28, DIP20A, DIP20B, DIP14 or DIP8),

» **SW2** selects the type of microcontroller (27 microcontrollers are currently supported, but only those that match the selected case will be listed),
» **SW3** selects the command (Read, Write, Edit or Erase) and
» **SW4** executes the selected command.

Press SW1 briefly to continue, and then use SW1-SW3 to select a socket, a microcontroller and a command. The LCD display shows the currently-selected items as shown in Figure 6. When you are satisfied with the selection, press SW4 to execute the selected command and display the result. If properly inserted in the appropriate socket, the microcontroller to be programmed will receive all necessary control signals and data according to Atmel's recommendations. All pins are under program control and the voltage on any pin is present only during the programming session, i.e. a short period after the SW4 has been pressed. This means that the microcontroller can be inserted to or pulled out from the socket even when the unit is still powered-up.

Commands

??

Prompt to select a command.

Read

The program reads the fuse bytes of the inserted microcontroller and displays their values in hexadecimal

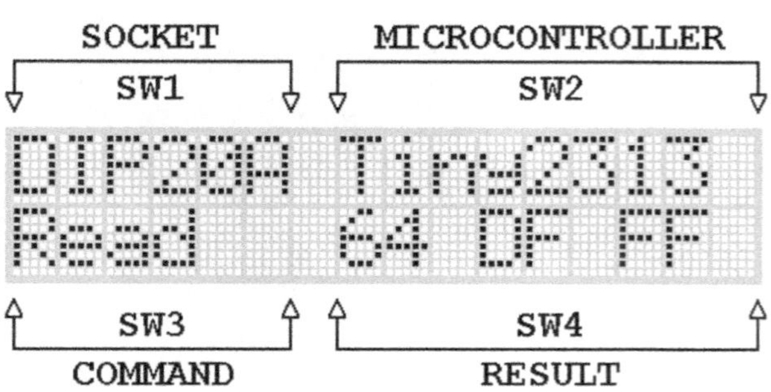

Figure 6: LCD display shows the selected items and the result of the executed command

form, in the following sequence: *low*, *high*, *extended*. Only those fuse bytes that actually exist in the selected microcontroller are displayed. After 4 seconds, the display is cleared and a new command is expected.

Write

When you select this command the program displays the default contents of the fuse bytes for the selected microcontroller. The values are shown in hexadecimal form, in the following sequence: *low*, *high*, *extended*. Following the command execution a status message will be displayed. The status will be "OK" if the command has been successfully executed and the result verified or "Error xx" if an error has occurred. "xx" is an error code shown as a hexadecimal number. Any set bits have the following meaning:

» bit 0: hardware error (no microcontroller?)
» bit 1: *low* byte has not been written correctly
» bit 2: *high* byte has not been written correctly
» bit 3: *extended* byte has not been written correctly

An error can occur if a wrong microcontroller has been selected (i.e. if the selected microcontroller does not match the inserted one) or if the microcontroller has been locked. After 4 seconds, the display is cleared and a new command is expected.

Edit

Use this command if you want to program fuse bytes with an arbitrary combination of bits. When you select this command, the program shows the default contents of the fuse bytes for the selected microcontroller. The values are shown in hexadecimal form, in the following sequence: *low*, *high*, *extended*. Only those fuse bytes that actually exist in the selected microcontroller are displayed. When the Edit command starts, a blinking cursor is displayed under the first hexadecimal digit. You can edit the value of the selected digit by briefly pressing the SW3 push-button as many times as necessary. You

CAUTION

There are some microcontrollers with one or more non-existent bits within a particular fuse byte. If you try to program (set to "0") a non-existing bit, an error will be displayed after the command has been executed because verification has failed. I don't know if you can destroy the microcontroller this way. Therefore, it is recommended that you study the datasheet before a non-default fuse bit configuration is written.

NOTE

The four-second interval during which a message is displayed can be shortened if you press any push-button.

can move the cursor between the digits by pressing the SW1 or SW2 push-buttons. When the desired combination is set, press SW4 to write it into the microcontroller and leave the Edit mode. To confirm the programming, the program displays the same messages as after the Write command.

Erase

Erase command erases lock bits. This is necessary if the flash memory of the microcontroller has been locked, because then the fuse bits will have been locked too. Caution: besides the lock bits, this command erases the whole flash memory, meaning that the program inside the microcontroller will be erased, too.

Following this command's execution, a status message will be displayed. The status will be "OK" if the command has been successfully executed or "Error 01" if an error has occurred (a wrong microcontroller has probably been selected or no microcontroller has been inserted). After 4 seconds, the display is cleared and a new command is expected.

NOTE

You can abort the Edit mode by resetting the control microcontroller.

MPIN	ATmega	ATtiny par.	ATtiny ser.	ATmega 8515 /161/162	ATmega 8535 /16/32	ATmega 8/48 /88/168	ATtiny 2313	ATtiny 26/ 261 /461/861	ATtiny 24 /44/84	ATtiny 13/25 /45/85
				DIP40A	DIP40B	DIP28	DIP20A	DIP20B	DIP14	DIP8
PA7	Data7	Data7		PB7 (8)	PB7 (8)	PC1 (24)	PB7 (19)	PA7 (11)		
PA6	Data6	Data6		PB6 (7)	PB6 (7)	PC0 (23)	PB6 (18)	PA6 (12)		
PA5	Data5	Data5		PB5 (6)	PB5 (6)	PB5 (19)	PB5 (17)	PA5 (13)		
PA4	Data4	Data4		PB4 (5)	PB4 (5)	PB4 (18)	PB4 (16)	PA4 (14)		
PA3	Data3	Data3		PB3 (4)	PB3 (4)	PB3 (17)	PB3 (15)	PA3 (17)		
PA2	Data2	Data2		PB2 (3)	PB2 (3)	PB2 (16)	PB2 (14)	PA2 (18)		
PA1	Data1	Data1		PB1 (2)	PB1 (2)	PB1 (15)	PB1 (13)	PA1 (19)		
PA0	Data0	Data0		PB0 (1)	PB0 (1)	PB0 (14)	PB0 (12)	PA0 (20)		
PC7	PAGEL			PD7 (17)	PD7 (21)	PD7 (13)				
PC6	XA1	XA1/BS2		PD6 (16)	PD6 (20)	PD6 (12)	PD6 (11)	PB2 (3)		
PC5	XA0	XA0		PD5 (15)	PD5 (19)	PD5 (11)	PD5 (9)	PB1 (2)		
PC4	BS1	BS1/PAGEL		PD4 (14)	PD4 (18)	PD4 (6)	PD4 (8)	PB3 (4)		
PC3	WR	WR	SDI	PD3 (13)	PD3 (17)	PD3 (5)	PD3 (7)	PB0 (1)	PA6 (7)	PB0 (5)
PC2	OE	OE	SII	PD2 (12)	PD2 (16)	PD2 (4)	PD2 (6)	PB5 (8)	PA5 (8)	PB1 (6)
PC1	RDY/BSY	RDY/BSY	SDO	PD1 (11)	PD1 (15)	PD1 (3)	PD1 (3)	PB6 (9)	PA4 (9)	PB2 (7)
PC0	BS2		SCI	PA0 (39)	PA0 (40)	PC2 (25)			PB0 (2)	PB3 (2)
PD7	XTAL1	XTAL1		XTAL1 (19)	XTAL1 (13)	XTAL1 (9)	XTAL1 (5)	XTAL1 (7)		
PD6	5V	5V	5V	VCC (40)	VCC (10,30)	VCC (7,20)	VCC (20)	VCC (5,15)	VCC (1)	VCC (8)
PD5	12V	12V	12V							
PD4	HV	HV	HV	RESET (9)	RESET (9)	RESET (1)	RESET (1)	RESET (10)	RESET (4)	RESET (1)
GND	GND	GND	GND	GND (20)	GND (11,31)	GND (8,22)	GND (10)	GND (6,16)	GND (14-11)	GND (3,4)

Table 1: Control and data signals for various AVR microcontrollers

Program upgrade

The program HV_AVR_programmer.bas supports most modern ATmega and ATtiny microcontrollers produced in dual inline packages (PDIP). It will support new microcontrollers, too, if they are pin-compatible with current ones and if they support the same or similar programming procedures. You will be able to program these new microcontrollers in one of the following ways:

Programming a similar microcontroller (no program editing is necessary)
If a new microcontroller is pin-compatible with a currently-supported one and has the same programming procedure, as well as the same number of fuse bytes (check a datasheet), then program it as if the supported microcontroller had been inserted. If the default values or meanings of some fuse bits differ between the two microcontrollers, then use the Edit command to update values.

Programming a new microcontroller (no program editing is necessary)
Use the following procedure if a new microcontroller is pin-compatible with a currently-supported one and has the same programming procedure, but the number of fuse bytes is different: Select the appropriate package style (with SW1) and then press and hold SW2 for more than 3 seconds. A "LO HI EX" identification will be displayed instead of the microcontroller's name as in the following example:

```
DIP20A LO HI EX
??
```

In this example, a microcontroller in the DIP20A socket with 3 fuse bytes has been selected. If you keep the SW2 pressed, the number of fuse bytes will change in a "LO HI EX" -> "LO HI" -> "LO" -> "LO HI EX" sequence. Release the SW2 when a suitable number of fuse bytes is displayed. Execute the Edit command; the default values of all fuse bits in this instance will be "1" (not programmed).

Entering a new microcontroller in the program's data base (requires a minor program update)
The programming data for each microcontroller are listed in the table *UC* at the end of the program. An entry in this table looks something like the following example:

```
Data 4 , 2 , 3 , &B01100100 , _
&B11011111 , &B11111111 , "Tiny2313"
```

The first item, "4", designates the socket. All available sockets are listed in the table *DIP*:

```
Dip:                ' available sockets
Data ""
Data "DIP40A"
Data "DIP40B"
Data "DIP28"
Data "DIP20A"
Data "DIP20B"
Data "DIP14"
Data "DIP8"
Data "*"
```

The first entry in this table has an index of 0 and, therefore, index 4 would correspond to the DIP20A socket. The second item from the *UC* table, "2", designates a programming procedure. Three different procedures have been programmed:

- 1, parallel HV programming for ATmega microcontrollers (valid for all ATmegas),
- 2, parallel HV programming for ATtiny microcontrollers (valid for 20-pin ATtinys) and
- 3, serial HV programming for ATtiny microcontrollers (valid for 8- and 14-pin ATtinys).

The third item from the *UC* table, "3", shows how many fuse bytes the selected microcontroller has. In this example, it would have all three bytes: *low*, *high* and *extended*. The following three bytes from the *UC* table define default values for *low*, *high* and *extended* fuses, respectively. It's necessary to define all three bytes, no matter how many fuse bytes the microcontroller really has (non-existing bytes must be filled with "1").

The last entry in the *UC* table is a string with the microcontroller name. The string can be 1 to 9 characters long.

If you enter a new entry in the *UC* table, its data structure has to be respected. The first entry in the table is always *Data 0*, while the last is always *Data 255 , 0*. The *Data* lines that define a particular microcontroller are located between these two lines:

```
Uc:
Data 0              'mandatory content of the
                    '1st entry
Data ...            'here enter data that
                    'describe...
Data ...            '...each microcontroller
Data 255 , 0        'mandatory content of the
                    'last entry
```

The entry for a new microcontroller can be inserted anywhere between the first and the last entry. Its position within the table, determines the order in which that microcontroller is listed on the display. No byte within the table should be equal to &B00000000, because this value disrupts the table searching algorithm.

Program ID	
Name:	HV_AVR_programmer.bas
Microcontroller:	ATmega8515 or ATmega8535
MiniPin compatibility:	yes (ATmega8535), with the programmer module
MegaPin compatibility:	yes, with the programmer module
The program enables HV programming of the fuses of most contemporary microcontrollers. This way, a "dead" microcontroller can be revived	

UART to RS232 or USB adapters

By Bojan Kovač

The abbreviation UART stands for Universal Asynchronous Receiver/Transmitter. It is a serial data interface with a defined speed. Regardless of the actual voltage level of the RS232 signals, these RS232/RS482 devices present signals to the microcontroller as a logical 0 or 1.

This protocol sends data to the microcontroller serially, which means the data stream must be converted back to parallel (which is the function of the UART block in the microcontroller). A block diagram of such a data transfer is shown in Figure 1.

Data transfer via the USB bus is similar to RS232 with a some differences: USB is a faster transfer method, and to interface it with a microcontroller, we can use a USB to UART bridge, such as the FT232RL made by Future Technology Devices International LTD (FTDI) [1].

There are a variety of different asynchronous serial adapters available on the market. Bascom-AVR communicates with all of these with one statement meant to send data to the AVR's UART- the *Print* statement.

Probably there is no other microcontroller language with as simple a statement to control the UART, as Bascom/AVR. There are numerous UART parameters that must be configured, but many of them are changed very infrequently, so we can often just use the default settings.

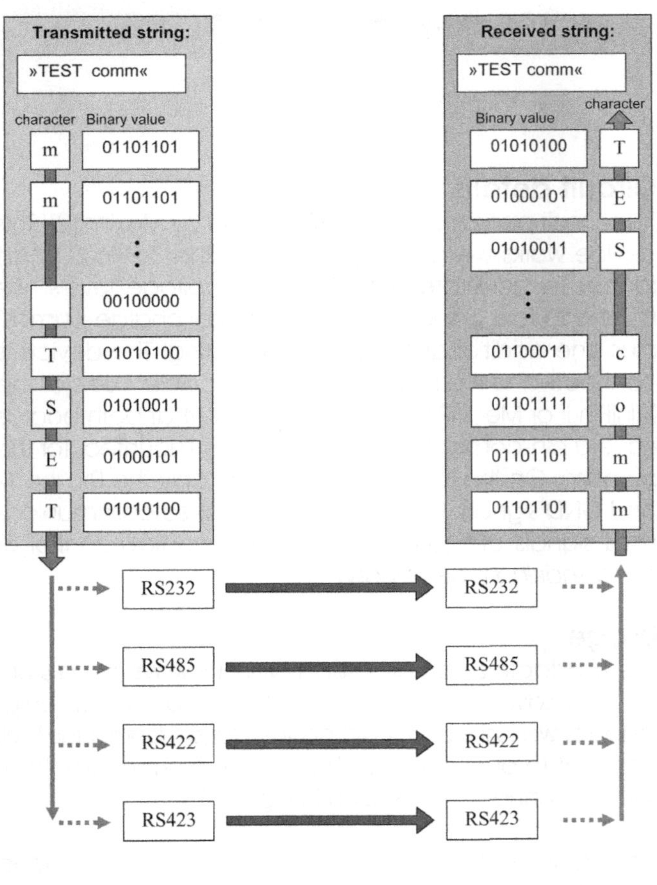

Figure 1: UART data

When designing a new device, I always reserve pins for serial communications. That allows me to easily change program parameters, not to mention being able to externally store data from the microcontroller.

Logic levels amongst digital devices vary. Usually a logical 1 is either 5.0 V or 3.3 V (and more recently, 1.8 Volts). Generally the logic levels depend upon the microcontroller's power supply voltage rating. This can present a problem, as not all microcontrollers and peripheral devices work at the same voltage. So, for example, a simple connection between your mobile phone and a USB or RS232 port may be problematic. The solution to this is to use level-shifting devices (usually ICs) that present suitable logic levels to both sides of the communications link.

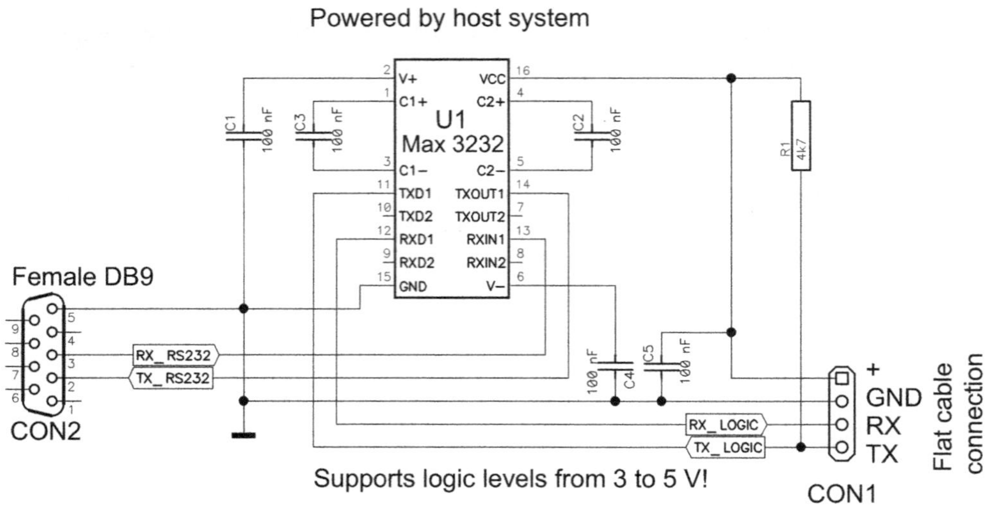

Figure 2: Schematic of an RS232 to UART adapter

For serial communications we use two signals: Rx and Tx, both of which are referenced to GND.

UART to RS232

This type of adapter will work when we want to establish serial communication between a microcontroller device (using logic level signals of 3.3 or 5.0 volts) and a PC with an RS232 port. This adapter gets its power from the microcontroller side, which generally uses a power supply of either 3.3 or 5.0 Volts. It converts the logic signals into those that are compatible with the RS232 protocol. This type of adapter can be totally enclosed within the DB9 female connector that is used to mate with the PC's RS232 port.

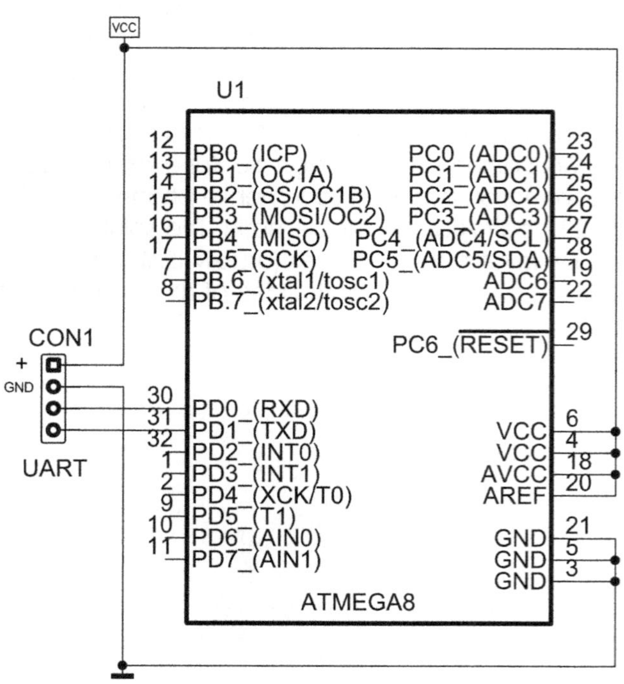

Figure 3: Example of an adapter connection to the microcontroller

Circuit details

This circuit contains a MAX3232 made by Maxim [2]. This device works well with logic levels in the 3.0 to 5.5 Volt range. To generate suitable RS232 voltage levels, we must add four capacitors (for its internal charge-pumps) plus one additional capacitor for filtering. The device is connected to the host using a 4-wire cable. Users of the MiniPin II or MegaPin boards will notice that both boards have a pin-compatible IDC connector mounted, for this purpose. On the RS232 side we have only the Rx, the Tx and GND signals. In most instances, these communications signals are sufficient (i.e. when no flow-control or *hand-shaking* is necessary).

Usage

These adapters can be used in various ways. For a start, we can save PCB space by not using an RS232 chip. Instead, we just put a 4-pin connector on-board that will connect to our adapter, when needed. An example of such a connection is shown in Figure 3.

Another very interesting use is to connect our cell-phone to a PC via this adapter. Using AT commands, we can access all cell phone functions, and there are a lot of

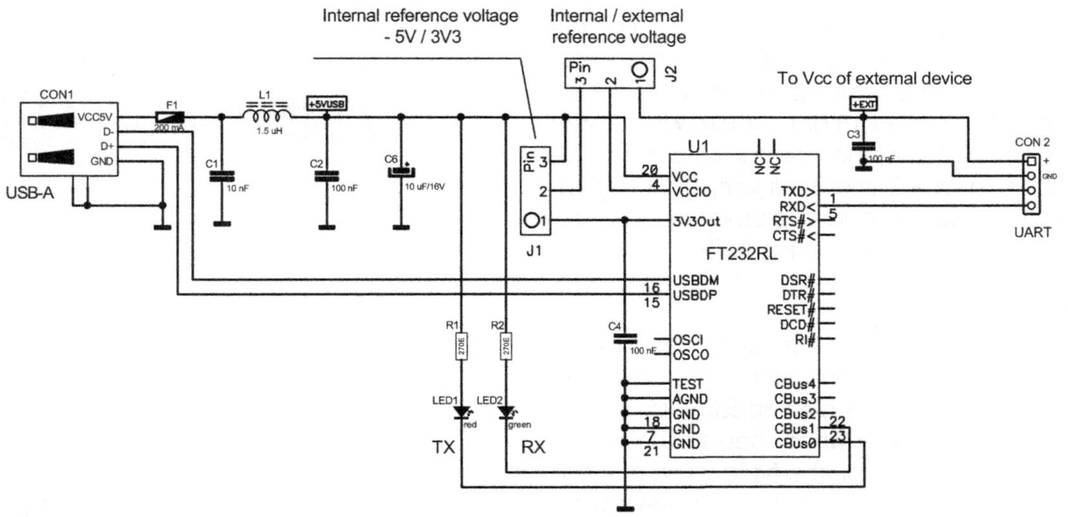

Figure 4: Schematic diagram of UART to USB adapter

them! We can make our device into a remote controller via SMS. All cell-phones have Rx, Tx, GND & V_{cc} pins available on a connector. Using these pins, we can connect a cell-phone to MiniPin II or to a PC.

UART to USB

The second type of adapter is similar in function to the first one mentioned, but is intended to be connected to a PC only. All modern PC laptops contain a USB port, but virtually none contain a built- in RS232 port. This may be a problem if we happen to need one. A solution to this problem is the UART to USB adapter.

Circuit details

We have used the FT232RL USB to UART chip made by FTDI. If this is the first time you have used a device containing this FTDI chip, you'll have to install FTDI Windows drivers on your PC. After the drivers are installed, the device shows up as a COM port, and is used in the same manner as the UART to RS232 adapter mentioned earlier. You still have to find out which COM port has been assigned to our adapter (the driver installation, as well as the COM port determination, just mentioned, is all described at the beginning of the MegaPin Chapter). The schematic diagram of this adapter is shown in Figure 4.

The FT232RL has an input pin labelled V_{cc} IO. This power

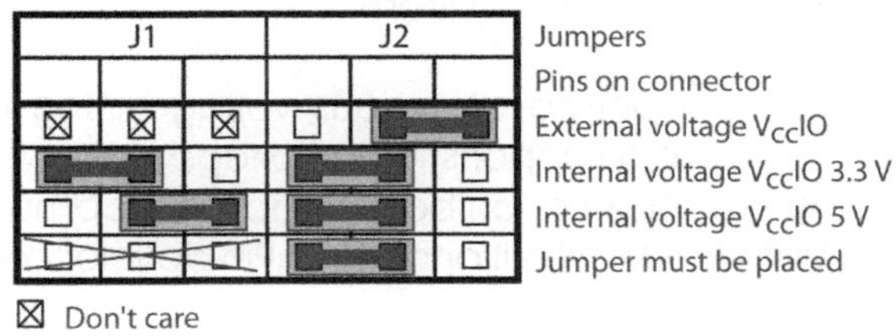

Table 1: Setting V_{cc}IO voltage with jumpers J1 and J2

supply input defines the voltage level for the logic signals. The remainder of the chip gets its power from the USB port itself (5V). This schematic shows the standard configuration of the FT232RL, with two jumpers added to set the logic levels. With jumper J2 we select between an internal or external V_{cc}IO voltage, while jumper J1 sets which of the internal voltages is to be used: 3.3 or 5.0 Volts. This chip also supports logic levels down to 1.0 Volts, so we can connect it to most modern microcontrollers.

Usage

The concept is same as with the RS232 to UART adapter, except that data is being transferred via the USB bus. The IDC connector has the same configuration as on the RS232 to UART adapter and is compatible with MiniPin II and MegaPin boards.

If the target circuit board contains a suitable power supply, we will connect all four pins of the IDC connector

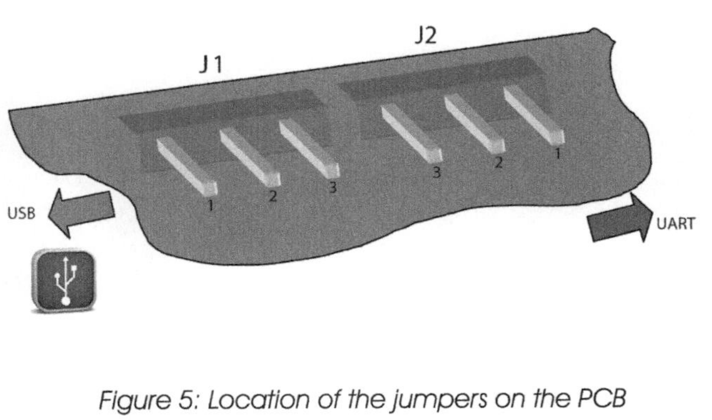

Figure 5: Location of the jumpers on the PCB

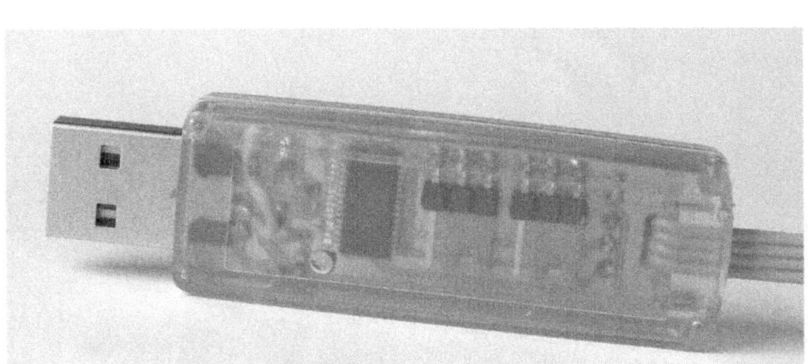

and short pins 1 and 2 on jumper J2. In this mode, the power supply voltage goes directly to $V_{cc}IO$ pin. If the target circuit can't supply power, then we have to measure it and try to get as close to it as possible, with jumper J1. On jumper J2, we select the internal voltage source for $V_{cc}IO$, by shorting pins 2 and 3. All jumper combinations are shown in Table 1, and a picture showing the location of the jumpers is shown in Figure 5.

Conclusion

To do two-way communications, you don't need to design a special circuit, if this communication is only done infrequently. With the adapters described, you can establish communication only when needed. You just have to pick a suitable adapter. The typical use of these adapters is for debugging, when data from the microcontroller is sent to the PC using Bascom's *Print* statement. When you design your device, all you have to add is a four pin connector. wired to $+V_{cc}$, GND, Rx and Tx. It doesn't matter whether or not you use them: they will be there when we need them.

Both adapters operate at various voltages: the USB to UART board also supports logic voltages below 1.0 Volt. The IDC connector on both adapters is compatible with both the MiniPin II and MegaPin development boards.

Notes:
1. www.ftdichip.com
2. www.maxim-ic.com

LCD adapter for 16x2 and 8x2 LCD modules

By Jurij Mikeln

Many years ago there were problems obtaining LCD modules. If you were lucky enough to buy a certain module at a reasonable price, you could be disappointed few months later when you couldn't buy the same or even a compatible LCD module. What was offered might have a different pinout, not to mention different physical dimensions.

Back then, it was really a nightmare buying LCDs, because you would never know what you might get. For that reason, we developed a universal LCD adapter, which was cleverly designed to handle most of the pinouts of available LCDs. Now it's different: we can buy many types of LCDs and there isn't the problem described above. Lately, we purchased some very attractive 8x2 blue LCDs that were both cost-effective and very nice looking. However they had a strange pinout that we have never seen before, so we had to make a new, universal PCB, which will suit both the standard 2x16 and the new 8x2 LCDs.

Schematic diagram

The schematic diagram shown in Figure 1 is very simple. You will see that it supports two LCDs (but only one

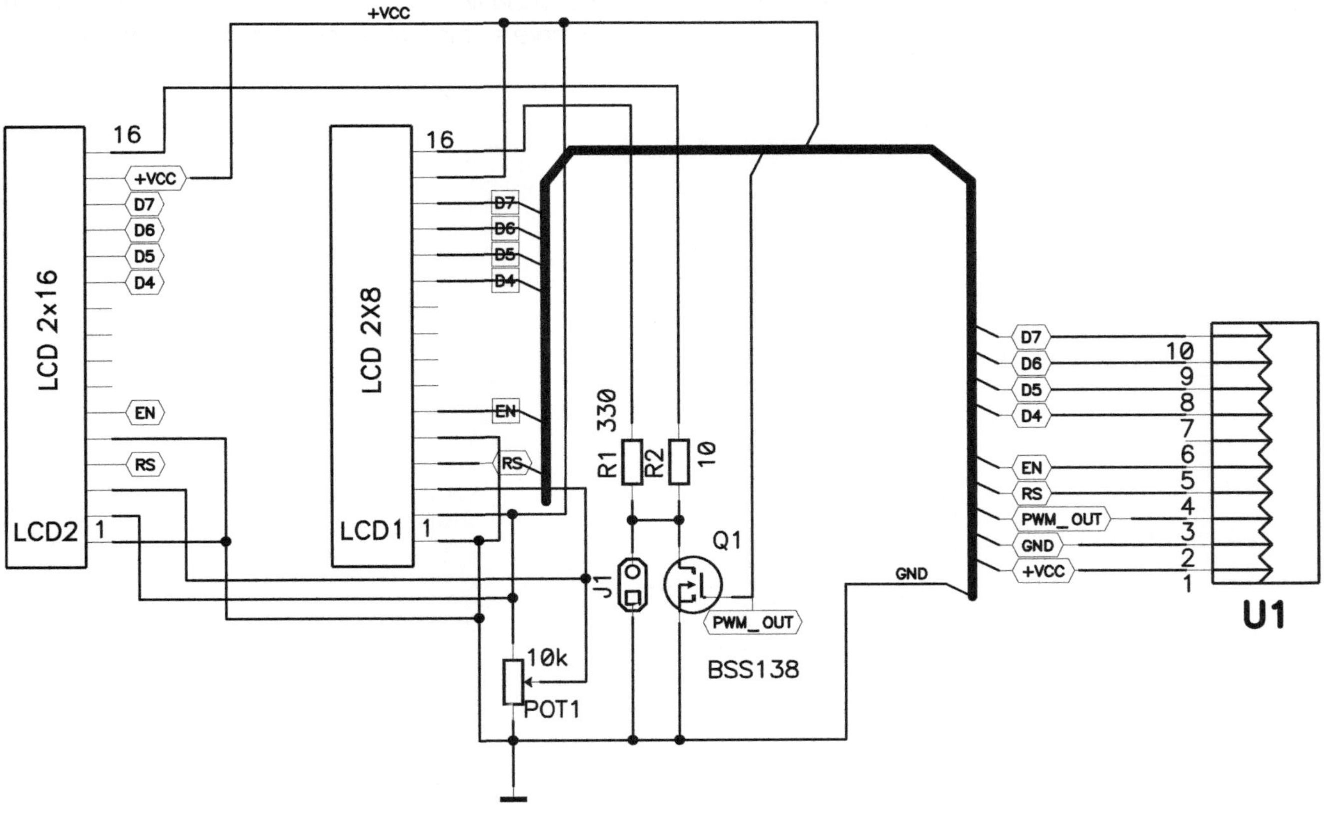

Figure 1: Electrical schematic diagram of 2x8 and 2x16 LCD adapter

at a time!), and has a MOSFET for driving the LCD's backlight

The adapter has an IDC socket for easier connection to the MiniPin II, MegaPin development boards or any other circuit where you might want to use this LCD module. The first and second pin on the connector are +5V and GND, while others are PortX.0 to PortX.7, in that order. On the adapter side, the control pins are connected as follows (see Figure 2).

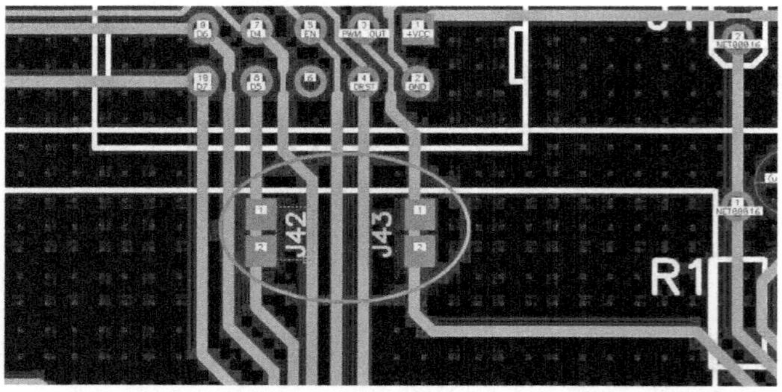

Figure 2: Changing Backlight drive connections using jumpers J42 & J43

D7-D4 pins are connected to PortX.7 – PortX.4, Enable pin at PortX.2 and Register Select pin at PortX.1. So, Bascom's LCD configuration statement would be:

```
Config Lcdpin = Pin , Db7 = Porta.7 ,_
Db6 = Porta.6 , Db5 = Porta.5 ,_
Db4 = Porta.4 , E = Porta.2 , Rs = Porta.1
```

On the board, there is also one pin which drives the LCD backlight connected to PortX.5.

This LCD board works with either 2x8 or 2x16 LCDs and, in either case, can drive the backlight through a MOSFET. The PCB is single-sided.

If we want to drive the backlight with an AVR microcontroller, note that some AVR's have a PWM pin on PortD.5 (ATmega16/32 etc.), whereas others use PortD.0. To accommodate this, we can cut the PCB shunts at J42 & J43, and add 2 wire jumpers to reverse the two connections. The PCB jumpers can be seen in Figure 2.

If you make this board change, you will also have to change the Bascom program so that Data5 is now assigned to PortX.0, as shown below:

```
Config Lcdpin = Pin , Db4 = Portb.4 ,_
Db5 = Portb.0 , Db6 = Portb.6 ,_
Db7 = Portb.7 , E = Portb.2 , Rs = Portb.1
```

Careful observers will notice that each LCD has its own series resistor for backlight current limiting. For R2 on the 2x16 LCD we have used 10 Ohms, while for R1 on the 2x8 LCD backlight, we use a 330 Ohm resistor. With jumper J1 in place, we short out the MOSFET, which turns the backlight on at full-brightness, constantly.

Conclusion

The old "universal" LCD adapter will make way for our new LCD adapter. Our web page shows it with a 2x8 LCD module mounted. This 2x8 LCD module is very bright, much more so than what shows up in the photos.

Practical projects

161

There should be many practical projects in every book for programmers and this book is no exception. Bascom-AVR, in conjunction with AVR microcontrollers, is a winning combination when designing a simple (but very powerful) I2C analyzer. Other projects, like a Frequency generator, Frequency counter, a simple but accurate clock and a Metal detector are just a few of the projects that can be found in this chapter.

> AVR microcontrollers are user-friendly,
> so get to know them better!

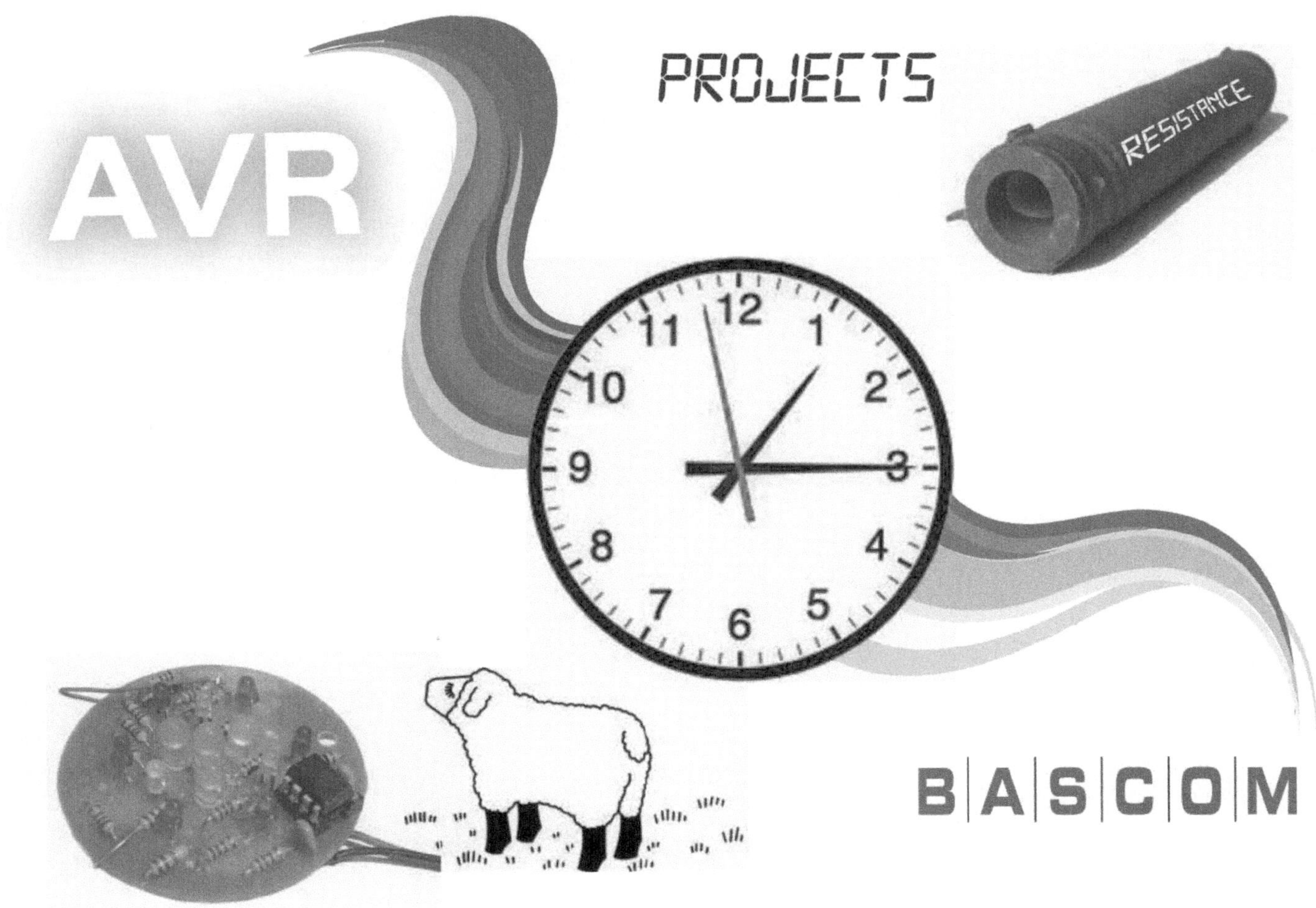

I²C monitor

By Vladimir Mitrović

Integrated circuits within telecommunications and industrial electronic devices and complex consumer devices (for example, in a TV set) often communicate using the I²C protocol. This article describes a simple device that can monitor traffic on the I²C bus. Let's find out what kind of messages these chips exchange!

I²C fundamentals

The I²C bus is a simple bidirectional 2-wire bus for efficient **i**nter-**IC c**ontrol (which is where the abbreviation I²C comes from). These two lines are called the serial data line (SDA) and the serial clock line (SCL). Serial, 8-bit bidirectional data transfers can be made at up to 100 kbit/s in the standard mode or up to 400 kbit/s in the fast mode. The traffic on the bus is controlled by the master IC (usually a microcontroller) that generates clock signals and initiates and terminates a transfer. Each slave device connected to the bus is software addressable by a unique address and will only respond if addressed by the master.

Communication begins with the START condition, generated by the master. The START condition is indicated by a *High* to *Low* transition on the SDA line while the SCL is *High*. The bus is considered to be busy after the START condition. Following the START condition, the master will address one of the slave ICs connected to the I²C bus. The address is a 7-bit number. The 8th bit is a R/W bit. If this bit is *Low*, the master will send one or more blocks of instructions or data to the addressed slave. If this bit is *High*, the master is ready to receive one or more blocks of data from the addressed slave. The data transferred via the I²C bus consists of 8-bit packets, each followed by the 9th - acknowledge bit. The data is transferred with the most significant bit (MSB) first and the number of bytes that can be transmitted per transfer is not restricted. The new bit is placed on the SDA line while SCL is *Low*. The master ends the communication with a *Low* to *High* transition on the SDA line while SCL is *High*, which is considered the STOP condition. The STOP condition releases the addressed slave and the I²C bus.

The 7-bit addressing scheme, explained above, allows up to 112 different addresses. Most new chips use a 10-bit addressing scheme, which provides more address combinations and thus more unique addresses. The 10-bit addressing scheme uses two bytes for addressing purposes and does not affect compatibility with 7-bit addressing in any way. Thus 7- and 10-bit devices can be connected to the same I²C bus.

Let's see how this communication works, using for example the AT24C02 serial EEPROM. Assuming that all the address pins on the device have been wired to a logic *High*, this serial EEPROM will have an I²C address of "AE". We want to write an "11" at EEPROM address "00" (addresses and data in this example are given as hexadecimal numbers). The communication will look like that shown in the following example (see Table 1).

Reading the same data from the AT24C02 is shown in the following example, (see Table 2).

The acknowledge bits are omitted from this example for simplicity. In reality, the receiving device confirms the reception of each byte with an ACK bit.

I²C monitor

An ATtiny2313-based I²C monitor looks very simple, but all the "clever things" are hidden in the microcontroller's program. The program is written in Bascom-AVR with several embedded assembler routines. Assembler routines are written for monitoring the traffic on the I²C bus, where all events take place at high speed. For example, in I²C fast mode, with a bit rate up to 400 kHz, the program has only 2.5 μs to read and process each bit. Simultaneously, the program must properly react to not only the expected data patterns, but to accidental START and STOP conditions, which can also occur during communication. To simplify the hardware, the START and STOP conditions are handled by software, which also

START	master->all devices	
AE	master->all devices	Address is recognised by the AT24C02 (it is assumed that address pins A0 -A2 are set to "1"). As the 8th address bit is "0", the master will send data to the slave.
00	master->AT24C02	Master sends the address of a byte within AT24C02 memory space where data is to be written.
11	master->AT24C02	Master sends data to be written.
STOP	master->AT24C02	

Table 1

START	master->all devices	
AE	master->all devices	Address is recognised by the AT24C02 (it is assumed that address pins A0-A2 are set to "1"). As the 8th address bit is "0", the master will send data to the slave.
00	master->AT24C02	Master sends the address of a byte within AT24C02 memory space where data is to be read is memorised.
START	master->all devices	This is repeated START, which is necessary if the new address is to be sent during the same communication session.
AF	master->all devices	Address is recognised by the AT24C02 (it is assumed that address pins A0-A2 are set to "1"). As the 8th address bit is "1", the master will read data from the slave.
11	AT24C02->master	AT24C02 sends requested data.
STOP	master->AT24C02	

Table 2

dictates specific programming requirements. To speed up program execution, a 20 MHz crystal is used in the final version of the monitor, although a somewhat simpler version of the monitor, written during development, worked well even with an 8 MHz crystal.

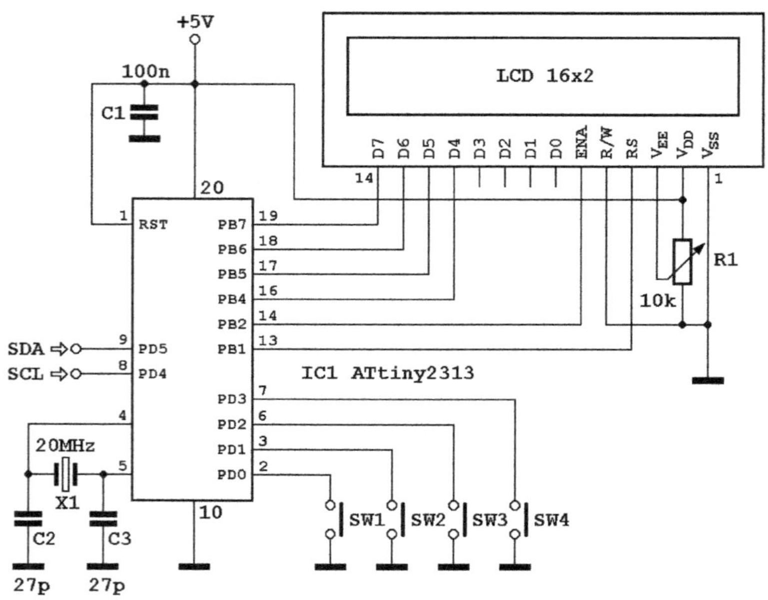

Figure 1: The ATtiny2313 used as an I²C monitor

The I²C monitor should be connected to the device, whose I²C communication is to be monitored, using three connecting wires: besides the SCL and SDA lines, we need a ground wire as well. You can find the SCL and SDA lines on the PCB of the device by finding an I²C IC and then connecting the monitor to its SCL, SDA and GND pins. If you have the schematics for the device, you can even supply power to the monitor directly from the device itself (a stable 5 volts @ 15 mA is needed to supply the monitor).

The I²C monitor does not generate any signals of its own on the I²C bus, and should in no way affect the I²C communication of the monitored device. However, the connecting cables will have a certain capacitance, and should be as short as possible (20-40 cm is OK).

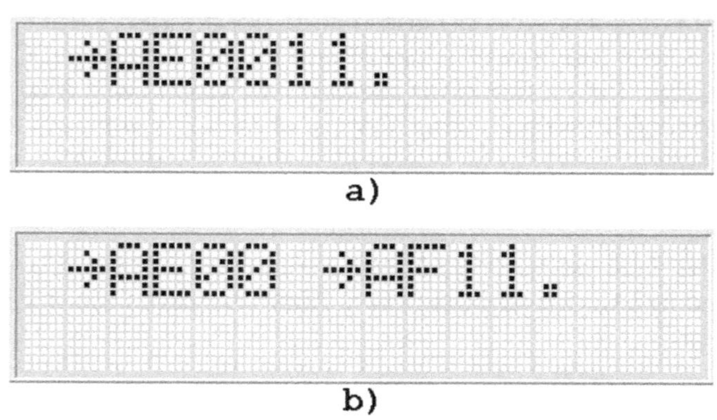

Figure 2: Display examples: writing a byte to the AT24C02 serial EEPROM (a) and reading the same byte from the AT24C02 (b)

After power-up, the program displays an initial message and continues to loop until the START condition is detected. As soon as this happens, the program starts to monitor and store the traffic on the I²C bus. Monitoring will end when:

- the STOP condition is detected or
- 16 bytes are stored (START conditions are counted, too) or
- more than 4 seconds have elapsed since the last START condition has occurred.

The first case is the most common under normal circumstances. The second case happens if the message is too long: 16 bytes is the limit because this is how many characters can be displayed (in hexadecimal form) on the 16x2 LCD display. The third case indicates a communication error: any message should last less than 4 seconds.

After monitoring has finished, for any of the above reasons, the program displays the stored communication as a series of hexadecimal numbers. Each byte is shown as a two-digit hexadecimal number, while START and STOP are shown as an arrow and a dot, respectively. Figure 2 shows the previously-explained example of writing and reading a byte to or from the AT24C02 serial EEPROM. If the message is longer than 8 bytes, the display continues on the second line. If the message storage has been interrupted (i.e. the message was too long or lasted more than 4 s), there will be no STOP condition (as shown by a dot) in the display.

Additional functions

The program will work as explained if no push-buttons are closed (SW1-SW4 in Figure 1). Pressing one of these buttons will activate additional functions:

- **SW1** (the push-button is checked when the START condition is detected): Instead of monitoring the traffic on the I²C bus, the program measures and displays the frequency of the SCL, i.e. the transmission bit rate. The measurement starts with the first SCL line level change following the START condition and lasts for 8 cycles. After this, the program calculates and displays the frequency and starts a new measurement. The process is repeated for as long as SW1 is pressed.
- **SW2** (push-button is checked when the START condition is detected) switches on address filtering. In this mode, the detected I²C address (the 1st byte after the START condition; only 7-bit addressing is supported) is compared to the memorised I²C address (filter). The state of the 8th, R/W bit, is irrelevant. If the two addresses don't match, the program ignores the traffic until the next START condition occurs. If they match, the program continues to store the traffic as described before. An exception is filter address "00", which will match any received I²C address (i.e. the program will act as if the address filtering has not been activated).
- **SW2** also allows for entering and updating the filter address. The microcontroller stores the filter address in the 1st byte (address 0) of the microcontroller's internal EEPROM. This byte can be written during the flash-programming procedure, or at any later time, by using SW2. If you press SW2 and keep it closed for the duration of the message "I2Cmonitor" (displayed when the program starts), you will force the program to enter an interactive mode for updating the filter address. In this mode, an "I2C address:" message, followed by the actual filter address, is displayed on the lower line of the LCD display. In the example shown in Figure 3, this address is "00" and the cursor is displayed under the first digit. By briefly pressing SW2, as many times as necessary, you will increment the first digit to the desired value. After hexadecimal "F", the selected digit rolls over to "0". Pressing SW2 for a longer time shifts the cursor to the second digit. You can change its value in steps of 2 (only even numbers are allowed, because the last bit of the filter should be a "0"). Pressing SW2 for a longer time once again, terminates the interactive mode. The new filter address is stored in the EEPROM and will be available whenever the filter addressing mode is activated in the future.
- **SW3** (push-button is checked when the START condition is detected) disables the Watchdog timer. The purpose of the Watchdog is to limit the monitoring to 4 seconds after a START condition has been detected. A normal communication, that begins with the START and ends with the STOP condition, lasts considerably less than 4 s even at low bit rates. However, it has been observed that the master sometimes generates a new START condition, immediately after the STOP condition, even with no further communication. In this case, the microcontroller would erase the display after 4 seconds and display the new message that contains only the START symbol. To maintain the last meaningful message in the display, keep SW3 pressed.
- **SW4** holds the previous message on the display for as long as it is kept pressed. The button is checked just before the new message is about to be displayed. If pressed, the display of the new message will be postponed until the button is released. This enables

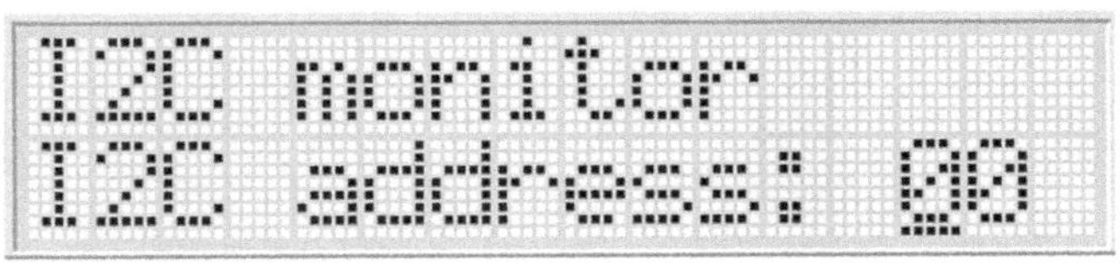

Figure 3: Interactive mode for the filter address update (current address is "00")

Figure 4: I²C monitor displays the traffic on the I²C bus of a satellite receiver (the MiniPin development system is used here instead of the stand-alone circuit shown in Figure 1)

maintaining an interesting message on the display for as long as necessary. The subsequent message will be stored and displayed, with this delay, but any further messages will be lost.

Possible modifications

The Program I2Cmonitor.bas has been written for the analysis of I^2C communication. It contains functions that I consider useful. The program uses almost the entire flash memory of the ATtiny2313 (2028 Bytes). Therefore, any serious modification would require a more powerful microcontroller, e.g. ATtiny4313. With a more powerful microcontroller, one could consider the use of a larger display (16x4 or 20x4). This would allow you to display larger messages, keeping more than one message in the buffer, scrolling thru the messages and other enhancements.

Example program ID	
Name:	I2Cmonitor.bas
Microcontroller:	ATtiny2313 and other more powerful AVRs
Testing circuit:	Figure 1
MiniPin compatibility:	yes (with appropriate μC)
MegaPin compatibility:	yes
The program monitors and displays the traffic on the I^2C bus with data rates up to 400 kbit/s.	

Programmable IR sender/receiver

By Vladimir Mitrović

It's normal for satellite, TV and hi-fi audio receivers, various recorders and players, air conditioning and many other devices to have remote controls. Some remotes have been designed for one specific device, whereas others are universal and tend to combine the functions of many remote controls in just one unit.

Most contemporary remote controls use an infra-red (IR) beam to transfer information to the IR receiver contained in the associated device. The way the information modulates the IR beam differs from device to device - otherwise other devices could respond in an undesired fashion, when you try to change the volume on your TV set, for example. This device discrimination was achieved by choosing different protocols and by giving various addresses to different devices.

Philips RC-5 and RC-6, Sony SIRC, NEC, RCA, Sharp, etc. - these are official names or nicknames given to modern, frequently-used protocols for IR communication. They differ in both carrier frequency and the type of modulation. Regardless of what type of modulation and carrier frequency is used, every message contains the address of the device for which it is intended. The receiving device will ignore all messages which carry unknown addresses, and react only to the messages sent by a matching remote control.

A remote control is basically a microcontroller which controls an infrared LED. Depending on the button being pressed, the microcontroller switches the transmitting LED on and off according to some pattern. The IR receiver, contained in the receiving device, receives these IR flashes, converts them into a series of electrical pulses and forwards them to the central microcontroller for further processing.

Remote controls and receivers are built around dedicated integrated circuits that perform this job reliably. However, a general-purpose microcontroller like the ATtiny2313 can also do the same job, and Bascom-AVR has several statements for this purpose. Currently, these are intended for receiving messages according to the RC-5 protocol (*GETRC5*) or sending messages according to the RC-5, RC-6 and Sony protocols (*RC5SEND, RC6SEND, SONYSEND*). This project goes further and enables the user to receive and send IR messages which follow other frequently-used protocols.

Part 1: Let's read an IR message

An IR-receiver for remote control systems is usually a dedicated IC such as the SFH506, TSOP1138 or their relatives. The IC is built in a black-coloured case, designed to filter out ambient light, and includes a photodiode, a preamplifier, an automatic gain control (AGC), a bandpass filter and a demodulator. However, for test purposes, we need an IR receiver without the bandpass filter, capable of receiving IR signals modulated on carriers of different frequencies. Such a receiver can be built from discrete components, as shown in Figure 1. Besides decoding the information, which is encoded as a series of pulses, this receiver will also separate the carrier and send it to another output. A high sensitivity is neither necessary nor preferred: by bringing the remote control close to the receiving photo-transistor, ambient light interference is greatly reduced.

If photo-transistor T1 (BPY62 or similar) is not illuminated by daylight or a strong artificial light, a negligibly small current flows thru R1 and T2 will be switched off. The voltage drop across R1 will be sufficient to turn on T2 only if T1 is illuminated by a pretty strong light. The appropriate level of illumination will be achieved if the transmitting IR diode of a remote control is held very close and precisely directed towards T1.

A remote control transmits flashes of IR light that represent a series of pulses. The information is encoded in the pulse width and/or the pulse distance. A single pulse is not continuous, but consists of a short sequence of repeating flashes.

The frequency of these flashes (called the carrier frequency) is generally in the 30-60 kHz range. This high-frequency carrier contains no information and should be removed by the receiver. In the circuit shown in Fig 1, this is partially done by overdriving T1 (by placing the IR sender very close) and the remaining carrier is filtered out by C1.

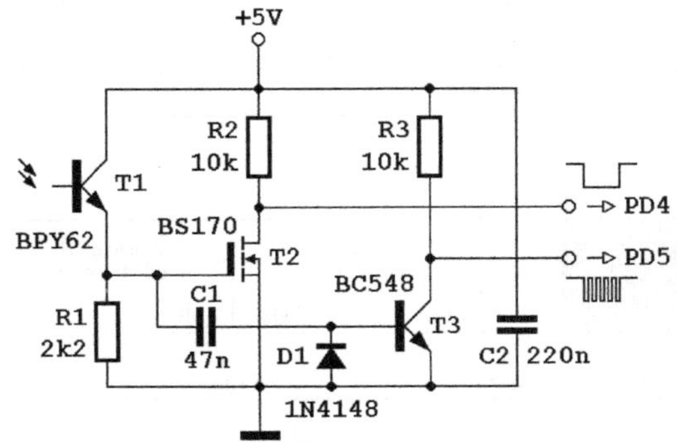

Figure 1: An IR-receiver built from discrete components

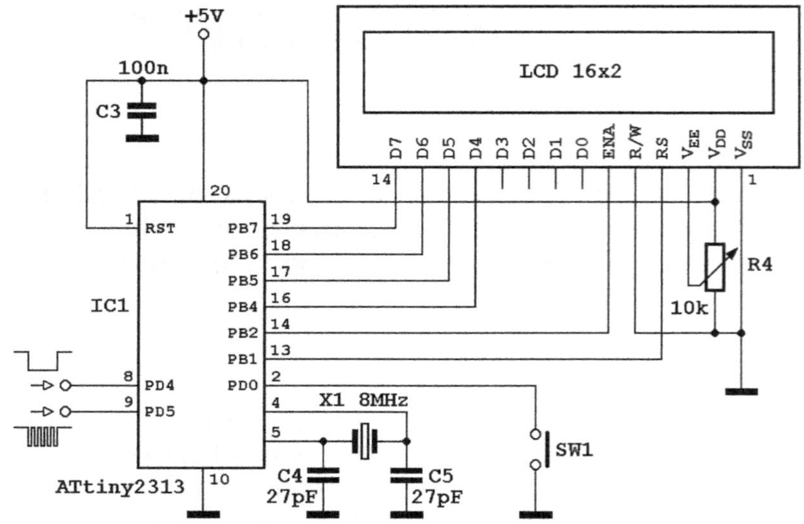

Figure 2: ATtiny2313 microcontroller analyses signals from the IR receiver and displays received messages

pulses are used for measuring the carrier frequency.

The ATtiny2313 microcontroller, in the circuit shown in Figure 2, analyses signals from the IR receiver and displays received messages. Instead of building a stand-alone circuit, as shown in Figure 2, development boards like the MiniPin II and MegaPin, fitted with an appropriate microcontroller, could also be used.

NEC protocol

The NEC protocol uses pulse distance encoding of the bits (Figure 3). Each pulse is a 562.5 µs (= 1T) long 38 kHz carrier burst. A logic "0" is coded as a 1T long carrier burst followed by a 1T space (no signal). A logic "1" is coded as a 1T long carrier burst followed by a 3T space. Thus, a logic "0" transmission lasts for 1125 µs, while a logic "1" lasts for 2250 µs.

If a remote control is close enough and transmits a light-pulse, there will be a DC voltage drop across R1 close to 4 V. This DC bias voltage keeps T2 conducting as long as T1 is illuminated, and the junction of R2 and T2 will be near 0 V. The remaining carrier has an amplitude of about 1.2 Vpp and has no impact on T2. As soon as the light-pulse has finished, T1 and T2 stop conducting current and the voltage at the junction of R2 and T2 rises to 5 V. This generates a number of negative-going pulses which correspond to the IR pulses transmitted by the remote control.

The carrier itself is sent via C1 to the base of transistor T3, which amplifies it and restores its rectangular wave shape. Therefore, when the remote control sends an IR carrier with a pulse train modulating it, there will be a series of rectangular pulses corresponding to the carrier frequency present at the collector of transistor T3. These

Figure 3 below shows a typical NEC protocol pulse train. A message is started by a 9 ms AGC burst, followed by a 4.5 ms space, an 8-bit address and an 8-bit command. With this protocol, the LSB is transmitted first. The address and command are transmitted twice: once in the original form and once in an inverted form (i.e all bits are inverted). This allows for verification of the received message and, as a bonus, all messages are the same length (each message contains 16 logic "0"s and 16 logic "1"s). A message ends with a 1T long carrier burst, followed by a space. The total length of a message, including the ending space, is 110 ms.

If a button on the remote control remains pressed, every 110 ms a repeat code is transmitted (i.e. the message itself is not repeatedly sent). The repeat code consists of a 9 ms AGC pulse, followed by a 2.25 ms space and a 1T burst.

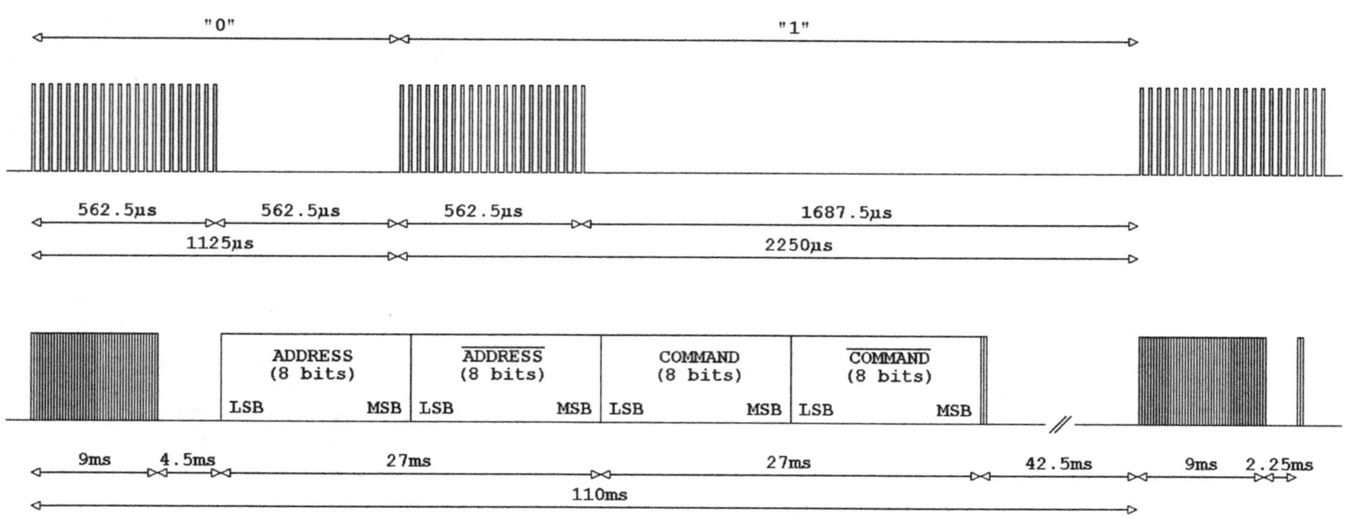

Figure 3: NEC protocol

The Extended NEC protocol uses 16-bit addressing, but without the repetition of the address bits. By sacrificing this address redundancy, the address range is considerably extended. In order to maintain fixed-length messages, only addresses that contain 8 logic "0"s and 8 logic "1"s are used. The command redundancy is preserved.

Please note that there are versions of this protocol that slightly differ from the one described here.

The Get_NEC.bas program

The Get_NEC.bas program decodes a message coming from the IR receiver to the microcontroller's pin PD4, in the form of negative pulses. The program waits for the starting AGC burst and the following space to occur, and then starts sampling the input signal. A sample is taken every 562.5 μs. For a 32-bit message containing 16 logic "0"s and 16 logic "1"s, it's sufficient to take 96 samples, but the program takes slightly more: a total of 128 samples are taken. These samples are stored in the *Nec(17)* array. The first 16 bytes of this array are treated as one 128-bit long variable, each bit of which contains one sample. An assembler routine has been written, which enables quick sampling and storing of the samples in the variable.

See Note for more information.

When the sampling has finished, the program briefly displays the collected samples in the form of a hexadecimal number. For closer examination of this message, you can extend the display time by pressing the SW1 push-button.

Next, the program starts to analyse the collected samples. Every "10" combination is interpreted as logic "0", while every "1000" combination is interpreted as logic "1". Any other combination is treated as an error, which stops the analysis. Any message length that differs from the expected 32 bits will also be considered as an error. The decoded "0"s and "1"s are combined into variables, and represent the address and the command in normal and inverted form. The contents of these variables are shown in Figure 4a.

NOTE

A logic *Low* at the PD4 pin indicates an existence of the carrier burst, while *High* corresponds to space. This "inverted logic" can be confusing. Therefore, during the sampling procedure, the program complements the sampled bits. In the program, a logic "1" stands for a carrier burst and a logic "0" for a space.

The meaning of the specific fields is as follows:
- A1: 8-bit address
- A2: inverted 8-bit address (or extended address in the case of 16-bit addressing)
- C1: 8-bit command
- C2: inverted 8-bit command

All data is in hexadecimal form. In this example, the address is "16", the command is "A7" and the other data are their complements. We can conclude that this message has been transmitted using the basic NEC protocol, and interpreted correctly. The message is displayed for 8 seconds, after which the program is ready to decode the next message.

If an error is detected in the received data (an illegal bit combination, a too short or too long message etc.) the program displays an "Error xx" message, where "xx" denotes the error type. You will have to analyse the program's source code to determine the cause of the error.

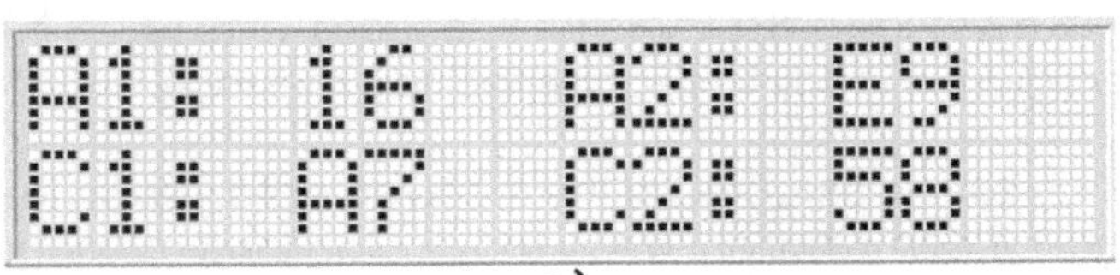

a)

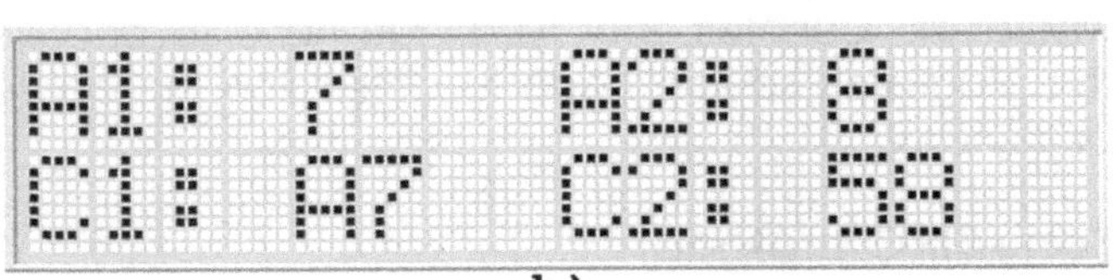

b)

c)

Figure 4: Messages received in the NEC, RCA and SONY protocols (top to bottom)

RCA protocol

The RCA protocol also uses pulse distance encoding of the bits (Figure 5). The principle is similar to the NEC protocol, but the carrier frequency and time intervals differ. Here, the basic time interval 1T lasts 500 μs, while the carrier frequency equals 56 kHz. A logic "0" is coded as a 1T long carrier burst followed by a 2T space (no signal). A logic "1" is coded as a 1T long carrier burst followed by a 4T space. Thus, the transmission of a logic "0" takes 1500 μs, while a logic "1" takes 2500 μs.

The RCA protocol is a 12-bit protocol, with the message containing a 4-bit address and an 8-bit command. The address and command are transmitted twice: once in the original and once in the inverted form (i.e. all bits are inverted). This allows for verification of the received

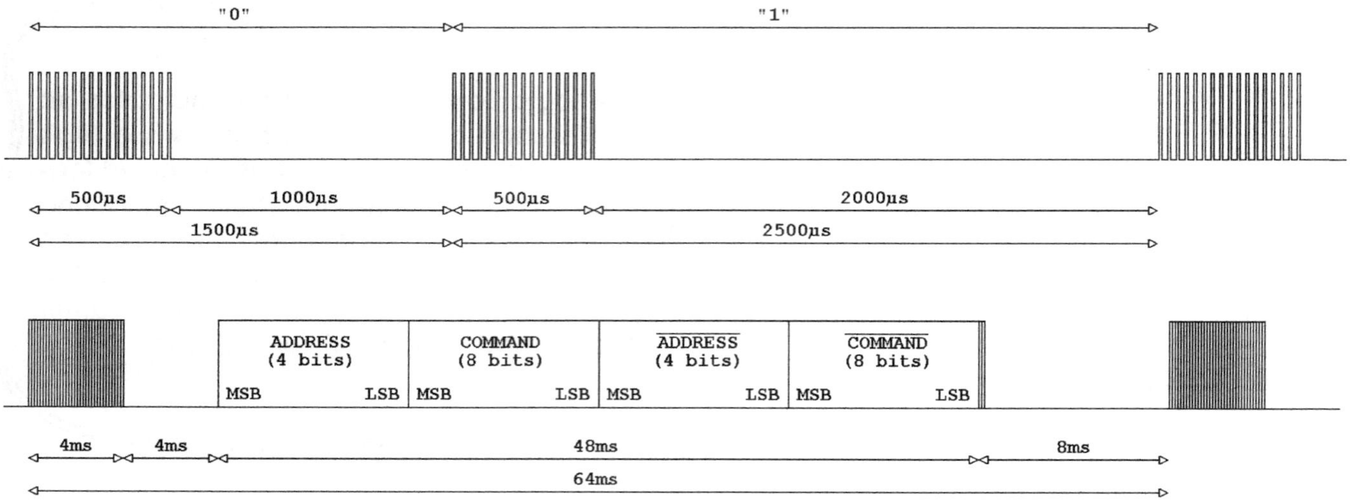

Figure 5: RCA protocol

message and, as a bonus, all messages have the same length (each message contains 12 logic "0"s and 12 logic "1"s).

Figure 5 down shows a typical RCA protocol pulse train. A message starts with a 4 ms burst, followed by a 4 ms space. In the following four transmitted blocks (comprised of 4, 8, 4 and 8 bits) an address, a command, an inverted address and an inverted command are transmitted. The MSB is transmitted first. A message ends with a 1T long carrier burst, followed by a space. The total length of a message, including the ending space, is 64 ms.

The same message is repeated every 64 ms, for as long as the remote control's button is pressed.

Please note that there are versions of this protocol that slightly differ from the one described here.

The Get_RCA.bas program

The Get_RCA.bas program decodes a message coming from the IR receiver to the microcontroller's pin PD4, in the form of negative pulses. The program waits for the starting AGC burst and the following space to occur, and then starts sampling the input signal. A sample is taken every 500 µs. For a 24-bit message which contains 12 logic "0"s and 12 logic "1"s, it is enough to take 96 samples, but the program takes slightly more: a total of 128 samples are taken. These samples are stored in the *Rca(17)* array. The first 16 bytes of this array are treated as one 128-bit long variable, each bit of which contains one sample. An assembler routine has been written which enables quick sampling and storing of the samples in the variable.

See Note for more information.

When the sampling has finished, the program briefly displays the collected samples in the form of a hexadecimal number. For closer examination of this message, you can extend the display time by pressing the SW1 push-button.

Next, the program starts to analyse the collected samples. Every "100" combination is interpreted as a logic "0", while every "10000" combination is interpreted as a logic "1". Any other combination is treated as an error, stopping the analysis. Any message length that differs from the expected 24 bits will also be considered as an error. Decoded "0"s and "1"s are combined into variables and represent the address and the command in normal and inverted form. The contents of these variables are shown in Figure 4b.

The meaning of the specific fields is the following:

- A1: 4-bit address
- A2: inverted 4-bit address
- C1: 8-bit command
- C2: inverted 8-bit command

All data is in hexadecimal form. In this example, the address is "7", the command is "A7" and the other data are their complements. We can conclude that this message has been transmitted and interpreted correctly. The message is displayed for 8 seconds, after which the program is ready to decode the next message.

If an error is detected in the received data (i.e. an illegal bit combination, a too short or too long message etc.) the program displays an "Error xx" message, where "xx" denotes error type. You have to analyse the program's source code to determine the cause of the error.

Sony SIRC protocol

The Sony SIRC protocol uses pulse width modulation for encoding bits (Figure 6). A logic "0" is coded as a 600 µs carrier burst followed by a 600 µs space (T = 600 µs). A logic "1" is coded as a 2T burst with a 1T space. Thus, the transmission of a logic "0" takes 1200 µs, while a logic "1" takes 1800 µs.

There are three versions of the Sony SIRC protocol: 12, 15 and 20-bit versions. The structures of these versions are shown on the right side of Figure 6. With this proto-

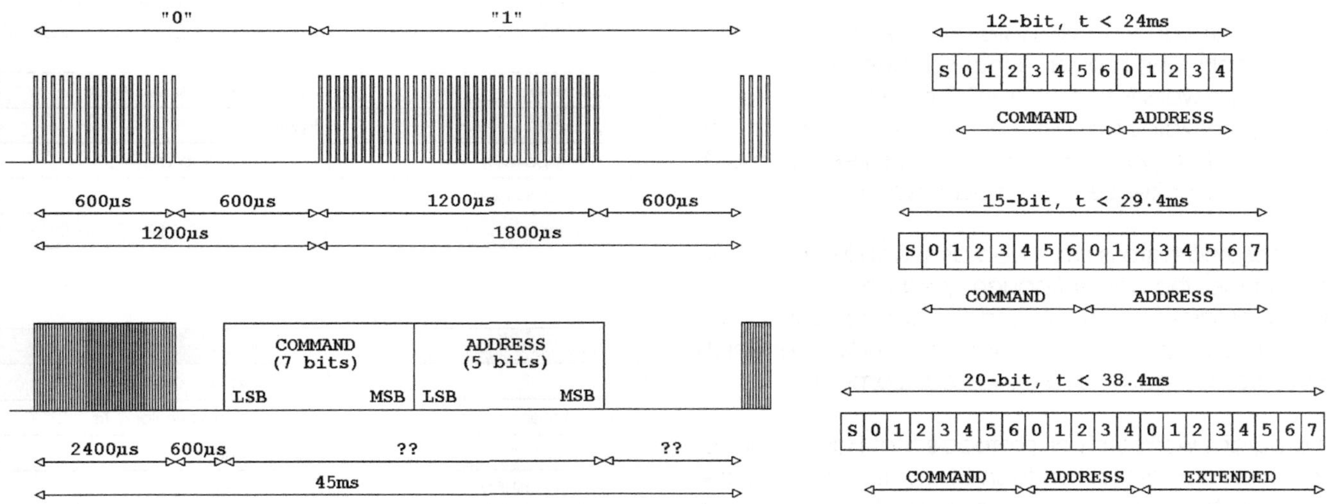

Figure 6: SONY SIRC protocol

col, every field is transmitted only once. The bottom left side of Figure 6 shows the structure of the 12-bit message in detail. The message starts with a 4T burst, followed by a 1T space, a 7-bit command block and a 5-bit address block. The LSB is transmitted first. 15- and 20-bit messages have a similar structure, but individual blocks last longer. The total message length depends upon the protocol version and message content. 12-bit messages last up to 24 ms, 15-bit messages up to 29.4 and 20-bit ones up to 38.4 ms.

The same message is repeated every 45 ms, for as long as the remote control's button is pressed.

The Get_Sony.bas program

The Get_Sony.bas program decodes a message sent from the IR receiver to the microcontroller's pin PD4, in the form of negative pulses. The program waits for the starting AGC burst and a following space to occur and then starts sampling the input signal. A sample is taken every 600 µs. For the longest 20-bit message, containing only logic "1"s, it's necessary to take 60 samples, but the program takes slightly more: a total of 64 samples are taken. These samples are stored in the *Sony(9)* array. The first 8 bytes of this array are treated as one 64-bit long variable, each bit of which contains one sample. An assembler routine has been written which enables quick sampling and storing of the samples in the variable.

See Note for more information.

When the sampling has finished, the program briefly displays the collected samples in the form of a hexadecimal number. For closer examination of this message, you can extend the display time by pressing the SW1 push-button.

Next, the program starts to analyse the collected samples. Every "10" combination is interpreted as a logic "0", while every "110" combination is interpreted as a logic "1". Any other combination is treated as an error, stopping the analysis. Any message length that differs from the expected 12, 15 or 20 bits will also be considered as an error. Decoded "0"s and "1"s are combined into variables and represent the address, the command and the extended word (only for 20-bit messages). The contents of these variables are shown in Figure 4c.

The meaning of the specific fields is as follows:

» upper row: 12-, 15- or 20-bit, depending on message length
» C: 7-bit command
» A: 5- or 8-bit address
» E: 8-bit extended word

All data is in hexadecimal form. In this example, the message is 20-bits long, the command is "30", the address is "17", and the extended word is "F0". Field "E:" is displayed for 20-bit messages only. Without redundancy fields, we cannot conclude whether this message has been transmitted and interpreted correctly or not. The message is displayed for 8 seconds, after which the program is ready to decode the next message.

If an error is detected in the received data (i.e. an illegal bit combination, invalid message length etc.) the program displays an "Error xx" message in which "xx" denotes the error type. You have to analyse the program's source code to determine the cause of the error.

Carrier frequency and start signal length

The program Get_Start.bas measures carrier frequency and the lengths of the start signal and the first space

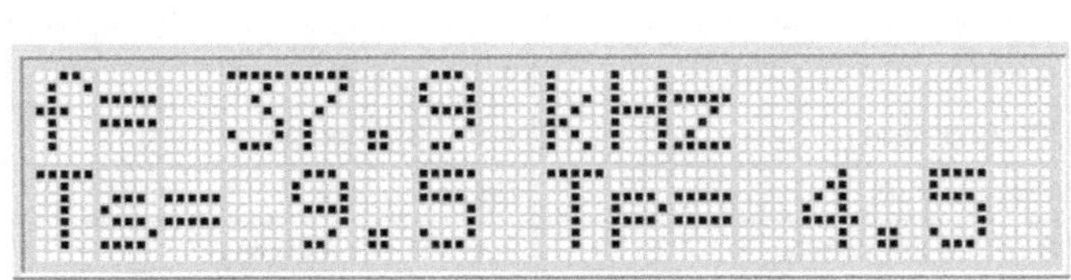

Figure 7: START signal basic parameters

after the start signal. These data can help you to detect the protocol of the message that has been transmitted. The program waits for an initial AGC burst (= START signal) and then activates two parallel processes: the start signal and the first space lengths are measured by Timer0, while the carrier frequency is measured by Timer1.

The measured data is displayed as shown in Figure 7. In this example, the carrier frequency equals 39.7 kHz, the start signal lasts for 9.5 ms and the space lasts for 4.5 ms. The message is displayed for 5 seconds, after which the program is ready for a new measurement.

The program works with all protocols that have an initial burst which contains more than 50 cycles of the carrier frequency. The carrier frequency must be higher than 4.8 kHz to be correctly measured. If an error is detected in the received data the program briefly displays an "Error x" message, where "x" denotes the error type. You have to analyse the program's source code to determine the cause of the error.

Closing remarks

It's not a simple task to write a program that can identify the protocol being sent. An identification method can be comparing the measurement results obtained with the Get_f.bas program to the known characteristics of various protocols. The three examined protocols have specific start signal lengths and can be distinguished by this parameter only. This specificity is used in the Get_NEC_RCA_Sony.bas program, which combines programming techniques used in the four previously-explained programs, to identify the protocol and to read, decode and display the message.

All programs wait for the start signal, which triggers sampling. A button on the remote control can be pressed any time the program is ready, for a new measurement. This is indicated by the word "ready" in the lower row of the display. Keep the button pressed for as short a time as possible, to avoid sending a repeated message.

The IR receiver shown in Figure 1 has intentionally been designed for low sensitivity to prevent ambient lighting interference from affecting measurements. Due to the low sensitivity, it's necessary to find an optimal position of the remote control with respect to the photo-transistor. An optimal position implies a 1-3 cm distance and it can be determined by the "Get_start.bas" program: the position is good if the same or similar results are obtained during several consecutive measurements.

Example program ID	
Name:	Get_NEC.bas
Microcontroller:	ATtiny2313 and similar AVRs
Testing circuit:	Figure 1 and 2
MiniPin compatibility:	yes (with appropriate μC)
MegaPin compatibility:	yes
The program decodes IR messages sent according to basic and extended NEC protocol	

Example program ID	
Name:	Get_RCA.bas
Microcontroller:	ATtiny2313 and similar AVRs
Testing circuit:	Figure 1 and 2
MiniPin compatibility:	yes (with appropriate μC)
MegaPin compatibility:	yes
The program decodes IR messages sent according to 12-bit RCA protocol	

Example program ID	
Name:	Get_Sony.bas
Microcontroller:	ATtiny2313 and similar AVRs
Testing circuit:	Figure 1 and 2
MiniPin compatibility:	yes (with appropriate μC)
MegaPin compatibility:	yes
The program decodes IR messages sent according to 12-, 15- and 20-bit RCA protocol	

Example program ID	
Name:	Get_Start.bas
Microcontroller:	ATtiny2313 and similar AVRs
Testing circuit:	Figure 1 and 2
MiniPin compatibility:	yes (with appropriate μC)
MegaPin compatibility:	yes
The program measures basic characteristics of the IR message: carrier frequency and lengths of the start signal and the first space after the start signal	

Example program ID	
Name:	Get_NEC_RCA_Sony.bas
Microcontroller:	ATtiny4313 and similar AVRs
Testing circuit:	Figure 1 and 2
MiniPin compatibility:	yes (with appropriate μC)
MegaPin compatibility:	yes
The program decodes IR messages sent according to NEC, RCA and Sony protocols	

Part 2: Let's transmit an IR message!

Now that we have explored the basic characteristics of several widely-used protocols, we are ready to generate and transmit IR messages using these protocols. Note: Bascom-AVR has several statements for generating messages according to RC5, RC6 and Sony protocols. These statements will not be considered here.

IC transmitter

A universal IR transmitter, built around the ATtiny2313 microcontroller, is shown in Figure 8. R2 limits the current thru IR LED D1 to 15 mA, a value which ATtiny can sink with ease. The usable range of this simple transmitter is up to 0.5 meters: just enough for testing purposes. You can extend the range of the transmitter considerably if you replace R2 and D1 in Figure 8 with the BS250-based driver shown in Figure 9. The R2 resistance is now significantly lower and current pulses thru D1 reach 100-200 mA. In spite of these high-current pulses, the average

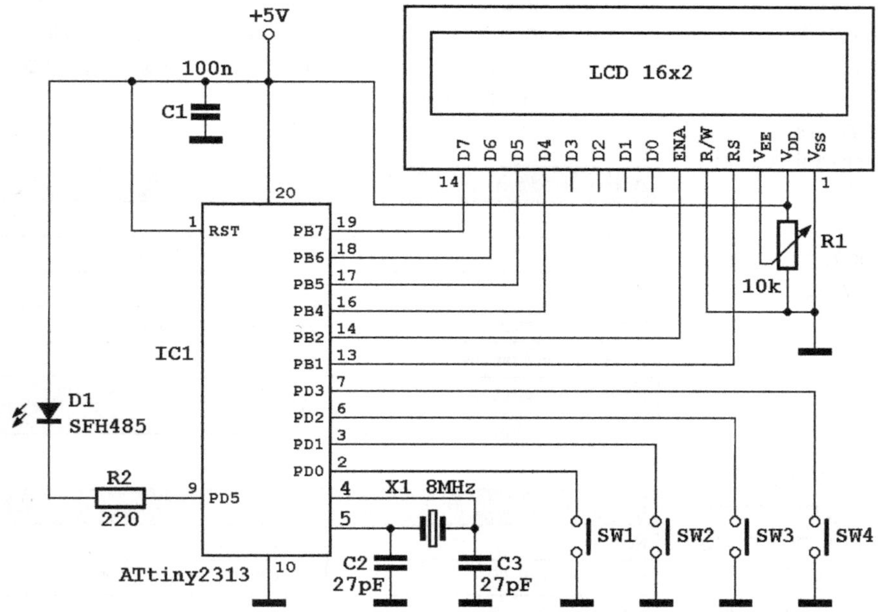

Figure 8: Universal IR transmitter with ATtiny2313

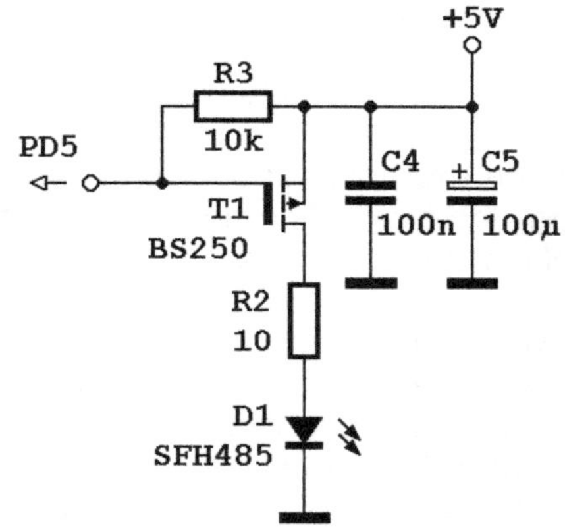

Figure 9: Extended range IR transmitter

power consumption of the circuit shown in Figure 9 during active periods is under 50 mA and drops to 0 mA when the circuit is inactive (PD5 = 1).

Both transmitter versions are controlled by the ATtiny2313 microcontroller and one of the following programs:

- NEC protocol: Send_NEC.bas
- RCA protocol: Send_RCA.bas
- Sony SIRC 12-bit protocol: Send_Sony_12.bas
- Sony SIRC 15-bit protocol: Send_Sony_15.bas
- Sony SIRC 20-bit protocol: Send_Sony_20.bas

All of these programs follow the same pattern:

- use push-buttons SW1 and SW2 to select one of the available commands (commands are displayed on the display in sequence);
- use push-button SW4 to execute the selected command;
- use push-button SW3 to generate a series of 500 µs carrier bursts (pulses), separated by 250 µs spaces.

Carrier frequency, device address and available commands are coded within the program itself and correspond to the devices I have tested. You should change the following program lines to adapt the program to some other device:

```
'***** configuration *****
Const Carrier_freq = 58000
                         'f_carrier = 58kHz
Const Address = &H07     'Address = xxxxAAAA
Const Command_no = 11    'number of commands
'*************************
```

Constant *Carrier_freq* determines the carrier frequency.

Constant *Address* determines the device address.

Constant *Command_no* determines the number of commands that the program can transmit (the commands themselves are defined in the table *Commands*).

The example is taken from the program Send_RCA.bas, which sends the 4-bit addresses according to the protocol. The comment in the address row explains the way in which the address has to be defined. In this example, the four most significant bits can be of any value, and the address is defined by the four least significant bits. In the program Send_NEC.bas, which is configured for the extended NEC protocol, the address is defined using two constants:

```
Const A_low = &B00000001      'Address low
Const A_hgh = &B11111101      'Address high
```

In the 20-bit Sony protocol you have to define an extended field besides the address:

```
Const Address = &H1A      'Address = xxxAAAAA
Const Extended = &H49     'Extended
                          'field = EEEEEEEE
```

In all programs, the available commands are defined in the table *Commands* at the end of the program:

```
Commands:                     'MSB->LSB
Data &B10000111               '0
Data &B10010010               '1
Data &B10010011               '2
Data &B11001100               '3
Data &B10001110               '4
Data &B10001111               '5
Data &B11001000               '6
Data &B10001010               '7
Data &B10001011               '8
```

```
Data &B11000100                        '9
Data &B11011100                        'ON/OFF
Data &B11001110                        'OK
```

In this example, which was taken from the Send_NEC.bas, there are 12 commands in the table and the value of the *Command_no* constant should be 12.

If you want to adapt any of the five example programs to your device, you have to know the following:

» which protocol it uses,
» what the carrier frequency is,
» the address of the device and
» command codes.

This information can be found on various internet sites or it can be determined with the Get_xxx.bas programs, as explained in Part 1 of this chapter. Fill the *Command* table with the desired command codes, update configuration parameters, compile the program and program the microcontroller. The circuit from figures 8 and 9 will now be able to control your device instead the original remote control.

Possible applications

What's the use of a homemade remote control, when one can buy a universal remote control for no more than 10 EUR? One possible application would be to use an unused remote control to control lighting, curtains or other homemade devices. In such case, use a SFH506, TSOP1138 or similar IR receiver IC instead of the circuit from Figure 1. It's much more sensitive and has far better interference suppression characteristics. Always use an IR receiver IC that matches the carrier frequency: the SFH506-36 for the 36 kHz carrier, the SFH506-38 for the 38 kHz carrier, etc. To write your own receiving program, use one of the "Get_xxx.bas program as a template (use one that handles a similar protocol, of course). The program should be modified in the following way: instead of displaying a message on the display, you would analyse the received message and take some action dependent upon the message that has been received. In most cases, this will mean setting the state of an output pin properly, thus activating an external device connected to this pin.

The other possible use is for IR-communication between two devices. I have used it to establish communications between a DVB-T set-top box and an HDD recorder. Once successfully implemented, the HDD recorder gained the ability to change the program setting on the DVB-T set-top box to match the program setting on the recorder. You can think of similar applications for yourself. Bear in mind, however, that such an application is a very challenging task and you must thoroughly understand how both devices work.

Example program ID	
Name:	Send_NEC.bas
Microcontroller:	ATtiny2313 and similar AVRs
Testing circuit:	Figure 8 and 9
MiniPin compatibility:	yes (with appropriate μC)
MegaPin compatibility:	yes
The program sends IR messages according to basic and extended NEC protocol	

Example program ID	
Name:	Send_RCA.bas
Microcontroller:	ATtiny2313 and similar AVRs
Testing circuit:	Figure 8 and 9
MiniPin compatibility:	yes (with appropriate μC)
MegaPin compatibility:	yes
The program sends IR messages according to 12-bit RCA protocol	

Example program ID	
Name:	Send_Sony_12.bas
Microcontroller:	ATtiny2313 and similar AVRs
Testing circuit:	Figure 8 and 9
MiniPin compatibility:	yes (with appropriate μC)
MegaPin compatibility:	yes
The program sends IR messages according to 12-bit Sony SIRC protocol	

Example program ID	
Name:	Send_Sony_15.bas
Microcontroller:	ATtiny2313 and similar AVRs
Testing circuit:	Figure 8 and 9
MiniPin compatibility:	yes (with appropriate μC)
MegaPin compatibility:	yes
The program sends IR messages according to 15-bit Sony SIRC protocol	

Example program ID	
Name:	Send_Sony_20.bas
Microcontroller:	ATtiny2313 and similar AVRs
Testing circuit:	Figure 8 and 9
MiniPin compatibility:	yes (with appropriate μC)
MegaPin compatibility:	yes
The program sends IR messages according to 20-bit Sony SIRC protocol	

"Bare-bones" programmable electronic load

By Jurij Mikeln

Not long ago, I was testing a PWM power supply and its characteristics. For basic tests, an ordinary 100W ceramic power resistor – a souvenir from my student days, was enough. Finding a similar resistor nowadays would be nearly impossible task. Probably one can find it at radio amateur "flea markets". Even if we found a suitable resistor, this is not a good solution if we want to perform measurements over wide range power supply voltages/currents. For that purpose one would need to buy either a powerful rheostat or a programmable electronic load.

Neither of the choices mentioned above is too cost-effective for an electronic hobbyist, so we need a different approach. While testing the PWM power supply, I tested my first prototype of a PWM electronic load, consisting of a MegaPin board and one MOSFET power transistor. That prototype proved the concept very well. Using a selection of different output transistors I could select a resistance in the range of a couple of Ohms down to milliOhms.

When testing the PWM power supply, I needed resistance values ranging from 1,500 Ohms down to about 7.5 Ohms. Using these, and some intermediate resistances, we could check the performance of our power supply.

As mentioned, MOSFET transistors worked very well in our first prototype. With our next circuit we wanted to go one step further. We used an ATtiny85 in our circuit (one can also use an ATtiny 25, but we had ATtiny85s on-hand). The ATtiny85 has enough output pins to drive the PWM electronic load, but not enough left for driving an LCD display. So we decided to drive the LCD via the SPI bus, as described elsewhere in this book. That minimized the part count, yet made our PWM electronic load fully functional with a LCD display and two buttons to set the load value. Perfect for a "bare-bones" electronic load!

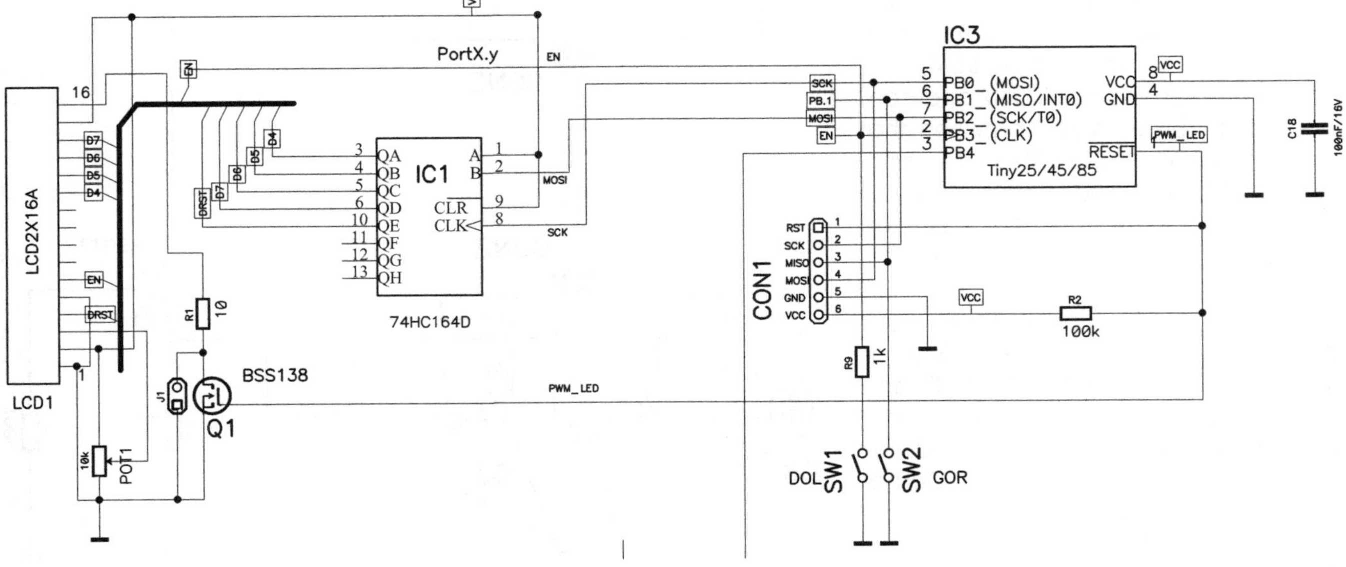

Figure 1: Drive electronics of electronic load

The Circuit

The device was split to two parts: the drive electronics and the power control. The drive electronics consists of ATtiny85 that scans two buttons SW1 & SW2, drives the LCD and MOSFET Q5, which drives the high-power MOSFETs. The ATtiny85 also has one available pin (PORTB.5 = RST) which could drive the LCD's backlight. However, once you program that pin to be a regular I/O pin (and not the -RESET pin), you can no longer program the ATtiny85 with an ISP programmer- you then have to use a parallel programmer.

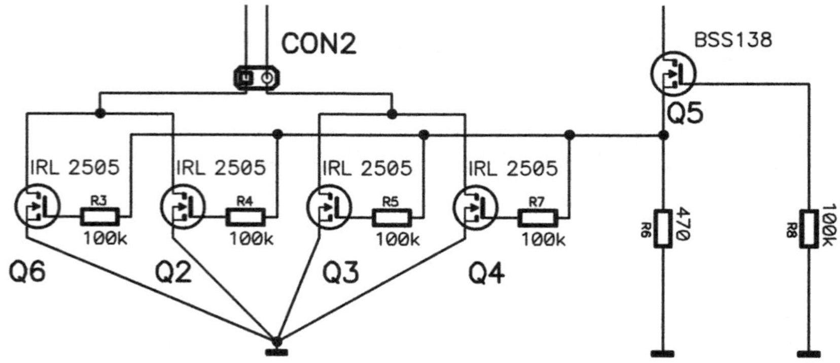

Figure 2: Power circuit of electronic load

You'll likely notice in Figure 1, IC1 (74HC164D), which is needed to drive the LCD via SPI. There are more details about this in another chapter of the book. Because the electronic load is really "bare-bones", SW1 is also connected to SPI bus. One might expect an interaction with the LCD display, but due to the inclusion of R9 in the circuit, there is no interaction at all. Without R9, the LCD would not display correctly while SW1 was pressed.

There are quite large currents flowing to our "bare-bones" electronic load (up to several Amps.), so we designed a double-sided PCB with wide tracks. We designed the circuit with four output transistors connected in pairs. One can use only one pair of them, like Q4 and Q3 for example, or just one transistor, if only modest currents loads are needed.

The Electronic load can be connected to the power source under test, in 3 ways:

1. connect the power source to CON2. The Total resistance will be the sum of the internal resistances of the parallel-connected MOSFETs Q6, Q2 plus parallel-connected MOSFETs Q3, Q4. See Figure 3.
2. connect the power source between one terminal of CON2 and GND. The total resistance will equal the resistance of parallel-connected Q6, Q2 or Q3, Q4 respectively. See Figure 4,
3. short both terminals of CON2 and connect the power source between that connection and GND. The total resistance will be equal to internal resistances of all MOSFETs connected in parallel (Q6 II Q2 II Q3 II Q4). See Figure 5.

The PCB is double-sided. Most parts are placed on the component side, including the ATtiny85. Only the LCD and switches are placed on the solder side. The four output transistors should be mounted on a suitable heat sink. Do not forget to electrically isolate them using a Mica insulating KIT.

The PCB is designed to withstand currents up to 15A, but don't overload it. If you need an even greater current capacity, then solder some thick wires to the current-carrying PCB tracks. Also bear in mind that the output power transistors have limitations: the IRF-3708PBF is rated for a maximum of 30 Volts.

Bascom software

The software is also "bare-bones", Note that the program requires that the "`lcd-spi.lib`" file is placed in the Bascom/LIB folder. The following are important lines in the program:

```
Tccr1 = &B00000001
Gtccr = &B01100000

$lib "lcd-spi.lib"          'SPI library used
Const Lcd_e = 3             'Enable pin
```

The first two statements configure ATtiny85's Timer properly. The last four statements load and configure the

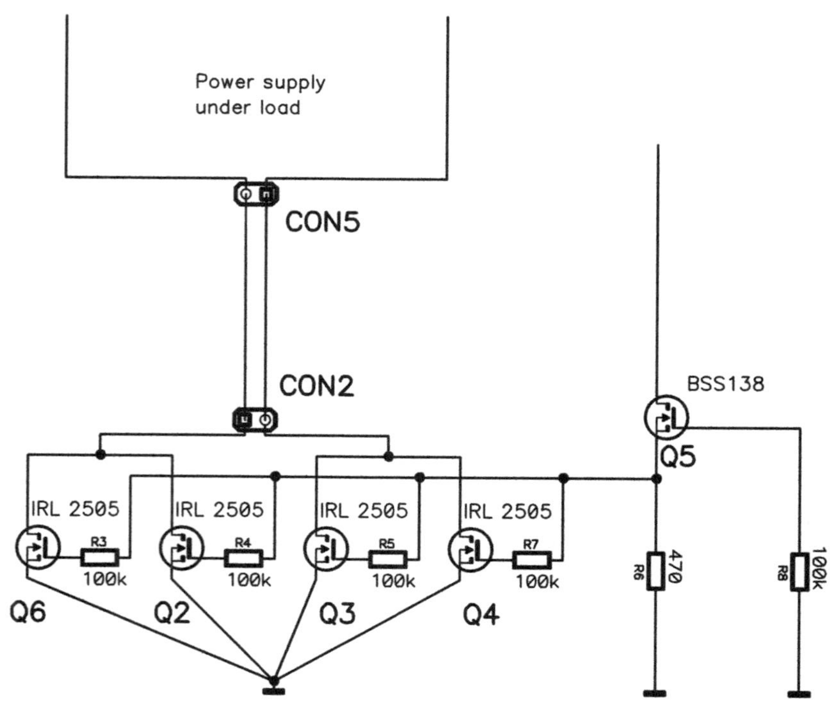

Figure 3: Connection of electronic power load

lcd-spi library, enabling the LCD display to work. Without these statements the PWM electronic load will not perform correctly and LCD will not display anything.

As it stands, this program does not display on the LCD the internal resistance of the power transistors. That is a drawback, but you have to bear in mind that each power output transistor has its own internal resistance depending upon the Gate-Source drive voltage. That would mean that we would have to incorporate these internal resistance figures into a table in the program, and change the table if other transistor were used. That would be very impractical, so we decided that the LCD will show PWM drive value ranging from 0 to 255, which represents the highest and lowest resistance respectively.

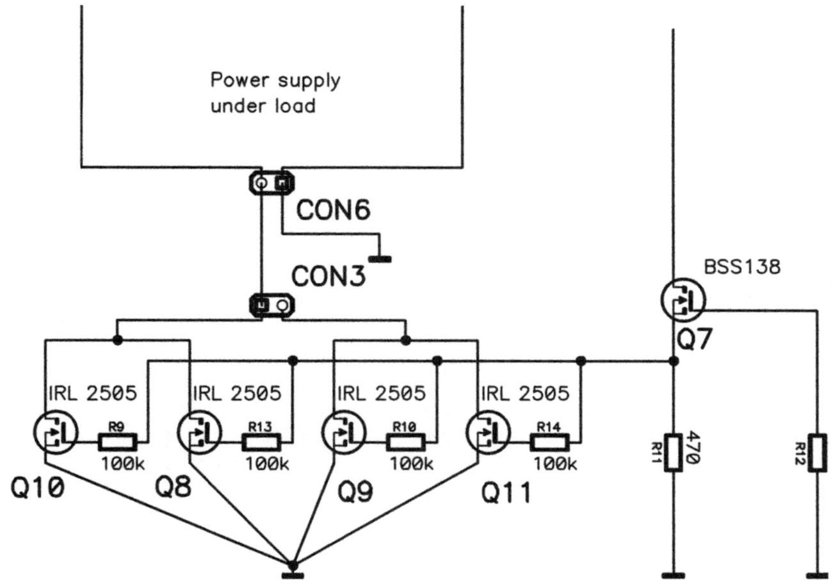

Figure 4: Connection of two parallel MOSFETs to GND

Possible improvements

When testing the electronic power load, we noticed that the heat was not evenly distributed amongst the output transistors. That was due to the temperature dependence of the MOSFET's internal resistance.

To improve that we could measure temperature and change PWM drive signal accordingly. A good solution is to connect a low Ohm resistance from the Source of each transistor to ground. The resistance should be 0.5 Ohms or less.

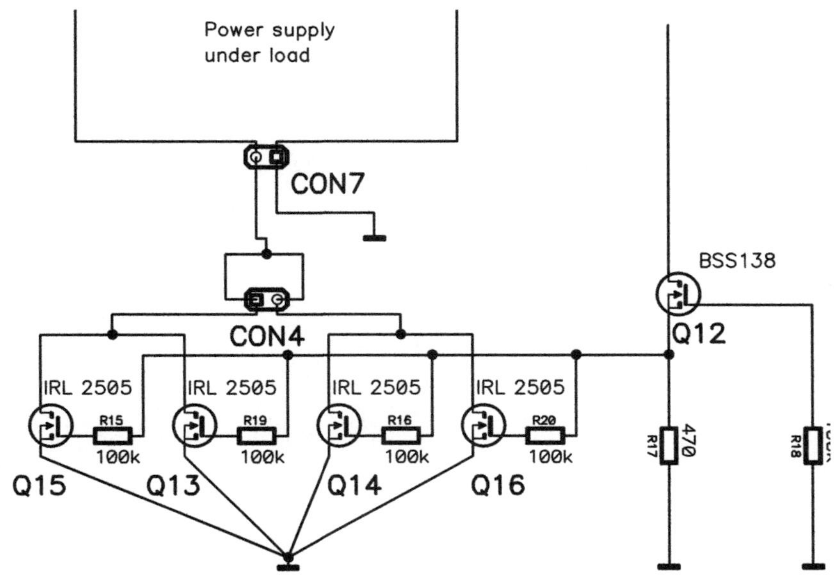

Figure 5: Parallel connection of all MOSFETs

Conclusion

This project is "bare-bones" in both circuitry and software. The LCD displays only the PWM value and not the resistance, because setting/displaying the MOSFET's internal resistance would be very impractical as it changes with each transistor and with temperature. For those of you who would like to use this electronic load with larger currents, let me tell you that I have successfully tried the IRFP4368PBF, which is rated for 350 A! I wish you successful "electronic loading"!

Example program ID	
Name:	PWM load.bas
Microcontroller:	Any ATtiny AVRs
Testing circuit:	Figure 1
MiniPin compatibility:	/
MegaPin compatibility:	/
Use multi_lcd-SPI.lib	

Example program ID - Library	
Name:	lcd-spi.lib
Microcontroller:	/
Testing circuit:	/
MiniPin compatibility:	/
MegaPin compatibility:	/
Library for use with above	

A Frequency Reference Using the ATtiny2313

By Vladimir Mitrović

The ATtiny2313-based frequency reference produces a series of rectangular pulses with a 50% duty cycle. The frequency of these pulses is very stable, while the frequency range covers a full 10 decades, ranging from 0.001 Hz to 10 MHz.

Basic methods of frequency generation

The circuit shown in Figure 1 is very simple, because everything is done inside the microcontroller. A 20 MHz quartz crystal is used as the microcontroller's clock source to allow the highest possible upper frequency limit. The clock frequency is divided inside the microcontroller by various division factors, to obtain the range of output frequencies mentioned above. As all the output frequencies are obtained strictly by frequency division, they are as stable and accurate as the crystal is.

The following microcontroller resources are used for frequency division:

1. The 8-bit system clock prescaler divides the system clock by division factors of 1, 2, 4, 8, 16, 32, 64, 128 or 256. This affects the CPU clock and thus slows down the program execution proportionally.
2. The 10-bit prescaler module divides the actual system clock by 1, 8, 64, 256 or 1024 for Timer/Counter0 and Timer/Counter1. The two Timers/Counters can have different prescaler settings.
3. Timer/Counter0 counts the appropriately prescaled system clock pulses in *Clear Timer on Compare* (CTC) mode. In this mode, the counter is cleared to zero when its value matches the value in the OCR0A register. If the value in the OCR0B register is the same as the value in OCR0A, and the Timer/Counter has been properly configured, the output OC0B (PD5) will toggle whenever the counter is cleared. Values between 0-255 in the OCR0A and OCR0B registers will result in division factors of 2-512.
4. Timer/Counter1 counts the appropriately prescaled system clock pulses in CTC mode. The counter is cleared to zero and the output pin OC1A (PB3) toggles whenever the counter value matches the value in the OCR1A register. Values 0-65535 in the OCR1A register will result in division factors of 2-131072.
5. Timer/Counter1 counts clock pulses at input pin PD5 in CTC mode. The counter is cleared to zero and the output pin OC1A (PB3) toggles whenever the counter value matches the value in the OCR1A register. Values 0-65535 in the OCR1A register will result in division factors of 2-131072.

For higher output frequencies, only options 1) and 4) are used. The clock prescaler and the Timer/Counter1 are connected as shown in Figure 2, while the output frequency can be calculated using the following formula:

$$f = \frac{fosc}{2 * clock\_prescale * (1 + OCR1A)}$$

With a 20 MHz crystal frequency, the maximum and minimum output frequencies will equal 10 MHz and

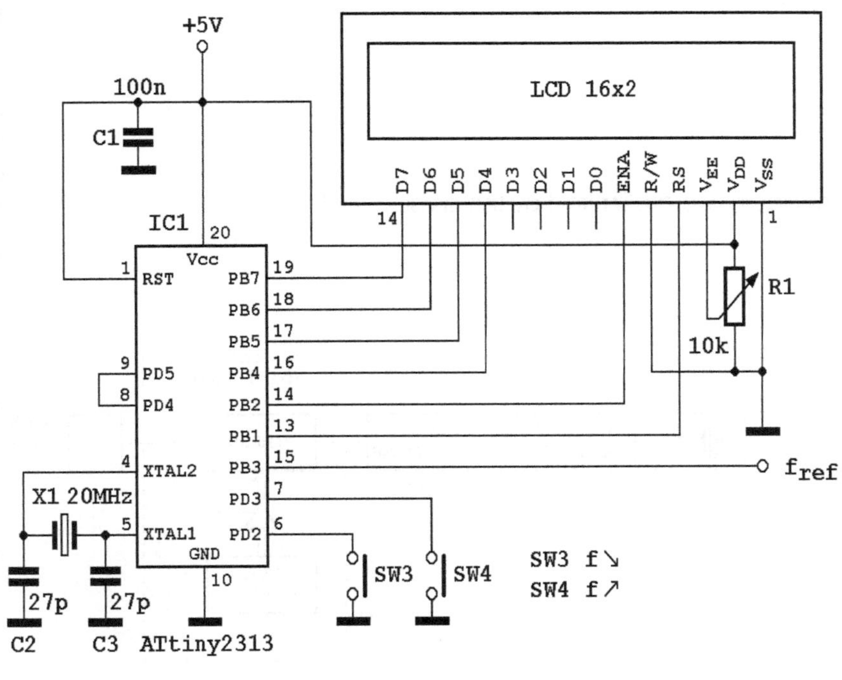

Figure 1: The circuit is very simple because everything is done inside the microcontroller

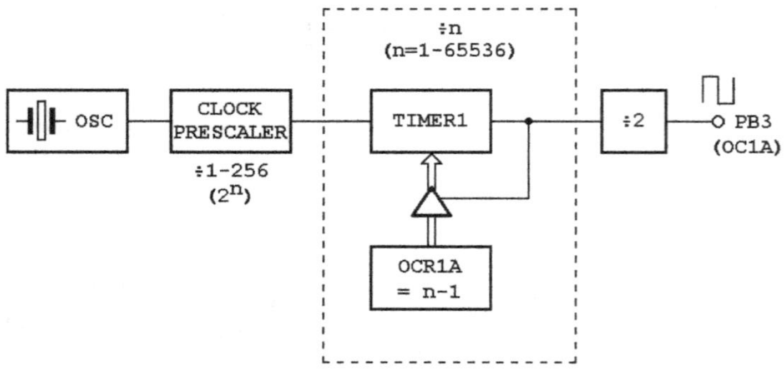

Figure 2a: The clock prescaler and Timer/Counter1 are used for the generation of frequencies down to 5 Hz

around 0.6 Hz. However, if we want to generate frequencies with a 1-2-5 step (10 MHz, 5 MHz, 2 MHz, 1 MHz, ...), the lowest frequency will be 5 Hz. This is due to the fact that the 1-2-5 step is obtained only by the division factors 2^n and 5^n: the clock prescaler is used for division factors 2^n, whereas division factors 5^n are realised by the Timer/Counter1. This narrows the choice of values for the clock prescaler and the OCR1A register and therefore the maximum division factor is somewhat lower than expected.

For frequencies lower than 5 Hz, options 1), 2), 3) and 5) are used. The Timer/Counter1 clock input is now connected to the Timer/Counter0 OC0B output pin and it counts the pulses from that pin. In this way, two timers are cascaded via OC0B and the overall division factor is increased by a factor of 1000. The output frequency can be calculated by using the following formula:

$$f = \frac{fosc}{4 * clock\_prescale * Timer0\_prescale * (1 + OCR0A) * (1 + OCR1A)}$$

Here again, we are limited by the division factors 2^n and 5^n, which limit the lowest frequency to 0.005 Hz. If we want to extend the range to a full 10 decades, two frequencies are still needed: 0.002 Hz and 0.001 Hz. They are achieved by choosing the value of 212 for OCR0A and 5730 or 11461 for OCR1A:

$$f = \frac{20000000}{4 * 256 * 8 * (1 + 212) * (1 + 5730)} = 0.002Hz$$

$$f = \frac{20000000}{4 * 256 * 8 * (1 + 212) * (1 + 11461)} = 0.001Hz$$

Although the calculated values deviate slightly from the expected ones, the error in both cases is less than 0.00001%, which can be ignored.

The Program

The program generates a set of predefined frequencies which are interactively selected by the SW3 and SW4 push-buttons. Immediately after the power has been switched on, the program starts to produce a 1 kHz signal on the f_{ref} output and waits in a loop for the push-buttons SW3 and SW4 to be pressed. When one of them has been pressed, the program reconfigures the timers to produce the previous or next predefined frequency. The current frequency is displayed on the LCD display in the form "f = 1.000 kHz".

In the program, all configuration values for clock and timer prescalers, as well as Timer/Counter0 and Timer/Counter1 division factors, are stored in appropriately named tables. The program uses the *F* variable as an index into these tables.

» *Clock_prescale_table* contains division factors for the clock prescaler. The value fetched from the table is converted to the value that needs to be written in the CLKPR register in order to achieve the desired division factor (for example, a division factor of 256 is achieved when &B00001000 is written into CLKPR):

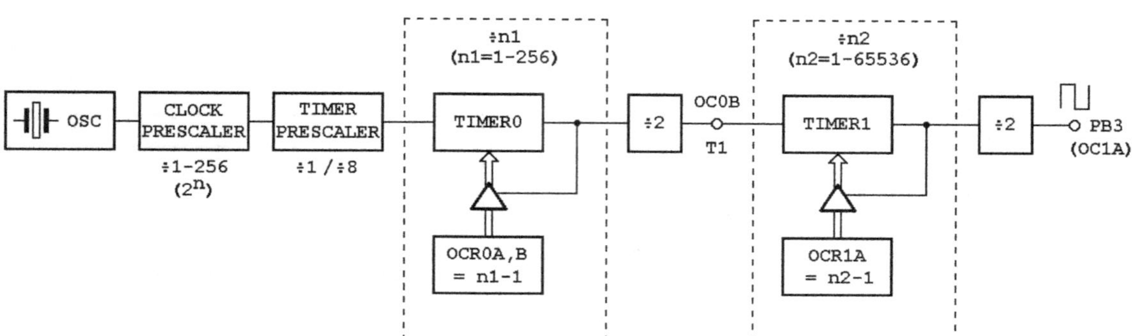

Figure 2b: The clock and timer prescalers as well as both timers are used for the generation of lower frequencies

```
Clock_prescale=Lookup (f,Clock_prescale_table)
Clkpr_prescale = 0
While Clock_prescale > 1
   Shift Clock_prescale , Right
   Incr Clkpr_prescale
Wend
Clkpr = &B10000000
Clkpr = Clkpr_prescale
...
Clock_prescale_table:        '[1-256]
Data 1%                      '0: 10 MHz
Data 2%                      '1: 5 MHz
Data 1%                      '2: 2 MHz
...
Data 64%                     '28: 0.005 Hz
Data 256%                    '29: 0.002 Hz
Data 256%                    '30: 0.001 Hz
```

» *Ocr1a_table* contains the division factors needed by Timer/Counter1. The program decrements the value fetched from the table by 1 and writes it into the OCR1A (= Output Compare1A) register:

```
Ocr1a_value = Lookup(f , Ocr1a_table)
Decr Ocr1a_value
Compare1a = Ocr1a_value
...
Ocr1a_table:        '[1-65535],
Ocr1a = Ocr1a_table_entry - 1
Data 1%                      '0: 10 MHz
Data 1%                      '1: 5 MHz
Data 5%                      '2: 2 MHz
...
Data 15625%                  '28: 0.005 Hz
Data 5731%                   '29: 0.002 Hz
Data 11462%                  '30: 0.001 Hz
```

» *Ocr0a_table* contains the division factors needed by Timer/Counter0. The program decrements the value fetched from the table by 1 and writes it into the OCR0A and OCR0B registers:

```
Ocr0a_value = Lookup(f , Ocr0a_table)
Decr Ocr0a_value
Ocr0a = Ocr0a_value
Ocr0b = Ocr0a_value
...
Ocr0a_table:        '[1-255, 0=not used]
Data 0                       '0: 10 MHz
Data 0                       '1: 5 MHz
...
Data 125                     '28: 0.005 Hz
Data 213                     '29: 0.002 Hz
Data 213                     '30: 0.001 Hz
```

» *Timer0_prescale_table* contains the division factors for the timer prescaler:

```
Timer0_prescale=Lookup(f,Timer0_prescale_table)
If Timer0_prescale = 1 Then
   Config Timer0 = Timer , _
      Prescale = 1 , _
      Compare B = Toggle , _
      Clear Timer = 1    'start Timer0
Else
   Set Gtccr.psr10
                         'reset Timer
                         'prescaler
   Config Timer0 = Timer , _
      Prescale = 8 , _
      Compare B = Toggle , _
      Clear Timer = 1    'start Timer0
End If
...
Timer0_prescale_table:   '[1-8-64-256-1024,
                         '0=not used]
Data 0                   '0: 10 MHz
Data 0                   '1: 5 MHz
...
Data 1                   '27: 0.01 Hz
Data 8                   '28: 0.005 Hz
Data 8                   '29: 0.002 Hz
Data 8                   '30: 0.001 Hz
```

The *Config Timer0* statement configures and simultaneously starts the Timer/Counter0. For higher frequencies, the Timer/Counter1 is configured to act as a timer:

```
Config Timer1 = Timer , _
   Prescale = 1 , _
   Compare A = Toggle , _
   Clear Timer = 1        'start Timer1
```

For lower frequencies, the Timer/Counter1 is configured to act as a counter:

```
Config Timer1 = Counter , _
   Edge = Falling ,_
   Compare A = Toggle ,_
   Clear Timer = 1        'start Timer1
```

In both cases, the *Config Timer1* statement configures and simultaneously starts the Timer/Counter1.

» *Disp_table* contains messages to be displayed on the display. The displayed message corresponds to the currently-selected frequency:

```
Aux_string = Lookupstr(f , Disp_table)
Home L
Lcd "f= " ; Aux_string ; "Hz"
...
Disp_table:
Data "10.00 M"
Data "5.000 M"
Data "2.000 M"
Data "1.000 M"
Data "500.0 k"
Data "200.0 k"
...
```

As frequency generation is performed entirely in hardware, the program has nothing much to do, after the prescalers and timers have been configured. It just waits for one of the push-buttons to be pressed, and then fetches another configuration from the tables, which it uses to reconfigure the prescalers and timers for the new frequency. This push-button monitoring is handled by external interrupts INT0 and INT1. Using *Debounce* statements is not applicable in this instance, because the program changes the CPU speed as needed, and this would have a huge impact on the *Debounce* execution time.

Two interrupt service routines have been written, *Int0_sub* and *Int1_sub*. The first one is executed when the SW3 push-button has been pressed, while the second one reacts to SW4. Both routines check the state of the associated input pin twice, to eliminate switch "bounce", just as the *Debounce* statement does.

```
Int0_sub:
   Gosub Waitms_25
   If Pind.2 = 0 Then
      If F < 31 Then
         Incr F
         Gosub Set_freq
      End If
   Set Eifr.intf0
   End If
Return

Waitms_25:
   Clkpr_prescale = Clkpr
   Aux_word = 256
   While Clkpr_prescale > 0
      Shift Aux_word , Right
      Decr Clkpr_prescale
   Wend
   While Aux_word > 0
      Waitus 96
      Decr Aux_word
   Wend
Return
```

	Frequency [Hz]	Division factor	Clock prescale	Timer1 div. factor	Timer0 prescale	Timer0 div. factor
"high frequencies " onlyTimer1 is used, connected according Fig. 2a	10 000 000	2	1	1	0	0
	5 000 000	4	2	1	0	0
	2 000 000	10	1	5	0	0
	1 000 000	20	2	5	0	0
	500 000	40	4	5	0	0
	200 000	100	2	25	0	0
	100 000	200	4	25	0	0
	50 000	400	8	25	0	0
	20 000	1 000	4	125	0	0
	10 000	2 000	8	125	0	0
	5 000	4 000	16	125	0	0
	2 000	10 000	8	625	0	0
	1 000	20 000	16	625	0	0
	500	40 000	32	625	0	0
	200	100 000	16	3125	0	0
	100	200 000	32	3125	0	0
	50	400 000	64	3125	0	0
	20	1 000 000	32	15625	0	0
	10	2 000 000	64	15625	0	0
	5	4 000 000	128	15625	0	0
"low frequencies " both timers are used, connected according Fig. 2a	2	10 000 000	32	625	1	125
	1	20 000 000	64	625	1	125
	0.5	40 000 000	128	625	1	125
	0.2	100 000 000	64	3125	1	125
	0.1	200 000 000	128	3125	1	125
	0.05	400 000 000	256	3125	1	125
	0.02	1 000 000 000	128	15625	1	125
	0.01	2 000 000 000	256	15625	1	125
	0.005	4 000 000 000	64	15625	8	125
	0.002	10 000 000 000	256	5731	8	213
	0.001	20 000 000 000	256	11462	8	213

Table 1: Parameters for program "Fgen_20MHz"

Note here that an ordinary *Waitms 25* has been replaced by the *Waitms_25* subroutine, which delays approximately 25 ms, regardless of the actual system clock frequency (which is changed by the program).

The *Int1_sub* differs from the one above in just one line: the index variable *F* is decremented instead of being incremented.

Two programs have been written, following the principle explained above: Fref_20MHz.bas and Fref_16MHz.bas. The first one uses a 20 MHz crystal and generates frequencies in the 0.001 Hz to 10 MHz range using 1-2-5 steps. The second one uses a 16 MHz crystal and generates frequencies in the 0.001 Hz to 8 MHz range using 1-2-4-8 steps.

Tables 1 and 2 summarize the configuration parameters for both programs. A lot of other frequencies can be obtained by changing these parameters and the crystal frequency. Keep in mind, however, that the overall division factor has to be an even number.

	Frequency [Hz]	Division factor	Clock prescale	Timer1 div. factor	Timer0 prescale	Timer0 div. factor
"high frequencies " onlyTimer1 is used, connected according Fig. 2a	8 000 000	2	1	1	0	0
	4 000 000	4	2	1	0	0
	2 000 000	8	4	1	0	0
	1 000 000	16	8	1	0	0
	800 000	20	2	5	0	0
	400 000	40	4	5	0	0
	200 000	80	8	5	0	0
	100 000	160	16	5	0	0
	80 000	200	4	25	0	0
	40 000	400	8	25	0	0
	20 000	800	16	25	0	0
	10 000	1 600	32	25	0	0
	8 000	2 000	8	125	0	0
	4 000	4 000	16	125	0	0
	2 000	8 000	32	125	0	0
	1 000	16 000	64	125	0	0
	800	20 000	16	625	0	0
	400	40 000	32	625	0	0
	200	80 000	64	625	0	0
	100	160 000	128	625	0	0
	80	200 000	32	3125	0	0
	40	400 000	64	3125	0	0
	20	800 000	128	3125	0	0
	10	1 600 000	256	3125	0	0
	8	2 000 000	64	15625	0	0
	4	4 000 000	128	15625	0	0
	2	8 000 000	256	15625	0	0
	1	16 000 000	256	31250	0	0
"low frequencies " both timers are used, connected according Fig. 2b	0.8	20 000 000	64	15625	1	5
	0.4	40 000 000	128	15625	1	5
	0.2	80 000 000	256	15625	1	5
	0.1	160 000 000	256	31250	1	5
	0.08	200 000 000	64	15625	1	50
	0.04	400 000 000	128	15625	1	50
	0.02	800 000 000	256	15625	1	50
	0.01	1 600 000 000	256	31250	1	50
	0.008	2 000 000 000	256	15625	1	125
	0.004	4 000 000 000	64	15625	8	125
	0.002	8 000 000 000	128	15625	8	125
	0.001	16 000 000 000	256	15625	8	125

Table 2: Parameters for program "Fgen_16MHz"

Notes:

- The accuracy of the generated frequency depends entirely on the clock crystal's accuracy and stability. Alternatively, one can use a crystal oscillator module, the output of which should be connected to the XTAL1 input pin. In this case, omit X1, C2 and C3.
- Set the *Flash Fuse* bits CKSEL3...0 to correspond to the selected crystal option. The factory default clock source setting is the Internal RC Oscillator with the longest start-up time and an initial system clock prescaling of 8, resulting in a 1 MHz system clock. You can't use this when a crystal oscillator or an oscillator module is used!
- It is sometimes difficult to reprogram a microcontroller that is running with a high clock prescaler setting. This applies to both of the frequency reference programs (i.e. the 16 and 20 MHz versions). If such a problem occurs, reset the microcontroller manually *just prior to* the start of the programming session.
- The programs were originally written for the ATtiny2313 in the circuit shown in Figure 1. This is functionally fully compatible with the MegaPin development system. The names of the push-buttons SW3 and SW4 are chosen to match the names of the MegaPin push-buttons. Other AVR microcontrollers can be used as long as they have ATtiny2313-compatible timers and clock prescaler. Minor program changes are necessary if the microcontroller chosen has an 8-bit Timer/Counter0 with only one Output Compare Register (OCR). For those microcontrollers whose Timer/Counter0 output pin OC0, OC0A or OC0B is not the same as Timer/Counter1's input pin (T1), these two pins must be wired together, externally.

Example program ID	
Name:	Fref_20MHz.bas
Microcontroller:	ATtiny2313 and some other AVRs with the same timer architecture and clock prescaling capabilities
Testing circuit:	Figure 1
MiniPin compatibility:	no (yes if adapter board for ATtiny2313 is used)
MegaPin compatibility:	yes
The program generates frequencies from the 0.001 Hz to 10 MHz range with 1-2-5 steps	

Example program ID	
Name:	Fref_16MHz.bas
Microcontroller:	ATtiny2313 and some other AVRs with the same timer architecture and clock prescaling capabilities
Testing circuit:	Figure 1
MiniPin compatibility:	no (yes if adapter board for ATtiny2313 is used)
MegaPin compatibility:	yes
The program generates frequencies from the 0.001 Hz to 8 MHz range with 1-2-4-8 steps	

An ATtiny2313 Frequency meter

By Vladimir Mitrović

The ATtiny2313-based frequency meter shown in Figure 1 can measure frequencies from 1 Hz to almost 10 MHz with a 4 to 5 digit accuracy. The accuracy depends primarily on the exact frequency of the X1 crystal, which can be fine-tuned by the variable capacitor C5. A 74HCT4520 (IC3) is used as a digital low-pass filter, which signals the microcontroller if the measured frequency exceeds the upper limit. A two line LCD display is used to show the result. Therefore, the frequency and the period can be displayed simultaneously.

The input signal should be TTL or CMOS compatible, with an amplitude of at least 2 Vpp. Diodes D1 and D2 limit the input voltage if its amplitude exceeds 5 Vpp. S2 is used as a display-hold button.

How we can measure high frequencies

We can measure high frequencies by counting input pulses within a precisely-defined time interval. In its simplest form, it can be done as shown in this example:

```
Counter1 = 0
Config Timer1 = Counter , Edge = Falling
Wait 1
Stop Timer1
```

The 16-bit Timer/Counter1 is configured as a counter, counting pulses on the T1 input pin. The counting starts as soon as the counter has been configured and stops after 1 second. If the initial value in the Counter1 register is 0, as is the case here, its value after one second will match the frequency of input pulses. Very simple indeed, but such a simple program has two limitations:

- Counter1 is a 16-bit register and can only count up to 65535, at which point it overflows and starts counting again from 0;
- The Wait command is not accurate enough for precise measurements.

Therefore, an assembler routine has been written which lasts exactly one second. Apart from being accurate, this routine also counts the number of Counter1 overflows. The final result is a 32-bit number and is accurate to +/-1 digit:

```
frequency =
number_of_overflows * 65536 + Counter1
```

The highest frequency that could be measured as de-

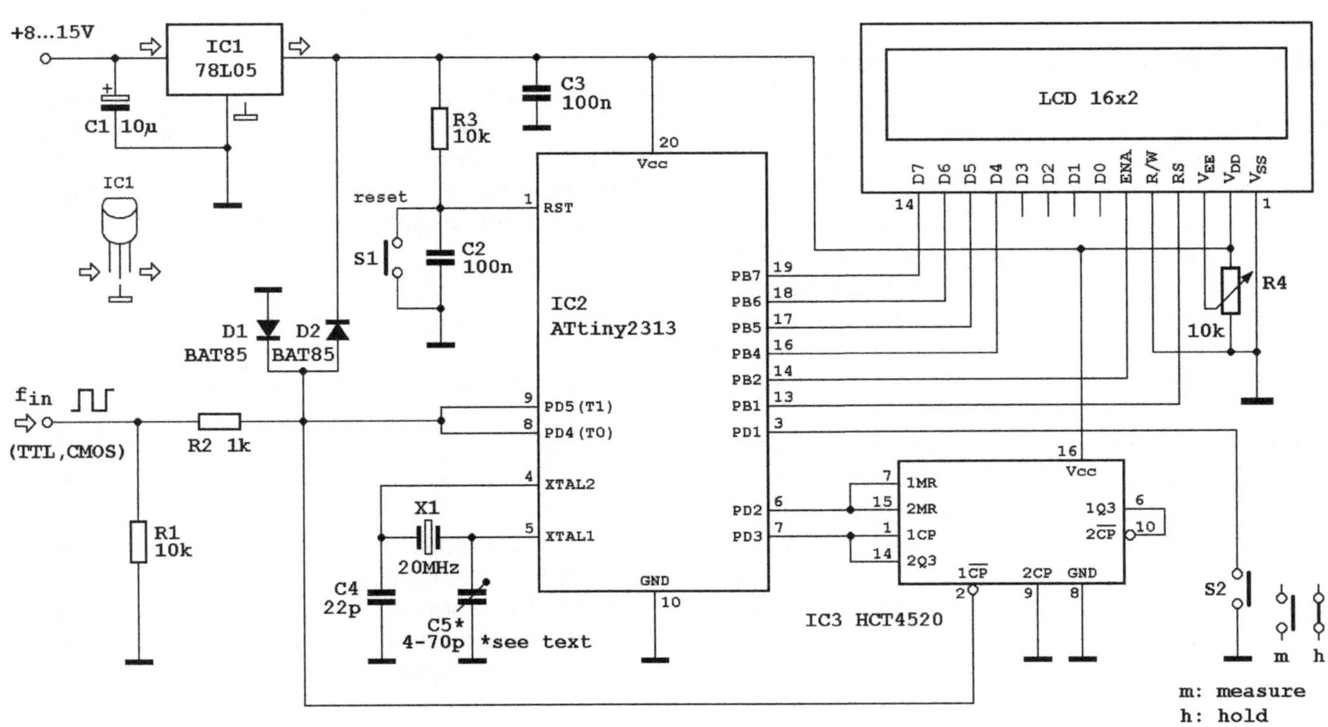

Figure 1: The ATtiny2313 Frequency meter

scribed above is 2^{32}, i.e. about 4 GHz. Such a high frequency cannot be measured with this microcontroller. With a 20 MHz crystal, the microcontroller can measure frequencies up to 10 MHz. It should be noted that the microcontroller itself cannot accurately measure frequencies that are beyond the upper frequency limit. For example, a frequency of 10.2 MHz will be measured as 9.8 MHz. This error is caused by the way the microcontroller detects level changes at the input pin and it cannot be detected by software.

The problem has been solved by the dual 4-bit synchronous binary counter 74HCT4520 (IC3). The microcontroller normally holds its PD2 output pin *High*, which resets the IC3 counter, setting all its outputs *Low*. Being in Reset, the IC3 counter cannot count pulses at its input (pin 2). Just before each measurement, the microcontroller produces a 13.5 µs negative pulse on its PD2 output pin. This pulse "unlocks" the counter, which then starts to count input pulses. Two things can happen:

» if the input frequency is lower than approximately 9.4 MHz, IC3 will count less than 128 pulses during the 13.5 µs and the most significant counter output pin, 2Q3, will still remain *Low*;
» if the input frequency is higher than approximately 9.4 MHz, IC3 will count more than 128 pulses during the13.5 µs and the most significant counter output pin, 2Q3, will go *High* (this disables further counting).

After this negative pulse has finished, the microcontroller reads the state of the 2Q3 output pin and finds out whether the input frequency is too high (PD3 = 2Q3 = 1) or whether it is within the measuring range (PD3 = 2Q3 = 0). The upper limit is rounded to 9 MHz by software.

How we can measure lower frequencies?

We have just seen how frequencies up to 9 MHz can be measured. The measurement accuracy equals the crystal accuracy +/-1 digit. The crystal accuracy, especially when fine-tuned by C5, will be enough for most amateur measurements. However, this "+/-1 digit" measuring error becomes more significant the lower the measuring frequency. We could reduce the error by extending the measuring period to 10 or 100 seconds, which is not very convenient - one has to wait too long for a result to be displayed.

So, lower frequencies cannot be measured precisely by counting input pulses over a reasonably long time interval. Instead, we usually measure them indirectly, by measuring the duration of one (or more) cycles (i.e. the period). Assuming that the input pin is still T1 (PD5), a simplified measurement could be done, as in the following example:

```
Counter1 = 0
Bitwait Pind.5 , Set
Bitwait Pind.5 , Reset
Config Timer1 = Timer , Prescale = 1
Bitwait Pind.5 , Set
Bitwait Pind.5 , Reset
Stop Timer1
```

After the Counter1 register has been cleared, the program waits for the falling edge of the input pulse and then starts the Timer/Counter1. Timer/Counter1 is configured to count clock pulses, which it will do until the next falling edge is detected. At that instant, the Counter1 register contains the number of clock pulses it has counted. The duration of each clock pulse depends on the clock frequency, and equals 0.05 µs for a 20 MHz crystal. In this case, the input frequency can be calculated using the following formula:

$$f=\frac{1}{Counter1*0.05*10^{-6}}$$

This program has several disadvantages:

» Counter1 is a 16-bit register and can only count up to 65535, at which point it overflows and continues counting from 0. Therefore, the lowest frequency we could measure in this way is about 300 Hz;
» As the frequency increases, the number in Counter1 becomes progressively smaller and thus the calculation error becomes greater;
» In the absence of an input signal, the program execution remains blocked at one of *Bitwait* statements.

Therefore, an assembler routine has been written which counts Counter1 overflows and therefore expands the counting register to 32 bits. As a result, the lower frequency limit is moved downwards and low frequencies are measured with better accuracy. The measuring interval is limited to 2 seconds to avoid possible program blockings if there is no input signal.

Both timers are used for this measurement. Timer/Counter0 counts pulses at the measurement input pin T0 (PD4) which, in turn, controls Timer/Counter1 (which counts 20 MHz clock pulses). Timer/Counter0 is configured to overflow after each single input pulse:

```
Counter0 = 255
Config Timer0 = Counter, Edge = Falling
```

or to overflow after each one hundred pulses

```
Counter0 = 156
Config Timer0 = Counter, Edge = Falling
```

The first configuration is appropriate for input frequencies in the 1 - 100 Hz range, while the second one is better suited to somewhat higher frequencies: 100 Hz - 10 kHz. In both cases, the timer recognises the *High* to *Low* transition on the input pin.

The first Timer0 interrupt starts the measurement, while the second one stops the measurement. The measured result falls within the 200000 - 20000000 range, with an error of +/-10 counts. Such an error is fully acceptable because the software scales this result to the actual 10000-100000Hz range, which reduces this error to +/-1 digit.

The program

The program is written in Bascom-AVR with several embedded assembler routines. There are three measuring ranges (see Table 1) and each of them uses the optimum measuring procedure for the applicable frequency range. These procedures have been explained earlier.

Each measuring procedure is programmed within its own *While-Wend* loop:

```
Do
   While Range = 1
      ...
   Wend
   While Range = 2
      ...
   Wend
   While Range = 3
      ...
   Wend
Loop
```

Within each *While-Wend* loop is program code that configures timers, initiates measurement, checks and displays the result and, finally, initiates the new measurement. Depending on the previous result, this new measurement can be carried out according to the same or another procedure. The following situations are possible:

- In range 1 (10 kHz - 9 MHz), the number of cycles during 1 second is counted:
  - if the frequency is too high, message "f >>" is displayed and the measurement is repeated;
  - if the frequency is within the range, the result is displayed and the measurement is repeated;
  - if the frequency is too low, the next measurement will be in range 2.

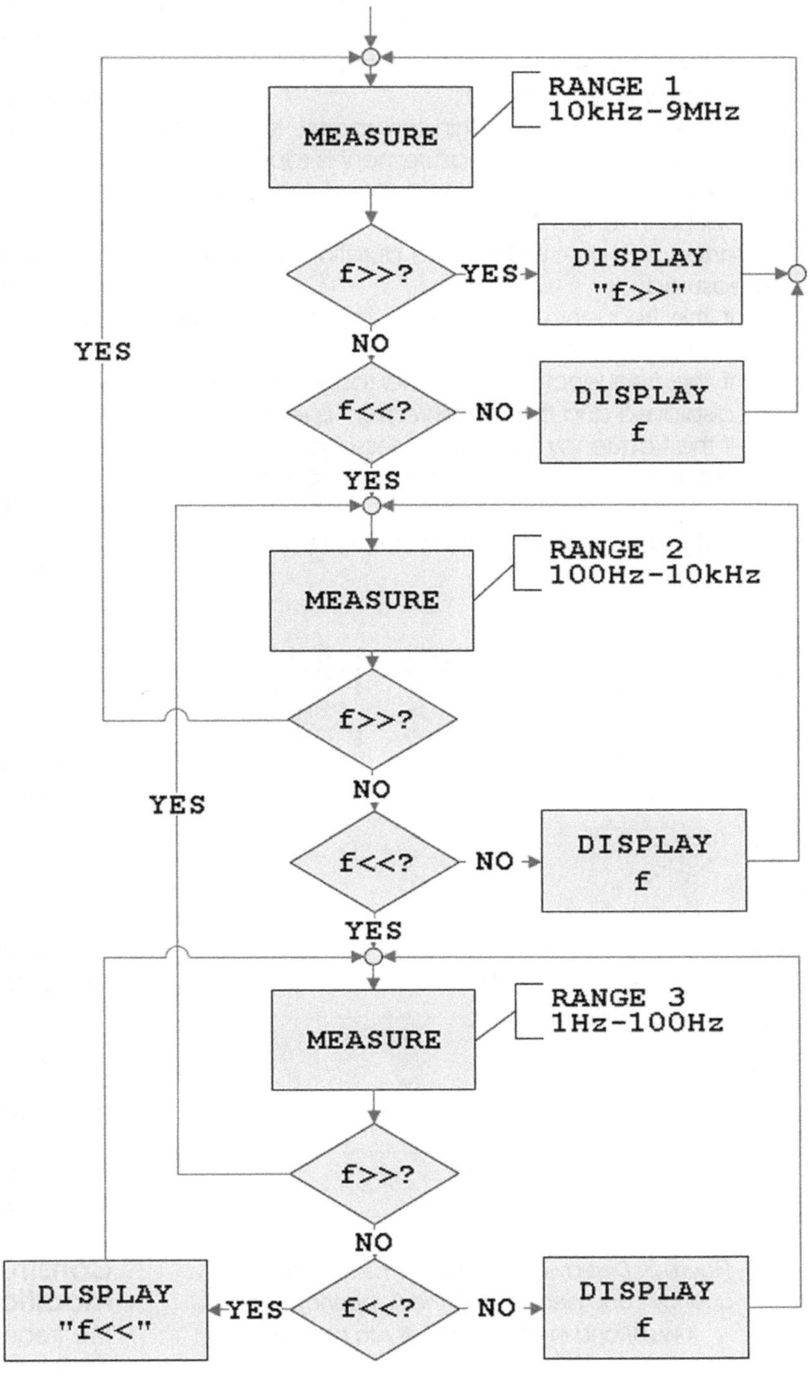

Figure 2: Program logic

f	variable "Freq"		PD3	measuring range	note
	min	max			
> 9,4 MHz	-	-	1	1,2,3	f >>
> 9 MHz	9000001	-	0	1	f >>
9 MHz - 10 kHz	10000	9000000	0	1	
10 kHz - 100 Hz	200000	20000000	0	2	
100 Hz - 1 Hz	200000	20000000	0	3	
< 1 Hz	-	-	0	3	f <<

Table 1. Measuring ranges

- In range 2 (100 Hz - 10 kHz), the duration of 100 cycles is measured:
  - if the frequency is too high, the next measurement will be in range 1;
  - if the frequency is within the range, the result is displayed and the measurement is repeated;
  - if the frequency is too low, the next measurement will be in range 3.
- In range 3 (1 Hz - 100 Hz), the duration of 1 cycle is measured:
  - if the frequency is too high, the next measurement will be in range 2;
  - if the frequency is within the range, the result is displayed and the measurement is repeated;
  - if the frequency is too low, message "f <<" is displayed and the measurement is repeated.

Simplified program logic is shown in Figure 2. What isn't shown though is that before each new measurement, the program briefly turns on the digital filter IC3 to see if the frequency is higher than 9.4 MHz. As explained earlier, these frequencies cannot be measured with this instrument. If the digital filter detects too high a frequency, the message "f >>" is displayed and the check is repeated until the frequency drops into range.

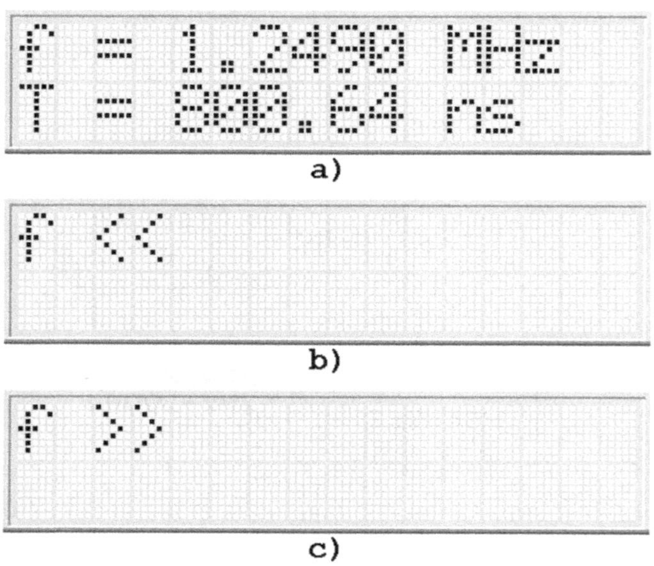

Figure 3: Display examples: the measured frequency f and period T (a), the frequency is too low (b) and the frequency is too high (c)

The most complex part of the program is the preparation of the results, before they are shown on the LCD display. Two results are displayed: the signal frequency and the period (the duration of one cycle). Besides these values, appropriate error messages are displayed if the frequency is too high or too low. Typical examples are shown in Figure 3.

In the 1st range, the frequency is obtained directly from the measurement and the period is calculated by the following formula:

$$T = 1/f$$

In the 2nd and the 3rd range, the period is measured directly while the frequency is calculated by the following formula:

$$f = 1/T$$

Both results are always shown as 5-digit decimal numbers (10000-99999). The directly-measured value (frequency or period) is accurate to +/-1 digit. The accuracy of the calculated value is 0.01% or better. If the S2 switch is pressed, the measurement in progress will be finished and, after the result is displayed, the program will wait in a loop until S2 is opened. This condition is indicated by an "H" (for hold) being displayed as the last character on the upper line of the display.

Construction, adjustment and possible modifications

The frequency meter is best built on a PCB, as shown in Fig 4a and Fig 4b. The push-buttons S1 (reset) and S2 (hold) can be placed directly on the PCB or mounted

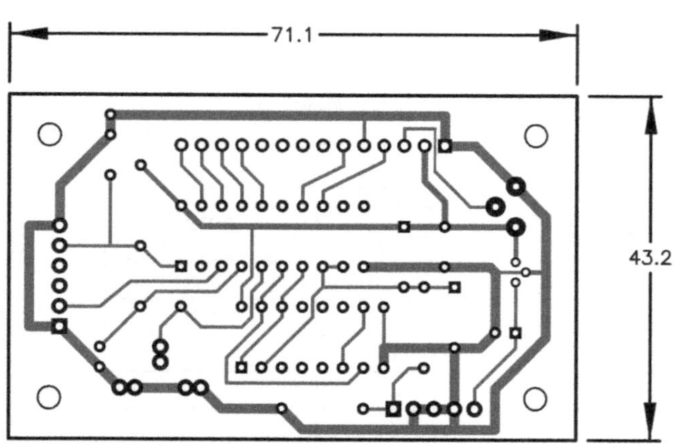

Figure 4a: PCB design, bottom layer

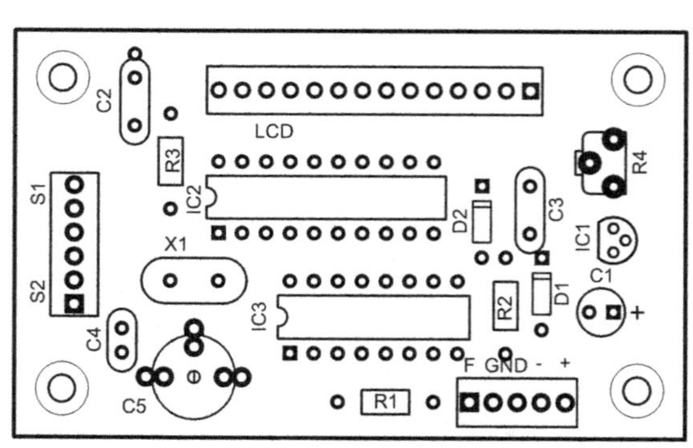

Figure 4b: Component layout

on the panel beside the display. Alternatively, they can be replaced by appropriate jumpers. Use C5 to adjust the frequency meter's accuracy. You will need a known, precision frequency reference or another precise frequency meter for this adjustment. In the first case, measure that frequency reference, and adjust C5 until the display matches that of the reference. In the latter case, connect both instruments in parallel, measure the frequency of some source and keep adjusting C5 until both instruments show the same result. The adjustment can be carried out on any frequency within the measuring range. If you have no precise frequency meter available, set C5 approximately to 1/3 of its full capacity and rely on the crystal's accuracy.

The frequency meter software can be tested using the MegaPin or MiniPin II development systems (MiniPin II with an appropriate microcontroller). If the high-frequency limit check is not necessary, you can omit IC3. In this case, it is necessary to short the PD3 input pin to ground. The program is written for a 20 MHz or a 10 MHz crystal. If the latter is used, replace the

```
$crystal = 20000000
```

line with the following line

```
$crystal = 10000000
```

and recompile the program. Conditional compilation directives will automatically tailor the measuring constants and routines to the new clock frequency. However, bear in mind that the highest measurable frequency with a 10 MHz crystal is 4.5 MHz.

Example program ID	
Name:	Fmeter.bas
Microcontroller:	ATtiny2313 and some other AVRs with the same timer architecture
Testing circuit:	Figure 1
MiniPin compatibility:	yes (with an appropriate microcontroller)
MegaPin compatibility:	yes
The program measures frequencies from the 1 Hz to 9 MHz range.	

Simple RTC - Real Time Clock

By Jurij Mikeln

Some AVR microcontrollers have Timer2 which can operate in asynchronous mode. These AVRs are the ATmega8, ATmega168 and ATmega16 etc. With some help from simple Bascom code, one can make an accurate clock which will display date and time.

Bascom-AVR offers many "goodies", one of which is certainly the RTC clock. I've met many Bascom programmers and seen many programs, where a real time clock was used. None of those programmers used the RTC clock that is described in this chapter. Programmers seem to love generating 1 second pulse with a timer interrupt service routine which increments the values of variables for second/hour/day etc. The sample code described here, is very practical, uses very little of the microcontroller's resources and to top it off, generates an accurate clock. This program will perform well on both the MegaPin and MiniPin II development boards. It should perform well in your device too, providing that you connect it up accordingly. Possibly you might use an ATmega168P, which, according to its datasheet, promises very low energy consumption during sleep mode. That would make this microcontroller ideal for a low-power clock.

Software

The author of the Bascom software, Mr. Mark Alberts, has already written a basic sample program Megaclock.bas that can be found in the Program Files/MCS/Bascom-AVR/Samples folder. The main part of that short program is this statement:

```
CONFIG CLOCK = soft /USER
 [, GOSUB = SECTIC]
```

This statement is thoroughly described in the Bascom-AVR Help. For our use, the statement will look as follows:

```
Config Clock = Soft
```

With this statement, we have set all of the necessary registers in the AVR to allow Timer2 to work in asynchronous mode. Place an ATmega32 (or any of the above-mentioned AVR microcontrollers) on the MegaPin (or MiniPin II) board and set the fuse bit to Internal RC – this is important! Place a 32,768 kHz crystal into the appropriate socket (J18 at MegaPin, J7 at MiniPin II), disconnect jumper (J5 at MegaPin; J3 at MiniPin II) on PortC. Then load the program into the microcontroller and our RTC clock will work.

The Megaclock.bas sample shows to us how to set the date/time using the following statements:

```
Date$ = "11/11/00"
Time$ = "02:02:00"
```

This statement is rather impractical, as it will set the date/time contained in the two strings, not the current date/time. Therefore we need a manual way to set/change the date and time. We can do this by (individually) changing the following internal variables:

```
_day , _month, _year , _sec, _hour, _min
```

We can now display the date and time on an LCD:

```
Lcd Date$ ; "  " ; Time$
```

Actually, apart from the clock configuration statement described earlier, the whole program is very short:

```
Do
   Home Upper
   Lcd Time$
   Lowerline
   Lcd Date$
   Powersave
 Loop
```

What you don't see above, is that, in the background, all of the necessary variables are being updated, by an Assembly language procedure (contained in an interrupt service routine), generated automatically by the Bascom compiler.

Can the generation of a precise clock/calendar be much simpler than that? I don't think so! Of course one must add routines for initially setting the date/time and possibly routines for an alarm. You can even make yourself a unique clock with multiple alarms, at different times on different days.

The *Powersave* command was added for lowering the power consumption of the microcontroller. It means that the microcontroller is in sleep mode, most of the time, except when the RTC wakes it up once per second, to perform a short Assembly language updating routine.

Conclusion

In this short chapter, we have shown you that it's about time to move forward and start using solutions that make our programming easier. One such solution is surely Bascom's built-in RTC clock routine that was written for AVR microcontrollers which have the Asynchronous Timer2 feature. This clock will be as accurate as the crystal is.

NOTE

If you decide to incorporate the AVR RTC in your project, you should be very careful in the physical layout of your PCB, in the vicinity of the 32,768 KHz crystal. Place the crystal as close to the TOSC1 and TOSC2 pins as possible. It's a good idea to provide a ground plane on the opposite side of the PCB if possible. Try to route any digital lines, which change state often, as far away from the crystal and connecting traces as possible. If these steps are not taken, it is quite likely your clock will "gain time", as the oscillator circuit picks up stray noise. There have been numerous AVR forum notes about this problem, in the past.

We have written a program, where you can set the time in seconds, minutes and hours.

Example program ID	
Name:	Megaclock.bas
Microcontroller:	AT MEGA 32 or any AVR with Async Timer 2
Testing circuit:	/
MiniPin compatibility:	Yes
MegaPin compatibility:	Yes
RTC clock, basic functions	

Example program ID	
Name:	Megaclock1.bas
Microcontroller:	AT MEGA 32 or any AVR with Async Timer 2
Testing circuit:	/
MiniPin compatibility:	Yes
MegaPin compatibility:	Yes
Advance program with the possibility to set the time	

The RFM12B expansion board

By Bojan Kovač

The RFM12B expansion board offers MiniPin II and MegaPin users a cheap platform for developing short-range RF communication using RFM12B transceiver modules. The RFM12B is a low-power version of RFM12 module. It operates from 2.2 to 3.8 Volts.

RFM12B are half-duplex [1] transceivers that communicate on the 433 MHz UHF band. These very small and cost-effective modules are capable of transmitting and receiving on presettable channels with a defined bandwidth. All of these parameters will be configured by our program. To start off, let's learn more about RFM12B modules. A block diagram of the RFM12B is shown in Figure 1.

The RFM12 module is rated for 10 mW output power, corresponding to ITU standards for the 433 MHz band. There is also a high-power version, the RFM12BP, which is intended for the 868 MHz band and delivers 0.5W of output power. Typical use of RFM12B would be:

- remote control,
- home security,
- wireless keyboards and other PC peripherals,
- toy remote control,
- wireless key,
- telemetry,
- smart meters etc..

Main features:

- stable and accurate FSK modulation with presettable frequency deviation,
- programmable receiver bandwidth resolution,
- differential antenna connection,
- SPI compatible serial interface,
- analog and digital signal strength indicator and many other features as described in [2].

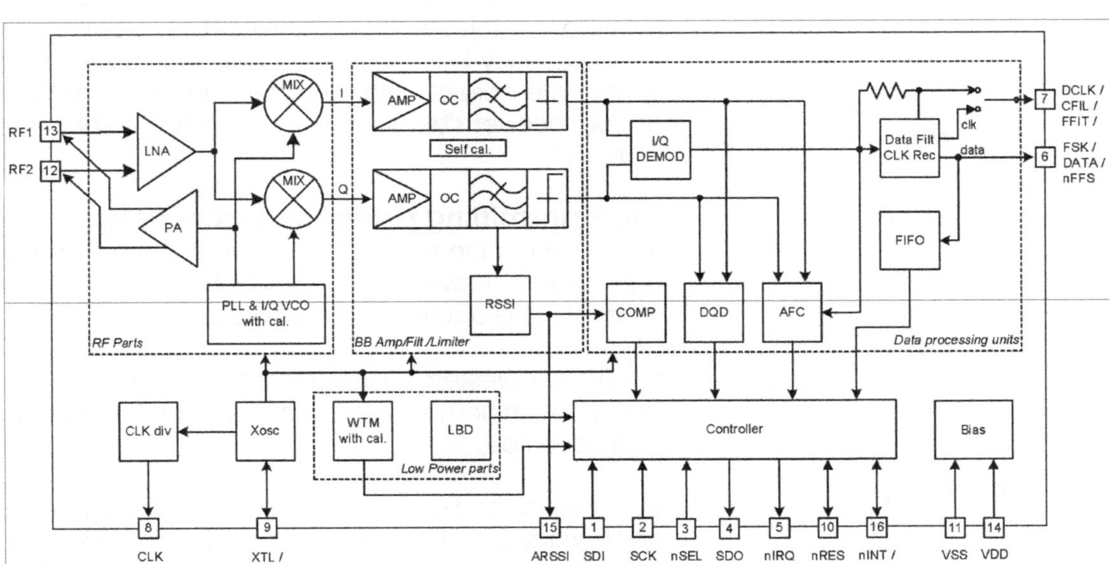

Figure 1: Block diagram of the RFM12B

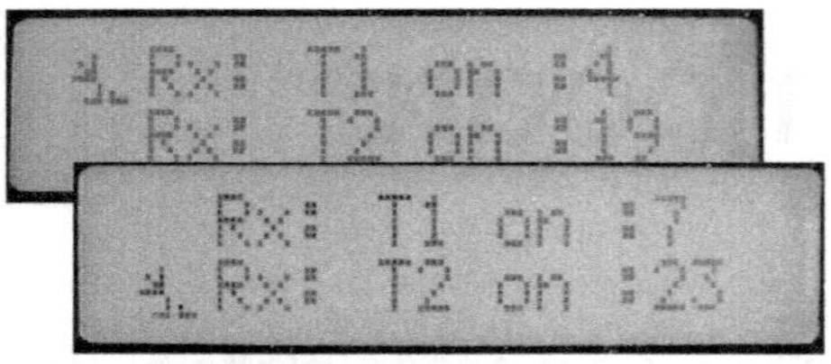

Figure 2: Displaying data on LCD

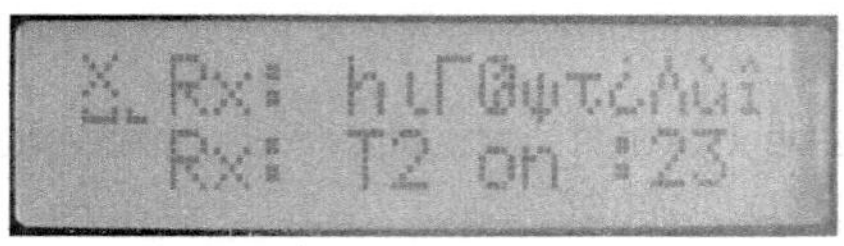

Figure 3: Data was not received correctly

The RFM12B has a built-in microcontroller which accepts external commands, enabling it to perform reliable communication. On its own, the module will not transmit or receive: it needs parameters loaded into it. With the help of our Bascom program, it will become a fully-operational communications device.

Description of the RFM12B Expansion board (EB)

The RFM12B EB features transmission and reception of message blocks. The communication reliability depends mostly upon the antenna used, the distance separating the transmitter and receiver and the presence of interference (a strong, nearby transmitting station on a close frequency) or the terrain (tall buildings, trees etc.).

The RFM12B EB module has a built-in PCB antenna. This may not be the most effective antenna, but it should serve our purposes. The RFM12B EB is connected to either a MiniPin II or MegaPin board via two IDC connectors wired up to two free ports on the development board. We have chosen PortB and PortD. PortB was chosen as it contains the AVR's SPI port while PortD contains the INT0 and INT1 interrupt inputs.

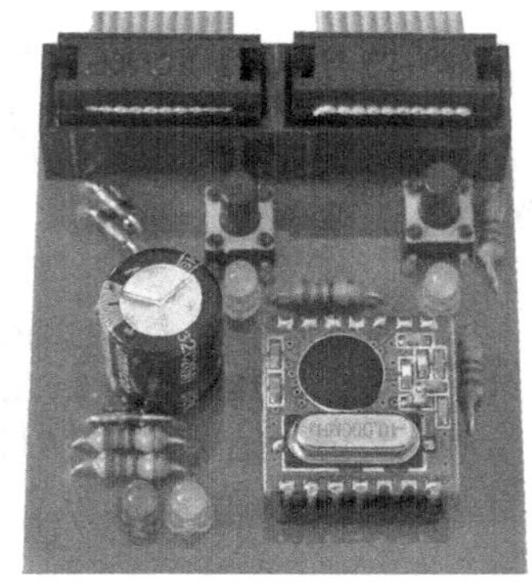

There are two built-in LEDs to indicate the receive/transmit signals, and an additional two LEDs to serve as status indicators (i.e. if the received data is correct, then turn on an LED).

The RFM12B EB has also two built-in switches, which can be used to trigger a data transmission.

We can only use one RFM12B EB with a MiniPin II / MegaPin board, at a time. If we want to test communication between two MiniPin II / MegaPin dev. boards then we would load different programs into each of the boards. We have written two programs: one for receiving and one for transmitting.

It is convenient to do this at our Bascom seminars, where two participants establish a communications link between each other's dev. boards. A sample of the resulting LCD displays can be seen in Figure 2. The transmitter program contains a counter (0 to 255). If we press a switch on the transmitter module (triggering a transmission) and the received data is correct, then this data is displayed, along with the description of the pressed switch (T1 or T2). Also, a special character is displayed at the far left of the LCD, which indicates that reception was OK. However, if the data was not received correctly, then that data is not processed by our program, however it is still displayed as shown in Figure 3.

You can see in Figure 3 that a symbol resembling an "x" is displayed, which indicates that the reception contained errors. This is not such a coincidence, as the 433 MHz frequency band is rather crowded. Our task is to receive the correct data, analyze it and perform tasks on the receiver side, such as turn an LED on/off, or a relay etc.

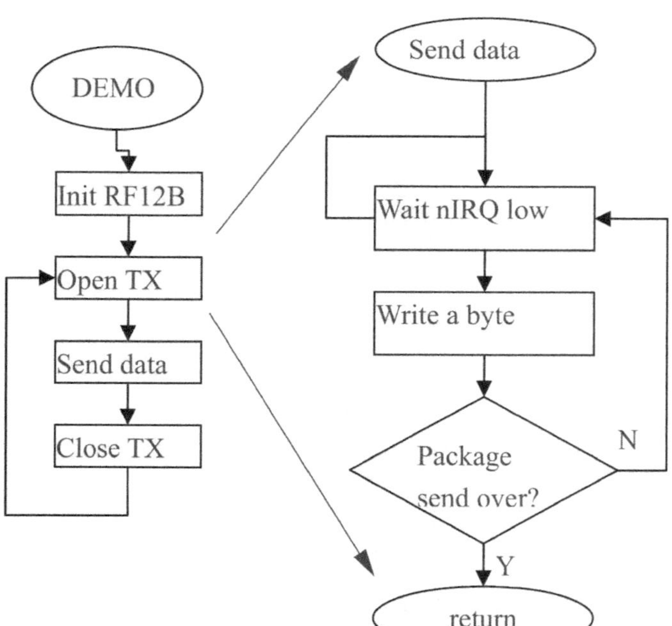

Figure 4: Transmit flowchart

The Transmitting program description

A flowchart of the transmitting program is shown in the Figure 4 (not shown is a routine which checks to see if either of the two switches was pressed).

If a switch is pressed, a message is transmitted, containing the switch name (T1 of T2) as well as the value of the 0-255 counter.

We have added a simple function to this program, which waits until the T1 switch is depressed and then sends the data only once. When pressing the T2 switch, we will send data repeatedly for as long as this switch is pressed.

Now let's look at the software.

The RFM12B module is configured once, at the start of the program. A description of all the commands can be found in the RFM12B datasheet. In the **configuration** section of the datasheet, a list of the various settings is given (channel No., Baud rate etc.). The same initialization settings must also be included in the receiver program as well.

After configuration, the program will flash both the Tx and Rx LEDs as a status indication.

Following initialization, the main program loops continuously: checking both the state of the switches as well as the packet "transmission complete" flag. Based upon those checks, it calls the appropriate routines.

A Short description of the subroutines

Subroutine for switch 1 (sends only one data packet when switch is pressed):

- transmits "T1 on....." and displays the same message on the LCD,
- checks the state of switch T1,
- wait until T1 switch is released,
- return to main loop.

Subroutine for switch 2 (sends data continuously while T2 switch is pressed):

- sends "T2 on ....." and displays the same message on the LCD,
- check the state of switch 2,
- if switch T2 is still pressed then go back to the start of this subroutine,
- else return to main loop.

The Receiving program description

The receiving program follows the flowchart shown in Figure 5. (Not shown is the routine which displays data on the LCD.)

The received data is analyzed and if it matches one of the acceptable patterns, a suitable subroutine is executed.

The receiving module configuration is similar to that of the transmitting module. It's done once at power-up. After configuration, the Rx and Tx LEDs are flashed, as a status indication. In the main loop, the *Test* flag is checked, to see whether an acceptable data pattern was received. If not, then the program returns to a start of the main loop. If the flag is set, then we analyze the received data in a suitable subroutine.

A Short description of the other subroutines

An Interrupt subroutine is executed every time a byte is received. This byte is added to a string. When the byte equals a CR (ASCII value = 13), then this indicates the end of the string, and we set the *Test* flag. Then the subroutine returns to the main program loop.

The String analyze subroutine compares the incoming string, and takes action according to the value of the string. It also displays the data on the LCD.

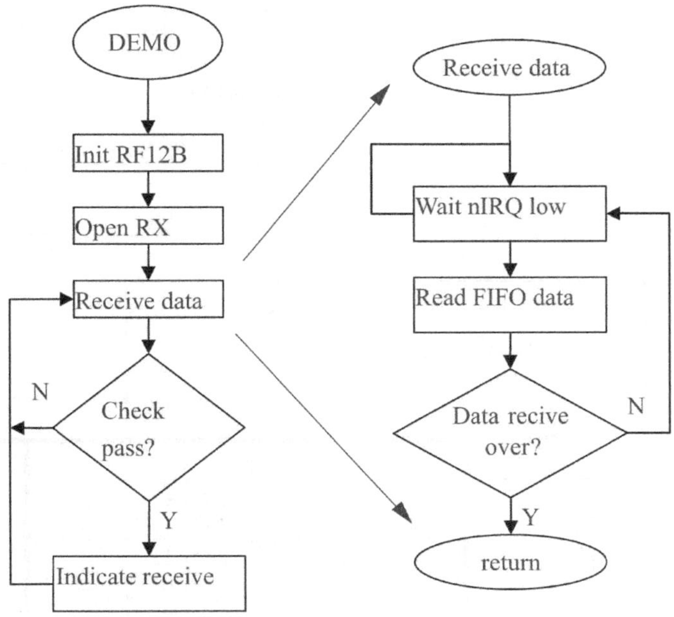

Figure 5: The Receiving program flowchart

The RFM12B EB schematic diagram

The schematic diagram, shown in Figure 6, is simple. The board contains two IDC male connectors that mate with the MiniPin II/Megapin board using flat cables. It gets its power from the host development board. You'll notice three diodes (U4, U5 & U6) in the circuit, which are needed to lower the power supply from 5V to the 3.2 Volts needed by the RFM12B module.

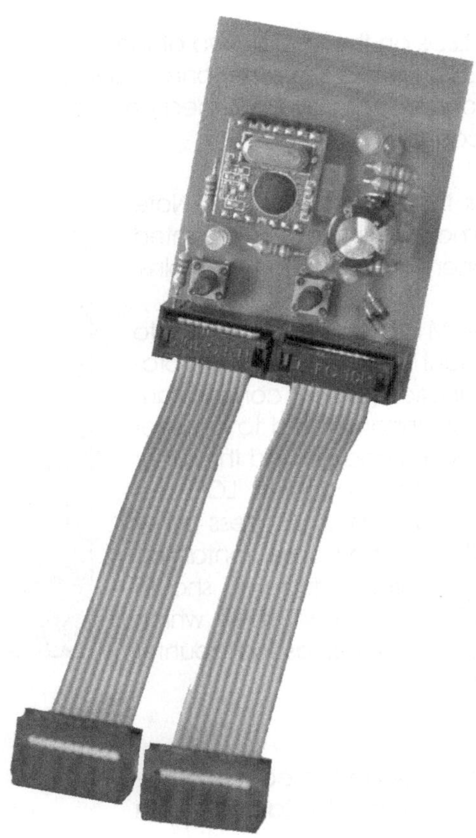

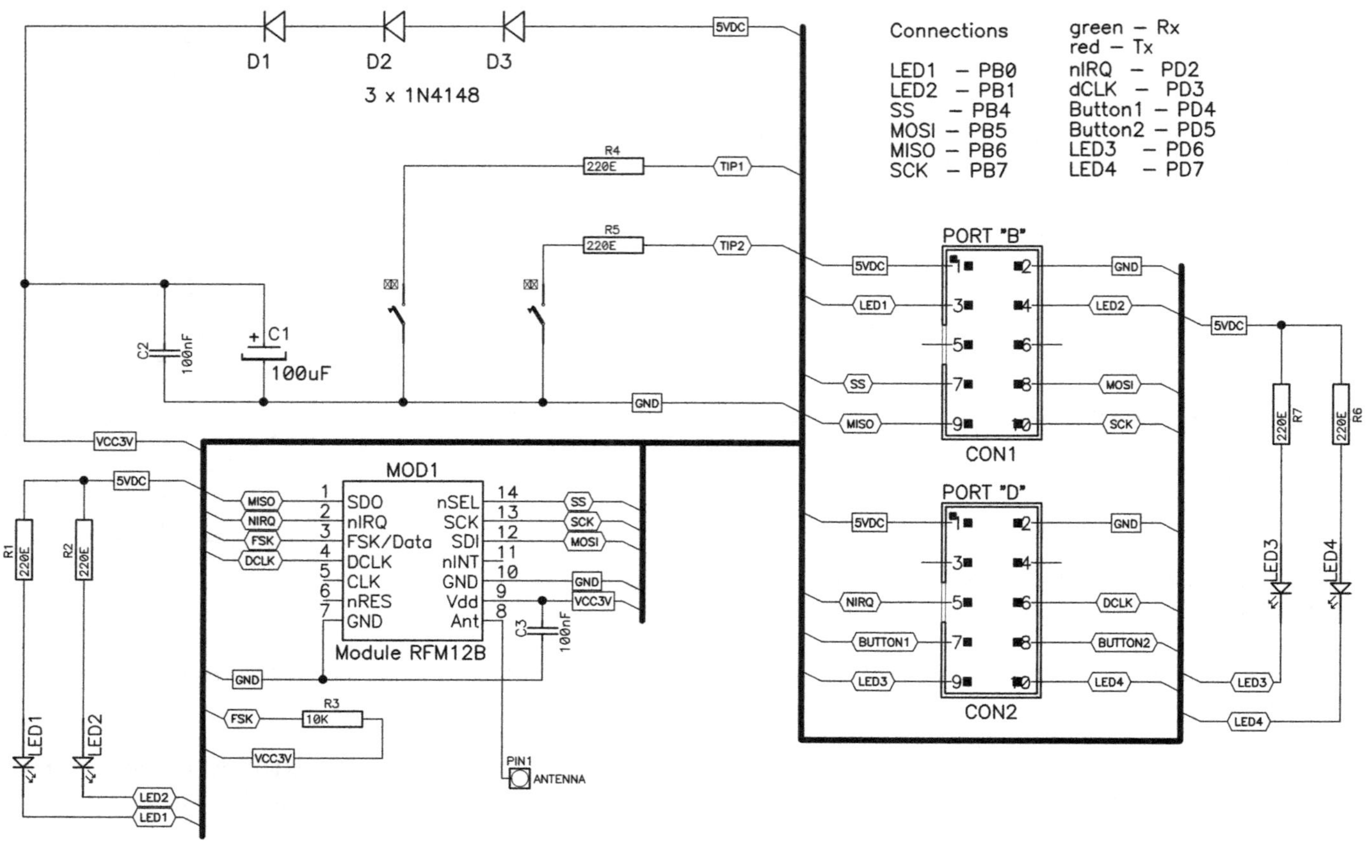

Figure 6: The RFM12B expansion board schematic diagram

The antenna is a PCB trace. You will notice the terminal labelled **Pin1,** on the PCB. Here you can optionally solder a wire antenna to improve communication. If you do so, then cut off the remaining PCB antenna trace, with a sharp knife.

There are four LEDs on the board. Two of them are Rx/Tx LEDs (LED1 & LED2), while the other ones (LED3 & LED4) are status indicators that can be turned on and off under program control, if desired.

Figure 7 shows the single-sided PCB. Note that the RFM module should be mounted on the component side using the short pins.

Connect the RFM12B expansion board to your development board, upload the program for one function (i.e. Rx), connect another RFM12B extension board to another development board and upload the other program (i.e. Tx). Then connect LCD displays to PortC, and off you go. Press either the T1 or T2 switch on the board containing the transmitter program, and you should see that the LCD display will show which switch was pressed as well as the counter value (0 to 255).

Conclusion

The RFM12B may not be the easiest module for a Bascom newbie to start with. With the help of our programs, you can start interfacing them and experimenting with different settings for the channel number and other such parameters. If you are ambitious enough, you could combine these two programs into one making the RFM12B perform as a transceiver.

1. http://en.wikipedia.org/wiki/Duplex_%28telecommunications%29#Half-duplex
2. http://www.hoperf.com/rf_fsk/cob/RFM12B.htm

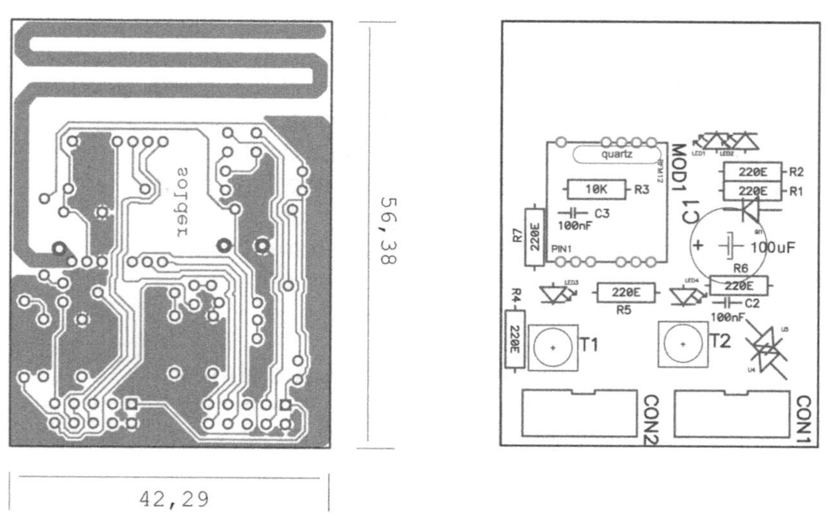

Figure 7: The RFM12B expansion board PCB (dimensions in mm)

	Control Command	Related Parameters/Functions	Related control bits
1	Configuration Setting Command	Frequency band, crystal oscillator load capacitance, baseband filter bandwidth, etc.	el, ef, b1 to b0, x3 to x0
2	Power Management Command	Receiver/Transmitter mode change, synthesizer, xtal osc, PA, wake-up timer, clock output can be enabled here	er, ebb, et, es, ex, eb, ew, dc
3	Frequency Setting Command	Data frequency of the local oscillator/carrier signal	f11 to f0
4	Data Rate Command	Bit rate	cs, r6 to r0
5	Receiver Control Command	Function of pin 16, Valid Data Indicator, baseband bw, LNA gain, digital RSSI threshold	p16, d1 to d0, i2 to i0, g1 to g0, r2 to r0
6	Data Filter Command	Data filter type, clock recovery parameters	al, ml, s1 to s0, f2 to f0
7	FIFO and Reset Mode Command	Data FIFO IT level, FIFO start control, FIFO enable and FIFO fill enable	f3 to f0, s1 to s0, ff, fe
8	Receiver FIFO Read Command	RX FIFO can be read with this command	
9	Synchron Pattern Command	Synchron pattern	b7 to b0
10	AFC Command	AFC parameters	a1 to a0, rl1 to rl0, st, fi, oe, en
11	TX Configuration Control Command	Modulation parameters, output power, ea	mp, m3 to m0, p2 to p0
12	PLL Setting Command	CLK out buffer speed, low power mode of the crystal oscillator, dithering, PLL loop delay, bandwidth	ob1 to ob0, lpx, ddit, ddy, bw1 to bw0
13	Transmitter Register Write Command	TX data register can be written with this command	t7 to t0
14	Wake-Up Timer Command	Wake-up time period	r4 to r0, m7 to m0
15	Low Duty-Cycle Command	Enable low duty-cycle mode. Set duty-cycle.	d6 to d0, en
16	Low Battery Detector and Microcontroller Clock Divider Command	LBD voltage and microcontroller clock division ratio	d2 to d0, v4 to v0
17	Status Read Command	Status bits can be read out	

Figure 8: RFM12B control commands

Example program ID	
Name:	TX_RFM12B_Minipin.bas
Microcontroller:	ATmega AVRs
Testing circuit:	/
MiniPin compatibility:	Yes
MegaPin compatibility:	Yes
Program sends data on the Channel 8 when push button is pressed	

Example program ID	
Name:	RX_RFM12B_Minipin.bas
Microcontroller:	ATmega AVRs
Testing circuit:	/
MiniPin compatibility:	Yes
MegaPin compatibility:	Yes
Program waits on the Channel 8 to receive data	

Shepherd's fire

By Bojan Kovač

Pulse-width modulation is really useful. One of my ideas was to make a real electronic flame that was modulated with PWM. Many of you probably help decorating a Christmas tree or making a nativity scene, containing a shepherd's fire near the shed at Bethlehem.

As a child, I wondered how to make a shepherd's fire near the Holy shed. At that time, I did it with a small lamp covered with red paper, surrounded with some small, slightly burnt wooden branches. The lamp was battery-powered which, unfortunately, did not last very long. Also, I was not pleased with a "fire" that glowed constantly. A few years later, as my electronics knowledge grew, I designed a blinking fire – more like a car's turn indicator...

Now I know enough to make an electronic flame that flutters like a real one. The prototype is shown in Figure 2, and is powered by a 5V mobile phone adapter. Because of this, I didn't bother to include a 5V regulator on the board, but there is a place for one if you need it.

Figure 1

Properties of Flames

If one watches a real fire for an extended time, you'll notice that it's unpredictable in terms of the fluttering, intensity and colour of the flame. To address this, I have designed an electronic solution that is programmed into a small ATtiny45 microcontroller using Bascom-AVR. The ATtiny45 microcontroller contains plenty of PWM outputs. If we change the PWM parameters then we can simulate a really unpredictable fire. The PWM parameters that I change are the PWM frequency, duty cycle and direction –either rising or falling. On each of five output pins, I change all of these parameters independently, which really mimics the effect of an unpredictable flame. In this circuit, I have used eight LEDs connected as shown in the schematic diagram (Figure 3). On the PCB, the LEDs are placed in a circle, as a flame is normally circular in shape as well. In the center there are four yellow LEDs that represent the main flame and should be brighter. Around the perimeter are mixed yellow and red LEDs as desired.

Software

A project normally starts with the microcontroller selection, in terms of the number of pins and available functions etc. For this project I have chosen the ATtiny45: an 8-pin AVR with five (or six) I/O ports which is supported by the MegaPin & MiniPin II development boards. Because ATtiny45 is small and comes in a PDIP package, it's ideal for those who do not like SMD parts. It's also attractive to electronic newbies because it shares the same case as the popular NE555, yet offers much more!

When designing shepherd's fire, I had a few surprises. The first was that one I/O pin is connected to the microcontroller's Reset pin, which means that if I use this pin as an I/O pin then I can no longer program it using an SPI programmer. Great!

So, I settled on using only five I/O pins. Then I started testing Timer0 and Timer1 individually. Timer0 performed

Figure 2

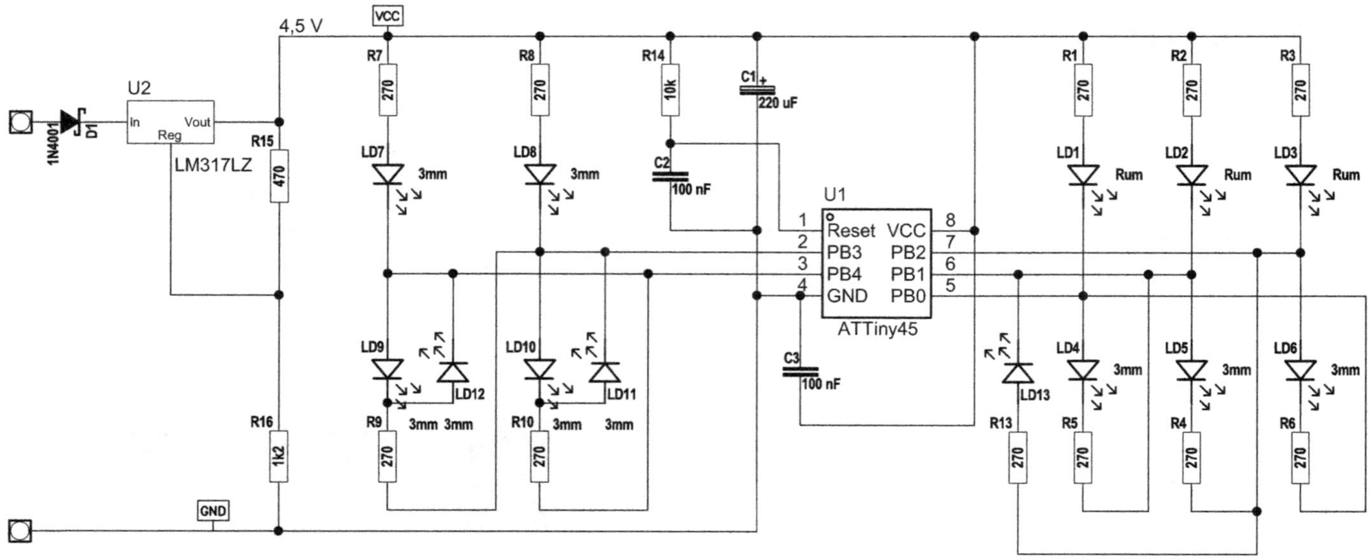

Figure 3: Schematic diagram for shepherd's fire

normally, but Timer1 did not. The reason for this is that Timer1 is an 8-bit Timer and not the usual 16-bit Timer normally found in AVRs. Therefore, Bascom-AVR refused to compile my code. After a thorough reading of the datasheet, I discovered the proper settings for Timer1. In the TCCR1 register you must set a clock prescale factor, after which Timer1 will perform as it should.

```
'Tccr1 = &H00      'Prescale = 0, Timer stops
'Tccr1 = &H01      'Prescale = 1
'Tccr1 = &H02      'Prescale = 2
'Tccr1 = &H03      'Prescale = 4
'Tccr1 = &H04      'Prescale = 8
'Tccr1 = &H05      'Prescale = 16
Tccr1 = &H06       'Prescale = 32
'Tccr1 = &H07      'Prescale = 64
'Tccr1 = &H08      'Prescale = 128
```

Also, I must define an interrupt service routine and enable interrupts:

```
On Timer1 Interrupt_timer1
Enable Ovf1
Enable Interrupts
```

The next unpleasant surprise occurred when I realized there are not five PWM outputs, but only two, along with their negated outputs.

Given these limitations, I changed my plans and decided to incorporate a pure software-based PWM for all five outputs. For the main PWM function, I chose Timer0. The PWM variables are declared at the start of the program. Of course not all PWMs are same – which is one source of the random flashing.

```
Dim Pwm_chip_foot2 As Byte
Dim Pwm_chip_foot3 As Byte
Dim Pwm_chip_foot5 As Byte
Dim Pwm_chip_foot6 As Byte
Dim Pwm_chip_foot7 As Byte

'starting values for PWM variables
Pwm_chip_foot2 = 40
Pwm_chip_foot3 = 10
Pwm_chip_foot5 = 80
Pwm_chip_foot6 = 92
Pwm_chip_foot7 = 24
```

At each Timer0 interrupt, I increment all five variables by one. When any of them reach a value of 100 we reset it to 1, which means that it starts counting over again. At the same time, I set the appropriate output pin Low, which turns that LED on. With values from 1 to 100, I get a duty-cycle in the range of 1 to 100%.

```
Interrupt_t0:
Incr Pwm_chip_foot2
Incr Pwm_chip_foot3
Incr Pwm_chip_foot5
Incr Pwm_chip_foot6
Incr Pwm_chip_foot7

If Pwm_chip_foot2 > 100 Then
   Pwm_chip_foot2 = 1
   Noga2 = 0
End If
If Pwm_chip_foot3 > 100 Then
   Pwm_chip_foot3 = 1
   Noga3 = 0
End If
'......... And so on for all 5 output pins
Return
```

But there is more. We have to turn on the next source of randomness, by introducing Timer1. At each Timer1 interrupt, a subroutine for each PWM output pin is run, in which we read a value from a 256 element lookup table. If the value is 255, we change the prescale factor for Timer1, ranging in value between 1 and 8.

```
'** Timer 1 interrupt routine **********
Interrupt_timer1:
Addon = Lookup(pointer_addon , Plus_val)
Incr  Pointer_addon
     If Pointer_addon = 255 Then
         Incr Incr Prescaler_timer1
            If Incr Prescaler_timer1>8 Then
               Incr Prescaler_timer1= 1
            End If
     End If
```

Last variable gets last value that is present on Pin No. 2,

```
Tempora = Switch_val2
'** If flag for addition is set …
If Add_val2  = 1 Then
```

then I check the sum to see whether to add it to a value from the Lookup table:

```
Summ = Switch_val2 + Addon
If Summ > 75 Then
      Incr Switch_val2
       If Switch_val2 > 98 Then
         Add_val2 = 0
       End If
End If
If Summ = 75 Then
      Incr Switch_val2
End If
If Summ < 75 Then
    If Tempora < 35 Then
             Incr Switch_val2
    End If
    If Tempora > 35 Then
             Switch_val2 = Summ
    End If
     If Tempora = 35 Then
             Incr Switch_val2
    End If
  End If
End If
```

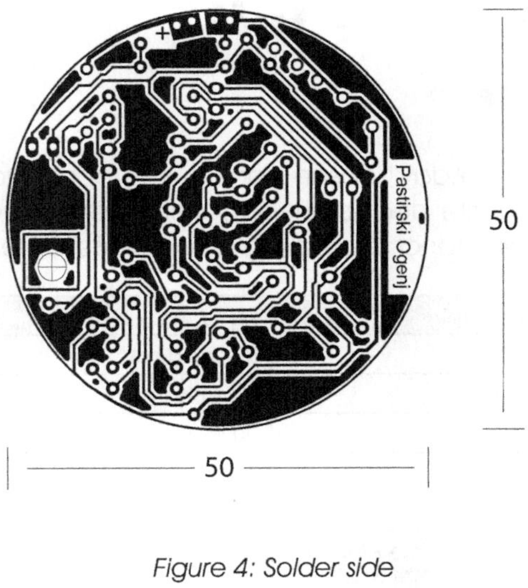

Figure 4: Solder side

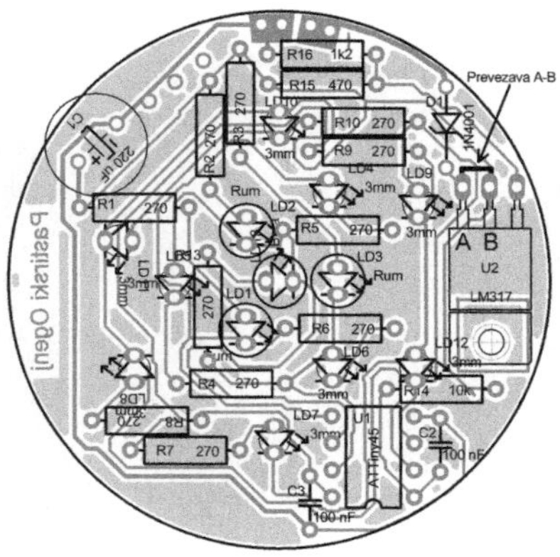

Figure 5: Assembly of PCB

In the above section of the program, I decide what value to add to the temporary sum. If the result is between 35 and 75 then I make the addition. If the sum is between 75 and 99, then I add only 1 and not the value read from the Lookup table. Doing this, I insure the smooth passing from minimum to maximum values and exclude the flashing which would occur when crossing from 0 to 255. Around both extreme values (0 and 255) I slow down the increase or decrease of the duty-cycle. If the value is larger than 99, then I change direction by resetting the *Add_val* flag – which is different for each of the five PWMs. If the direction is changed and the result of the temporary sum is from 75 to 35, then read value is deducted from the actual switching value. If the value is between 35 and then I subtract a 1. When values near zero are approached, I change direction again by setting the *Add_val* flag.

```
If Add_val2  = 0 Then
Summ = Switch_val2 - Addon

  If Summ  > 30 Then
     Switch_val2 = Summ
  End If
  If Summ  = 30 Then
     Decr Switch_val2
  End If
  If Summ  < 30 Then
     Decr Switch_val2
     If Switch_val2  < 2 Then : _
        Switch_val2 = 1 : End If
  End If
End If
'......... we do that for all 5 outputs
Return
```

These are the routines that are performed when Timer0 and Timer1 interrupts occur. In the main loop, we will check if the value of *Pwm_chip_footx* (which is being incremented by 1 at each Timer0 interrupt) is smaller or larger than the switching value. If it's larger, then we leave the

Figure 6: Assembled top

appropriate output at its present state: if it's not then we toggle its logical level. This gives us five PWM outputs all with varying duty-cycles between 0 and 100%.

```
Do
  If Pwm_chip_foot2  > Switch_val2  Then
    Chip_foot2  = 0
  End If
If Pwm_chip_foot2  < Switch_val2  Then
    Chip_foot2  = 1
End If
'**************
'and so on  for all 5 outputs
Loop
```

In the time it takes for one Timer1 interrupt, there are between ten and a few hundred Timer0 interrupts, depending upon which prescale factor is in force. The actual duty cycle values are being refreshed quickly and are occurring in the main loop at all times. With this program, running at 8 MHz (from the internal RC oscillator) I have achieved a PWM frequency of a little above 46 Hz, with duty-cycles varying with a step size of 1%. That is sufficient for my goal of driving the LEDs. Connecting additional LEDs in different combinations brought about a third source of randomness, which depends upon the actual voltage relationship between any two outputs. This changes due to direction (turning on/off), rise and speed (defined by the timer prescale factor).

The Circuit

The electronic circuit is not complicated, provided that you know how to solder correctly. This circuit can be built in less than one hour. It operates from 3.0 to 5.2 Volts. The board is circular in shape like a real fire. The LEDs are placed in two concentric circles. Series resistors are used to set the LED current, for a power supply of 5V. However if the circuit is powered from another voltage, you will have to re-calculate their value. Keep in mind that the circuit uses no voltage regulator, so do not power it with voltages higher than 5 Volts. As mentioned previously, I used an old mobile phone charger to power my circuit. You should check to see if the voltage from your phone charger is higher than 5 Volts: if so use an LM317 or other 5V regulator IC. If you use a phone charger directly, then place a small jumper wire between points A & B (see assembly plan) on the PCB. The LM317 circuit has two resistors that define the output voltage. In this case it will be 4.6 Volts. Diode D1 protects the circuit from connecting up a battery or other power source backwards, by mistake. The ATtiny45 microcontroller should be programmed using the MiniPin II or MegaPin development board, or a parallel programmer, prior to placing it in-circuit. R14 and C2 act as a simple reset circuit for the AVR at power-up. The PCB itself is shown in Figure 4.

Conclusion

The LEDs themselves are only a light source. To mix the colours and diffuse them evenly, you have to spread wax on top of the cover. After that, we get very realistic glowing fire. With the prototype, I took plastic egg holders that were cut and glued to a yogurt plastic cup – as shown in Figure 6. Everything was dipped in molten wax which was scraped a bit while still warm and then waxed again (Figure 7).

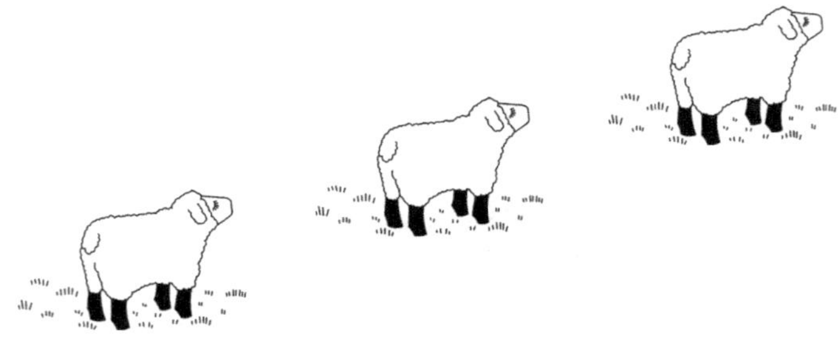

When the holiday season comes, you can place your shepherd's fire near a shed, cover it with some small stones and branches, making a very realistic fire.

Example program ID	
Name:	Sheppard.bas
Microcontroller:	AT TINY45
Testing circuit:	Figure 3
MiniPin compatibility:	yes
MegaPin compatibility:	yes
Program that emulates real fire with multiple LEDs using 3 ch. PWM on ATtiny45	

Figure 7: Assembled and waxed

Metal detector

By Tomislav Berend

Did you ever want to discover a hidden treasure? One of the first devices that I built as a child was a simple metal detector. Later, I built various different metal detectors from plans published in electronics magazines. Today, the prices for metal detectors vary from a few hundred to a thousand Euro, and therefore I have decided to design one of my own – an improved version of the "pulse induction" metal detector.

Introduction

With technology advancing every day, metal detectors have also improved. All of them are now based on microcontrollers that also handle the analogue circuitry. In this chapter, I will describe a "pulse induction" metal detector that is very sensitive and easy to assemble. However, it does have a drawback: it does not distinguish different metals. Let's look at the history of metal detectors.

History

Long ago, people wanted an instrument that would help them discover precious treasures. The first notes can be found in 1830, with experiments by geologist R.W. Fox. The first detectors detected only the conductivity of the soil and the minerals within.

In the 1879, Prof. D.E. Huges introduced the first "induction balance – IB" metal detector. This detector was used in a London hospital to find metal parts within injured people. This principle is still used by many modern metal detectors.

In the 1881, Alexander Graham Bell used a metal detector to find a bullet that hit President James Garfield. The first portable metal detectors appeared in 1925, invented by Gerhard Fischer, who later founded the A&S Company, which manufactured metal detectors commercially.

The principles of metal detectors have not changed much. Only the data interface has changed, which has improved the sensitivity and accuracy of metal detec-

Figure 1: First attempts to use a metal detector

Figure 2: One of the first commercial metal detectors

tors. The principle used is based upon the fact that a coil's inductance changes in the presence of a metal object.

Metal detector Methods

There are a few methods used in metal detectors which I will describe.

Induction Balance (IB)

Figure 3 shows the block diagram of an IB metal detector. This is one of the oldest methods that is still in use today. The detector operates at very low frequencies between15 and 25 kHz. An oscillator produces an electromagnetic field in the search coil. This magnetic field travels through the air to the receiver coil. This signal is amplified, and then rectified by a peak detector. The resulting DC signal is amplified again by a DC amplifier. That DC signal is then chopped at an audio rate, changing it into an audible tone, with a volume proportional to the level of the DC signal itself. After the chopper, an audio amplifier is used to amplify the signal so it can feed a loudspeaker or a headphone.

When a metal object comes near the search coil, it will disrupt the inductive balance between the search coil and the receiver coil, causing a higher voltage to be induced in the receiving coil. The greater the DC output voltage fed to the chopper, the stronger the audio signal will be. Note that the frequency of the audio doesn't change-just the amplitude changes in response to the proximity of metal to the coils. The advantage of this method lies in its better sensitivity, while its drawback is that precise tuning is required during manufacture. Also, the construction and alignment of the search/receiver coils is somewhat critical. It should be noted that this detection method is affected quite markedly by soil conductance (such as the presence of salt-water in the soil).

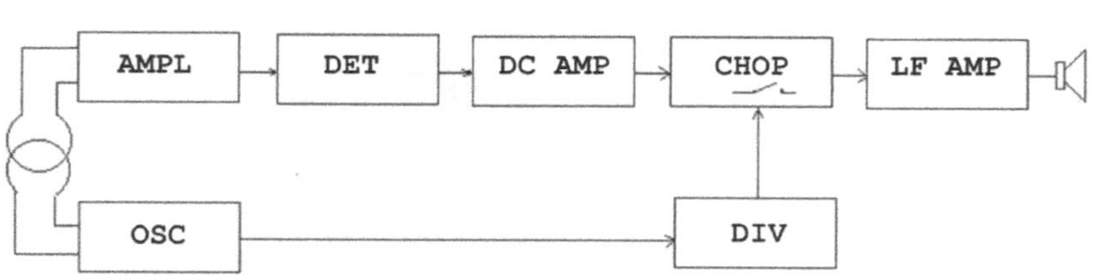

Figure 3: Block diagram of an IB metal detector

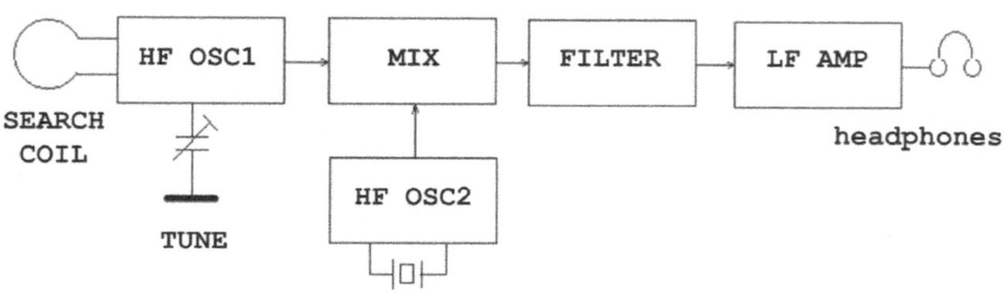

Figure 4: Block diagram of a BFO metal detector

Beat Frequency Oscillator (BFO)

Figure 4 shows the block diagram of a BFO metal detector. This is one of the oldest metal-detection methods. Its operation is quite simple. Oscillator No. 1 contains the search coil as part of its resonant circuit. Its frequency depends upon the search coil's inductance as well as the value of a variable capacitor, which is also a part of that resonant circuit.. Oscillator No. 1 is tuned to a frequency that is virtually the same as the frequency of oscillator No.2. Oscillator No. 2 uses a quartz crystal, which gives it a highly accurate, fixed frequency. When a metal object approaches the search coil, its inductance changes, therefore the oscillator frequency changes as well. Signals from both oscillators are fed to a mixer whose output consists of several frequencies: both input frequencies, their sum, and the difference between the two (as well as some higher harmonic frequencies). Only the difference frequency is within the human hearing range. We amplify that difference frequency, which can be heard as a high pitch tone, that will rise in pitch in proportion to the change in inductance of the search coil, brought about by the presence of a metal object.

Using the variable capacitor connected to oscillator No. 1, we can set a frequency difference which results in a tone within the audible range. If, for example, both oscillators are tuned to 200 kHz and the inductance changes by 0.01 %, then the output frequency changes by 20 Hz. To achieve higher difference frequencies, we need to use oscillators with higher frequencies. Doing this, however, raises an oscillator stability issue, so we have to strike a balance between stability and higher frequency to achieve the best performance.

The advantage of this type of metal detector is simple construction of both the device and the search coil, but a drawback is the high influence of soil conditions to the detector's performance.

Transmit/Receive (T/R)

Figure 5 shows a block diagram of T/R type metal detector. T/R metal detectors are very similar to IB metal detectors. An oscillator signal is sent to a search coil and also sent separately to a limiter (which turns it into a square wave of fixed amplitude). The signal from the receive coil is amplified and sent to another limiter. Both signals will now have the same amplitudes (because of the limiters), but are normally 180 deg. out of phase. These two signals are fed to a phase detector. Under normal conditions, the phase detector output is zero. If a metal object approaches the search coil, the signal's phase will change, giving a DC signal at the output of the phase detector. A drawback of this design involves the difficulty of tuning the coils, as well as the major effect of soil conductivity.

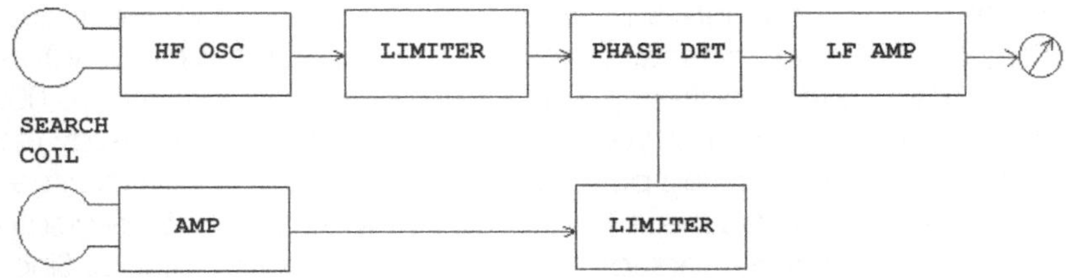

Figure 5: Block diagram of T/R type metal detector

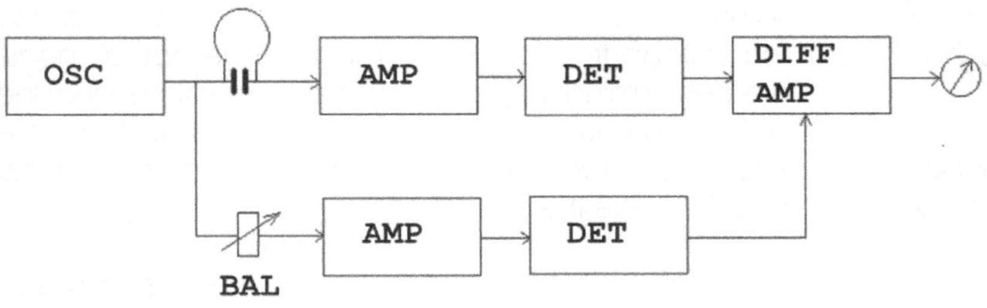

Figure 6: Block diagram of the OR metal detector

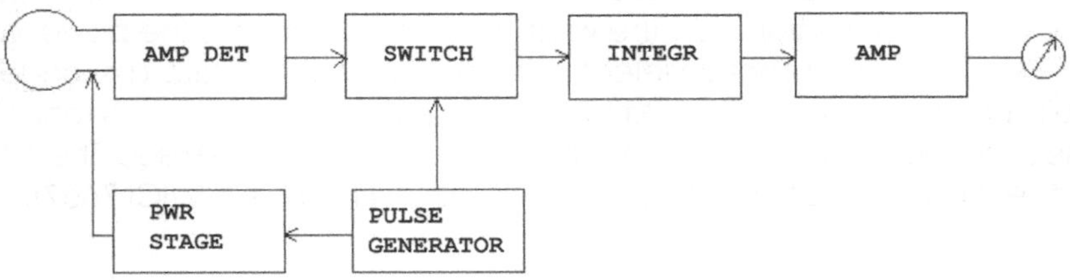

Figure 7: Block diagram of the PI metal detector

Off-resonance (OR)

Figure 6 shows the block diagram of the OR metal detector. With this metal detector, a signal from the oscillator is passed through a stop-band resonant circuit (a "trap") to an amplifier. From the other side of the resonant circuit, a signal is taken through a balance circuit to another amplifier. The stop-band resonant circuit is tuned to the oscillator frequency, which means that it attenuates that signal greatly. Signals from both amplifiers are passed on to detectors and from there to a differential amplifier. When the circuits are in a balanced state, the output signal will be zero. Any metal presence near the search coil will change its inductance, thus changing the oscillator's frequency. This new frequency will pass through the stop-band resonant circuit much more readily, causing a change in the DC signal at the output of the differential amplifier.

Pulse Induction (PI)

Figure 7 shows the block diagram of the PI metal detector PI metal detectors operate on a totally different principle, although they still depend upon the principle of the changing inductance of a search coil when metal is near it. You can see in Figure 7 that a pulse generator creates pulses. The pulses are amplified and connected to an electronic switch. When this pulse is connected to the coil, a magnetic field occurs around it. In Figure 8 you can see the waveform of this pulse.

When the current through the coil is interrupted, the magnetic field around the coil is also interrupted. Due to self-inductance, we will see a strong pulse of reverse-polarity coming from the coil. To prevent self-oscillation, we add a damper resistor to the circuit. When metal comes near the search coil, the reverse-polarity pulse (occurring when the drive current is interrupted), will take longer to decay than normal. This longer pulse, although relatively small, is still large enough to be detected. To boost it, we take many successive measurements, and feed the reverse-polarity decay signals to an integrator. The integrator's voltage output is amplified and fed to an indicator.

The advantage of this type of metal detector is the simple construction of the search coil and the fact that soil conditions do not affect the detector unless there are minerals present in the ground. The drawback of this method is that it does not distinguish amongst different types of metals. Also, the search coil head must not include any metal parts. Another drawback is the higher power consumption and a rather complicated design.

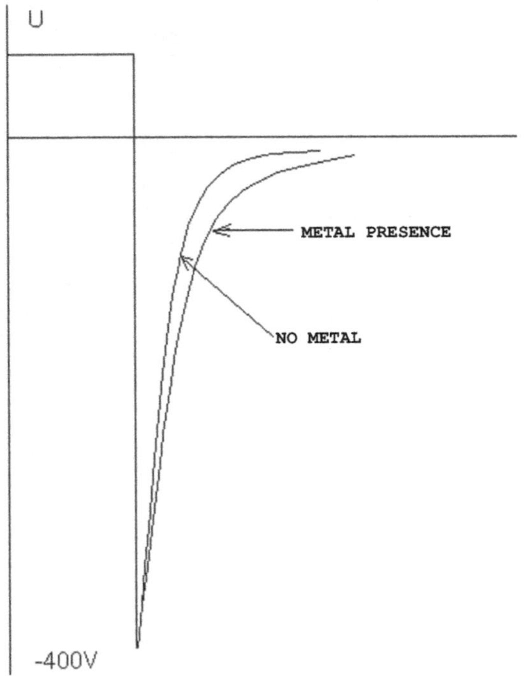

Figure 8: The pulse that is fed to the search coil

Microcontroller - based PI metal detector

If a microcontroller is used for a PI metal detector, it can handle many of the functions. A microcontroller can generate accurate pulses, measure time and time - dependant responses. In place of an integrator, we can use its fast A/D converter to acquire voltages with precise timing.

At the heart of this metal detector, I've chosen an ATmega8, which has all the functions needed. It can operate with a 16 MHz clock, has six A/D converter inputs, enough RAM & Flash memory and enough I/O pins to connect to the peripheral devices. A standard 2x16 LCD was used for the display.

The schematic diagram of a microcontroller-based PI metal detector is shown in Figure 9. The schematic can be divided into a few sections:

» the power supply unit,
» the microcontroller with both a display and configuration switches,
» pulse amplifier,
» search coil,
» detector and amplifier.

Circuit description

Voltage from the battery is fed to the circuit through choke L1 that suppresses interference caused by the search coil pulses. After the choke is a protective diode that shunts out negative spikes arising from self-induction in the search coil. This also protects the circuitry from wrong battery polarity. C2 is a large capacitor (10,000 µF), which is very important: it serves as an energy reservoir during pulse generation. The circuit just described provides the +12V power. A three-terminal 5V regulator provides regulated power for the microcontroller. Since the operational amplifier requires a negative power supply, I've used an ICL7660 charge-pump (U2) to provide -5V (on pin 5).

As mentioned, timing is very important when measuring the voltage from our searching coil. The actual measurement timing depends upon the coil itself and the width of the pulse fed to it. The wider the pulse, the more energy is stored in the coil, and the slower the voltage decay across the coil will be.

To adjust the timing parameters, there are switches to set width+, width-, delay+, delay-.

PortC.0 is configured as an output. The microcontroller generates a short pulse (100 to 450 µsec) on this pin. That pulse is used to create the magnetic field within the search coil. The width of this pulse defines the power of our metal detector. Wider pulses will create a stronger magnetic field thereby increasing the detector's range. The pulse width can be varied in steps of 50 µsec. The microcontroller pulse is fed to a PFET driver U5 (ICL7667).

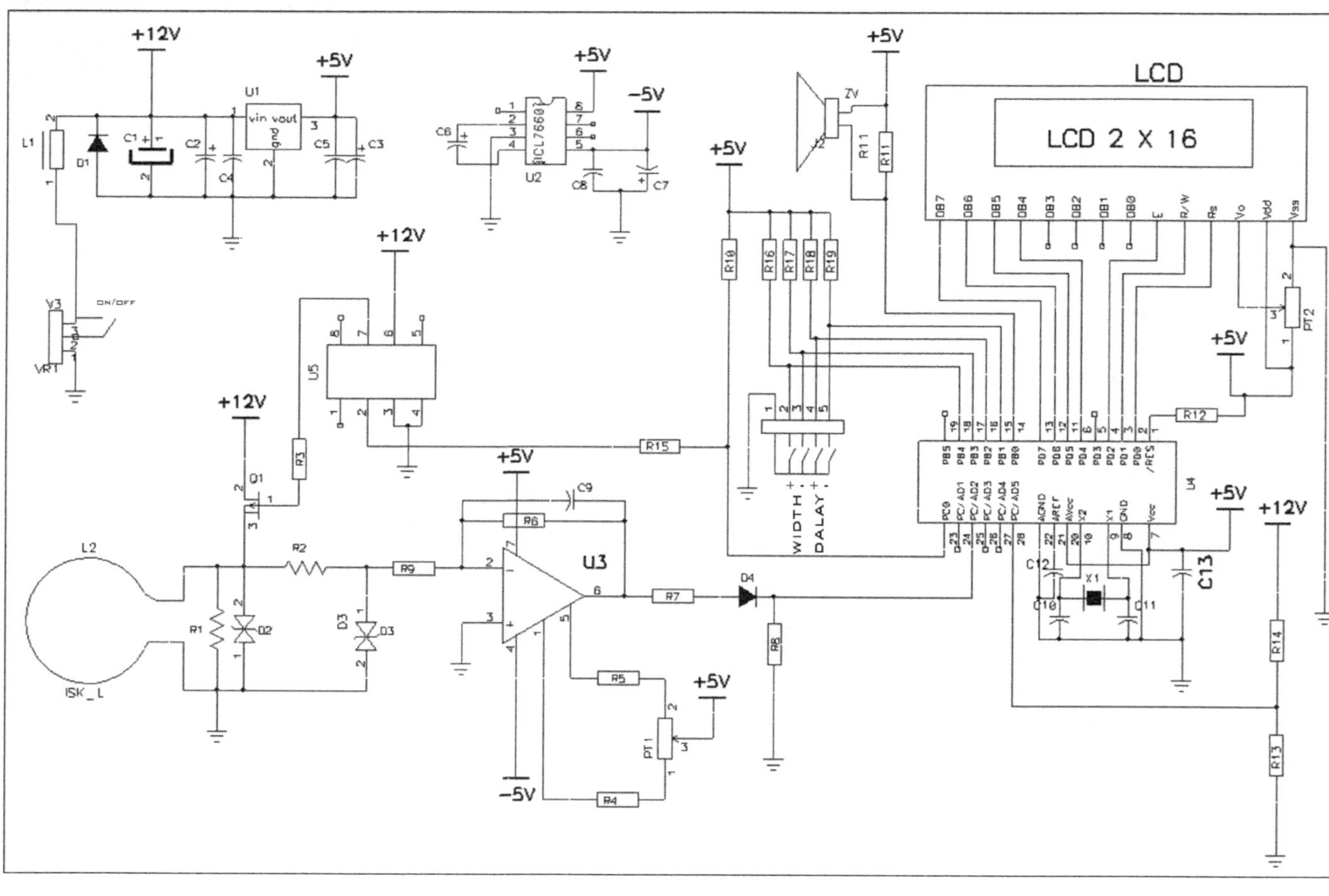

Figure 9: Schematic diagram of a microcontroller-based PI-metal detector

Maybe you will wonder why I have used a PFET here. If we have used NFET instead then our voltage of interest would swing around +/- 12 Volts. That would mean that we would have to adapt power supply for U3 to be +/- 12 Volts too. Maybe you'll wonder why I have used a PFET here. I used a PFET, because the coil decay waveform is best measured with respect to ground, by U3, and a PFET is best suited for this type of switching.

An IRF9630 PFET (Q1) acts as the power stage. It can withstand a maximum voltage of -200 Volts. The MPT2P50E is much better, with maximum voltage rating of -400 Volts, but it is hard to obtain. The PFET **must** be mounted on a heat sink – especially if the search coil is poorly-wound. The search coil is connected to the PFET's source pin, a bi-directional suppressor diode PKE6KE400CA is connected in parallel with the coil. This diode protects the PFET transistor from excessive negative voltage spikes generated by the coil. The pulse waveform is shown in Figure 10.

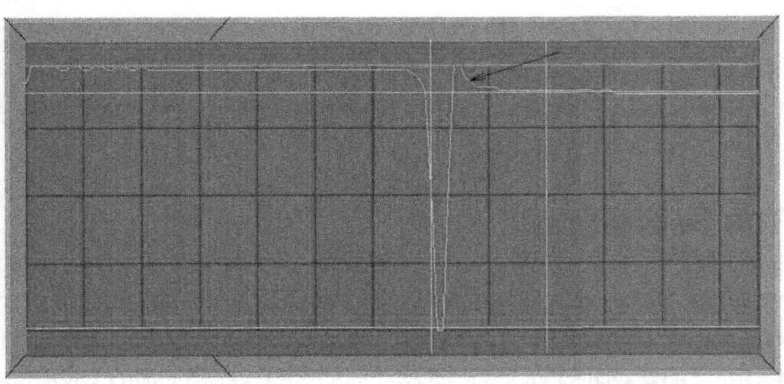

Figure 10: Waveform of the pulse across the search coil (50V/div, 50 µsec/div)

Also connected to the search coil are resistor R2 and diode D3 (a bi-directional suppressor diode PKE6KE-400CA) which limits the signal at the op-Amp negative input pin.

The preamplifier is an LF356 op-amp (the LF357 or LM318 are not quite as good, but still suitable). With PT1, the balance potentiometer connected between pins 1 and 5, we can shift the signal from the positive to the negative power rails. This sets the "zero point" of our detector. The op-amp's output waveform is shown in Figure 11 and Figure 12.

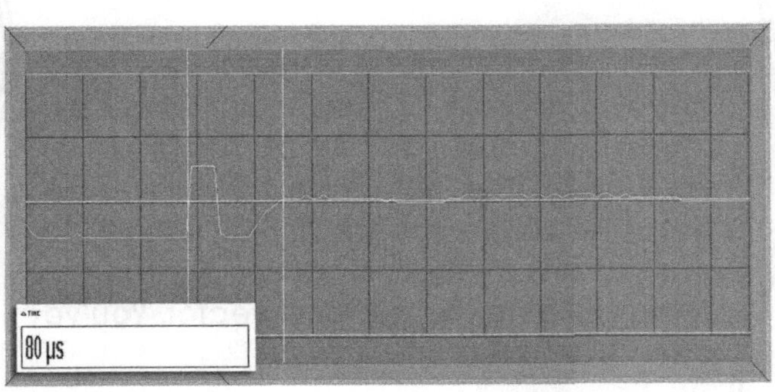

Figure 11: U3 op-amp output signal without metal parts nearby

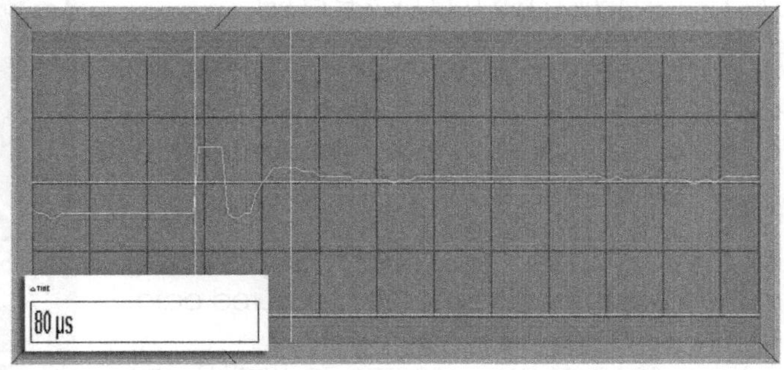

Figure 12: U3 op-amp output signal with metal coin nearby

Because the A/D converter can only handle positive voltages, a protective diode D4 is added in series with the input pin. I recommend that you use a Schottky diode here, for its lower voltage drop.

The signal is fed to the ADC2 pin. I've used 5 Volts as the A/D reference voltage.

The pulse voltage will be measured at a time delay set by the "Zak+" and "Zak-"switches. This delay must be optimized with respect to the coil used and the pulse power fed to the coil. The delay (from the end of the applied power pulse) can be set in 5 µsec steps from 40 to 85 µsec. The detector pulse power can be adjusted with switches "Sir+" and "Sir-" to the following settings: 100, 200, 300, 350, 400 and 450 µsec.

ADC5 monitors the power supply voltage through a voltage divider network. The software checks that voltage every 30 seconds. If the power supply drops lower than 9 Volts, the detector will notify the user that the voltage is too low and the detector will stop working.

The LCD display is connected to PortD in a somewhat unique way. In time-critical programs, Bascom's regular LCD commands are too slow - they take a lot of time just displaying simple information. To avoid that, I have used:

```
$lib "lcd4busy.lib"
Const _lcdport = Portd
Const _lcdddr = Ddrd
Const _lcdin = Pind
Const _lcd_e = 2
Const _lcd_rw = 1
Const _lcd_rs = 0
```

Using this configuration, the LCD display was much quicker (due to the fact that the **lcd4busy** library routines poll the display to see when it has finished a command, instead of just waiting a fixed, *conservative*, time for that command to complete).

The quicker display makes it possible to move the detector over the surface more quickly.

Note that the R/W pin is connected to PortD.1 and not to GND as is usually the case.

The LCD displays all necessary data. The first line shows the power supply voltage, followed by the pulse width and the measurement delay, both in μsec.

On the second line we have bar graph, and a numeric representation of the measured data.

A Piezo speaker is connected to PortB.0. This speaker is very handy, making it un-necessary to watch to display constantly. The speaker generates a frequency which varies according to the presence of metal. In normal operation, we just hear a "click" every second or so.

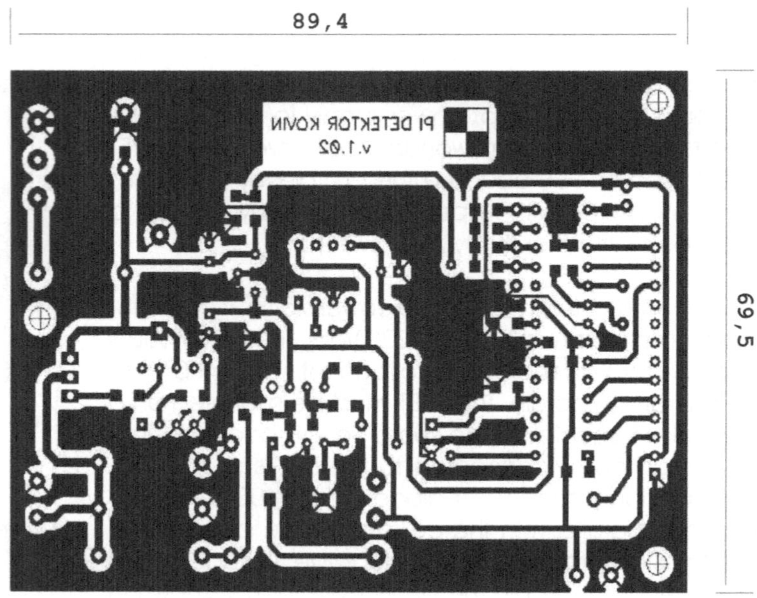

Figure 14: Metal detector PCB layout

The Software

At the start of the program, we configure the microcontroller's Ports. At reset, all AVR ports are in a high-impedance state, which could damage the PFET. Therefore, PortC.0 is immediately configured as an output and set to a low logic state. After this, the program configures the A/D converter, Timer0 (for creating sound) and the LCD display.

Near the beginning of the program the power supply voltage is checked and if it measures less than 9 Volts, the program jumps to a subroutine where a warning is displayed on LCD. Then the program simply loops, disabling the detector from any further operation.

If power supply voltage is OK then the program jumps to the main loop which is repeated 40 times. Within the main loop, a pulse is generated. After that pulse generation, we wait out a fixed (user –specified) time delay, after which time a measurement is performed. All 40 measured results are averaged. This value is displayed on the LCD in the form of "bar graph" as well as its numerical value, which is more precise. At the same time, we vary the tone going to the built-in speaker, according to the measured value. The program also polls the switches periodically, to see if either the "Power" or "Width" settings have been changed. Unless these settings have changed, we do not refresh the display, which saves precious time. The power supply voltage is checked every 30 seconds.

Figure 13: Metal detector LCD display

The Search coil

Making the search coil is not too difficult. The easiest way to make it is to draw a circle 20 cm in diameter on a piece of wood. Divide that circle into sixteen equal parts, and put a nail at each spot (covered with protective heat-shrink tubing). On that template, wind 30 turns of copper "magnet" wire (with a diameter of 0.6 mm).

After the coil is wound, bind it up with string. Then solder a coaxial cable (not longer than 2 meters) to the two coil leads. Connect the other end of the coaxial cable to the detector's input. Finally, the coil should be mounted to a suitable holder.

A smaller coil is better for searching for smaller metal parts, but it will have a shorter range. You can also ex-

ATTENTION

When using this metal detector, you may discover military objects, which may explode and hurt you, if you try to excavate them. The author and publisher do not take any responsibility or liability in case of any injury or damage done while using/building the metal detector. You've been warned!

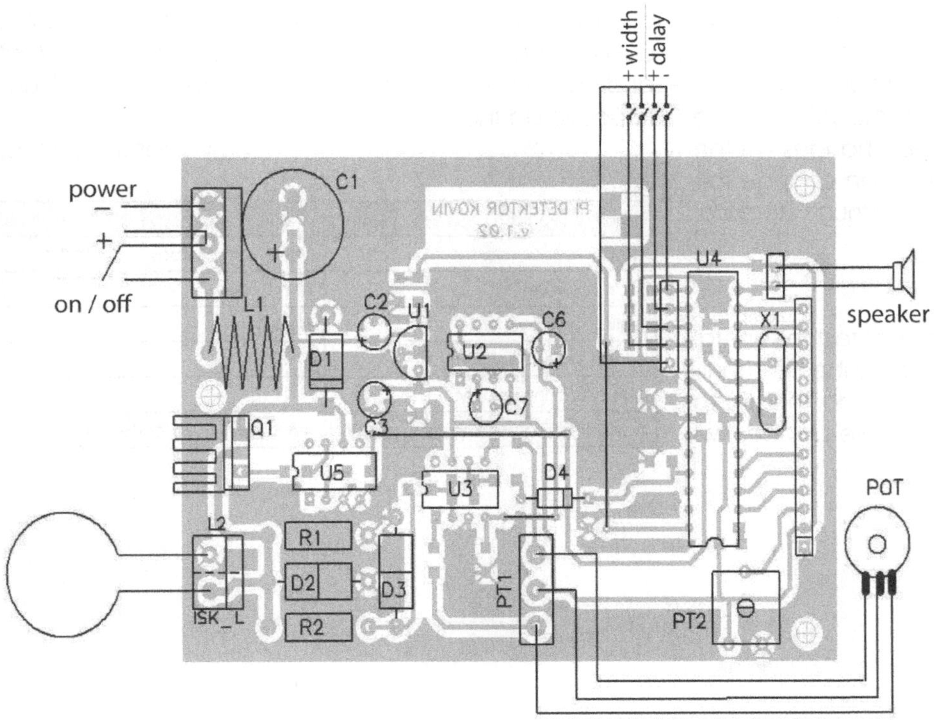

Figure 15: Component layout on the top side of PCB

periment with other coil shapes, but I didn't try this myself. I tested both 20 and 30 cm coils and found that a 20 Cent coin was detected at a distance of 20 cm. It's very important that the coil itself does not contain any metal parts. The coil's inductance should be approximately 400 μH - anything close to this value will be OK. If you decide to experiment with other coils, I suggest that you connect the metal detector to a "bench" supply and measure its current consumption. With this current measurement, you can see if your coil is within the desired range or not. Too few turns will increase both the current and the PFET heating. While experimenting, I suggest you perform your tests with a low pulse power.

Construction details

The Metal detector circuit is contained on a single-sided PCB with dimensions of 89.4 x 69.5 mm. To aid in construction, Figure 15 shows the components on the top of the board and Figure 16 shows the components on the solder side).

Start by mounting the SMD parts, followed by the three PCB jumpers, then mount the IC sockets and other components. The L1 choke can be wound on a small ferrite ring using 10 to 15 turns of magnet wire (0.6 mm diameter). You can also use a choke, salvaged from a cell-phone charger. Capacitor C1 should be mounted parallel to the PCB or else it won't fit into the enclosure. Q1, the PFET transistor should be mounted on a suitable heat-sink. Finally, connect the potentiometers, switches and the LCD display, and you're done.

To power the metal detector, I suggest to use rechargeable batteries because using ordinary alkaline batteries will cost you a fortune.

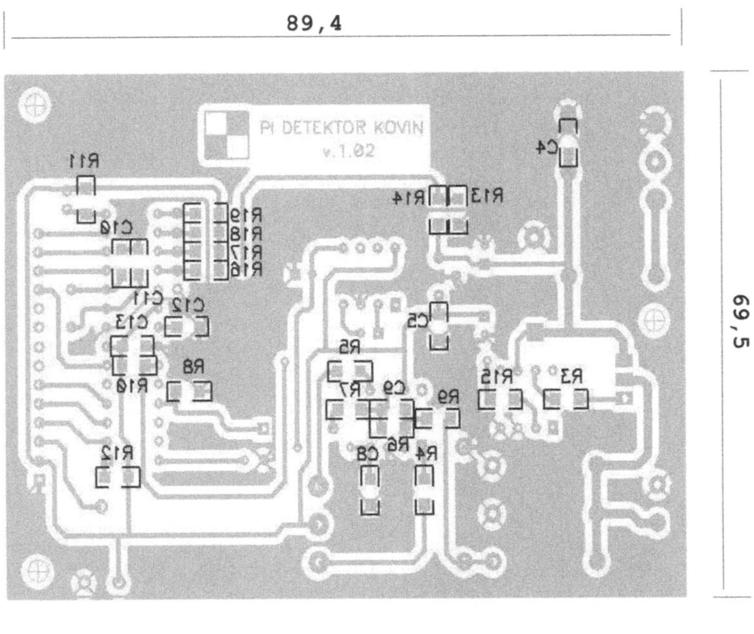

Figure 16: Component layout on the bottom (solder) side of PCB

Tune - up procedure and use

After final assembly, you'll have to check for common mistakes (poor solder joints, shorts etc.) under a magnifying glass. Mounting SMD parts can be tricky for a newbie.

After checkout, you can connect up the power supply **with the search coil disconnected**. The power drain should be in range of 40 to 50 mA, while the LCD display should show the introduction message. If you can't see this, adjust the contrast with PT2.

If that's OK, disconnect the power supply, connect the search coil and power up the detector again. After a few seconds you will hear some sound from the speaker and the LCD will display data as shown in Figure 13. The Search coil should be separated from metal parts by at least 1 meter: then set the frequency of the tone to approx. 1 Hz, using potentiometer P1. If this isn't possible, change the delay time using the delay switches. Then observe the numerical value on the LCD and adjust it to be in range of 5 to 8, using potentiometer P1. Move the search coil near a metal object and you should hear the pitch of the sound changing. You should also see changes on the LCD display as well. At this point, you can change the pulse power and delay to find the optimum detector sensitivity.

Conclusion

In closing, here is one suggestion: Do not test this metal detector near an older style cathode-ray tube PC monitor or TV screen which is powered-up. If you do, the strong electromagnetic signals given off by those devices will disturb the operation of this detector a lot! I found that out during my testing! My work bench is close to a TV set, and I lost a couple of hours troubleshooting the unit, until I discovered this.

Happy treasure hunting!

Example program ID	
Name:	Metal_detector.bas
Microcontroller:	ATmega 8
Testing circuit:	Figure 9
MiniPin compatibility:	/
MegaPin compatibility:	/
Advance program with the possibility to set the time; use lcd4busy.lib	

Pinout for the AVR microcontrollers

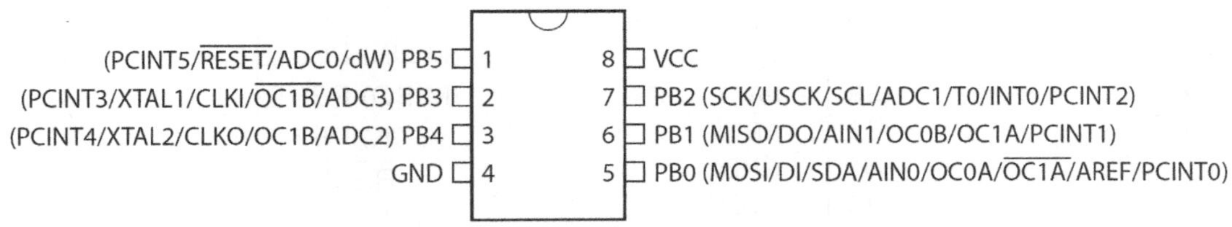

NOTE: TSSOP only for ATtiny45/V

ATTINY25 \ ATTINY45 \ ATTINY85

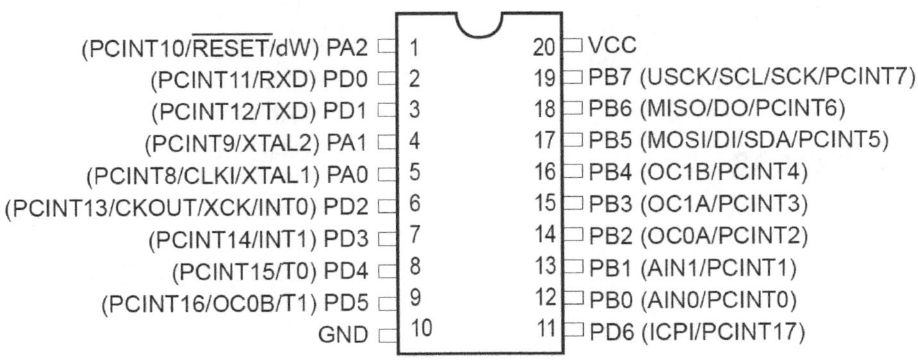

ATTINY2313 \ ATTINY4313

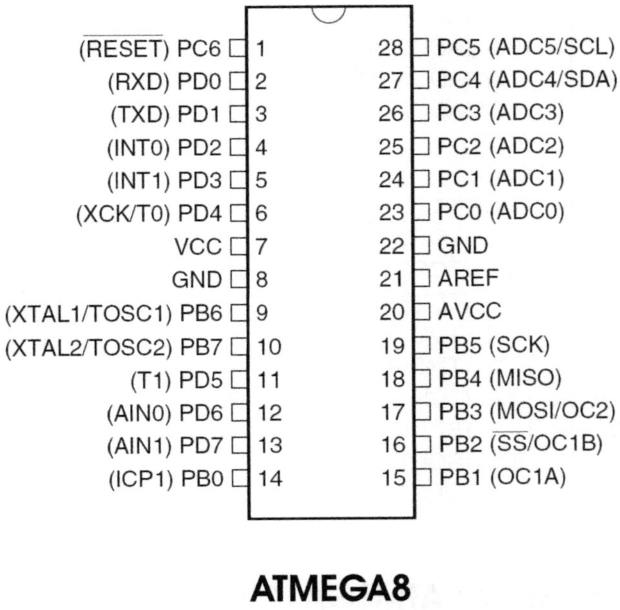

ATMEGA8

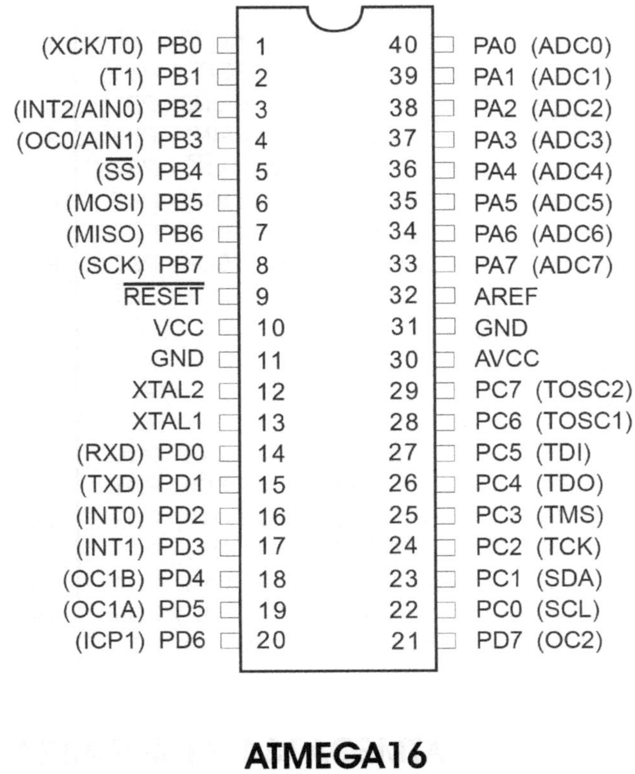

ATMEGA16

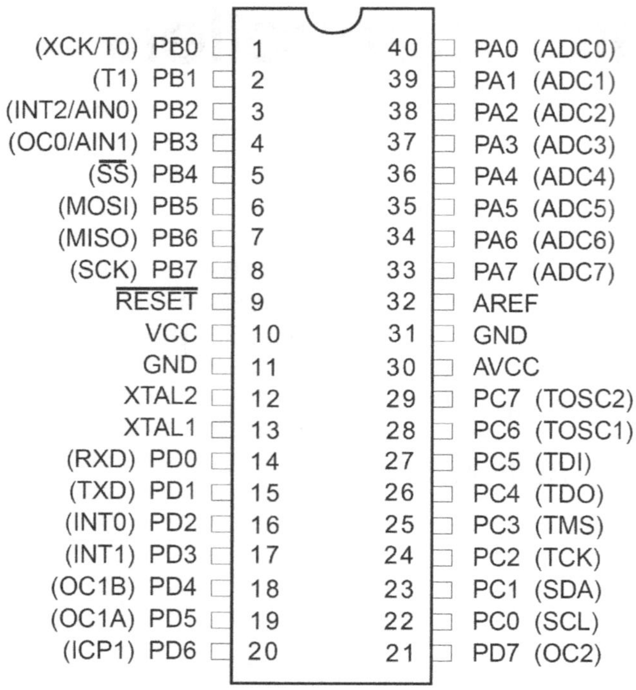

ATMEGA32

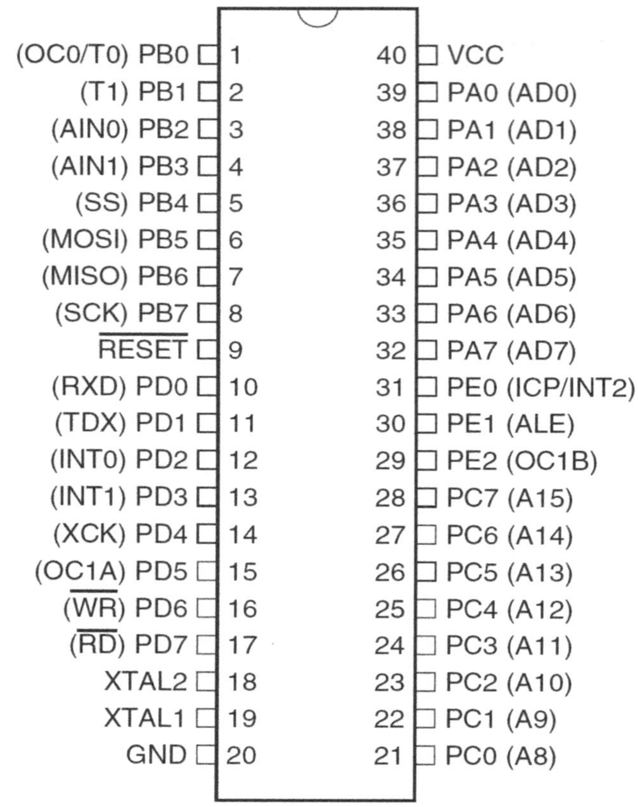

ATMEGA8515

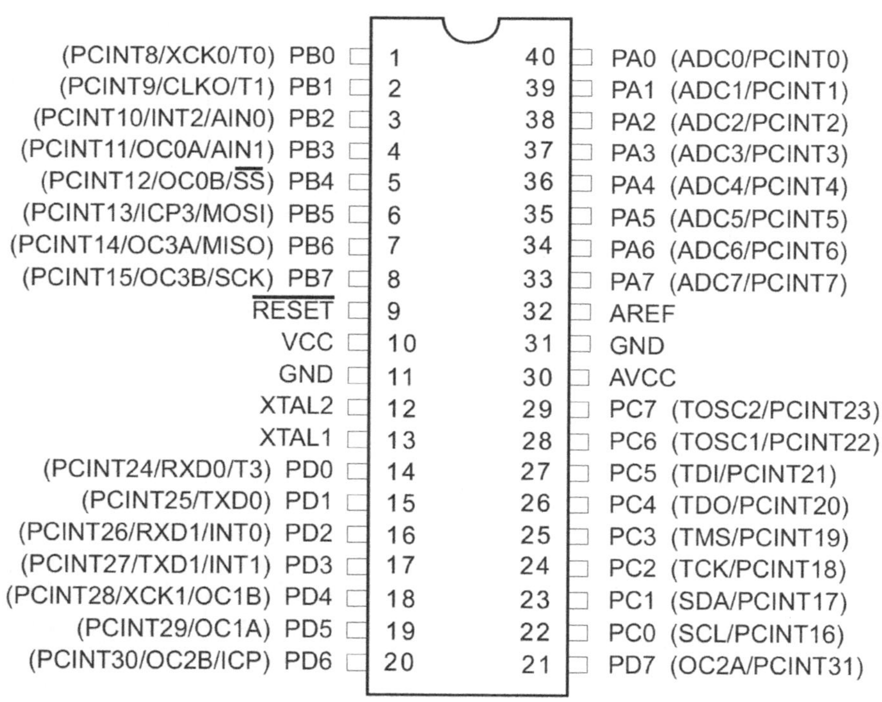

ATMEGA164 \ATMEGA324 \ ATMEGA644 \ ATMEGA1284

Notes:

CPSIA information can be obtained at www.ICGtesting.com
Printed in the USA
LVOW012054091012
302156LV00016B/2/P

9 789616 680042